WITHDR

COLONIAL CHESAPEAKE

COLONIAL CHESAPEAKE

New Perspectives

EDITED BY
DEBRA MEYERS
AND
MELANIE PERREAULT

LEXINGTON BOOKS

A Division of
ROWMAN & LITTLEFIELD PUBLISHERS, INC.
Lanham • Boulder • New York • Toronto • Oxford

LEXINGTON BOOKS

A division of Rowman & Littlefield Publishers, Inc.
A wholly owned subsidary of The Rowman & Littlefield Publishing Group, Inc.
4501 Forbes Boulevard, Suite 200
Lanham, MD 20706

PO Box 317
Oxford
OX2 9RU, UK

British Library Cataloguing in Publication Information Available

Library of Congress Cataloging-in-Publication Data

Colonial Chesapeake : new perspectives / edited by Debra Meyers and Melanie Perreault.
  p.   cm.
Includes bibliographical references and index.
ISBN-13: 978-0-7391-1091-1 (cloth : alk. paper)
ISBN-10: 0-7391-1091-8 (cloth : alk. paper)
ISBN-13: 978-0-7391-1092-8 (pbk : alk. paper)
ISBN-10: 0-7391-1092-6 (pbk : alk. paper)
  1. Chesapeake Bay Region (Md. and Va.)—History—17th century.   2. Chesapeake Bay
Region (Md. and Va.)—History—18th century.   I. Meyers, Debra, 1956–   II. Perreault,
Melanie.
F187.C5C64 2006
975.5'1802—dc22   2005012346

Printed in the United States of America

♾ ™ The paper used in this publication meets the minimum requirements of American National
Standard for Information Sciences—Permanence of Paper for Printed Library Materials, ANSI/
NISO Z39.48–1992.

CONTENTS

Acknowledgments

THE SEEDS OF THIS BOOK were planted at the Omohundro Institute of Early American History and Culture Eighth Annual Conference in College Park, Maryland, when a group of scholars interested in Chesapeake history presented a well-attended roundtable discussion on some of the latest research in the field. The participants—April Hatfield, Michele Hinton, Seth Mallios, Sarah Hand Meacham, Debra Meyers, Melanie Perreault, and Owen Stanwood—demonstrated a diverse array of methodologies and topics, and Lorena Walsh and Lois Carr—seminal figures in Chesapeake studies—offered valuable comments. The enthusiastic response of the participants and many conference attendees convinced the editors of this volume that a new collection of essays on the Chesapeake was in order.

The authors and editors would like to thank the copyright holders at the *Virginia Magazine of History and Biography* for their permission to reproduce "'They Will be Adjudged by Their Drinke, What Kind of Housewives They Are': Gender, Technology, and Household Cidering in England and the Chesapeake, 1690 to 1760." We would also like to thank the many other people whose contributions were essential to the completion of this project—Lexington's editors and reviewers as well as this volume's contributors—for their diligence, patience, and promptness. Additionally, members of the Kentucky Early American History seminar carefully read parts of this volume and offered many excellent suggestions. Finally, we would like to thank James Axtell, Lois Green Carr, Ruth Friedman, Karen Kupperman, Gloria Main, Russell Menard, Thad Tate, Lorena Walsh, and John J. Waters for their encouragement, support, inspiration, and guidance over the years; it is to them that we dedicate this volume.

Introduction

DEBRA MEYERS AND MELANIE PERREAULT

THIRTY-FIVE MILLION YEARS AGO, a meteor streaked through Earth's atmosphere, slamming into the Atlantic Ocean at 70,000 miles per hour. The impact dramatically transformed the surrounding landscape, devastating the east coast of North America, gouging a crater deeper than the Grand Canyon, and sending a shower of water as high as thirty miles into the atmosphere. Of course, no human observed the event, but the geologic history of the Chesapeake Bay is etched into the cracked bedrock deep below its waters. Millions of years later, the last glaciers retreated from eastern America, the melting ice cutting a series of channels that drained into the sunken earth encircling the impact zone. The first human inhabitants wandered into the Chesapeake Bay region around 18,000 years ago. Like all peoples, they must have shared stories about the past, but the tales went unrecorded save for the few clues left in their material possessions.[1]

Thousands of years later, new immigrants washed up on the shores of the bay and began building communities on the lands they called Virginia and Maryland. Where a geologic cataclysm had created a new environment, two civilizations collided in an epic struggle to determine the cultural landscape. The newest arrivals brought with them a formal system of writing, and thus the written history of the Chesapeake began. Like all accounts of the past, the history of the colonial Chesapeake has been subject to significant change and debate in the intervening four centuries after 1607, when the English established a tentative foothold on Jamestown Island. The wide range of interpretations is testimony to both the changing nature of the discipline itself, and the ingenuity and innovation of its practitioners.

The first written histories of the Chesapeake came from participants in the colonial venture, and offer us insights into the motivations and personal aspirations of some of the earliest settlers. Captain John Smith's *Generall Historie of Virginia, New England, and the Summer Isles* (1624), Father Andrew White's *Declaratio Coloniae Domini Baronis de Baltimore* (1634), and John Hammond's *Leah and Rachel, or, The Two Fruitfull Sisters, Virginia and Mary-land* (1656) are invaluable histories of the earliest English settlements in the Chesapeake despite the inherent difficulties with using such accounts that were meant to encourage immigration. Writing at the end of the seventeenth century, Robert Beverley had more chronological distance for his *History and Present State of Virginia*, but the history was used largely as a springboard to criticize the current governor.[2] Similarly, John Leeds Bozman wrote a politically useful text for Maryland during the early decades of the nineteenth century. And with the rising anxiety among Protestant Marylanders faced with the huge influx of Catholic immigrants during the nineteenth century, other Maryland historians attempted to use their craft to claim Maryland's founding to justify their own religious superiority. A more "objective" history would have to wait until the twentieth century.

By the end of the nineteenth century, history was "professionalized." The founding of the American Historical Association in 1884 led to the adoption of professional standards for research and writing, and universities began offering Ph.D.'s in history. Since most of these universities were located north of the Mason-Dixon Line, it is not surprising that many of the historical narratives their graduates produced tended to emphasize the importance of New England. The history of colonial America in these accounts essentially began with the Pilgrims setting foot on Plymouth Rock, and ended with the battles of Lexington and Concord. Heavily focused on New England, the Pilgrims, Puritans, and intellectual history, these accounts viewed Virginia and Maryland as an afterthought, merely an interesting sidelight to the "real" history that took place in the colder climate to the north.[3]

When early-twentieth-century historians began looking at the Chesapeake as a region deserving serious study, they often began from a defensive position, determined to insert their work into the growing national narrative constructed in and focused on New England. Many of these early histories of Maryland and Virginia unwittingly fell into an argument about the region's "contribution" to American history rather than asserting its singular significance.[4] Scholars searching for the origins of American liberty focused on the social and political order in the Chesapeake, alternatively stressing the importance of an emerging elite (the First Families of Virginia, known as the FFVs), or emphasizing the impact of social disruption in events such as Virginia's Bacon's Rebellion (1676) or the Associators' Revolution in Maryland (1689). Among the most important early-twentieth-century scholars of the Chesapeake was Thomas J. Wertenbaker, who argued that seventeenth-century society was essentially an unstable democracy dominated by small yeoman farmers until the expansion of slavery and the subsequent establishment of an elite planter class led to a more stable oligarchy by the end of the century. Other historians suggested slightly different timing for the changes, but the general pattern of Chesapeake history—that of a steady movement from chaos to stability—was set. Not surprisingly, the primary actors in these histories were white landholding men.[5]

During the social and political turmoil of the 1960s, historians began to ask new questions about the past. To get a more accurate picture of life in the past, some historians argued, one must look beyond the extraordinary—the presidents, the wealthy, and the highly educated—and instead focus on "pots and pans" history. In a sense, these scholars were redefining what it meant to be extraordinary, discovering in the often-mundane details of life a quiet nobility of purpose of everyday people confronting major crises as well as the routine challenges of daily existence. The most famous proponent of this new history was Fernand Braudel, a French scholar who spent several years in Nazi captivity during World War II and emerged with a rough draft of his magnum opus, *The Mediterranean and the Mediterranean World in the Age of Philip II*. In this and other works, Braudel sought to create what he called a "total" history. Braudel argued that the only way to capture the complexity of life was to analyze the past in terms of a three-tiered notion of time: long term (geographic and climatological); medium term (a decade or a generation); and short term (day-to-day life). By examining each of these time dimensions separately, Braudel believed, historians could create a complete picture of the past.[6]

American historians applauded Braudel's efforts to apply his theories to a massive study of the sixteenth-century Mediterranean, but chose more circumscribed topics for their own research. These historians sought to capture the *mentalité* or worldview of everyday Americans. This approach emphasizes the agency of people left out of the traditional power structures of society, and is based on the concept that individuals are driven by a collective mentality, whether they are conscious of it or not. Braudel's study of the Mediterranean also had an important impact on American historians by encouraging them to see the Chesapeake as a region with an integrated history rather than separate histories of Virginia and Maryland.

One of the central difficulties of studying nonelite peoples, of course, is that they left few written documents of their own. Without diaries, letters, or public speeches to analyze, historians had to become creative in their methodology to reconstruct the world of nonelites. Historians examined birth and death records, wills and probate inventories, land patents, and other seemingly trivial documents to uncover information about daily life in colonial America. By the late 1960s and early 1970s, scholars embraced an approach called "New Social History" that overwhelmingly emphasized statistical analysis as the key to producing objective, even scientific, accounts of the past. Scholars could identify demographic trends with mathematical precision and scientific objectivity. Not only could numbers reveal the average age at marriage for any given year or the increase in agricultural production over the course of a decade, but they could also determine whether there was a relationship between the two apparently unrelated figures. Did men tend to get married earlier when agricultural production was up? If so, what were the larger demographic consequences of a good harvest? And what might such statistics reveal about the mind-set of early American farmers?[7]

For many of the earliest social historians, the most appropriate unit of study seemed to be a single town. An assemblage of all of the relevant data for a town would be more manageable than for an entire colony, yet it would be large enough to allow significant statistical analysis. Kenneth Lockridge's study of Dedham, Massachusetts, inspired many subsequent New England town studies. Lockridge argued that the most salient feature of daily life in Dedham's first hundred years was its orderliness; indeed, he labeled the society a Christian Utopian Closed Corporate Community, highlighting the homogeneity and common sense of a higher purpose that seemed to characterize Puritan settlements. What was most revolutionary about these town studies was their focus on ordinary people rather than the Congregationalist ministers and governors who dominated earlier accounts of New England history. For practitioners of social history, the lack of traditional sources for historians—letters, diaries, sermons, government records, and other staples of a literate world—was no longer an obstacle to illuminating the past of even the most obscure American colonist. Indeed, the history of the nonliterate was considered a more accurate version of the past, portraying a more representative life than that of the elitist few.[8]

Inspired by the work of Lockridge, John Demos, and Philip Greven, the first social histories of the Chesapeake often used New England as the benchmark, chronicling the ways Virginia and Maryland deviated from what was perceived to be the norm. Usually, the Chesapeake did not fare well in these comparisons. Higher mortality rates and social fluidity seemed to indicate that the Chesapeake was a remarkably unattractive place to live, especially in the early years. If, as the social historians suggested, the story of New England was largely that of a steady decline from an early-seventeenth-century "golden age" of idealism to a more worldly materialism, then what would be the dominant narrative in the Chesapeake, which apparently skipped the utopian moment? The search for a common theme led researchers to the state and local archives, where every seemingly unimportant fact was dutifully recorded and placed in a category to be scrutinized later.[9]

Initially under the assumption that data would provide some objective truth about the past, scholars soon realized that the numbers left room for significant interpretive differences. On one side of the interpretive divide were those who saw in the Chesapeake a highly exploitative society that was marked by rampant individualism, unstable political and religious institutions, and constant social conflict. An important advocate of this version of Chesapeake history was Edmund S. Morgan, whose work *American Slavery, American Freedom: The Ordeal of Colonial Virginia* was one of the first book-length reassessments of southern society published in the 1970s. Morgan described a world where elite landlords and corrupt government officials dominated over a population of brutish colonists who were kept just under the boiling point for much of the seventeenth century. Other historians acknowledged that the region, particularly in the seventeenth century, suffered from significant turmoil, yet they found a surprising degree of cohesion in community networks and local government institutions. Perhaps the most explicit challenge to Morgan's conflict model of Chesapeake history is Darrett and Anita Rutman's *A Place in Time: Middlesex County, Virginia, 1650–1750*, which argues that family and community ties ameliorated the worst aspects of a potentially exploitative society.[10]

These two monographs were a rarity for the social history of the Chesapeake, which primarily came in the form of articles and essays. In part, the emphasis on shorter studies was a concession to the type of research and writing quantitative history demands. With narrative often taking second billing behind a dizzying array of statistics, charts, and graphs, brevity was required. Many of these studies can be found in one of the best collections of Chesapeake social history, Thad Tate and David Ammerman's *The Chesapeake in the Seventeenth Century*. The general theme of the essays in this volume is that of transformation, from a fragile society of sickly immigrants to a stable and profitable community dominated by a burgeoning native-born elite in the early eighteenth century. One of the central demographic factors the essays confront is the huge mortality rate in the Chesapeake, which had significant consequences for the entire society. Carville Earle's provocative essay on the dangerous disease environment in Jamestown explained that the ravages of typhoid fever and dysentery, not famine as some of the colonists themselves had supposed, were responsible for mortality rates near 40 percent in the early years. Those who survived, Lois Green Carr and Russell Menard show, could expect a much shorter life than their counterparts in Europe. High mortality and early death had a significant impact on family structure, according to Lorena Walsh's study of marriages in Maryland, since they worked together with a drastically unequal sex ratio (men outnumbered women 6:1 in some areas) to make it difficult to transfer traditional English family life to the Chesapeake.[11]

Despite the demographic disaster documented in these essays, the authors generally disagree with Morgan's notion of an exploitative society on the verge of chaos by the mid-seventeenth century. Instead, they describe an adaptive community that met the challenges of establishing a colony in a decidedly unhealthy environment. Eventually, Earle shows, the colonists figured out the geographic component of the disease environment and moved away from the most dangerous areas. And even though the death rate remained high, the settlers did not abandon the idea of family life entirely. The traditional nuclear family was a rarity, Walsh argues, but quasifamilies of relatives and neighbors performed many of the same functions. The decision to immigrate to the Chesapeake was not one of desperation, and many colonists found opportunities for social and economic advancement that were limited in England. The emergence of a native-born elite by the end of the century gave the settlers a sense of cohesion and confidence in their future.

The key to the developing economic, social, and political stability in the Chesapeake, the authors agree, was the development of a tobacco economy and a slave labor force by the turn of the eighteenth century. But the collection had surprisingly little to say about the subject. The authors also largely ignore the existence of Native Americans in the Chesapeake, focusing instead upon the struggle of English settlers to establish themselves on land previously occupied by Indians. This omission was due in part to the types of sources that comprised the bulk of raw material for social historians. African slaves and Native Americans rarely left wills, probate inventories, and deeds to be quantified.[12]

A new wave of historiography in the 1980s sought to place the Chesapeake in a broader context, examining the roles of Native Americans and African Americans (both slave and free), while also giving greater attention to the region's role in the larger Atlantic system. One of the most innovative works to come out of this period was Rhys Isaac's book *The Transformation of Virginia, 1740–1790*. In an effort to capture the *mentalité* of the Chesapeake populace during the tumultuous years surrounding the American Revolution, Isaac embraces an approach that might be best characterized as "dramaturgical ethnography." Heavily influenced by cultural anthropologists such as Clifford Geertz, Isaac emphasizes the importance of symbolic meaning and rituals in shaping the everyday life of Virginians, from the rhythmic drumbeats of an African song to the architecture of a colonial courthouse. Through an intense analysis of a series of brief vignettes, Isaac describes a society transforming from a rigid patriarchy to one that emphasized the autonomous power of individuals.[13]

While Isaac claimed that evangelical religion was a significant factor in shaping Chesapeake culture, Allan Kulikoff argues that material conditions were the primary determinant of people's everyday lives and larger social changes. In *Tobacco and Slaves: The Development of Southern Cultures in the Chesapeake, 1680–1800*, Kulikoff places the most important transformation of the Chesapeake a half century earlier than Isaac's reckoning. The period from 1680 to 1750, Kulikoff suggests, marks the consolidation of the slave-based Chesapeake plantation system that determined virtually every aspect of daily life for slaves and free men and women alike. Kulikoff combined the commitment to quantified analysis of the early social historians with an eye toward the multicultural approach Isaac favored, creating a sweeping overview of colonial Chesapeake history. Changes in demographic structures both reflected and caused changes in the dominant plantation culture, Kulikoff argues, resulting in a patriarchal society marked by class and racial division.[14]

More traditional than Isaac in their approach to studying the past, the contributors to *Colonial Chesapeake Society*, published in 1988, seek to capture the complexity of a diverse colonial world. This collection includes many of the same scholars as Tate and Ammerman's earlier work, but represents a maturing of the methodology and writing of social history. The eleven essays in this book still were primarily concerned with the general theme of community in colonial Maryland and Virginia, and were heavily focused on labor history. Reflecting a growing interest in comparative history, the authors find evidence of strong economic, political, and familial ties that connected across the Atlantic and even crossed the growing racial divide. With almost two decades of quantitative research behind them, the historians could make comparisons that would have been impossible earlier. And by including additional methodological approaches, especially historical archaeology and anthropology, the authors began to construct a more complete narrative of the colonial Chesapeake. When considered as a whole, they argue, suddenly the Chesapeake no longer appeared to be the odd deviation from the New England norm. In fact, the Puritans were starting to look like the exception.[15]

The most comprehensive articulation of this position was Jack Greene's *Pursuits of Happiness: The Social Development of Early Modern British Colonies and the Formation of American Culture*. In his sweeping argument, Greene contended that English colonies essentially fell into two models: declension and developmental. As Greene defined it, a declension model of social development shows a society moving from cohesion to fragmentation, from traditional to modern. A developmental society, however, moves from the simple to the complex. A comparison of settlements in New England, the Chesapeake, the Middle Colonies, and the Lower South, as well as those in Ireland, Bermuda, and the West Indies, Greene argues, reveals that virtually every colony *except* those in New England followed the developmental model. While Greene does not suggest that this finding negates the importance of New England, he maintains that those in search of the origins of American culture would be better served by starting in the Chesapeake. With Greene's work, the historiography of the Chesapeake had come full circle, from the defensive, "contribution" approach characteristic of the early twentieth century to a much more nuanced acknowledgment of the complexity and significance of the region's past. The "New Social" history had succeeded in moving the Chesapeake from the periphery of American history to the center.[16]

The most recent scholarship on the Chesapeake, including that of the contributors to this collection, reflects a growing interest in asking new questions about the social construction of race, class, and gender, while situating the Chesapeake in its Atlantic context. These histories do not discard the important insights of previous studies of the Chesapeake; in fact, the debts owed to the social historians mentioned above will be clear to any careful reader. Perhaps one of the most important changes has been the interdisciplinary nature of the research. Historians with an interest in anthropology and archaeology have embraced ethnohistory as a means of studying the Anglo-Indian relationship. Environmental historians have incorporated their knowledge of scientific evidence with the more traditional written sources to examine the interdependence of humans and their environment. And the influence of literary analysis has sent historians back to the archives to tease out the subtle, often unconscious meaning of language, finding power relationships hidden in the words written hundreds of years earlier.

Many Chesapeake historians interested in race have adopted this interdisciplinary perspective to examine the intricacies of a region where peoples of European, African, and Native American heritage were crucial participants in the formation of society. Ethnohistorians such as James Axtell, Karen Kupperman, and Frederic Gleach have drawn attention to the important role of the Anglo-Indian relationship in the seventeenth century. One of the important goals of ethnohistory is to emphasize the agency of Native Americans in constructing the past—they were not simply passive observers watching European colonists create the "real" history. The powerful Powhatan Indians dominated the early history of the Chesapeake, and the Europeans were inserting themselves into a historical narrative that had been developing over many years. Though the "scientific" categories of race were not clearly articulated until the eighteenth century, the effort to categorize the "other" as inferior was an important source of power for Europeans desperate to establish their superiority in a distant land.[17]

Other historians interested in issues of race have turned their attention to the slave plantations to examine the origins of the "peculiar institution" in America.

Lois Green Carr, Russell Menard, and Lorena Walsh combine their deep knowledge of Chesapeake social history to write *Robert Cole's World: Agriculture and Society
in Early Maryland.* By using Cole's life as a case study for larger trends, the authors
seek to breathe life into the typically statistic-laden histories of seventeenth-
century planters without abandoning a commitment to demographic analysis.
Then, in 1997 Lorena Walsh published *From Calabar to Carter's Grove: The History of
a Virginia Slave Community.* Using the scant available documents and archaeological
evidence, Walsh continues her effort to prove the existence of strong community
networks in the Chesapeake, arguing that despite the brutal conditions of slavery,
African Americans were able to construct a resilient culture blending traditional
African elements with those of the New World. Philip Morgan's even more ambitious study, *Slave Counterpoint: Black Culture in the Eighteenth-Century Chesapeake and Lowcountry,* appeared a year after Walsh's book. Morgan divides this lengthy (almost
700 pages) examination of slavery in the Chesapeake and the Carolinas into three
sections: the first is the closest to traditional social history, and consists of a
detailed quantitative analysis of the material conditions of slavery; the second part
focuses upon interactions between slaveholders and slaves; finally, the third section traces the development of a distinct African-American culture in the late
eighteenth century. The sheer magnitude of Morgan's work is impressive, but
equally important is his effort to unite the best methodologies of social, cultural,
and even psychological analysis.[18]

James Horn also emphasizes the benefits of integrating multiple methodologies in his monograph *Adapting to a New World: English Society in the Seventeenth-Century
Chesapeake.* Using a combination of community studies and comparative analysis,
Horn revisits many of the issues that had dominated social history for the previous twenty years, but argues that the Chesapeake must be understood in its transatlantic context. For Horn, the "chaos to stability" model of social development
that dominated earlier historiography missed the very important continuities
between English lifestyles and institutions and the society that developed in early
Maryland and Virginia. In the Chesapeake, Horn argues, the conditions of colonization caused the original settlers to develop simplified versions of English
labor relationships, religious beliefs, and family life. As society became more stable by the end of the seventeenth century, these institutions grew in complexity
and began taking on a distinct Chesapeake cast.[19]

Since social historians were interested in presenting an inclusive version of the
past, it is not surprising that gender has been at the center of many studies. Wom-
en's history was just beginning to become accepted as an important field when
Lois Carr and Lorena Walsh drew attention to the particular challenges facing
women in the early colonial Chesapeake in their article "The Planter's Wife: The

Experience of White Women in Seventeenth-Century Maryland." As women's history developed, some historians pointed out that gender roles were significant not only for women, but for men as well. Kathleen Brown's book, *Good Wives, Nasty Wenches, and Anxious Patriarchs* sought to untangle the complicated web of race, class, and gender in colonial Virginia. Brown argued that the construction of ideas about race in the Chesapeake was deeply connected to ideas about gender. Elite white men, concerned about the difficulty in establishing their authority in a fluid society, forged a patriarchal structure over the region by systematically relegating blacks and white women to an inferior status. By the mid-eighteenth century, white masculine power was deemed a natural right and the formerly "anxious" patriarchs asserted a confident authority over their society.[20]

Building upon the strong foundation outlined above, the cutting-edge collection of essays in this volume represent the vast array of experiences in the Chesapeake region, encompassing the racial, class, ethnic, and gender diversity that characterized life in early Maryland and Virginia. The authors in *Colonial Chesapeake: New Perspectives* emphasize the rise (and importance) of power relations, reproductive politics, and identity politics, along with a new understanding of the more traditional political history. Equally significant are the new primary sources being utilized and the interdisciplinary methods of analysis coupled with a transatlantic perspective.

Each of the essays in this volume builds on the methods and early interdisciplinary work of the New Social historians as well as those who followed them. Consequently, they use both unconventional and traditional primary sources in inventive ways. In order to uncover, more fully, the world of the early modern Chesapeake, contributors consider such sources as historical narratives, ships' logs and paybooks, poems, legislation, wills, court records, recipe books, account books, advice literature, diaries, almanacs, newspapers, census records, land and tax records, architecture, city planning, and education policies. This volume makes a significant contribution to the growing interest in the Chesapeake as an accurate indication of the English customs, rituals, and beliefs men and women brought to the New World while posing new questions of other English colonies and the mother country. Ultimately, this study suggests that the multicultural Chesapeake created significant cultural, intellectual, and social norms that have shaped the diverse world of the American people.

Notes

1. For a detailed explanation of the most recent geological studies of the development of the Chesapeake Bay, see C. Wylie Poag, "The Chesapeake Bay Bolide Impact: A

Convulsive Event in Atlantic Coastal Plain Evolution," *Sedimentary Geology* 108 (1997): 45–90. For a discussion of the first human residents of the Chesapeake, see Helen Roundtree and E. Randolph Turner, *Before and After Jamestown: Virginia's Powhatans And Their Predecessors* (Gainesville: University Press of Florida, 2002).

2. The best edition of Smith's history can be found in Philip Barbour, ed., *The Complete Works of Captain John Smith*, 3 vols. (Chapel Hill: University of North Carolina Press, 1986). For Beverley's history, see Louis B. Wright, ed., *The History and Present State of Virginia* (Chapel Hill: University of North Carolina Press, 1947). Although the English established the first permanent European settlement in the Chesapeake, they were not the first Europeans to *attempt* to do so. As Seth Mallios's essay in this collection reveals, the Spanish efforts to establish a Jesuit mission predates the English arrival by more than thirty years.

3. For a discussion of the development of the American historical profession, see Peter Novick, *That Noble Dream: The "Objectivity Question" and the American Historical Profession* (New York: Cambridge University Press, 1988). On the veneration of the Pilgrim myth in American history, see James and Patricia Scott Deetz, *The Times of Their Lives: Life, Love, and Death in Plymouth Colony* (New York: W. H. Freeman, 2000). One of the important exceptions to the northern location of history Ph.D. programs was that of Johns Hopkins University in Baltimore, where students were educated in the "scientific" approach to studying history.

4. The concept of studying the "Chesapeake" as a distinct region did not take hold until the late 1960s. For the most part, historians in the first half of the twentieth century viewed the history of Virginia and Maryland as separate endeavors owing to the different political and religious backgrounds of the colonies.

5. Thomas J. Wertenbaker, *Patrician and Plebian in Virginia* (Charlottesville, 1910). In the 1930s, Charles Andrews argued that Maryland, far from being the religious haven its leaders advertised, was much more like Virginia than New England. Maryland, he argued, was actually a business venture gone wrong and was just as venal and chaotic as its neighbor along the Chesapeake. Thad Tate's exhaustive essay on seventeenth-century Chesapeake historiography is an excellent starting point for historiography through the 1970s. See Tate, "The Seventeenth-Century Chesapeake and its Modern Historians," in *The Chesapeake in the Seventeenth Century: Essays on Anglo-American Society*, eds. Thad Tate and David Ammerman (Chapel Hill: University of North Carolina Press, 1979), 3–50.

6. Fernand Braudel, *The Mediterranean and the Mediterranean World in the Age of Philip II*, trans. Sian Reynolds (New York: Harper and Row, 1972). Braudel's interest in social history began before the war, when Marc Bloch and Lucien Febvre began publishing their influential journal, *Annales d'histoire économique et sociale* (Annals of economic and social history).

7. The dedication to assembling massive databases of numbers is particularly remarkable given the crude state of technology at the time. Those scholars fortunate enough to have access to the first computers had to wrangle with a punch-card system where each bit of data had to be cut into a piece of cardboard and fed into a reader. Needless to say,

the process was rather laborious and left plenty of room for error. Among the first scholars to recognize the value of the computer for social history was John J. Waters, whose pathbreaking work on family life in colonial Guilford, Connecticut, inspired many similar studies. See Waters, "Family, Inheritance, and Migration in Colonial New England: The Evidence from Guilford, Connecticut," *William and Mary Quarterly* 39 (1982), 64–86.

8. Kenneth Lockridge, *A New England Town: The First Hundred Years* (New York: Norton, 1970). Lockridge was not alone in arguing that New England's history was best seen as a steady decline from a seventeenth-century "golden age" of utopian idealism to a more materialistic, competitive society. See also Michael Zuckerman, *Peaceable Kingdoms: New England Towns in the Eighteenth Century* (New York: Knopf, 1970) and Philip Greven, *Four Generations: Population, Land and Family in Colonial Andover, Massachusetts* (Ithaca, N.Y.: Cornell University Press, 1972).

9. Bernard Bailyn was one of the earliest proponents of this view of early Chesapeake history. According to Bailyn, "A veritable anarchy seems to have prevailed at the center of colonial society," with frequent social and political upheaval preventing any chance of establishing a stable society. The division of power between a developing local oligarchy and a royal government imposed from outside Virginia made conflict inevitable. See Bailyn, "Politics and Social Structure in Virginia," in *Seventeenth-Century America*, ed. James Morton Smith (New York: W. W. Norton & Company, 1959), 90.

10. Edmund S. Morgan, *American Slavery, American Freedom: The Ordeal of Colonial Virginia* (New York: Norton, 1975); Darrett B. and Anita H. Rutman, *A Place in Time: Middlesex County, Virginia, 1650–1750* (New York: Norton, 1984).

11. Thad Tate and David Ammerman, eds., *The Chesapeake in the Seventeenth Century: Essays on Anglo-American Society* (Chapel Hill: University of North Carolina Press, 1979).

12. Gloria Main's *Tobacco Colony: Life in Early Maryland, 1650–1720* (Princeton, N.J.: Princeton University Press, 1982) emphasized the importance of tobacco in shaping the social and economic development of Maryland.

13. Rhys Isaac, *The Transformation of Virginia, 1740–1790* (Chapel Hill: University of North Carolina Press, 1982).

14. Allan Kulikoff, *Tobacco and Slaves: The Development of Southern Cultures in the Chesapeake, 1680–1800* (Chapel Hill: University of North Carolina Press, 1986). Kulikoff's analysis occasionally verged on economic determinism, emphasizing the extent to which material conditions affected virtually every action and thought in the Chesapeake.

15. Lois Green Carr, Philip D. Morgan, and Jean B. Russo, eds., *Colonial Chesapeake Society* (Chapel Hill: University of North Carolina Press, 1988).

16. Jack P. Greene, *Pursuits of Happiness: The Social Development of Early Modern British Colonies and the Formation of American Culture* (Chapel Hill: University of North Carolina Press, 1988).

17. Among the many works of these scholars, see James Axtell, *The Invasion Within: The Contest of Cultures in Colonial North America* (New York: Oxford University Press, 1986); Karen Kupperman, *Indians and English: Facing Off in Early America* (Ithaca, N.Y.: Cornell University Press, 2000); Frederic Gleach, *Powhatan's World and Colonial Virginia: A Conflict of Cultures* (Lincoln: University of Nebraska Press, 1997).

18. Lorena S. Walsh, *From Calabar to Carter's Grove: The History of a Virginia Slave Community* (Charlottesville: University Press of Virginia, 1997); Philip D. Morgan, *Slave Counterpoint: Black Culture in the Eighteenth-Century Chesapeake and Lowcountry* (Chapel Hill: University of North Carolina Press, 1998). More recently, Anthony Parent has argued that the adoption of slavery in the Chesapeake was not an "unthinking decision," as some earlier historians had suggested, but was a conscious decision of the gentry class designed to solidify their elite social and economic status. See Anthony Parent, *Foul Means: The Formation of a Slave Society in Virginia, 1660–1740* (Chapel Hill: University of North Carolina Press, 2003).

19. James Horn, *Adapting to a New World: English Society in the Seventeenth-Century Chesapeake* (Chapel Hill: University of North Carolina Press, 1994).

20. Lois Green Carr and Lorena Walsh, "The Planter's Wife: The Experience of White Women in Seventeenth-Century Maryland," *William and Mary Quarterly* 34 (October 1977), 542–71; Kathleen M. Brown, *Good Wives, Nasty Wenches, and Anxious Patriarchs: Gender, Race, and Power in Colonial Virginia* (Chapel Hill: University of North Carolina Press, 1996). The apparent confidence in men's authority may have been more imagined than real, as Woody Holton has argued that the plantation patriarchy of the late eighteenth century rested on rather shaky foundations. See Holton, *Forced Founders: Indians, Debtors, Slaves, and the Making of the American Revolution in Virginia* (Chapel Hill: University of North Carolina Press, 1999).

MEMORY: COLONIAL NARRATIVE AND ETHNIC IDENTITY

I

ONE OF THE PRIMARY GOALS of this essay collection is to encourage readers to think about the similarities and differences among people living in the Chesapeake by focusing on race, ethnicity, class, gender, and sexuality. Thus we begin the collection with a section entitled "Memory: Colonial Narrative and Ethnic Identity" that includes the innovative work of Seth William Mallios—who reminds us that the English were not the first Europeans to settle in the Chesapeake—and Melanie Perreault's work on intercultural violence.

Using a unique approach—archaeological seriate analysis—Seth Mallios recovers information about the Chesapeake using traditional historical narratives in new and exciting ways. Seriations, long utilized by archaeologists to identify stylistic change over time, can be employed to analyze Jesuit narratives by treating the texts as "artifacts." Mallios argues that because previous scholars have not recognized the inherent problems with using Ajacan Jesuit narratives, they have added to the fictionalization of the first European attempt to settle in the Chesapeake. Like the New Social historians, Mallios insists upon research methods that are empirically based and thus sheds new light on the 1571 murder of the Ajacan Jesuits by stripping away the martyrdom myth to uncover "the politics of oppression."

Melanie Perreault's essay also interprets historical change in narrative texts to uncover the true meaning behind the escalating Anglo-Indian violence during the first half of the seventeenth century. Using promotional tracts and colonial narratives, Perreault argues that the bloodshed caused the colonists to question their identity as English men and women. Forced to confront their own potentially "savage" behavior, the English used religious discourse to reassert their sense of self and their superiority. By redefining even the most horrific examples of violence as an effort to restore their identity, the English maintained their distinction from the Spanish (who were described as indiscriminate murderers of Indians) while avoiding suggestions that they were degenerating into the perceived barbarism of the Native Americans. This interpretation of English identity goes well beyond Edmund Morgan's earlier theme that the English saw themselves as Native American liberators from the Spanish papists.

Seth William Mallios's "The Creation of Ajacan's Martyrs: Employing a New Analytical Technique on Early Colonial Chesapeake Narratives" and Melanie Perreault's "'We Washed Not the Ground With Their Bloods': Intercultural Violence and Identity in the Early Chesapeake" utilize primary sources in innovative ways. Readers have an opportunity to analyze, for themselves, transcribed documents from the periods discussed: Juan Rogel's letter to Francis Borgia (1572) and Edward Waterhouse's "A Declaration of the State of the Colony and . . . a Relation of the Barbarous Massacre" (1622).

Letter to Francis Borgia (1572)

JUAN ROGEL

Our Most reverend Father in Christ,

At the end of last June, I wrote to Your Paternity from Havana, telling how, under an order of holy obedience, I made ready to make this journey in search of Ours who had come to these parts. . . . Thus, on July 30, we left San Agustín for this purpose, and after staying at Santa Elena for five days, we arrived at the Bay of the Mother of God. . . . Reaching this bay, the Governor immediately ordered us to search for Alonso, the boy who came with Father Baptista. He has not died, according to what we heard from one of the Indians of this region, who was captured by the pilot on his second trip. This Indian has been brought along in chains. Anchoring the fleet in a port of this bay, the Governor sent an armed *fragatilla* with thirty soldiers to a fresh-water stream where Ours disembarked when they came here. . . . The order of the Governor was to take the uncle of Don Luis, a principal chief of that region, as well as some leading Indians. On taking them, we were to ask them to give us the boy and we would let them go. Everything happened in excellent fashion, for within an hour after our arrival, he took the chief with five of his leaders and eight other Indians.

This was the method of capture. After we had anchored in the middle of the narrow stream, Indians soon appeared on the bank and some entered the boat. To these the Spaniards gave gifts and made some exchanges. When they left the boat very contentedly, others arrived. With a third group came the chief and his leaders; one of them wore as a decoration or trinket a silver paten that Ours had brought. At once the Spaniards seized them and forced them down into the boat, and dressing the ship, passed to the mouth of the stream three leagues away by oar. On the way, the soldiers killed some Indians who were trying to shoot arrows at us and had wounded a soldier.

At the mouth of the river, which was very wide, we anchored again an arquebus shot away from the shore. Canoes of Indians came in peace, and they said that the boy was in the hands of a leading chief who lived two days journey from there, near this port. They asked that we give them time to send for him and bring him. This we did and we gave them trinkets to give the chief who held the boy and we stayed there waiting for him. It seems that as soon as the chief learned of the capture of the others and about the fleet and the imminent death of the Indians, he sought to curry favor with the Governor. For he did not want to let the boy be brought to our ship, but he sent him to this port with two Indians . . .

When the Indians did not bring the boy, we fought off an ambush of many canoes loaded with archers ready to attack the vessel. First there came two large canoes filled with Indians who were so concealed that no one was seen except the two who steered and they pretended they brought us oysters. Before they got aboard the watchman discovered them. We made ready and the others retreated. At my request, the steersmen were not fired upon, for we were still not certain whether it was an ambush or whether they came in peace. When the time was up and the boy did not come we waited for a night and further into midday and finally we set sail with our captives. By way of farewell, the pilot steered the ship towards land with the excuse that he wanted to speak to them, and then he ordered a blast from the arquebuses into the group of Indians who were standing crowded together on the shore. I believe many of them were killed, and this was done without any knowledge of mine until it happened. Then we returned to this port.

Now I will relate to Your Paternity how Ours who were here suffered death, as this boy tells it. After they arrived there, Don Luis abandoned them, since he did not sleep in their hut more than two nights nor stay in the village where the Fathers made their settlement for more than five days. Finally he was living with his brothers a journey of a day and a half away. Father Master Baptista sent a message by a novice Brother on two occasions to the renegade. Don Luis would never come, and Ours stayed there in great distress, for they had no one by whom they could make themselves understood to the Indians. They were without means of support, and no one could buy grain from them. They got along as best they could, going to other villages to barter for maize with copper and tin, until the beginning of February. The boy says that each day Father Baptista caused prayers to be said for Don Luis, saying that the devil held him in great deception. As he had twice sent for him and he had not come, he decided to send Father Quirós and Brother Gabriel de Solís and Brother Juan Baptista to the village of the chief near where Don Luis was staying. Thus they could take Don Luis along with them and barter for maize on the way back. On the Sunday after the feast of the Purification, Don Luis came to the three Jesuits who were returning with other

Indians. He sent an arrow through the heart of Father Quirós and then murdered the rest who had come to speak with him. Immediately Don Luis went on to the village where the Fathers were, and with great quiet and dissimulation, at the head of a large group of Indians, he killed the five who waited there. Don Luis himself was the first to draw blood with one of those hatchets which were brought along for trading with the Indians; then he finished the killing of Father Master Baptista with his axe, and his companions finished off the others. This boy says that when he saw them killing the Fathers and Brothers, he sought to go among the Indians as they inflicted the wounds so that they might kill him too. For it seemed better to him to die with Christians than live alone with Indians. A brother of Don Luis took him by the arm and did not let him go. This happened five or six days after the death of the others. This boy then told Don Luis to bury them since he had killed them, and at least in their burial, he was kind to them.

The boy stayed in the same hut for fifteen days. Because of the famine in the land, Don Luis told him that they should go and seek grain. Alonso came in this way with him to the chief where he remained. The chief told the boy to stay and he would treat him well and hold him as a son. This he did. Finally Don Luis distributed the clothes of the Fathers among himself and his two brothers who shared in the murders. The boy took nothing but the relics and beads of Father Baptista, which he kept till now and handed over to us. After this Don Luis went away very anxious to get hold of the boy to kill him, so that there would be no one to give details of what happened to Ours, but because of his fear of the chief with whom the boy was staying, he gave up the idea.

When he had learned the truth, the Governor acted in this fashion. He told the captured chief that he must bring in Don Luis and his two brothers for punishment, and if he did not do this, the Governor would punish all those captured. Since three had been killed in that chief's lands, he could not escape blame for the murders. The chief promised that he would bring them within five days. We are waiting for this time to elapse, and I am not sure whether the Governor will send us on our trip to the island of Cuba before the time is up. He will report to Spain, God willing, whatever action he will have taken. The country remains very frightened from the chastisement the Governor inflicted, for previously they were free to kill any Spaniard who made no resistance. After seeing the opposite of what the Fathers were, they tremble. This chastisement has become famous throughout the land, and if this further one is done, it will be all the more famous. I have noticed something about this region. There are more people here than in any of the other lands I have seen so far along the coast explored. It seemed to me that the natives are more settled than in other regions I have been and I am confident that should Spaniards settle here, provided they would frighten the natives that threaten harm, we could preach the Holy Gospel more easily than elsewhere. We are keeping this boy with us. He is very fluent in the language and had almost forgotten his Spanish. After he was freed from his captivity, we asked him if he wished to be with us, or go with his father who is also here. He said that he wanted to be with us only. In order to make sure that he retains the language and does not forget it, I am debating whether to bring along with me an Indian boy, who has come along with Alonso, leaving his parents and home to be with him. Thus he might train in the language, unless, meanwhile, Your Paternity or Father Provincial order otherwise.

For my part, I can say to Your Paternity that if it is judged in Our Lord that this enterprise ought to be begun, and if you desire that the task should fall to me, I would consider myself most fortunate. I fear that there will be the same difficulty among these people in making conversions, as has been found in the places where we have been. If there is to be some fruit here, it will have to be by wearing them away like water on a rock. . . .

When this boy was with Don Luis, following the death of the others, Don Luis left the vestments and books and everything else locked up in chests. On returning, they took up their share of spoils. He said that a brother of Don Luis is going around clothed in the Mass vestments and altar cloths. The captured chief told me that Don Luis gave the silver chalice to an important chief in the interior. The paten was given to one of those Indians we captured, while the other images were thrown away. Among other things there was a large crucifix in a chest; some Indians told this boy that they do not dare approach that chest since three Indians who wanted to see what was in it, fell down dead on the spot. So they keep it closed and protected. About the books, Alonso said that after pulling off the clasps, the Indians tore them all up and threw them away . . .

From the Bay of the Mother of God in Florida, August 28, 1572. Your Paternity's unworthy son and servant in Our Lord,

JUAN ROGEL

A Declaration of the State of the Colony and . . . a Relation of the Barbarous Massacre (1622)

EDWARD WATERHOUSE

O N THE FRIDAY MORNING (the fatal day) the 22 of March, as also in the evening, as in other days before, they [the Indians] came unarmed into our houses, without bows or arrows, or other weapons, with Deer, Turkeys, Fish, Furs, and other provisions, to sell and truck with us, for glass, beads, and other trifles: yea, in some places, sat down at breakfast with our people at their tables, whom immediately with their own tools and weapons, either laid down, or standing in their houses, they basely and barbarously murdered, not sparing wither age or sex, man, woman, or child: so sudden in their cruel execution, that few or none discerned the weapon or blow that brought them to destruction. In which manner they also slew many of our people then at their several works and husbandries in the fields . . . they well knowing in what places and what quarters each of our men were, in regard of their daily familiarity. . . . And by this means that fatal Friday morning, there fell under the bloody and barbarous hands of that perfidious and inhumane people, contrary to all laws of God and men, of Nature and Nations, three hundred and forty-seven men, women, and children, most by their own weapons; and not being content with taking away life alone, they fell again upon the dead, making as well as they could, a fresh murder, defacing, dragging, and mangling the dead carcasses into many pieces, and carrying some parts away in derision, with base and brutish triumph.

Neither yet did these beasts spare those amongst the rest well known unto them, from whom they had daily received many benefits and favors, but spitefully

"A Declaration of the State of the Colony and . . . a Relation of the Barbarous Massacre," 1622. *Records of the Virginia Company*, vol. 3, ed. Susan Myra Kingsbury (Washington, D.C.: Government Print Office, 1906–1935), 551–53.

also massacred them, without remorse or pity, being in this more fell than Lions and Dragons, which (as Histories accord) have been so far from hurting, as they have both acknowledged, and gratefully requited their Benefactors; such is the force of good deeds, though done to cruel beasts, as to make them put off the very nature of beasts, and to put on humanity upon them. But these miscreants, contrariwise in this kind, put not off only all humanity, but put on a worse and more than unnatural brutishness. One instance of it, amongst too many, shall serve for all.

That worthy religious gentleman, Master George Thorpe, Esquire, . . . did so truly and earnestly effect their conversion, and was so tender over them, that whosoever under his authority had given them the least displeasure or discontent, he punished them severely. . . . He was not only too kind and beneficial to the common sort, but also to their King, to whom he oft resorted, and gave many presents which he knew to be highly pleasing to him. And whereas this king before dwelt only in a cottage, or rather a den or hog sty, made with a few poles and sticks, and covered with mats after their wild manner, to civilize him, he first, built him a fair house according to the English fashion, in which he took such joy, especially in his lock and key, which he so admired, as locking and unlocking his door a hundred times a day, he thought no device in the world was comparable to it.

Thus insinuating himself to this King for his religious purposes [Thorpe] conferred with him oft[en], and intimated to him matters of our Religion; and thus far the Pagan confessed, moved by natural Principles, that our God was a good God, and much better than theirs, in that he had with so many good things above them endowed us. He [Thorpe] told him, if he would serve our God, he should be partaker of all those good things we had, and of far greater than sense or reason ever could imagine . . . [And both he [the Powhatan leader] and his people for the daily courtesies this good Gentleman did to one or other of them, did profess such outward love and respect unto him, as nothing could seem more: but all was little regarded after this Viperous brood, as the sequel showed: for they not only willfully murdered him, but cruelly and felly, out of devilish malice, did so many barbarous despites and foul scorns after to his dead corpse, as are unfitting to be heard by any civil ear. One thing I cannot omit, that when this good Gentleman upon his fatal hour, was warned by his man (who perceived some treachery intended to them by these hellhounds) to look to himself, and withal ran away in fear of the mischief he strongly apprehended, and so saved his own life; yet his Master, out of conscience of his own good meaning, and fair deserts ever towards them, was so void of all suspicion, and so full of confidence, that they had sooner killed him, then he could or would believe they meant any ill against him. Thus the sins of these wicked Infidels, have made them unworthy of enjoying him, and the eternal good that he most zealously always intended to them.

And thus these miserable wretches, not he, hath lost by it, who to the comfort of us all, hath gained a Crown of endless bliss, and is assuredly become a glorious Martyr, in which thrice-happy and blessed state we leave him. But these miscreants, who have thus despised God's great mercies so freely offered to them, must needs in time therefore to be corrected by his justice.

The Creation of Ajacan's Martyrs: Employing a New Analytical Technique on Early Colonial Chesapeake Narratives

SETH WILLIAM MALLIOS

Introduction

February 5, 1571: Somewhere near modern-day Williamsburg, Virginia

An Indian neophyte entered a meager missionary settlement, home to a handful of Jesuits that occupied the northern extreme of Spain's *La Florida* territory. This convert had been born a Chesapeake Algonquian prince only to be later trained in Catholicism and renamed Don Luis. After first joining the Spanish in 1561, he traveled with them to Europe and other parts of North America. Don Luis ultimately returned to his original home of Ajacan in 1570 with the purported intent of converting his native kin. The missionaries and Ajacan Algonquians got along well at first, but a few months into the settlement, Don Luis and the other Algonquians deserted the Jesuits. Father Segura, the cleric in charge of this missionizing endeavor, received no explanation for the abandonment. He had not seen Don Luis for months, until this morning.

Don Luis was unarmed as he approached the missionary settlement. The few natives who joined him also carried no weapons. Don Luis told Segura that he had come back to Ajacan to construct a church for the missionaries. Segura was thrilled with the offer; he immediately handed his metal axes to the neophyte to begin the building process. Don Luis promptly beheaded Segura with one of the axes as his native followers killed the other clerics. The only survivor of this attack was a young Spanish boy named Alonso de Olmos, whom the Algonquians decided to spare.

Seriate analyses of narrative elements in sixteenth- and seventeenth-century historical records revealed how Spanish stories of the Chesapeake's Ajacan Jesuits grew from direct reports of indigenous murder to elaborate constructions regarding the missionaries' purported divine sacrifice. A comparison of details from the seven existing contemporary sources demonstrated how and when Father Segura and his followers came to be celebrated by their peers and followers as martyrs. Seriations, traditional archaeological techniques used to identify stylistic change, showcased meaningful transformations in narrative styles and themes. In treating texts as artifacts, this approach unified a critique of specific written attributes with a diachronic perspective on the narratives. The following analysis detailed how the different stories of Ajacan evolved. They changed from 1) descriptive reports to 2) embellished accounts to 3) cautionary tales to 4) moralistic fables. These four groupings of distinct writing styles and agendas corresponded with the following four narrative phases of clerical apotheosis: 1) pre-martyrdom, 2) proto-martyrdom, 3) martyrdom, and 4) super-martyrdom. Fifty years after the 1571 murder of the Jesuits, contemporary Western writers told the history of the first European attempt at settling the Chesapeake exclusively in the context of the missionaries' alleged martyrdom. Once created, the myth of the Ajacan Jesuits' sacred self-immolation gained acceptance regardless of previously established contradictory historical details.

The following analysis begins with a brief discussion of seriate analyses and other historical anthropological investigations of change over time. It also offers an overview of Spanish colonization in the Chesapeake. These background discussions then give way to the heart of this chapter: the actual seriation of the historical texts detailing the failed mission at Ajacan.

Seriate Analysis and Historical Anthropological Investigations of Change over Time

Archaeologists have traditionally used seriate analyses to pinpoint stylistic change.[1] Most often used on large archaeological assemblages from disparate temporal or spatial contexts to identify sequences of cultural drift, this analytical technique pinpoints detailed changes in material culture, including design and technique.[2] Ordering the sequence of gradual change for multiple traits establishes chronology and often details how larger cultural phenomena transformed as well.[3]

Historical archaeologists have used seriations to study just about every artifact type. There is one notable exception, the historical texts themselves. For some reason the anthropological attention to change over time has not been readily extended into the realm of textual analysis. It is as if historical archaeologists have heeded James Deetz's declaration at the end of *In Small Things Forgotten*—"don't read what we have done; look at what we have done"—too literally.[4] It is not inappropriate to examine texts using the traditional tools of anthropological archaeology. Instead of reading Deetz's conclusion as merely a privileging of the authenticity of artifacts over historical records, it is argued here that texts should be seen as the same sorts of material productions, constructions, and creations as other artifacts. This interpretation transforms Deetz's statement into: "Don't merely read what we have written; look at what we have done; and look at what we have done with what we have written as well."

Historical Background of the Jesuits at Ajacan

Admiral Pedro Menendez de Aviles, the first governor of Spanish Florida, temporarily secured the territory for Spain with a series of military outposts during the 1560s. Desires of locating an accessible waterway to the Far East through North America, maintaining easily defended ports for ships that faced frequent looting, and acquiring valuable native goods kept Menendez eager to expand the Spanish territory northward past the entrance of the Chesapeake Bay.[5] Spanish clerics had been largely unsuccessful in their attempts at proselytizing to Florida's indigenous population during this period. In the late 1560s, Menendez secured the services of the newly formed Jesuit Order and encouraged the Jesuits to attempt a settlement in the Chesapeake. They agreed and brought along Don Luis de Velasco, a Chesapeake Algonquian neophyte who had joined the Spaniards in 1561. The clerics believed that Don Luis would serve as an interpreter and ensure friendly intercultural relations as a few other neophytes had done years earlier in *La Florida*.[6] The Jesuit crew that journeyed to the Chesapeake in the early fall of 1570 consisted of Segura; the neophyte Don Luis; Father Luis de Quiros; Brothers Gabriel Gomez, Sancho Zaballos, and Pedro Mingot de Linares; lay catechists Cristobal Redondo, Gabriel de Solis, and Juan Baptista Mendez; and Alonso de Olmos, the young son of a Santa Elena colonist. They traveled to Ajacan, Don Luis's former home, with no soldiers and only two priests with previous proselytizing experience. Segura chose his crew deliberately, omitting military personnel and jaded veteran priests, both groups that he blamed for previous missionary failures.

Segura and his followers sailed into the Chesapeake Bay and up what would later be deemed the James River. Their ship anchored, and the crew came ashore on September 10, 1570. Members of the native population promptly celebrated the return of Don Luis. Segura, confident in seemingly amicable relations with the natives, dispatched the nonreligious members of the Spanish crew. Segura asked the ship's pilot to deliver his initial report to Cuban Treasurer Juan de

Hinistrosa. His correspondence requested that King Philip II provide the missionaries with additional food supplies. As soon as the Spanish leader received the Jesuit letter, he sent Captain Vincente Gonzales with provisions to Ajacan. In his letter, Segura also gave explicit instructions for Spanish supply ships coming to the area. Native sentinels camped out along the James River would signal any European vessel they spotted and guide the ship to a location where further identification could be determined.

As soon as Gonzales and his crew sailed up the James in the spring of 1571, they spotted a group of natives wearing the missionaries' clothes and encouraging the Europeans to come ashore. Gonzales realized that Segura's instructions were not being followed and seized two natives for interrogation. He learned that two months earlier Don Luis and the Ajacan Algonquians had slain all of the Jesuits except for the boy Olmos. The Spanish supply ship immediately left the Chesapeake, and Gonzales informed his superiors of the Jesuit deaths. Menendez oversaw a visit to Ajacan a year and a half later in which the Spanish reacquired Olmos and killed several natives. That same year, 1572, the Society of Jesus gave up missionizing in the North American Southeast.[7]

Olmos informed Menendez of the events at Ajacan during 1570–1571. He explained that after a few weeks of seemingly pleasant interaction, Don Luis and the other Ajacan natives abandoned the Jesuits and took up residence in the interior. The missionaries survived for three or four months by trading with adjacent indigenous villages and scavenging for sustenance. Segura sent Quiros and two others to visit the neophyte in February of 1571. Following Segura's instructions, Quiros begged Don Luis to return to Ajacan and help the missionaries trade for corn on the way back to their settlement. Upon hearing Quiros's entreaty, the former neophyte and his Algonquian kin murdered the three Jesuits. They then journeyed to Ajacan and slew the five remaining missionaries, sparing only the boy Olmos.

Contemporary historical sources

In terms of the Spanish team that went to Ajacan, only Alonso de Olmos survived the attacks, and he never published an account of the Ajacan venture. As the lone European witness of the doomed mission, Olmos provided the only primary testimony of Ajacan events, on which all later texts directly and indirectly drew. This analysis examines all seven of the existing contemporary postmurder historical sources to scrutinize how the deaths of Segura and his followers were related. If a source was written within fifty years of the mission's 1572 demise, it was deemed contemporaneous. Nearly all of these texts were written in sixteenth- and seventeenth-century Spanish by Jesuits for a predominantly Jesuit audience. Listed chronologically, the seven contemporary written accounts are:

1) **Rogel's August letter (1572)** While aboard Menendez's ship during the 1572 Spanish mission of vengeance to the Chesapeake, Father Juan Rogel wrote a letter on August 28, 1572, to Francis Borgia, general of the Society of Jesus.

2) **Rogel's relation (1590–1595)** Father Rogel also wrote a relation sometime between 1590 and 1595 that shared many details with his earlier letter.

3) **Ribadeneyra's account (1592)** Father Pedro de Ribadeneyra, a Jesuit member, scholar, and administrator, described the demise of the Ajacan Jesuits in his book, *The Life of Father Francis Borgia, Third General of the Society of Jesus*, which was published in 1592.

4) **Carrera's relation (1600)** A relation written in 1600 by Father Juan de la Carrera, the outfitter of the Ajacan mission, also discussed Segura's fate and included details of a heated dispute between himself and Segura over what items to take on the journey.

5) **Martinez's relation (1610)** Bartolome Martinez's relation is unique in that it purportedly drew on direct conversations between Ajacan survivor Alonso de Olmos and the author of the historical text.

6) **Ore's relation (1617–1620)** Father Luis Geronimo de Ore wrote a narrative including the details of the Ajacan mission sometime between 1617 and 1620.

7) **Sacchini's relation (1622)** Father Francisco Sacchini wrote a book entitled *Borgia, the Third Part of the History of the Society of Jesus*, in 1622.

Historian David Beers Quinn claimed that the narratives listed above regarding the Ajacan venture are "so overlaid with hagiographical invention, and the authentic data so scarce, that little more can be said."[8] This analysis and others like it examine the existing details in these narratives and use this information to answer questions other than simply what happened at Ajacan.[9] In treating texts like artifacts with an infinite number of possible attributes, the scholarly task becomes finding the right question to ask of the correct set of attributes. The work presented here disputes Quinn's notion that Ajacan's narratives possess a dearth of authentic data. These data are inauthentic only when scholars fail to ask meaningful questions that they can answer.

Ajacan Seriation

Applying a seriate analytical technique to narrative plots from the historical accounts of the Spanish Jesuit mission at Ajacan revealed two significant patterns.

First, it corroborated the temporal sequence of the relations as expected. Second, and more importantly, it showed how Jesuit ideas of the missionaries' martyrdom developed. The myth of their martyrdom was a later creation that gradually emerged into being during the end of the sixteenth century and the start of the seventeenth century. Contrasting details from each of the contemporary sources that described the death of the missionaries revealed how and when the Ajacan clerics came to be lauded as martyrs. The seriate analysis displayed stylistic change, in this case a gradual change in the narrative styles and themes of the contemporary Jesuit chroniclers of Ajacan.

For the most part, the historical texts concerning Segura's Ajacan venture corresponded. Analysis of an identical series, one based on their many similarities, would offer little insight. The key to pinpointing changes in the way the stories were narrated was in how the accounts were dissimilar. In selecting the attributes on which to analyze the narratives, there were two types of concerns: practical and substantial. A successful seriation of texts needed story elements that actually varied between the seven existing historical accounts. In addition, these narrative attributes had to be tied to the plot of the story. A sufficiently divisive attribute that was unimportant to the story's thematic essence—like whether or not the narrative was written in Spanish or Latin—would be less likely to pinpoint a meaningful transformation. As a result, narrative attributes, the units of analysis for this study, were chosen on the basis of how the core events at Ajacan were described and the characterizations of those performing the historical actions. In addition to distinguishing the narratives from one another, they had to detail either what happened or how the people involved were behaving.

The narrative elements that were ultimately chosen included general storytelling techniques and historical specifics. The transformation was regular and gradual for both. An example of a general storytelling technique that was incorporated in the seriation was the use of religious comparisons and analogies. The two earliest sources, Rogel's letter from August of 1572 and his later relation, were the lone narratives that did not label the Chesapeake Jesuits as "martyrs." Only Rogel's letter failed to specify that Don Luis acted like a "pagan." Likewise, Ribadeneyra's 1592 account and Rogel's texts were distinct from the others in that they failed to liken Don Luis to the New Testament's Judas or portray the missionaries as "sheep" and the Algonquians as "wolves."

Alterations in historical specifics also followed a uniform and linear pattern. An example of this was in how the narratives related the Jesuits' food procurement strategies once Don Luis and his followers abandoned the clerics. Rogel's initial letter stated that the missionaries survived by bartering with neighboring native villagers. His later relation and the other two narratives written around

1600 avowed that the clerics scavenged the area for nuts and berries. Martinez, Ore, and Sacchini's post-1609 accounts completely omitted these subsistence matters. Evidently, in the eyes of the historical authors these issues had become an unimportant part of the story or one that did not now support the narrative's transformed theme.

Placing the historical accounts and story attributes on separate axes of a grid illustrated the gradual change in the narratives over time. The vertical axis listed the historical accounts in chronological order, and differing story elements segmented the horizontal axis (table 1.1). When a relation included a particular narrative element, an "x" marked their intersection on the grid. When the account omitted the detail, an "o" was placed at their crossing point. If this presence/ absence seriation revealed theoretically perfect gradual change, the grid would include a series of "x"s diagonally from top left to bottom right (table 1.2). The bottom left and top right parts of the grid would be entirely "o"s. The "x" pattern would bow out in the middle because some visionary writers would anticipate change and others would lag behind the current trends.

A detailed examination of the seriation of Ajacan historical accounts and individual story elements revealed a nearly perfect diagonally elliptical presence/ absence pattern (table 1.1). The seriate analysis pinpointed four general changes in the Ajacan narratives. The first account described how the missionaries bartered with the neighboring villages once they had been abandoned. Years later, historical narrators altered the details, suggesting that the Ajacan clerics scavenged for food during the lean times. The stories transformed again years later as details of missionary activity during the native desertion were omitted. In parallel fashion, the texts began identifying the Jesuits as martyrs only once they included references to the former neophyte acting like a pagan. In addition, metaphors comparing historical figures at the temporary Spanish Chesapeake settlement to wolves and sheep corresponded with allusions to Don Luis as the Bible's Judas. Both of these storytelling tactics were restricted to Ajacan's latest narratives.

Four narrative phases paralleled stages in the construction of the martyrdom myth (table 1.1). Phase one consisted of the account that only reported events and lacked an overall moral. It corresponded to the "premartyrdom" Ajacan narrative stage as no mention was made of Segura's purported holy self-sacrifice. Rogel's 1572 letter did not assess the Jesuits' legacy and was limited to succinct description. Rogel's later relation did not moralize like later narratives, but as part of the second "protomartyrdom" stage, it altered and likely romanticized certain details. Ajacan narratives with significantly embellished themes formed the third "martyrdom" phase. The transformation from protomartyrdom relations to accounts of martyrdom was based on the change from peripheral to thematic

Table 1.1.   Seriation of Narrative Elements from Ajacan Historical Records. "X" denotes presence of trait; "O" denotes absence of trait.

Source	Bartering to survive	Don Luis would barter on the way back	Scavenging to survive	Don Luis acting like a pagan	Martyrdom	Use of wolf and sheep metaphor	Don Luis called Judas	Phase of mythical martyrdom construction
1572 (August) Rogel letter	X	X	O	O	O	O	O	(1) Premartyrdom
1590–1595 or 1607–1611 Rogel relation	O	O	X	X	O	O	O	(2) Protomartyrdom
1592 Ribadeneyra account	O	O	X	X	X	O	O	(3) Martyrdom in historical perspective
1600 Carrera relation	O	O	X	X	X	X	X	(4) History in context of martyrdom
1610 Martinez relation	O	O	O	X	X	X	X	(4) History in context of martyrdom
1617–1620 Ore relation	O	O	O	X	X	X	X	(4) History in context of martyrdom
1622 Sacchini relation	O	O	O	X	X	X	X	(4) History in context of martyrdom
Narrative approach	(1) Peripheral (economic) reality	(1) Peripheral (economic) reality	(2) Peripheral fabrication	(3) Thematic fabrication	(3) Thematic fabrication	(4) Embellished thematic fabrication	(4) Embellished thematic fabrication	

Table 1.2.   Theoretically Perfect Presence/Absence Seriation. "X" denotes presence of trait; "O" denotes absence of trait.

Time/Form	A	B	C	D	E
1	X	X	O	O	O
2	O	X	X	O	O
3	O	X	X	X	O
4	O	O	X	X	O
5	O	O	O	X	X

embellishment. Narrators went from obscuring secondary details to switching the story's theme. Ribadeneyra's protomartyrdom relation was the initial account to label the Jesuits as "martyrs," yet he did not employ emotional metaphors to support this theme. These sorts of thematic embellishments constituted the fourth, "supermartyrdom," phase. The authors used religious and metaphorical images, like Jesus, Judas, and a wolf in sheep's clothing, to tell a history of Ajacan in the context of the martyrdom. The historical perspective had been sacrificed for the ethical concerns of the underlying moral. Whereas Ribadeneyra's approach presented the martyrdom in historical perspective, Carrera and later writers told historical accounts in the context of the martyrdom. The narratives began and ended with the premise that the Jesuits had been martyred.

Conclusion

This study employed an old analytical technique—seriate analysis—in a new way. Using a traditional archaeological tool on sixteenth- and seventeenth-century texts to pinpoint the development and transformation of a historical myth provides us with a different sort of history, namely, archaeological history. Since the technique of seriate analysis spawned from the earliest tenets of anthropological thought, use of this methodology on historical records emphasizes the benefits of interdisciplinary approaches to issues in history, archaeology, and anthropology. It can also synthesize methodological approaches that are both empirically based and sensitive to marginalized perspectives and the politics of oppression.

Notes

1. For example, George W. Brainerd, "The Place of Chronological Ordering in Archaeological Analysis," *American Antiquity* 16 (1951): 301–13; Philip, J. Phillips, A. Ford, and J. B. Griffin, "Archaeological Survey in the Lower Mississippi Alluvial Valley, 1940–47," *Papers of the Peabody Museum* (1951); Clement W. Meighan, "A New Method for the Seriation of Archaeological Collections," *American Antiquity* 25 (1959): 203–21; James Deetz and Edward Dethlefsen, "The Doppler Effect and Archaeology: A Consideration of the Spatial Aspects of Seriation," *Southwestern Journal of Anthropology* 21 (3)(1965): 196–206; Frank Hole and Mary Shaw, "Computer Analysis of Chronological Seriation," *Rice University Studies* 53 (1967); William B. Craytor and Leroy Johnson, Jr., "Refinements in Computerized Item Seriation," *Museum of Natural History, University of Oregon, Bulletin* 10 (1968); Leroy Johnson, Jr., "Item Seriation as an Aid for Elementary Scale and Cluster Analysis," *Museum of Natural History, University of Oregon, Bulletin* 15 (1968); Robert C. Dunnell, "Seriation Method and its Evaluation," *American Antiquity* 35 (1970): 305–19.

2. Archaeologists have repeatedly isolated gradual stylistic transformations through

seriations, from Flinders Petrie's inaugural Diospolis Parva sequence of ceramic jars from predynastic Egyptian tombs (W. M. Flinders Petrie, *Seventy Years in Archaeology* [New York: Greenwood Press, 1932] to James Deetz and Edwin Dethlefsen's celebrated New England colonial gravestone analysis (Deetz and Dethlefsen, 1965: 196–206; Edward Dethlefsen and James Deetz, "Death's Heads, Cherubs, and Willow Trees: Experimental Archaeology in Colonial Cemeteries" *American Antiquity* 31(4)(1966): 502–10; James Deetz, *In Small Things Forgotten* [New York: Doubleday, 1996]).

3. A major underlying assumption of scholars who employ traditional anthropologically archaeological seriations is in the belief that change and drift are relatively gradual and result in intermediate forms. The concepts of gradual change and physical intermediacy shaped the discipline of anthropology at its inception (Georges Comte de Buffon, *Natural History* [Halifax: Milner and Sowerby, 1749]; James Hutton, *Theory of the Earth, or, An Investigation of the Laws Observable in the Composition, Dissolution and Restoration of Land Upon the Globe* [Edinburgh: The Society, 1785]; Charles Lyell, *Elements of Geology* [J. Murray: London, 1830]; Charles Darwin, *The Origin of Species* [Chicago: Rand, McNally, 1859]; Charles Darwin, *On the Contrivances by Which British and Foreign Orchids are Fertilized by Insects* [New York: D. Appleton and Company, 1862]; Charles Darwin, *Descent of Man* (New York: D. Appleton and Company, 1871]). The historical anthropological attention to gradual geological, biological, and cultural change (Herbert Spencer, *On Social Evolution* [Chicago: University of Chicago Press, 1857]; E. B. Tylor, *Primitive Culture* (New York: Harper, 1871); Lewis Henry Morgan, *Ancient Society* (Cambridge: Belknap Press of Harvard University Press, 1877) and necessary intermediary forms was the context for later developments in seriate analyses of materials uncovered at prehistoric archaeological sites (e.g., Alfred Kidder, *An Introduction to the Study of Southwestern Archaeology* [Andover, Mass.: Phillips Academy, 1924]). In addition, many early historical archaeologists, including Harrington (J. C. Harrington, "Dating stem fragments of seventeenth and eighteenth century clay tobacco pipes," *Quarterly Bulletin, Archaeological Society of Virginia* 9(1)(1954): 10–14) and his innovative analysis of gradually changing pipestem bore diameters, used these sorts of material studies in series to examine their assemblages as well (e.g., Adrian Oswald, "English Clay Tobacco Pipes," *The Archaeological Newsletter* (1951); Deetz and Dethlefsen, 1965).

4. Deetz, *In Small Things Forgotten*, 260.

5. Eugene Lyon, *The Enterprise of Florida: Pedro Menendez de Aviles and the Spanish Conquest of 1565–1568* (Gainesville: University Press of Florida, 1976), 165; Clifford Lewis and Albert Loomie, *The Spanish Jesuit Mission in Virginia 1570–1572* (Chapel Hill: University of North Carolina Press, 1953), 5.

6. Woodbury Lowery, *The Spanish Settlements Within the Present Limits of the United States: Florida, 1562–1574* (New York: G. P. Putnam's Sons, 1911), 339–58; Lewis and Loomie, *Spanish Jesuit Mission*, 93.

7. Paul Hoffman, *A New Andulucia and a Way to the Orient: The American Southeast during the Sixteenth Century* (Baton Rouge: Louisiana State University Press, 1990), 265–66.

8. David B. Quinn, *North America from Earliest Discovery to First Settlements, the Norse Voyages to 1612* (New York: Harper & Row/Harper Colophon Books, 1977), 283.

9. Seth Mallios, "In the Hands of 'Indian Givers': Exchange and Violence at Ajacan, Roanoke, and Jamestown. (Ph.D. diss., University of Virginia, Charlottesville, 1998). University Microfilms International, Ann Arbor, MI (1998); Seth Mallios, "Exchange and Violence at Ajacan, Roanoke, and Jamestown," in *Native Americans of the Chesapeake Region in the Age of Contact: Archaeological Perspectives*, eds. Dennis Blanton and Julia King (Gainesville: University of Florida Press, 2004a); Seth Mallios, "Gift Exchange and the Ossomocomuck Balance of Power: Explaining Carolina Algonquian Socioeconomic Aberrations at Contact," in *Searching for the Roanoke Colonies: An Interdisciplinary Collection*, eds. E. Thomson Shields and Charles Ewen (N.C.: North Carolina Department of Cultural Resources, Division of Archives and History, Historical Publications Section, 2004b).

References

Brainerd, George W. 1951. The place of chronological ordering in archaeological analysis. *American Antiquity* 16:301–13.

Comte de Buffon, Georges. 1749. *Natural History*. Halifax: Milner and Sowerby.

Craytor, William B. and Leroy Johnson, Jr. 1968. Refinements in computerized item seriation. *Museum of Natural History, University of Oregon, Bulletin* 10.

Darwin, Charles. 1859. *The Origin of Species*. Chicago: Rand, McNally.

Darwin, Charles. 1862. *On the Contrivances by Which British and Foreign Orchids Are Fertilized by Insects*. New York: D. Appleton and Company.

Darwin, Charles. 1871. *Descent of Man*. New York: D. Appleton and Company.

Deetz, James. 1996. *In Small Things Forgotten*. New York: Doubleday.

Deetz, James, and Edward Dethlefsen. 1965. The Doppler effect and archaeology: a consideration of the spatial aspects of seriation. *Southwestern Journal of Anthropology*. 21 (3):196–206.

Dethlefsen, Edward, and James Deetz. 1966. Death's heads, cherubs, and willow trees: experimental archaeology in colonial cemeteries. *American Antiquity*. 31(4):502–10.

Dunnell, Robert C. 1970. Seriation method and its evaluation. *American Antiquity*. 35:305–19.

Harrington, J. C. 1954. Dating stem fragments of seventeenth and eighteenth century clay tobacco pipes. *Quarterly Bulletin, Archaeological Society of Virginia*. 9(1):10–14.

Hoffman, Paul. 1990. *A New Andulucia and a Way to the Orient: The American Southeast during the Sixteenth Century*. Baton Rouge: Louisiana State University Press.

Hole, Frank, and Mary Shaw. 1967. Computer analysis of chronological seriation. *Rice University Studies* 53.

Hutton, James. 1785. *Theory of the earth, or, An investigation of the laws observable in the composition, dissolution and restoration of land upon the globe*. Edinburgh: The Society.

Johnson, Leroy, Jr. 1968. Item seriation as an aid for elementary scale and cluster analysis. *Museum of Natural History, University of Oregon, Bulletin* 15.

Kidder, Alfred. 1924. *An Introduction to the Study of Southwestern Archaeology*. Andover, Mass.: Phillips Academy.

Lewis, Clifford, and Albert Loomie. 1953. *The Spanish Jesuit Mission in Virginia 1570–1572*. Chapel Hill: University of North Carolina Press.

Lowery, Woodbury. 1911. *The Spanish Settlements within the Present Limits of the United States: Florida, 1562–1574*. New York: G. P. Putnam's Sons.

Lyell, Charles. 1830. *Elements of Geology*. London: J. Murray.

Lyon, Eugene. 1976. *The Enterprise of Florida: Pedro Menendez de Aviles and the Spanish Conquest of 1565–1568*. Gainesville: University Press of Florida.

Mallios, Seth. 1998. In the Hands of "Indian Givers": Exchange and Violence at Ajacan, Roanoke, and Jamestown. Ph.D. diss., University of Virginia, Charlottesville.

Mallios, Seth. 2004a. Exchange and violence at Ajacan, Roanoke, and Jamestown. In *Native Americans of the Chesapeake Region in the Age of Contact: Archaeological Perspectives*, Dennis Blanton and Julia King, eds. Gainesville: University of Florida Press.

Mallios, Seth. 2004b. Gift exchange and the Ossomocomuck balance of power: Explaining Carolina Algonquian socioeconomic aberrations at contact. In *Searching for the Roanoke Colonies: An Interdisciplinary Collection*. E. Thomson Shields and Charles Ewen, eds. North Carolina: North Carolina Department of Cultural Resources, Division of Archives and History, Historical Publications Section.

Meighan, Clement W. 1959. A new method for the seriation of archaeological collections. *American Antiquity* 25:203–11.

Morgan, Lewis Henry. 1877. *Ancient Society*. Cambridge, Mass.: Belknap Press of Harvard University Press.

Oswald, Adrian. 1951. English clay tobacco pipes. *The Archaeological Newsletter*.

Petrie, W. M. Flinders. 1932. *Seventy Years in Archaeology*. New York: Greenwood Press.

Phillips, Philip, J. A. Ford, and J. B. Griffin. 1951. Archaeological survey in the lower Mississippi Alluvial Valley, 1940–47. *Papers of the Peabody Museum*.

Quinn, David B. 1977. *North America from Earliest Discovery to First Settlements, the Norse Voyages to 1612*. New York: Harper & Row/Harper Colophon Books.

Spencer, Herbert. 1857. *On Social Evolution*. Chicago: University of Chicago Press.

Tylor, E. B. 1871. *Primitive Culture*. New York: Harper.

"We Washed Not the Ground with Their Bloods": Intercultural Violence and Identity in the Early Chesapeake

2

MELANIE PERREAULT

WHEN ENGLISH SETTLERS arrived in the Chesapeake in the seventeenth century, they entered into a complex, often violent relationship with the native peoples they encountered. The colonists who came to establish the Jamestown settlement were greeted on their first evening with a shower of arrows that wounded a sailor "in two places of the body very dangerous," and responded with their own volley of gunshot that sent the Indians scrambling for cover in the nearby woods. Periods of relative peace alternated with episodes of extraordinary violence, all catalogued in the often self-serving English accounts of their efforts to establish a permanent presence in the Chesapeake. John Smith included detailed descriptions of Indian efforts to poison, torture, and kill the English interlopers, yet he emphasized the restraint with which the English met each attack. Indeed, Smith acknowledged, some readers might find it "unpleasant that we washed not the ground with their bloods, nor showed such strange inventions, in mangling, murdering, ransacking, and destroying (as did the Spaniards) the simple bodies of those ignorant souls." Smith's comparison with the Spanish reveals a central theme of early English accounts of Anglo-Indian relations in the Chesapeake. English writers fashioned themselves as defenders of the Indians, offering protection from enemy Indian groups, indiscriminate Spanish violence, and eternal damnation.[1]

Implicit in these narratives was an effort to establish a distinct national identity, and the Chesapeake offered a prime testing ground where the English could contrast themselves with Indians and other Europeans. In the early seventeenth century, race was not yet a fixed category by which the English could establish

23

their identity. References to skin color were descriptive rather than discriminatory, particularly since most observers agreed that the environment, not some innate characteristic, determined the hue and general appearance of one's skin. Instead, English writers, like other Europeans, participated in a discourse that contrasted themselves from overseas others using religious identity—the others were invariably "heathens." Even as sixteenth-century England was experiencing the throes of internal disorder and division, based in part on religious faction, the early encounters with peoples who openly maintained vastly different notions of spirituality served to mute attention toward the longstanding schisms at home.[2]

Despite significant religious and political differences, a common Christian identity offered at least some sense of unified purpose for Protestants and Catholics in early modern England. The defeat of the Spanish Armada in 1588 and the absence of any large-scale Catholic revolts in England were sufficient evidence that God had selected the English for a special purpose distinct from those of other Christians. Colonial promoters appealed to that sense of unity as they argued for a cooperative effort to establish an English presence in the New World. In the dangerous, heathen lands of Virginia, the English could obscure their very real religious differences and begin the process of forging an English identity upon the land and its people. Richard Hakluyt acknowledged that such a work would take place gradually, only after the colonists "learned the language of the people . . . and by little and little acquaint themselves with their manner," but ultimately the English would succeed in "gaining the souls of millions of those wretched people, the reducing of them from darkness to light, from falsehood to truth, from dumb Idols to the living God, from the deep pit of Hell to the highest heavens." Economic concerns were at the forefront of colonial arguments in favor of overseas ventures, but the assurance that God had chosen the English for this task was a significant component of many promotional efforts.[3]

Of course, the Spanish could make equal claim to the desire to establish a Christian presence in "heathen" lands, and unlike the English, they could point to the presence of Spanish missionaries in the New World since the fifteenth century. These incontrovertible facts called for a further refinement of the English argument in favor of establishing distant colonies. In their promotional pamphlets and in their exploration narratives, English authors explicitly contrasted their behavior with that of their Spanish rivals. While many English advocates of colonization openly admired the Spanish organizational skills and the economic empire they established in the New World, even the most laudatory accounts noted the perverse pleasure the Spanish seemed to take in devising horrific deaths for their Indian victims. Although the "Black Legend" of Spanish violence in America had its origins in the protests of Las Casas in the early sixteenth century, anti-Spanish discourse intensified in Europe during the Revolt of the Netherlands (1565–1608). The publication of the first English translation of Las Casas in 1583 ignited a firestorm of criticism aimed at Spanish activities in Europe and the New World. Happily for the English, the alleged cruelty of the Spanish offered an opportunity to justify their entry into the scramble for America rather late in the game.[4]

Not surprisingly, some of the most vehemently anti-Spanish attitudes came from promoters of English colonization. Richard Hakluyt's "Discourse of Western Planting," written in 1584, argued that the Spaniards had so grievously assaulted the peaceful natives of the West Indies that they no longer had the moral authority to rule over the Indians. Quoting extensively from Las Casas, Hakluyt included graphic accounts of Spanish conquerors, who allegedly "took the little souls by the heels ramping them from their mothers' breasts and crushed their heads against the cliffs." Even more shocking than the alleged incidents of brutality, Hakluyt claimed, was the reception of these accounts in Spain. When presented with the graphic descriptions, "so passing strange and exceeding all humanity and moderation have they been that the very rehearsal of them drove diverse of the cruel Spanish which had not been in the West Indies into a kind of ecstasy and maze." Such a reaction indicated that the horrific violence might not simply be attributable to the indiscriminate actions of individual conquistadors, but instead reflected a larger character flaw of the Spanish people as a whole. Hakluyt's treatise was an unpublished document intended for the eyes of a few government officials, and could afford to be explicit about the author's feelings toward the Spanish rivals. The anti-Spanish rhetoric contained the seeds of a nascent notion of a distinct identity for the English, resting in part on their apparently "natural" aversion to indiscriminate violence, steeped in religious rhetoric.[5]

By the late sixteenth century, the English began openly to fashion themselves as protectors of the Indians, the role Las Casas sought for himself but ultimately failed to achieve. Walter Ralegh's efforts to establish an English colony in Guiana offered an opportunity for the English to compare their behavior in a region where the Spanish still struggled to exert control over the local population. Virtually every early account included testimony from native men begging the English to come protect them from the depredations of the Spanish. According to the English, everywhere they went they heard stories of sexual abuse, abduction, and murder at the hands of the Spanish. Thomas Masham reported that the Indians "made known their minds of the desire that they had to have the English come and kill the Spaniards." If killing their European rivals was not an option, Lawrence Keymis argued, the English could at least establish a permanent presence in Guiana, "as being the only help to put a bit in the mouth of the unbridled Spanish." The English further refined their unique identity by claiming an innate sense of justice, which stood in sharp contrast to the allegedly fiery-tempered Spanish.[6]

But all of these claims to the English status as divinely sanctioned protectors of Indians contained within them a potentially fatal flaw if the English participants failed to live up to the high standards such claims inevitably created. Advocates of an quasi-pacifist English presence in the New World faced a serious challenge in North America, where experience had already shown that plans hatched in England often did not prove effective in the distant lands across the ocean. Despite a stated desire to work peacefully with the natives of Roanoke Island, the military men who dominated English efforts to establish a colony there did not view nonviolent conflict resolution as a primary objective. Their leader, Ralph Lane, struggled to maintain discipline within the ranks of his own men while keeping an eye on the nearby Indians. In July 1585 the English claimed that an Indian had stolen a silver cup. The precipitating event seems minor, but in the highly charged atmosphere of distrust and fear that had developed in less than a year of colonization, the English reaction was swift and unrelenting. Not satisfied after requesting the return of the cup, the English "burnt and spoiled their corn, and town, all the people being fled." A series of raids from both sides ensued, with the Indians suffering the brunt of the injuries and deaths at the hands of Lane and his soldiers. Thomas Harriot explained that before Lane's colony abandoned Roanoke, "some of our company . . . showed themselves too fierce in slaying some of the people in some towns, upon causes that on our part might easily enough been borne withal." Although Harriot believed that the Indians recognized that the violence was "on their part justly deserved," and that the English were blameless, the failure to establish a successful relationship with the residents of Roanoke heightened concerns that colonization might be more difficult than its promoters suggested.[7]

If religion separated English from Indian, and unrestrained violence distinguished English from Spanish, how then could the English maintain their identity in a region that threatened to expose the fragility of such cultural markers? The rudimentary church established in early Virginia held only a tenuous control over the notoriously undisciplined colonists. And the powerful Powhatan Indians would not simply step aside and allow the newcomers to disrupt their efforts at empire building, an often bloody process that had been underway for years before the English arrival. Faced with a potentially unsettling choice of remaining true to a discourse of English pacifism or engaging in intercultural violence with the risk that they would lose their claim to Englishness, the colonists chose instead to redefine their acts of violence as a reassertion of a waning English identity, using religious rhetoric to justify their actions to themselves and to other potential critics. In the process, the English inhabitants of the Chesapeake unknowingly began developing their own identity distinct from that of their compatriots in England.[8]

When the English turned their attention from the failed efforts in Roanoke to the more promising environs of the Chesapeake in the seventeenth century, they already had a well-established rhetoric that justified English occupation of American lands as a bulwark against Spanish violence. Robert Johnson extolled the benefits of incorporating the Indians of Virginia into English society, "not by storms of raging cruelties (as West India was converted) with rapiers point and musket shot, murdering so many millions of naked Indians, as their stories do relate, but by fair and loving means suiting to our English natures." Recognizing that the Powhatan Indians had already had violent encounters with the Spanish at Ajacan, during his first meeting with Powhatan John Smith portrayed the English as fellow victims to Spanish aggression. When the Indian leader inquired about the purpose of the English visit, Smith explained that the English "being in fight with the Spaniards our enemy, being overpowered, near put to retreat, and by extreme weather [we] put to this shore." As soon as they fixed their pinnace, the English assured their nervous hosts, they would be on their way. Smith's lie not only offered an explanation for the English arrival, it also reasserted the association between the Spanish and violent behavior and sought to distinguish the apparently harmless English in the minds of the Indians.[9]

Despite their stated intention to leave, the English quickly began establishing a permanent presence in the Chesapeake. Initial plans called for a close integration between the Indians and the English in order to facilitate economic development. The ideal society called for daily interaction between the English colonists and their Indian neighbors; their experiences in other lands suggested that such a relationship, however difficult, would be mutually beneficial. The English would benefit from the creation of a reliable trading partner who could also serve as a vital informant about the land and its people. In a set of notes to Sir Humphrey Gilbert written in 1578, Richard Hakluyt the Younger advised that in a potential American colony "nothing is more to be endeavored with the inland people than familiarity. For so may you discover all the natural commodities of their country, and also all their wants, all their strengths, all their weakness, and with whom they are at war, and with whom confederate in peace and amity." Friendly Indians living near the English settlement could also provide a convenient food supply and an instant source of labor. The greatest benefit for the Indians, the English argued, would be that through the example of the colonists "they will daily by little and little, forsake their barbarous and savage living, and grow to such order and civility with us." Eventually, the Indians would come to adopt the identity of their superior neighbors, a development that would be as welcome as it was inevitable.[10]

Unlike the Puritans who would later establish Massachusetts Bay, or even the Jesuit missionaries in New France, the Anglican settlers who dominated the first two decades of Virginia's colonial development brought with them a religious ideology that explicitly mixed spiritual conquest with state-sponsored imperialism. But the settlers were not trying to establish some sort of religious utopia in Jamestown, and the leaders of the Virginia Company were careful to keep materialism at the center of the colony's activities. While religious turmoil tore apart Europe, Virginians settled for a more generalized ecumenical Christianity that emphasized Christian morality over a specific doctrine. By focusing on the *behavioral* value of Christianity, the Anglicans in the Virginia Company could control the worst impulses of their lower-class employees, and the Native Americans who might influence them, and simultaneously contrast themselves with their Christian rivals, whose violent behavior demonstrated the alleged flaws of the Catholic faith.[11]

After the initial skirmishes, incidents of violence between the colonists and the Indians before 1609 were limited in their scope and objectives. The English use of violence had two primary goals during this period: to punish for a perceived wrong and to force the natives to provide sustenance for the colony. For the Indians, violence served primarily as a means to test the strength of the English or as resistance to English aggression. There was no all-out attempt by either side to completely eliminate the other; neither the English nor the Indians believed they had the capability to achieve a total victory and each side still considered the other a potentially valuable ally. Since the Indians were to be a part of colonial society, they had to learn acceptable behavior quickly, and violence fit the English pedagogy. In many cases, the violence was intended more as a subtle reminder of English dominance rather than as an unfettered assault. During the first meeting with the Paspaheghs at Jamestown, one of the colonists caught an Indian stealing a hatchet, "whereupon he took it from him by force, and also struck him over the arm." John Smith was quick to use physical correction to chastise what he perceived to be uncooperative Indians. After being led around the woods in a fruitless search for a "glistering mineral stone," Smith refused to pay the previously agreed-upon copper to his guide, "but for his scoffing and abusing us," Smith reported, "I gave him twenty lashes with a rope." The relatively mild physical punishment stood in contrast with harsher treatment when the issue at hand was not hatchets or stones, but the more pressing English need for food.[12]

The violence associated with forcing the Indians to supply the English colony

with food arose out of a misunderstanding of the abundance of native food supplies, suspicion that the natives were deliberately withholding food as a means of
ridding themselves of the colony, and sheer desperation on the part of the hungry
colonists. The most famous incident, one that would have long-lasting ramifications for the Anglo-Indian relationship, occurred in January 1609, when Smith
confronted Powhatan, who appeared to be reneging on an agreement to trade for
corn. After issuing several only slightly veiled threats, Smith succeeded in having
his boat loaded with corn. Two days later, Smith challenged Powhatan's brother
Opechancanough to a one-on-one fight—the winner was to receive corn or copper. Opechancanough tried instead to ambush the English, but Smith "in such
rage snatched the king by his long lock [of hair] in the midst of his men, with his
pistol ready bent against his breast." The Englishman's grabbing of Opechancanough's scalplock was deeply offensive to the native leader; to the Algonquians,
the scalplock was sacred, a "physical manifestation of the soul." Smith then
addressed Opechancanough's people, declaring that "you promised to freight my
ship ere I departed, and so I shall, or I mean to load her with your dead carcasses."
Under Smith's leadership, the threat of violence accompanied by a small demon-
stration of force rather than unbridled violence was an effective means of forcing
the Indians to provide food for the English, and did not challenge the English
sense of themselves as protectors of the Indians. The beginning of what Frederick
Fausz has aptly named the "First Anglo-Powhatan War" forced the English to
reevaluate their position.[13]

Determined to remove the English from Jamestown, the Powhatan Indians
embarked upon a campaign of systematic violence in 1609. English accounts
offered lurid details of Indian activities, drawing readers into bloody scenes certain to evoke horror. With the fort under siege, George Percy sent messengers to
arrange a meeting with the surrounding Indians, but reported that "they were
sacrificed, and that their brains were cut and scraped out of their heads with mus-
sel shells." The notion that the Englishmen had been sacrificed in some sort of
Indian religious ritual tapped into a European trope of savagery that identified all
Indians as potential cannibals and viewed native American religions as a mere
synecdoche for the devil. John Smith was convinced that the Powhatans were
devil worshipers, claiming that their chief god "Oke" was the devil, whom they
served "more of fear than love." Many early English visitors to Virginia reported
that the Indians practiced child sacrifice as part of a yearly religious festival.
Surely, the English argued, a people so frightened by a god that they would kill
their own children to appease him would not hesitate to sacrifice the outsiders
who had recently arrived in their midst.[14]

In fact, the Powhatans acknowledged many different gods, the most powerful being the deity Smith knew as Oke. Since Oke had the power to reward people with good weather, a good hunt, and good health, or alternatively could punish transgressors with illness or a poor harvest, the Powhatans sought to appease the god through ritual offerings. The English interpreted native religious practices as demonic, failing to understand the immediate relationship between the Indians and the gods who could intervene in daily life. The alleged "child sacrifice" reported by several English observers was actually a coming-of-age ceremony called the *huskenaw*. The yearly event involved symbolic death rather than the gruesome stories spread by early English accounts.[15]

The belief that the Indians were somehow harnessing the power of mysterious evil forces helped explain not only their willingness to engage in bloody rituals, but also served as an explanation for their ability to defeat the allegedly superior firepower and tactics of the English soldiers. Evidence of the Indians' use of sorcery to fight the English came when Sir Thomas Dale and a group of gentlemen were sitting in an Indian's house, when suddenly "a fantasy possessed them, each man taking one another for an Indian, and so did fall pell-mell one upon another, beating one another down and breaking one of another's heads" before realizing their error. Confronted with such mysterious forces, the English responded with their own campaign of violence, often targeting Algonquian religious symbols. In a spree of destruction that recalled the Spanish annihilation of the Aztec temples during the conquest of Mexico, English soldiers "ransacked their temples, took down the corpse of their dead kings from off their tombs, and carried away their pearls, copper, and bracelets wherewith they do decore their kings' funerals." Clearly, the Anglo-Indian relationship had deteriorated significantly since Smith's departure a year earlier.[16]

The wave of violence threatened to erase the tenuous distinctions colonial promoters had begun delineating in their efforts to justify English settlements in America. At the same time, colonial leaders believed that a failure to respond quickly to the Indian attacks would invite more violence, severely undermining efforts to attract new settlers. To resolve the dilemma, the English engaged in a brutal campaign, including the killing of women and children, but were careful to cast their behavior in terms that actually reinforced their image as being interested in justice rather than bloodshed. After being appointed a marshal for the struggling colony, Thomas Dale pursued perceived enemies and "in a most severe manner caused [them] to be executed: Some he appointed to be broken upon wheels, others to be staked, and some to be shot to death." That the Indians were "executed" implied a legal foundation for the killings, even though no trials took place. William Strachey sought to downplay the significance of the English violence by offering a family metaphor. Quoting the preacher William Symonds,

Strachey argued: "'It is as much (saith he) as if a father should be said to offer violence to his child, when he beats him, to bring him to goodness." English violence, unlike that of the Spanish, was not motivated by greed or a character flaw, but was designed as a corrective to bad behavior, a domestic response to a wayward child who needed guidance.[17]

Indeed, Strachey argued, the English were uniquely positioned to understand and appreciate the use of violence not as mere punishment, but as a civilizing force. Any doubts as to its efficacy could be answered with a quick examination of England's own history. John White and Thomas Harriot, two of the participants in the failed Roanoke effort, included portraits of English ancestors, the Picts and the Britons, in their collection of drawings of Algonquians. Adorned in body paint, wearing little clothing, and carrying crude weapons, the English forebearers appear strikingly similar to the Indians, a not-so-subtle reminder that the "civilized" English were a recent development. Strachey pointed out that the transformation did not come peacefully, but that "had not this violence, and this injury, been offered unto us by the Romans . . . we might yet have lived [as] overgrown Satyrs, rude, and untutored, wandering in the woods, dwelling in caves, and hunting for our dinners." Violence should be limited in its scope, but was not necessarily antithetical to the English mission.[18]

While Strachey turned to his understanding of history to justify the increasingly violent Anglo-Indian relationship, many English observers turned to their religious beliefs to understand and explain the violence that plagued the colony. Although the early settlers of Jamestown developed a well-earned reputation for lawlessness, crude behavior, and materialistic motives, their worldview was also infused with religious imagery and practice. Each day offered constant reminders of the faith that, while the settlers often fell short of its ideals, shaped the rhythms of their lives. While John Smith was in charge, he reported, the colonists gathered for a daily prayer and a Psalm. Not surprisingly, a few of the settlers found it difficult to maintain their faith in the wilderness, particularly during times of severe stress. George Percy described an incident in 1609 when Hugh Pryce, "being pinched with extreme famine in a furious distracted mood did come openly into the market place Blaspheming exclaiming and crying out that there was no God. Alleging that if there were a God he would not suffer his creatures whom he had made and framed to endure those miseries." The other colonists saw their faith confirmed later that day when the Indians killed Pryce and wolves devoured his body.[19]

While Pryce apparently sealed his own fate through his public declaration of blasphemous words, the other colonists were not free from blame for God's apparent anger. Reflecting on the "starving time" that had just passed and the escalating violence in the colony, the Reverend Alexander Whitaker explained that "God hath heretofore most horribly plagued our countrymen with famine, death, the sword, etc., for the sins of our men were intolerable." Indeed, Whitaker wrote, "I marvel more that God did not sweep them away all at once than that in such a manner He did punish them." By attributing the Indian behavior to God's will, the English neatly avoided examining whether the native peoples had just cause to attack the colonists. The violence was due to a vague list of sins; notably absent was any mention of displacing an entire native population or stealing their primary means of sustenance. While God could use the Indians as instruments of punishment, He could also use them to relieve the English. George Percy marveled that at the height of the siege on Jamestown, a group of Indians arrived with food for the starving colonists. Percy claimed that "if it had not pleased God to have put a terror in the savages' hearts, we had all perished by those wild and cruel pagans, being in that weak estate as we were." By attributing the gift as an act of God, the English eliminated Indian agency, even in an act of mercy. Nonetheless, the timely arrival of the Indians suggested that there was still hope for a peaceful relationship with the Indians. The violence, while horrific, could be overcome with divine assistance and cooler heads on both sides.[20]

English accounts of the First Anglo-Powhatan War were careful to discount any comparison to the Spanish, and moved quickly to reestablish English identity as protectors of the Indians. Thomas Dale asserted that "this action of such price . . . should not die to the scorn of our nation, and to give cause of laughter to the Papists that desire our ruin." The real targets of English efforts to forge a successful presence in America were not only the Powhatans, but the Spanish as well. To remove any doubt that the English intended to prevent unrestrained violence against the Indians, Dale instituted a series of laws designed to limit the interaction between the Indians and the English. Although the separation meant the temporary end of the Virginia Company's plans to gain wealth through an integrated society, the risk of continued intercultural violence was greater than the potential rewards. Running off to live with the Indians was forbidden under pain of death, and even communication with the natives without the permission of the governor was prohibited. Any direct assault on the Indians would earn swift retribution. The laws declared that "whosoever shall willfully, or negligently set fire on any Indian dwelling house . . . or ill entreat the people of the country . . . except it be proclaimed, or without commandment of the chief officers shall be punished with death." Of course, the order allowed officially sanctioned violence to continue, but the proclamation was an attempt to reduce the worst abuses of the Indians.[21]

As it became increasingly clear that it would be impossible to avoid intercultural violence entirely, the English began to lay the groundwork for a justification for future conflict that would not undermine their identity as protectors. The Bible offered guidelines for a holy war that could be applied in the New World if necessary. In *A Good Speed to Virginia*, written just as the violence was escalating in 1609, Robert Gray pointed out that "David by way of prophecy, doth promise a blessing to those that shall take the children of the idolatrous Babylonians and dash them against the stone, and they that have taken arms against such people, are said to fight the Lord's battles." While the Spanish had also appealed to biblical precedent to explain their persecution of allegedly heathen Indians, the English were particularly well suited to engage in a genuine holy war since they were constitutionally opposed to indiscriminate violence. Spanish atrocities undermined their religious motives, Gray argued, but "far be it from the nature of the English, to execute any bloody cruelty amongst these people: far be it from the hearts of the English, to give them occasion, that the holy name of God, should be dishonored among the infidels." Violence in the name of God did not constitute "bloody cruelty" as long as it was administered with the correct frame of mind.[22]

After the marriage of Pocahontas to John Rolfe in 1614, tension between the English and Indians in the Chesapeake decreased, and it appeared as though each side was fulfilling the role the colonizers had intended. The peace, Francis Wyatt reported in November 1621, was "advantageous to both parts; to the savages as the weaker, under which they were safely sheltered and defended; to us as being the easiest way thought to pursue and advance our projects of buildings, plantings, and effecting their conversion by peaceably and fair means." To the new governor of the colony, the calm demeanor of the Indians was a welcome sign of their acceptance of their dependent status. Just as Pocahontas had placed herself legally under the identity of her English husband, so too had the Powhatans embraced the passive position of the defended.[23]

The peace came to a shattering end March 22, 1622, when the Powhatan leader Opechancanough led a surprise attack against the colonists. English accounts describe a pre-attack scene of intercultural tolerance and cooperation, where Dale's laws prescribing the separation of the races no longer seemed necessary. On the very morning of the attack, "in some places, [the Indians] sat down at breakfast with our people at their tables," demonstrating a casual intimacy that belied the bloodshed that was to follow. Without warning, the houseguests "immediately with their own [English] tools and weapons, either laid down, or standing in their houses, they basely and barbarously murdered, not sparing either age or sex, man, woman, or child." Although the colonists lived in a violent society, the sheer brutality of the attack left them struggling to understand what had happened. English accounts lingered over gory details, even as they claimed to be censoring the worst images of that day to spare readers the trauma of witnessing the bloodshed secondhand. The Indians "not being content with taking away life alone, they fell after again upon the dead, making as well as they could, a fresh murder, defacing, dragging, and mangling the dead carcasses into many pieces, and carrying some parts away in derision." Surely, these were the acts of inhuman predators, the English suggested.[24]

The Indian betrayal was magnified by the use of the victims' own weapons against them. By using English "tools and weapons" against their unsuspecting owners, the Indians appropriated symbols of English civility in an act of savagery. Caught in the very act of transforming the wilderness into a civilized "English" land, the unsuspecting colonists had little chance to defend themselves. The Indians attacked settlers who were "at their several works and husbandries in the fields, and without their houses, some in planting corn and tobacco, some in gardening, some in making brick, building, sawing, and other kinds of husbandry." After the initial surprise attack, the Indians continued to violate English space: "They have killed us in our own doors, fields and houses: thus we are not safe neither at home nor abroad." Frightened colonists searched desperately for some refuge from the violence, but found no safe place to hide.[25]

The blurred lines of identity increased English anxiety, as it was no longer clear who was friend and who was foe. Richard Frethorne's panic is palpable in a letter written shortly after the initial wave of violence. The Indians, Frethorne wrote, "have gotten pieces, armor, swords, and all things fit for war, so that they may now steal upon us and we cannot know them from English, [un]til it is too late, that they be upon us, and then there is no mercy."[26] Frethorne's fear reveals the shaky foundations of identity in the seventeenth-century Chesapeake—simply by adopting a few pieces of technology, the Indians could temporarily become English, just long enough to slip into the settlements and kill the "true" English. Indeed, a stunning reversal seemed to have taken place: the English integration plan designed to draw the Indians to "civility" backfired, and the colonists no longer could be certain that they were a distinct and superior people. After learning of the massacre, John Smith opined that "it hath oft amazed me to understand how strangely the Salvages hath been taught the use of our arms, and employed in hunting and fowling with or fowling pieces, and our men rooting in the ground about tobacco like swine." In Smith's estimation, the English had degenerated not just to a state of barbarism, but into animalistic behavior. How such a transformation had taken place in only fifteen years of colonization was a matter of great concern. If the causes were external, the settlers could overcome the degeneration by recommitting to maintaining an English space in the New World. If, however, the cultural decay was an indication of an inherent weakness in English identity, degeneracy would remain a constant threat in all colonial encounters.[27]

The English initially interpreted the bloodshed as a sign from God, just as they had the earlier attacks. Shortly after the attack, the Virginia Council reported to the Virginia Company that "it hath pleased God for our manifold sins to lay a most lamentable affliction upon this Plantation, by the treachery of the Indians." In a commission authorizing George Yeardley to lead a campaign against the Indians, Governor Francis Wyatt noted, "We must with all humbleness of mind, acknowledge the just hand of God to have fallen upon us for our sins." While Wyatt did not specify the sins that might have led to such punishment, the members of the Virginia Company in London did not hesitate to identify the behavior they believed to be responsible for God's wrath. The massacre, they explained, was "the heavy hand of Almighty God for the punishment of ours and your transgressions." In particular, they wrote, "We seriously advise and invite you and in particular earnestly require the speedy redress of those two enormous excesses of apparel and drinking." Not surprisingly, the Virginia Company had identified two moral shortcomings that cost the investors money, and demanded a quick correction of the allegedly extravagant behavior.[28]

Even more alarming was the suggestion that the Indians were acting as agents for their own demonic gods or even the devil. Joseph Mead claimed that the Indians did not really want to kill the settlers, but "their God will not let them alone but terrifies them and incites them against their wills to do this wrong." While the colonists in Virginia did not have the spiritual burden of establishing a "city on a hill," which might invite special scrutiny from both God and the devil, they did note that there was a diabolical element to some of their misfortunes. The primary suspects were Indian religious leaders, since "the devil had through the medium of the priests such an influence upon the natives that they only waited for a good opportunity to extirpate the foreigners." The surprise attack of 1622 was the result of a concerted effort of the Algonquian religious authorities ("tools of the Devil"), who "were constantly working upon the credulity and ignorance of this people to make them believe that the English had come to exterminate them in the same way as the Spaniard had done in other parts of the West Indies." Even the devil recognized that equating English designs with the Spanish cruelties in the New World would seriously undermine the entire colonial effort.[29]

Despite the potentially damning evidence that either God or the devil had been behind the bloodshed in Virginia, some reports were quick to point out that God also acted as a restraining force to prevent the total annihilation of the colony at the hands of the ruthless savages. After word of the massacre reached

London in June, the Reverend Joseph Mead lamented the news of more than three hundred deaths, but noted, "All had perished in like manner, had not our God, who is the best God, had more care of them, than they had of themselves." The clearest evidence of God's mercy was the alleged warning of an impending attack delivered by an Indian convert. Edward Waterhouse reported that "though three hundred and more of ours died by many of these Pagan Infidels, yet thousands were saved by the means of one of them alone which was made a Christian." If outward appearance, use of English tools, and location were no longer reliable markers of cultural identity, then the English could fall back on their remaining distinction between themselves and their attackers—religion.[30]

In their response to the Indian attack, the English used religious rhetoric to remove all restraints from their subsequent acts of violence. During "this last outrage of these infidels," Francis Wyatt recalled, "we were forced to stand and gaze at our distressed brethren frying in the fury of our enemies, and could not relieve them." Wyatt's sense of impotence would shortly give way to a plan of action. The Indians were "infidels," as opposed to the slightly less condemnable "heathens," and thus subject to the rules of a holy war. In a vitriolic condemnation that anticipated later racist diatribes, Christopher Brooke's "Poem on the Massacre in Virginia," written shortly after news of the attack arrived in London, suggested that the Indians might not even be humans:

> Consider what those Creatures are,
> (I cannot call them men) no Character
> Of God in them: Souls drown'd in flesh and blood;
> Rooted in Evil, and oppos'd in Good;
> Errors of Nature, of inhumane Birth,
> The very dregs, garbage, and spawn of Earth . . .
> Father'd by Satan, and the sonnes of hell.

After learning of the escalation of hostilities in Virginia, Francis Bacon pondered whether natural laws governed warfare. In *An Advertisement Touching an Holy Warre, Written in the Yeare 1622*, Bacon concluded that people who had "utterly degenerate[d], from the laws of nature" and had "taken in their body and frame of estate a monstrosity" could be justly eliminated. All Indians thus became potential targets—men, women, and children were equally guilty of religious offenses against a God whom they refused to recognize despite the English presence.[31]

Any good holy war requires a good martyr, and the Virginia Company found one in George Thorpe. Arriving in the colony just two years before the attack, Thorpe immediately set about establishing good relations with the Indians. But good relations came with a catch—to foster peace, the Indians would have to transform their society to conform to the English. Among the most noteworthy of Thorpe's accomplishments was the construction of a house for Opechanca-nough, complete with a door lock, to replace the "den or hog sty, made with a few poles and sticks, and covered with mats after their wild manner." Thorpe also fashioned himself as a special protector of the Indians, even publicly executing a couple of English mastiffs after a delegation of Indians complained about their use as weapons of terror. Yet Thorpe's efforts did nothing to save him from the Indians. In fact, he seemed to be a particular target of their wrath, since his killers "out of devilish malice, did so many barbarous despites and foul scorns to his dead corpse." Waterhouse observed that Thorpe, "to the comfort of us all, hath gained a crown of endless bliss and is assuredly become a glorious martyr, in which thrice-happy and blessed state we leave him."[32]

At the heart of the English accounts written in response to the attack, there was almost a sense of relief that the English no longer had to pay even lip service to protecting the Indians. As a result of the Indian violence, Waterhouse wrote, "our hands which before were tied with gentleness and fair usage, are now set at liberty by the treacherous violence of the savages, not untying the knot, but cut-ting it." Members of the Virginia Company advised that "since the innocent blood of so many Christians, doth in justice cry out for revenge . . . we must advise you to root out from being any longer a people, so cursed a nation, ungrateful to all benefit, and uncapable of goodness." Total destruction was the goal, the company recommended, "burning their towns, demolishing their tem-ples, destroying their canoes, plucking up their weirs, carrying away their corn, and depriving them of whatsoever may yield them relief." If the colonists could not totally wipe out their Indian foes, the company recommended "the removal of them so far from you, as you may not only be out of danger, but out of fear of them." All signs of Indian culture were to be removed from the region sur-rounding the English settlements, transforming them into a more clearly defined English space.[33]

The military men living in Virginia needed little encouragement to launch a counterattack. Even before the company's instructions to attack the Indians arrived in Jamestown, the colonists reported, "We have anticipated your desires by setting upon the Indians in all places." Traditional military assaults were not effective against foes who could so easily disappear into the woods, but the colo-nists promised to use starvation and "all other means that we can possibly devise [so that] we will constantly pursue their extirpation." Since all Indians had become legitimate targets for the English militias, there was no longer any need to make even the slightest justification for a blunt approach to the military strikes.[34]

Despite the rhetoric advocating genocide, complete destruction of the Indians was out of the question not only because it was an impractical goal, but also because it would eliminate a necessary source of food and might have unintended consequences for English identity. John Martin reasoned that the surrounding Indians "have ever kept down the wood and slain the wolves, bears, and other beasts (which are in great number)" so that by pursuing a policy of genocide "we shall be more oppressed in short time by their absence, than in their living by us both for our own security as also for our cattle."[35] Ironically, the destruction of the Indians would convert English space into Indian space by restoring the wilderness that threatened to envelop the young colony.

Violent behavior, which in earlier years threatened to undermine English identity by creating an uncomfortable comparison with the Spanish, now was constructed as a way to assert Englishness that had been gradually dissipating in the wild surroundings of Virginia. Samuel Purchas argued that the Indian violence "hath now confiscated whatsoever remainders of right the unnatural naturals had, and made both them and their country wholly English, provoking us, if we be our own, not base, degenerate, unworthy of the name of English." After setting out a strategy to respond to the massacre, John Smith made it clear that what was at stake was nothing less than a contest to determine whether England had the will to assert and maintain its own superiority. "I cannot choose but grieve," Smith wrote, "that the actions of an Englishman should be inferior to any, and that the command of England should not be as great as any monarchy that ever was since the world began, I mean not as a tyrant to torment all Christendom, but to suppress her disturbers, and conquer her enemies." Smith challenged the English to assume their rightful place in the grand scheme of world history, not as victims or evildoers, but as protectors.[36]

Like their counterparts in New England, the Chesapeake colonists were forced to confront their own brutal actions and reflect on the meaning of the bloodshed. In the religious stronghold of New England, anxiety over intercultural violence manifested itself as fear that they were "going native" and perhaps losing their Puritan identity. But settlers in the Chesapeake displayed little of the spiritual introspection that accompanied English soldiers in King Philip's War. Leaders of the Virginia Company encouraged the military campaigns as a reassertion of "Englishness" that previous colonists had let lapse as they became too comfortable with the native peoples. By redefining even the most horrific examples of violence as an effort to restore their identity, the English could maintain their distinction from the Spanish while simultaneously avoiding any suggestion that they were degenerating into the reputedly barbaric behavior of the surrounding Indians. Purchas argued that the dead bodies of the English established a special claim to possession of Virginia: "The dispersed bones of their and their countrymen's since murdered carcasses, have taken a mortal immortal possession, and being dead, speak, proclaim and cry, this our earth is truly English, and therefore this land is justly yours, O English." The spiritual dispossession of Indian lands had already taken place through the blood of the English colonists, Purchas suggested, leaving the living to claim the fields that had once been Powhatan hunting grounds and cornfields, but would soon host acres of tobacco and the African laborers whose own blood was shed in pursuit of the colonial dream.[37]

The transformation of the Virginia countryside into tobacco plantations was at best an imperfect replication of English landscapes, however, and the sense that the colonists were gradually losing their Englishness lingered under the surface of many accounts after 1622. The widely dispersed plantations pushed ever deeper into what remained of Indian lands, making church attendance a less frequent event. This is not to say that individual colonists were becoming less devout or abandoning Christianity altogether, for it is exceedingly difficult to measure private convictions. Christian morality and Anglicanism remained a significant component of the settlers' identities, but the opportunity to publicly affirm this aspect of their lives on a regular basis was greatly reduced. Despite Purchas's confident declaration, the settlers could not help but wonder, were they really creating an English space in Virginia even if the fields looked different from the farms of England? Did the bloodshed of the 1620s create an opportunity to re-create English society free from the influence of "savage" Indians, or did it herald a new lifestyle where intercultural violence would remain a permanent fixture? If living in Virginia would require a constant militaristic vigilance, it would be difficult to support any claims that settlers could establish English households in America.

In 1644, the Virginia colonists faced another surprise attack. This time, God apparently offered an unambiguous warning that bloodshed was imminent. According to an account published soon after the attack, a woman was washing her laundry when "of a sudden her clothes were all besprinkled with blood from the first beginning to the rinsing of them, at last in such abundance as if an hand should invisibly take handfuls of gore blood and throw it upon the linen." Understandably alarmed by the sight, the woman's husband interpreted it as a "premonition and warning from God having some kind of intimation of some design of the Indians" and began preparing a defense. When the predicted attack occurred, the outnumbered family was able to fight off an advancing group of twenty Indians.[38]

The divine warning this time came not in the form of a Christianized Indian, as it had in the attacks twenty-two years earlier, but in the most domestic English setting imaginable. Whereas the tranquil English households of 1622 were disrupted by the sudden appearance of "savages" in their midst, in 1644 the pools of blood were Heaven sent. Although the rest of the colony was not spared from the violence, the miraculous message offered protection and assurance that while God was not entirely pleased with the English settlers, perhaps this particular family was following the divine will to establish proper English households in the rapidly vanishing wilderness. The mundane act of washing clothes was transformed into an opportunity to witness God's power on earth. The attack of 1644 was the last stand for Opechancanough, and ultimately was the last significant effort of the Powhatan Indians to assert their power in a region they had once dominated.

Notes

1. George Percy, "A Trewe Relacyon," in *New American World: A Documentary History of America to 1612*, ed. David Beers Quinn, 4 vols. (New York: Arno Press, 1979) 5: 268–69. Hereafter cited as *NAW*. John Smith, *The Proceedings of the English Colonie in Virginia [1612]*, in *The Complete Works of Captain John Smith* (Chapel Hill: University of North Carolina Press, 1986), 1: 257. Hereafter cited as *CWJS*. In an effort to maintain readability without entirely sanitizing seventeenth-century writing, I have modernized all spellings but retained the idiosyncrasies of grammar.

2. On European notions about skin color, see Alden T. Vaughan, *Roots of American Racism: Essays on the Colonial Experience* (New York: Oxford University Press, 1995), 7–11; and Joyce E. Chaplin, "Natural Philosophy and an Early Racial Idiom in North America: Comparing English and Indian Bodies," *William and Mary Quarterly*, 3d ser., 54:1 (January 1997): 229–52. James Horn reminds us that there were significant variations in lifestyle and outlook within England and its developing empire, and that these differences played an important role in shaping colonial society. See Horn, *Adapting to a New World: English Society in the Seventeenth-Century Chesapeake* (Chapel Hill: University of North Carolina Press, 1994). Yet, especially for the chief promoters of colonization, the English muted differences in an effort to contrast themselves with the Spanish.

3. Edward Bond, *Damned Souls in a Tobacco Colony: Religion in Seventeenth-Century Virginia* (Macon: Mercer University Press, 2000), 3–11; Richard Hakluyt, *Discourse of Western Planting*, eds. David B. Quinn and Alison M. Quinn (London: Hakluyt Society, 1993), 8, 11.

4. Jonathan Hart, *Representing the New World: The English and French Uses of the Example of Spain* (New York: Palgrave, 2000), 69, 73, 82. For a discussion of the development of the Black Legend, see Charles Gibson, *The Black Legend: Anti-Spanish Attitudes in the Old World and the New* (New York: Knopf, 1971).

5. Hakluyt, *Discourse of Western Planting*, 52, 56; Hart, *Representing the New World*, 124.

6. Thomas Masham, *The Third Voyage Set Forth by Sir Walter Ralegh to Guiana*, in Richard Hakluyt, ed. and trans., *The Principal Navigations, Voyages, Traffiques, and Discoveries of the English Nation* (Glasgow: University of Glasgow Press, 1904) 11: 6. Hereafter cited as *PN*. Keymis, *A Relation of the Second Voyage to Guiana* in *PN* 10 in 481.

7. Anonymous, *The voyage made by Sir Richard Greenvile, for Sir Walter Ralegh, to Virginia, in the yeere 1585*, in *PN* 8: 316; Thomas Harriot, *A brief and true report of the new founde land in Virginia*, *NAW* 1: 153. Karen Kupperman argues that after Lane's experience, the English attitude toward natives was fundamentally altered: "There would be no grace period during which the Indians and the English would learn about each other." The English, according to Kupperman, had settled on force rather than kindness to get the Indians to do what they wanted. See *Roanoke: The Abandoned Colony* (Totowa, N.J.: Rowman and Allanheld, 1984), 105. Although the violence undoubtedly raised the level of suspicion on both sides of the encounter, future meetings in Roanoke and Jamestown continued to demonstrate that however slim the possibility, the Indians and the English often sought to find a nonviolent solution to their problems.

8. Michael Oberg has argued that the English efforts in Roanoke can be best understood as part of a larger effort to establish an English metropolis across the Atlantic, requiring the settlers to establish the often opposing forces of order and peace in the colonies. See *Dominion and Civility: English Imperialism and Native America, 1585–1685* (Ithaca, N.Y.: Cornell University Press, 1999). For a discussion of the development of the Powhatan chiefdom, see Helen Rountree, *The Powhatan Indians of Virginia: Their Traditional Culture* (Norman: University of Oklahoma Press, 1989), chap. 7.

9. Robert Johnson, *Nova Britannia [1609]*. (New York and Amsterdam: Da Capo Press, 1969), C2; Smith, *Proceedings of the English Colonie*, in *CWJS* 1: 53.

10. Richard Hakluyt, "Notes framed by a Gentleman heretofore to bee given to one that prepared for a discoverie, and went not," in *NAW* 3: 24, 30. George Peckham argued that English experience in nearby regions justified the hopes, noting that in the West Indies, the natives "are easily reduced to civility both in manners and garments, which being so, what vent for our English clothes will thereby ensue." See Peckham, *True Reporte of the late discoveries . . . by . . . Sir Humphrey Gilbert*, in *NAW* 3: 49. Edmund Morgan has argued that on the eve of colonization, the English "had not given up hope of a biracial community, in which indigent Englishmen would work side by side with willing natives, under gentle English government." The biggest obstacle to this goal, Morgan suggests, is that the English sent the wrong people to meet this goal. See Edmund S. Morgan, *American Slavery, American Freedom: The Ordeal of Colonial Virginia* (New York: W. W. Norton, 1975), 44.

11. Bond, *Damned Souls in a Tobacco Colony*, 142. Of course, Virginia did not escape the religious controversies entirely, and the political and religious crises of the 1640s forced the settlers to choose sides in the growing debates, but the first few decades were remarkably free of interfaith rivalries.

12. George Percy, "A Discourse of the Plantation of the Southern Colonie in Virginia," in *NAW* 5: 271; Smith, *Proceedings of the English Colonie, CWJS*, 1: 95. While, as Karen Kupperman has argued, massive retaliation was one of the guiding principles of Anglo-Indian relations in early Jamestown, the dependency of the English upon Indian food supplies and knowledge made such a policy unrealistic in practice. See Kupperman, *Indians and English: Facing Off in Early America* (Ithaca, N.Y.: Cornell University Press, 2000), 220.

13. Smith, *The Generall Historie of Virginia*, in *CWJS* 2: 202; *CWJS* 1: 253; James Axtell, *After Columbus: Essays in the Ethnohistory of North America* (New York and Oxford: Oxford University Press, 1988), 23; J. Frederick Fausz, "An 'Abundance of Blood Shed on Both Sides': England's First Indian War, 1609–1614," *Virginia Magazine of History and Biography* 98:1 (January, 1990), 3–56. The Indian leader may have remembered the incident as he planned the 1622 attack that killed 347 colonists. The Indian reluctance to trade food with the English may have been due to an unusually limited supply of corn. The region was experiencing a tremendous drought just as the undersupplied colonists arrived. See Dennis Blanton, "Drought as a Factor in the Jamestown Colony, 1607–1612, *Historical Archaeology* 34:4 (2000), 74–81.

14. Barlowe, *The first Voyage made to the coastes of America*, in *NAW* 3: 281; Smith, *A Map of Virginia*, 169. For descriptions of the apparent child sacrifice, see Whitaker, *Good Newes from Virginia*, 24, and Smith, *The Generall Historie*, 124.

15. Helen C. Rountree, *The Powhatan Indians of Virginia: Their Traditional Culture* (Norman: University of Oklahoma Press, 1989), 80–81, 136; Christian Feest, "Virginia Algonquians," in *Handbook of North American Indians*, ed. William C. Sturtevant. Vol. 15, *Northeast*, ed. Bruce G. Trigger (Washington, D.C.: Smithsonian Institution, 1988), 262. For the huskenaw ceremony, see Philip Barbour, "The Riddle of the Powhatan 'Black Boyes,'" *Virginia Magazine of History and Biography* 88 (1980): 148–54.

16. Percy was taken aback at the level of English violence, and drew the line at the execution of a captive Indian woman. As the soldiers debated the method of execution, Percy offered his opinion that "having seen so much bloodshed that day, now in my cold blood I desired to see no more." Despite Percy's protests, the woman was killed. Percy, *True Relation*, in Edward Wright Haile, ed., *Jamestown Narratives: Eyewitness Accounts of the Virginia Colony: The First Decade, 1607–1617* (Champlain, Va.: RoundHouse, 1998), 501, 510–11, 515. For a discussion of European fear of cannibalism, see Stephen Greenblatt, *Marvelous Possessions: The Wonder of the New World* (Chicago: University of Chicago Press, 1991), 44–45, 71–72.

17. Percy, *True Relation*, 578; Strachey, *The Historie of Travell into Virginia Britania*, eds. Louis B. Wright and Virginia Freund (London: Hakluyt Society, 1953), 24. While modern readers might find the sheer violence of the punishments reason enough to doubt their relationship to any sense of justice, criminals in England faced corporal punishment for a litany of crimes. William Harrison did not question the superiority of a legal system in which "Rogues are burned through the ears; carriers of sheep out of the land, by the loss of their hands; such as kill by poison are either boiled or scalded to death in lead or seething waters." See William Harrison, *The Description of England [1587]*, ed. Georges Edelen (Ithaca, N.Y.: Cornell University Press, 1968), 189.

18. Strachey, *Historie of Travell*, 24.

19. Smith, *Generall History of Virginia*, in *CWJS* 2: 171; Percy, *True Relation*, .

20. Alexander Whitaker, *Good Newes from Virginia*, in Haile, *Jamestown Narratives*, 550; Percy, *A Discourse of the Plantation of the Southern Colonie in Virginia*, *NAW* 5: 273.

21. Thomas Dale, *Jamestown Narratives*, 847; David Flaherty, ed., *Lawes Divine, Morall,*

and Martiall (Charlottesville: University of Virginia Press, 1989), 37; Edmund Morgan, *American Slavery, American Freedom* (New York: W. W. Norton, 1975), 80–81.

22. Gray, *A Good Speed to Virginia* (New York: Scholars' Facsimilies, 1937), CI, C2. Still, Gray argued, it would be better to convert than to kill the Indians, since "a wise man, but much more a Christian, ought to try all means before they undertake war" but "we are warranted by this direction of Joshua, to destroy willful and convicted idolaters, rather than to let them live, if by no other means they can be reclaimed" (C2).

23. Wyatt's letter was reported in Edward Waterhouse's *A Declaration of the State of the Colony And . . . A Relation of the Barbarous Massacre. Records of the Virginia Company*, ed. Susan Myra Kingsbury (Washington, D.C.: Government Print. Office, 1906–1935), 550. Hereafter cited as *VACO*.

24. Waterhouse, *Relation of the Barbarous Massacre*, in *VACO*, 551.

25. Waterhouse, *Relation of the Barbarous Massacre*, in *VACO*, 551; Samuel Purchas, *Purchas, His Pilgrimes* (Glasgow: James MacLehose and Sons, 1906), 18: 210.

26. Frethorne, in *VACO*, 61.

27. Vaughan, "Expulsion," 70; Smith, *Generall Historie of Virginia*, in *CWJS* 2: 285. Just a decade earlier, George Percy claimed that the Indians had no knowledge of European armor, when a group of soldiers arrived and the Indians "not being acquainted nor accustomed to encounter with men in armor, much wondered thereat, especially as they did not see our men fall as they had done in other conflicts." See Percy, *True Relation*, 515.

28. *VACO*, 612, 666, 678. While acknowledging that sinful behavior necessitated God's punishment of the colony, the council in Virginia defended themselves from the company's claim that alcohol and clothing were the root of the problem. The council "would to God that the covetousness of some at home, did not minister swell to our drunkenness here filling the country with wine *not* only in quantity excessive, but in quality base and infectious: for apparel we know no excess, but in the purists." *VACO*, 11. Nonetheless, Wyatt issued "A Proclamation Against Drunkenness" on June 21, 1622, establishing severe penalties for alcohol offenses. See *VACO* 3, 658.

29. Joseph Mead to Sir Martin Stuteville, July 13, 1622, ed. Robert Johnson. *Virginia Magazine of History and Biography*, Anonymous, *Two Tragicall Events*, etext.lib.virginia.edu/etc bin/jamestown-browse?id = J1022.

30. Robert C. Johnson, ed., "The Indian Massacre of 1622: Some Correspondence of the Reverend Joseph Mead," *Virginia Magazine of History and Biography*, 71:4 (1963): 408; *VACO*, 555.

31. *VACO*, 557, 656, 672; Christopher Brooks, "A Poem on the Late Massacre in Virginia," ed. Robert Johnson, *Virginia Magazine of History and Biography* 72:3 (July 1964): 285; Francis Bacon, *An Advertisement Touching an Holy Warre, Written in the Yeare 1622* (Amsterdam and New York: Da Capo Press, 1970), 134.

32. Alden T. Vaughan, "'Expulsion of the Salvages': English Policy and the Virginia Massacre of 1622," *William and Mary Quarterly* 1978 35(1): 71; *VACO*, 553. Vaughan has correctly argued that Governor George Yeardley's integration plan getting Opechancanough to bring entire families to live with the English, give them houses, clothes, and

cattle while kids went to school was a clear threat to Indian identity, but does not acknowledge that the blurred lines also threatened to undermine English identity.

33. *VACO*, 672. For a discussion of the rules of a holy war, see Jill Lepore, *The Name of War: King Philip's War and the Origins of American Identity* (New York: Alfred A. Knopf, 1998), 108–9.

34. *VACO*, 9–10.

35. Martin, *VACO*, 706.

36. Purchas, *Pilgrimes*, 229; Peter Hulme, *Colonial Encounters: Europe and the Native Caribbean* (New York: Methuen, 1986), 160; Smith, *CWJS* 2: 318.

37. Purchas, *Pilgrimes*, 228.

38. Joseph Frank, ed., "News from Virginny, 1644," *Virginia Magazine of History and Biography* 65 (1957): 86.

RACE: FAMILY AND MEMORY OF THE ENSLAVED

2

Kathleen Fawver, Thomas Brown, and Leah Sims—in part 2—concentrate on race and ethnicity as important historical variables of analysis in an effort to uncover colonial power relationships and identity politics of the Chesapeake slave society. The first essay in this section enters into the longstanding debate over the slave family and community building using traditional New Social History evidence, including census data and probate records. Kate Fawver's analysis of demographic data for Harford County, Maryland, suggests that there were important regional variations within the Chesapeake that determined the shape and character of slave families in the late eighteenth century. Fawver argues that although the numbers of slaveholding households increased throughout the eighteenth century, the number of plantations with more than six slaves declined. This development, in turn, hindered cohesive family structures. Yet despite the scarcity of large slave families residing on the same plantation, a free-black community grew substantially and developed a distinctive identity.

Thomas Brown and Leah Sims make extensive use of the testimony recorded in Chesapeake "freedom petitions" to explore community memory of black ethnic identity. Using a sociological concept of social capital, Brown and Sims find that both whites and blacks had vested interests in the construction of historical memories surrounding the ethnic identity of slaves; they distinguished African slaves from South Asian slaves and made more precise divisions among different African tribes. For the white slaveholders, some slaves were more valuable than others due to white stereotypes about the labor attributes of various ethnic groups. For blacks, ethnicity could play a significant role in their effort to obtain freedom. For example, Madagascarian slaves stood out from sub-Saharan slaves both in culture and appearance. Petitioners for freedom argued that since their ancestress was so different from the African-American population, she must have been enslaved illegally, and thus her descendants were entitled to freedom. Ethnicity thus constituted a significant type of human capital, and consequently motivated persistence of memory. In this examination of social memory, Brown and Sims reveal the fluidity of ethnic and racial categories in the eighteenth-century Chesapeake.

Kathleen Fawver's "The Black Family in the Chesapeake: New Evidence, New Perspectives" and Thomas Brown and Leah Sims's "'To Swear Him Free': Ethnic Memory and Social Capital in Eighteenth-Century Chesapeake Freedom Petitions" shed new light on race relationships in the Chesapeake using the tools of the New Social historians as well as some overlooked sources. Fawver's use of census data and probate records is best understood in the aggregate, manifest in her essay's tables. This data is difficult to analyze from small bits and pieces, but we have selected a tiny sample for inclusion here so that the reader might appreciate the inherent problems associated with extracting information about the enslaved from the extant records of the slaveholders. We have included a copy of the "Act for the Encourageing the Importacon of Negroes and Slaues into this Province" (1671)—downloaded from the searchable Archives of Maryland—to be used in conjunction with Brown and Sims's essay.

Coale William Sen.?	1	66		Crawford Mordecai	1	40
Sarah Cole	1	61		Susan? Crawford	1	39
Sarah Coale	1	30		James Crawford	1	17
Ann Ciale	1	26		Hannah Crawford	1	15
Skipwith Coale	1	22		Mordecai Crawford	1	10
Negroes				Jno Crawford	1	5
Mingo (no Tax)	1	66		Ruth Crawford	1	3
James	1	30		Negroes		
Sam	1	19		Jane	1	27
Bill	1	25		Cuff	1	13
Jesen	1	23		Tom	1	8
Poll	1	4		Ned	1	6
Lucy	1	2		Moses	1	4
Nanney Limo						
Dick	1	12		Chew Thomas	1	23
Coale Philip	1	40		Sarah Yates	1	49
Ann Coale	1	36		Susann Chew	1	25
Cassandria Coale	1	9		Sarah Yates	1	14
Frances Coale	1	7		Negroes		
Sarah Coale	1	5		Holiday	1	34
Richard Coale	1	3		Judy	1	30
Ann Coale	1	1		Suck	1	25
Elizabeth Tate	1	87		Rodger	1	13
Negroes				Hannah	1	7
James	1	65		Charles	1	5
Ned	1	17		Polley	1	3
				Lucy	1	3
				Geor...	1	1

An Act for the Encourageing the Importacon of Negros and Slaues into this Province (1671)

WHEREAS SEVERALL of the good people of this Prouince haue been discouraged to import into or purchase within this Prouince any Negroes or other Slaues and such as haue Imported or purchased any such Negroes or Slaues haue to the great displeasure of Almighty God and the prejudice of the Soules of those poore people Neglected to instruct them in the Christian faith or to Endure or permitt them to Receive the holy Sacrament of Babtisme for the Remission of their Sinns upon a mistake and vngrounded apprehension that by becomeing Christians they and the Issues of their bodies are actually manumited and made free and discharged from their Servitude and bondage be itt declared and Enacted by his Lordship the Lord and Proprietary of this Prouince by and with the advice and consent of the upper and lower houses of this present Generall Assembly and by the Authority of the same That where any Negro or Negroes Slave or Slaues being in Servitude or bondage is are or shall become Christian or Christians and hath or have Received or shall att any time Receive the Holy Sacrament of Babtizme before or after his her or their Importacon into this Prouince the same is not nor shall or ought the same be denyed adjudged Construed or taken to be or to amount vnto a manumicon or freeing Inlarging or discharging any such Negroe or Negroes Slaue or Slaues or any his or their Issue or Issues from his her their or any of their Servitude or Servitudes Bondage or bondages Butt that Notwithstanding any such Act or thing Acts or things And Notwithstanding any such becomeing Christian or Christians or Receiveing the Sacrament of Babtizme Every such Negroe and Negroes slaue and slaues and all and every the Issue and Issues of every such Negroe and Negroes Slaue and Slaues Is are and be and shall att all tymes hereafter be adjudged

---

From the *Proceedings and Acts of the General Assembly, April 1666–June 1676*, vol. 2, p. 272. Available online: www.mdarchives.state.md.us.

Reputed deemed and taken to be and Remayne in Servitude and Bondage and subject to the same Servitude and Bondage to all intents and purposes as if hee shee they every or any of them was or were in and Subject vnto before such his her or their Becomeing Christian or Christians or Receiveing of the Sacrament of Baptizme any opinion or other matter or thing to the Contrary in any wise Notwithstanding.

The Black Family in the Chesapeake: New Evidence, New Perspectives

3

KATHLEEN FAWVER

Part I: The Slave Family

This study forms part of a larger work that examined the best available evidence on household structure in early America—the 1776 Maryland census. The census data affords an unprecedented opportunity to test several theories about the structure and composition of Anglo-American households, the experience of women and children in a plantation economy, and the formation of the slave family. In this chapter, I reconstruct the black community on 258 plantations and thirteen slave quarters in the northern Chesapeake using the census returns, plantation records, tax lists, and genealogical data from Harford County to reexamine the best demographic evidence for the formation of a viable slave family. Using a data set such as the 1776 Census of Maryland instead of relying solely on plantation records provides a more comprehensive understanding of the regional patterns in slave demographics and of the free black community in the northern Chesapeake.[1]

Historians of slavery contend that demographic improvements served as the critical foundation for the formation of slave culture and an African-American communal identity in the eighteenth century. The first indications of a healthy and regenerative African-American community appear in the middle of the eighteenth century. Demographic improvements allowed for the emergence of the slave family, which served as the incubator of a unique African-American culture in the colonies. Historians attribute great significance to the role and function of the "slave family" in this context. Describing the slave family, John Blassingame wrote, "While it had no legal existence in slavery, [the family] was in actuality, one of the most important survival mechanisms for the slave. In his family, he found companionship, love, sexual gratification, sympathetic understanding of his sufferings; he learned how to avoid punishment, to cooperate with other blacks and to maintain his self-esteem. However frequently the family was broken, it was primarily responsible for the slave's ability to survive on the plantation without becoming totally dependent on and submissive to his master."[2] Children absorbed "attitudes, ideals and values" from their parents and not from the white planter family. The slave family raised the children, "cushioned the shock of bondage for them," and taught them "values different from those their masters tried to instill in them."[3] The slave family served as the lynchpin connecting the individual slave to a larger community and as a result, the slave did not lose his or her humanity to an inhuman system. While the image of the nurturing slave family is compelling, we must examine the demographic evidence in order to separate fantasy from reality.

Historians have divided the demographic history of slavery in Maryland into four distinct periods: 1660–1680, 1680–1710, 1710–1740, and 1740–1780. During the two periods between 1660 and 1710, the Maryland slave population grew due to the forced immigration, which produced a black population heavily skewed toward adult males. Early family and community formations faced the limitations of skewed sex ratios, high death rates, heavy immigration, and lower fertility. Although health conditions and sex ratios for blacks improved slightly around 1700, natural fertility alone could not sustain the population, and the numbers declined.[4]

In his work on four early slave counties, Russell Menard explained what a high sex ratio could mean in terms of population growth. He found that a high sex ratio indicated a high rate of immigration, reflecting the planter's preference for male adult labor. Between 1658 and 1710, the sex ratio rose to 1.446, meaning that adult males outnumbered adult females roughly by one and one-half to one. Combined with the small number per plantation, this ratio worked against healthy fertility rates. Additionally, the legal constraints of slavery worked against adult males' finding an available adult female and having their relationship legally defended.[5] Menard speculated that the lack of parity in the sex ratios indicates that the planters themselves did not recognize the profitability of natural reproduction.[6]

By 1720, the slave trade to the Chesapeake had lost momentum. Historians concur that by the 1720s and 1730s, the contours of the black population contrasted dramatically with the previous period. Despite high sex ratios, black women who had reached childbearing age during this period bore enough children to sustain natural population increase. In other words, the slave population grew from births and not from immigration. Stemming from a low age at conception and a short interval birth rate, native-born slave women could have many children with a higher survival rate than their predecessors. Allan Kulikoff found that improved sex ratios, rising fertility, improved mortality, and lower immigration rates resulted in a higher population density for blacks. This critical mass served as the foundation for a unique African-American society. He wrote, "Their social life centered around slave families, kin groups, quarters and neighborhoods. Most Afro-Americans lived with their immediate families, and slaves who lived in the largest quarters resided near numerous kinfolk."[7]

However, Jean Butenhoff Lee has identified a serious problem with this interpretation. Her work on Charles County suggested that the demographic improvements required for such cohesive community might not have existed everywhere. Lee challenged the population-density argument and suggested that Charles County simply lacked the requisite number of slaves living on large plantations. She found that most slaves lived on small plantations, and this situation kept their interaction with other slaves to a minimum. She concluded by calling for further research sensitive to regional variations in the demography of slaves.[8]

Philip Morgan used comparative data from plantations in South Carolina and the Chesapeake to assess levels of regional variation. Like Lee, Morgan found that plantations typically lacked slave-family formation in the early eighteenth century. On occasion, while living in close proximity to one another on large quarters in the Chesapeake, slaves might have had some semblance of two parent-children stability.[9] In South Carolina, slaves faced an even more depressing scene with sixty-six percent living alone. No matter how large or small, Chesapeake and Lowcountry estates in the early eighteenth century showed little evidence of family structure.[10] Morgan found that toward the end of the eighteenth century, slaves living on large plantations faced better chances for family formation. In the Chesapeake, "at least half, and in some cases two-thirds of adult slaves resided on units with evenly balanced numbers of men and women."[11] On large Chesapeake plantations, forty-five percent of the population lived in family structures. Likewise in South Carolina, low sex ratios on large plantations translated into a higher number of slave children living in two-parent households, and husband-wife-children living arrangements predominated by 1790.[12] Slaves living on smaller plantations in both regions did not fare as well. Analysis of small plantations in South Carolina revealed a majority of slaves living alone, while in the Chesapeake small plantations meant single-parent households.[13] Even the small Lowcountry plantations had more households headed by two parents since smaller plantations in South Carolina tended to be larger than small plantations in the Chesapeake. For Morgan, *plantation size* played just as important a role as improved demographics in affecting the number of slave families. Larger plantations meant that more slaves might have enjoyed the benefits of balanced sex ratios. Using the same demographic indicators, one may analyze the census returns for evidence of black population growth and slave families in Harford County.

Located in the Northern Chesapeake region, Harford County, named in honor of Henry Harford, the last lord proprietor of the Calvert family in Maryland, is an ideal place to examine the demographic evidence of black families.[14] In 1775, the Continental Congress ordered that all colonies raise revenue in anticipation of war with England. The extant portions of the enumeration include the following counties of Maryland: Prince George's, Frederick, Charles, Anne Arundel, Caroline, Dorchester, Queen Anne's, Talbot, and Harford.[15] Individual-level data exist from only six hundreds—Broad Creek, Deer Creek Lower, Susquehanna, Spesutia Lower, Harford Lower, and Bush River Lower—but aggregate figures for all fourteen hundreds have survived.[16] Harford's enumerators organized these data around the head of the household and provided the first and last names, age, race, and sex of the household inmates, including slaves. The 855 households in the six hundreds of Harford County contained nearly six thousand individuals. The census also includes demographic information on thirteen slave quarters, one forge, and one mill.[17]

The Demographic Parameters of Harford Slavery

In Harford County, African Americans constituted twenty-six percent of the total population in 1776. This figure increased to twenty-eight percent by 1790 and declined to twenty-six percent by 1850. The proportion of blacks in northern counties remained small compared to the southern counties, where the black population had grown to forty-eight percent by 1790. With the exception of Baltimore, whose total population was twenty percent black, neighboring counties had no more than thirteen percent of their population listed as black.[18] Within this context, Harford County deserves our attention since it contained the largest black population in northern Maryland.

Early returns reveal that most of the taxable slaves in Baltimore lived in the regions that became Harford County. Blacks constituted thirty-six percent of the total taxables in Deer Creek Hundred, thirty-eight percent in Spesutia Upper, thirty-seven percent in Lower Gunpowder River, and fifty percent in Spesutia Lower.[19] At the time the census was gathered, blacks still lived in the oldest parts of Harford County, specifically those hundreds that retained their original boundaries when Harford County separated from Baltimore County in 1773 (see table 3.1). The highest concentration of blacks lived in Spesutia Lower, an agricultural region along the mouth of the Chesapeake. In contrast, white populations

Table 3.1. Population Distribution by Hundred in Harford County, Maryland, 1776

Hundred	Whites	Blacks
Spesutia Lower	790	650
Spesutia Upper	767	340
Harford Lower	415	352
Harford Upper	548	194
Susquehanna	1,300	281
Bush River Lower	658	275
Bush River Upper	623	77
Deer Creek Lower	460	374
Deer Creek Upper	960	122
Eden	1,008	108
Broad Creek	318	24
Gunpowder Lower	683	331
Gunpowder Upper	893	214
N (%)	9,423 (74%)	3,342 (26%)

Source: Data for Harford County may be found in the Council of Safety (Census of 1776) MSA S961 1–18, Harford County, Maryland State Archives, Annapolis. Electronic version provided by the Minnesota Population Center, University of Minnesota. Janet Lindeman produced the electronic version for the Minnesota Population Center. I am grateful to Matt Sobek and Steven Ruggles for reference information. Nine cases could not be classified as male or female due to insufficient evidence.

dominated newer regions like Bush River Upper, Broad Creek, and Eden Hundred—one of the last regions incorporated. A distinct pattern emerges when we link the population distributions evident from the 1776 census and the tax of 1783. As populations grew, affordable land in the older and more developed areas in the tidewater region grew scarce (see table 3.1). White yeomen farmers migrated to the unincorporated interior region where they could purchase land. The scarcity of blacks in regions of cheap land and their concentration in the oldest parts of Harford is consistent with the fact that most blacks had no freedom to migrate and lived as chattel slaves.

Sex Ratios

Slaves in northern Maryland had a better chance of finding a partner of the opposite sex than in most counties. Lower sex ratios indicate a more balanced male-female population. In 1776, Harford's black male-female ratio was a surprising 1.2. Using the sex ratio of children as an indicator of future trends, we see that slaves would have experienced a gradual increase to 1.24 in the next few years.[20] Although the county-level evidence shows that sex ratios fluctuated dramatically during the eighteenth century depending on the immigration of new slaves or the demographic climate of the region, the sample from Harford suggests that slaves in the northern Chesapeake had a better chance of finding sexual partners among a small population than did slaves in southern counties. Yet, the improvement in sex ratios over the eighteenth century had less to do with the black population's growth than the next indicator, child-woman ratios.

Used as a raw indicator of population growth, a child-woman ratio provides an idea of how many children an average woman may have at a specific point in time. If one controls for migration, the larger the ratio, the better the chance that natural population growth occurred. For example, in 1776 Harford's white child-woman ratio flourished at a high rate of 1.64, which suggests that the large white population in the northern Maryland County resulted more from births than migration. Likewise, Harford's black child-woman ratio was 1.40. While it was lower than the ratio for whites, this ratio is comparable to that found in Prince George's, 1.5.[21] Both Harford and Prince George's counties fell below York County, which boasted a black child-woman ratio of 1.6 in 1620, and 2.0 by 1730. Harford had a much smaller ratio than York County, with fifty-one percent of the total black population listed as children.

One explanation for large black child-woman ratios is that many female slaves came into childbearing age. In 1740, only six percent (fifty-four) of the slave women were of childbearing age. By 1750, the number had increased to ten percent, and it stood at seventeen percent in 1760. By the time of the census, child-bearing females accounted for thirty-eight percent of all black women. The proportion is consistent with southern Chesapeake counties that vacillated between thirty and thirty-seven percent of the total black female population in the 1770s.[22] The age distribution of the black population indicated a strong fertility rate supported by low sex ratios. In other words, planters could look forward to the day when they would no longer be dependent upon the slave trade for labor. For a slave, it meant that family formation became a distinct possibility. Having the critical demographic indicators in place, we need to examine the individual plantations in Harford for evidence of the slave family.

Plantation Size

Philip D. Morgan argued that toward the end of the eighteenth century, plantation size affected the formation of slave families. Slaves living on a large plantation had a better chance of finding partners. Yet Jean Butenhoff Lee found that plantations in Charles County did not contain enough slaves for conjugal units to form.[23] Table 3.2 compares the plantation sizes in different regions in Maryland. Two distinct patterns of slaveholding appear. The first is the large number of plantations in the southern counties at the beginning of the decade. In nineteen years, Anne Arundel County increased its plantations by forty-seven percent. On average, twenty-six *new* plantations appeared every year. The second pattern is the high proportion of plantations that had more than twenty-one slaves. Not only did the total number of plantations grow, but the number of large plantations increased. In contrast, in Harford and Charles Counties the number of small plantations grew. While slaves appeared on thirty-one percent of all Harford plantations, fifty-seven percent lived on estates that owned between one and five slaves. By 1783, this number had increased to sixty-seven percent. Consistently, planters who owned more than five slaves lived in the oldest and wealthiest regions of Harford, Lower and Spesutia Lower Hundreds. Only nine percent of the total

Table 3.2. Plantation Size in Maryland 1721–1783

Place and Time	Percentage of Slaves Size of Unit (No. of Slaves)				
	1–5	*6–10*	*11–20*	*21+*	*Total*
Maryland					
Lower Western Shore 1721–1730 (N = 794)	17	19	29	40	100
Prince George's County 1731–1740 (N = 842)	17	26	34	24	100
St. Mary's County 1721–1730 (N = 484) 1731–1740 (N = 524)	26 32	21 22	25 35	28 11	100 100
Anne Arundel County 1700–1719 (N = 1,050) 1720–1739 (N = 1,549)	16 12	13 18	22 20	50 51	100 100
Charles County 1782 (N = 776)	57	22	14	6	100
Harford County 1776 (N = 278) 1783 (N = 558)	57 67	23 21	14 9	6 3	100 100

Sources: Data for Maryland Lower Western Shore, Prince George's, St. Mary's, Anne Arundel from Allan Kulikoff, *Tobacco and Slaves: The Development of Southern Cultures in the Chesapeake.* (Chapel Hill: University of North Carolina Press, 1986), Table 36, 331; data for Charles County from Jean B. Lee, *The Price of Nationhood: The American Revolution in Charles County* (New York: W. W. Norton and Company, 1994) Appendix Table 6, 271; data for Harford County 1776 from the Council of Safety (Census of 1776) MSA S961-1-18, Harford County, Maryland State Archives, Annapolis. Electronic version provided by the Minnesota Population Center, University of Minnesota; data for Harford County 1783 from the *Assessment of 1783: Harford County, Maryland* from the collection of the Maryland Historical Society, (Baltimore: Rhistoric Publications, 1976).

number of plantations in Spesutia Lower, Harford Lower, and Deer Creek Lower contained more than ten slaves. These findings reinforce the theory that in the northern counties, labor—not land—was a valuable commodity. Yet in Charles County, distinct for its large black population, most slaves simply did not live on plantations large or diverse enough to support families. Large plantations, a prerequisite for slave families, appeared *outside* of Harford County. As the overall number of plantations increased, the size of slave holdings decreased. According to the existing literature, this pattern of slaveholding would have inhibited slave-family formation.

The Structure of Slaves on Plantations

What did the predominance of small plantations mean for slave families? Table 3.3 compares slave-family formation in Harford with Prince George's County in 1776. Until they reached adult status, slave children lived in three different types of households depending on age and sex. Infants and toddlers required the most care, and the evidence from Prince George's and Harford show that they lived with their mothers. In Harford, which contained twice the number of infants and toddlers found in Prince George's County, two distinct patterns of living arrangements for children between the ages of zero and nine years appeared. Most children lived without family, while a second group lived in single-parent house-holds until they reached age nine. In contrast, Prince George's County planters preferred that mothers live with their young children. By age ten, the living arrangements of children dramatically changed and the proportion that lived with mothers fell to half the original number in both counties as more children found themselves living without family. As the child matured, his or her chances of living with immediate family members diminished. The increase in the percentage of children living alone at age fifteen and older suggests that at age ten, planters removed children from their mothers' care. At age fifteen and above, the majority of females lived alone. However, a significant number returned to live with their mothers, probably to assist in the care of younger siblings. Male children aged fifteen and older did not return to help with sibling care, as seventy-two percent in Prince George's and eighty-five percent in Harford faced a solitary existence. Slave marriages had no legal status. Slave children appeared as personal property, and very few planters allowed their slaves to live as domestic units (husband, wife, and children). Only seventeen percent in Prince George's County and a meager six percent in Harford lived in family units. Age and sex of the slave child played an important part in determining with whom that child lived.

Historians have argued that the lack of slave families may be a result of

Table 3.3. Slave Household Structure on Small Plantations in Prince George's and Harford Counties, 1776

Household Type	PG Children 0–9 (N = 325)	HA Children 0–9 (N = 690)	PG Children 10–14 (N = 162)	HA Children 10–14 (N = 267)	PG Males 15+ (N = 275)	HA Males 15+ (N = 467)	PG Females 15+ (N = 276)	HA Females 15+ (N = 405)	PG Total (N = 1,038)	HA Total (N = 1,831)
Husband-Wife										
Children	22	6.5	10	6.5	17	6.5	18	5.9	18	6.3
Mother-Children	56	25.2	29	17.6	2	2.7	35	28.1	32	18.7
Father-Children	4	2.1	1	3.6	2	5.4	a	.7	2	2.9
Siblings	6	6.2	17	5.0	7	a	5	a	8	3.2
No Family	12	60.1	43	67.8	72	85.1	42	64.9	41	68.9
Total Percent	100	100	100	100	100	100	100	100	100	100

Sources: Data for Prince George's County figures from Kulikoff, *Tobacco and Slaves*, Table 41, 372; data for Harford County from in the Council of Safety (Census of 1776) MSA S961 1–18, Harford County, Maryland State Archives, Annapolis. Electronic version provided by the Minnesota Population Center, University of Minnesota.

Note: a is less than 5% and other amounts have been rounded off.

uneven sex ratios on individual plantations. With Harford's demographic indicators, we could reasonably expect to find similar types of improvement encountered on large plantations in Chesapeake and South Carolina. Yet, in the northern county, only twenty percent of all households had balanced sex ratios (see table 3.4). When we examine the households with uneven sex ratios, we find that thirty-six percent of plantations had more women than men, while forty-four percent of all households contained more men than women. How might have plantation size affected family formation? Following Morgan, we might assume that larger plantations afforded slaves a better chance of cohabiting in families. However, on Harford plantations balanced sex ratios are found not on plantations with more than ten slaves, but on smaller plantations.[24] An even proportion of adult males and females lived on eighty-two percent of the plantations that can be classified as small. As plantation size grew, balanced sex ratios appeared less often, and this uneven distribution would have discouraged family formation. Even moderate-sized plantations, those containing six to ten slaves, showed better sex ratios than large plantations in Harford. In contrast to the pattern found on

Table 3.4.   Ratio of Adult Males to Adult Females on Harford County Plantations

| | | Percentage of Households | | | | | | |
| | | Size of Unit (Number of Slaves) | | | | | | |
	Difference	1–5		6–10		11–15	16–20	21+	Total
More Women than Men	−9							1 (.4)	1 (.4)
	−5	1 (.4)							1 (.4)
	−4			1 (.4)		1 (.4)	1 (.4)		3 (1.3)
	−3	2 (.9)		2 (.9)					4 (1.7)
	−2	13 (5.6)		5 (2.1)		1 (.4)	1 (.4)		20 (8.5)
	−1	51 (21.8)		3 (1.3)		1 (.4)			55 (23.5)
Balanced ratio	0	38 (16.2)		7 (3.0)		1 (.4)			46 (19.7)
More Men than Women	1	46 (19.7)		2 (.9)		2 (.9)		1 (.4)	51 (21.8)
	2	15 (6.4)		6 (2.6)		1 (.4)			22 (9.4)
	3	10 (4.3)		1 (.4)		1 (.4)			12 (5.1)
	4	2 (.9)		4 (1.7)		1 (.4)	1 (.4)		8 (3.4)
	5	2 (.9)		1 (.4)		2 (.9)		1 (.4)	6 (2.6)
	6					2 (.9)		1 (.4)	3 (1.3)
	7			1 (.4)					1 (.4)
	11					1 (.4)			1 (.4)
N (%)		180 (76.9)		33 (14.1)		14 (6.0)	3 (1.3)	4 (1.7)	234 (100)

Source: All figures for Harford County from the Council of Safety (Census of 1776) MSA S961 1–18, Harford County, Maryland State Archives, Annapolis. Electronic version provided by the Minnesota Population Center, University of Minnesota. For the purpose of this analysis, only households with adult slaves are included. Forty-four households had no adult slaves.

large plantations in South Carolina, smaller plantations in Harford revealed a higher chance for slave families than larger plantations. As Morgan cautions, slaves did not always find partners on the same plantation, yet nonetheless these findings suggest that slaves had a better chance of finding spouses on smaller plantations in Harford.

It is evident that the small plantations in Harford posed a demographic opportunity for many slaves in northern Maryland, but how does their experience compare to that of slaves living on small plantations in Virginia and South Carolina? In the north, twenty-four percent of all slave children under the age of fifteen lived within a single-parent household; twenty-one percent lived with their mothers.[25] Five percent lived with siblings and two percent lived alone. These living arrangements for children contrast with Virginia, where eighty-two percent lived with a single parent and twelve percent lived alone. South Carolina plantations appeared more sensitive to slave children, with fifty-six percent of all children residing with a single parent and only nine percent living alone. Sixty-one percent of all unfree children in Harford resided on plantations filled with unrelated slaves. This pattern of household structure suggests that planters in the northern county were less concerned with the maternal care of children than with the productive potential of their slaves.

The trend of building a plantation with unrelated individuals affected adult slaves as well. In Harford, the majority of adult males (seventy-nine percent) and females (sixty-one percent) lived on plantations with unrelated slaves. This pattern contrasts with small Virginia plantations, where most of the adult males lived alone while adult females lived as single parents. In South Carolina, seventy-nine percent of adult males and forty percent of adult females led a solitary existence. These comparisons show us how Harford plantations differed from other slave societies. We may conclude that very few slaves in the northern county could live as conjugal units with or without children.[26] Harford also stands out in that more if its slaves, young and old, lived with other unrelated slaves.

Finding a domestic partner may have been a difficult problem for many slaves. Forty-four percent of total plantations in Harford confronted the problem of having more men than women, and thirty-six percent had more women than men. Analysis of small plantations revealed that among those households with only one more adult male or one more adult female, the imbalance in sex ratios affected women disproportionately. In other words, on small plantations, the chance for balanced sex ratios was greater, but women had less chance of finding a domestic partner than men. In contrast, on larger plantations the absence of partners affected more men than women. The discrepancy is understandable given that large plantations in Harford were characterized by significant concentrations of adult males, unlike Virginia and South Carolina where large plantations translated into lower sex ratios. The smaller plantations of Harford may have provided slaves a better opportunity to find partners. However, on smaller plantations, women, not men, consistently found themselves without a partner. Increase in plantation size did not improve a slave's chance of finding a partner, because large plantations in Harford tended to have significantly more men than women.

Elderly Slave Women and Childcare

The lack of evidence for slave families leaves us with many questions. With fifty-one percent of the slave population under the age of sixteen, who cared for children in the absence of families? Where might the supervision and care of infants and adolescents have occurred if most lacked a parental figure? Instead of asking how the slave family looked, we might ask what the position of slaves in relation to other slaves on a plantation can tell us about patterns of childcare. Population growth due to childbirth produced a large number of slave children who required care. Analyzing the *position* of slave women over the age of forty-five (the traditional cutoff age for mothers) in relation to other adults produces a conjectural structure similar to that identified by Deborah Gray White on nineteenth-century plantations. "Senior" women who had become too old to work in the fields held the responsibility of caring for slave children during the day while their mothers labored in the fields.[27]

On Harford plantations, care of children was an age- and gender-specific occupation rather than the temporary babysitting White described. In the absence of a mother, children received care from unrelated adult slave women until they reached maturity. In 1776, the household of Joseph and Ann Hopkins reflected this type of surrogate mothering. The Hopkins' plantation included four adult males aged thirty to fifty-three; three adult women aged twenty-five to sixty; and nine children under the age of fifteen. The enumerator listed the four adult males first, and one adult woman (Nanny, aged thirty-five). Then he recorded Hannah, aged sixty; and two children, Will, aged fourteen, and Cesar, aged thirteen. Finally, he listed the third adult female (Hagar, aged twenty-five) and seven children. After Hagar, the enumerator listed fifteen-year-old Cumbo—too old to be her son. Given Hannah's capacity as an untaxed elderly slave, Hannah's position and that of the children appearing almost as a separate entity *before* Hagar and Cumbo—both taxable slaves—may have reflected an organization of caregiving.

Surrogate mothering occurred only in planter-households containing ten or more slaves. This pattern is consistent with the theory that the larger plantations would have had more need for elderly slave women because they contained the most children. The plantation of Jacob Giles gives us the most startling example of this type of arrangement. First, the plantation had a predominantly female slave population. Second, the location of Bethia (aged sixty) *after* the children (Sucke, aged fourteen, and Pall, aged six) suggests that they fell under her care. Although white children appeared in three households, they never numbered more than two. These examples suggest that children received primary caregiving and supervision from a full-time female occupant.[28]

The organization of plantations worked actively against family formation. The demographic evidence for Harford does not support the idea that slave families were common in the northern Chesapeake. Below, we will examine the evidence for family formation among free blacks in the northern Chesapeake.

Part II. The Free Black Community in the Chesapeake

In 1776, Bernard Preston lived on his plantation with his wife, Elizabeth, infant daughter, Sarah, and one sixteen-year-old slave named Jude. By 1783, Preston had increased his holdings to include five more slaves. Ten years later, Preston appeared at the Harford County court and declared that from "Diverse good causes and considerations," he claimed to be "consciously concerned to give and grant to the Negroes now in my possession their freedom and liberty." His submitted manumission ordered Ned, born in 1765, free in 1792; Sam, born in 1782, free in 1799; David, born in 1774, free in 1801; Charles, born in 1770, free in 1797; and Jack, "supposed to be thirty years of age," free in 1786. He also ordered the freedom of Cate, born in 1768, released in September 1795. With Cate's manumission, Preston attached the caveat "should she have issue within that space of time, such issue shall be free at the age of twenty one years."[29] Later that same year, he appeared again and registered his immediate manumission of one "Negro woman Prudence, aged about twenty-nine years" and the gradual manumission of Darby, age nineteen years, and Benjamin (age fifteen), both free at age twenty-five; and of three Negro girls—Sal (age thirteen), Tamar (age ten), and Hannah (age two)—to be freed at the age of twenty-five. Any children produced before the time of freedom would be required to serve until the age of twenty-one.[30]

Preston's pattern of manumissions reflected the "degrees of freedom" characteristic of the status of many blacks on Maryland plantations during the Early National period. An ambiguous status existed between freedom and bondage, whereby slave owners could assuage their republican scruples over their participation in a slave economy and slaves might anticipate a better future. Based on

manumissions such as Preston's, Maryland's free black population increased. Theoretically, free slaves could organize their own households, use the labor of their
free children, and accumulate property. Like the demographic events of birth and
death, manumission disrupted the structure of the planter household, and the
labor potential of slaves—not concerns over familial relationships—dictated the
timing of freedom.[31]

In their manumissions, planters paid little attention to the slave family. While
the planters may have employed republican rhetoric as justification for their decisions, black families as a unit received little consideration. In 1782, Harford
County planter John Bull submitted his manumission of "sundry slaves." He proclaimed that he was conscious "that the holding of Negroes in Perpetual slavery
and bondage to be pugnant [sic] to the laws of God and in consolidated consis-
tence with the strict rules of justice and equity and that freedom and liberty is
the unalienable right and providence of every person born in the world." His
beliefs and "divers other good causes and considerations," compelled him to free
thirty-five year old Thomas, on the twenty fifth day of December 1783 and
thirty-four year old Bet a year later. Perhaps conscious of the costs of freedom,
Bull included the condition that "any children produced by the said Negro Bet
to be manumitted when they had reached the age of twenty-one years." At the
same time, he prearranged the freedom for several boys and girls. Like Bet, any
children born to the girls would serve as slaves until they turned twenty-one.
Generously, Bull freed all the children born to the females after their manumission even though he possessed no legal claim to them.[32]

Bull's manumission record reflected a unique aspect of American slavery—
freedom was an individual status. Only the slave himself or herself received freedom through manumission. The essence of chattel slavery lay in the assumption
that all children of slaves, male or female, would themselves be slaves. From the
perspective of the slave owners, all children, now and in the future, belonged to
them and not to parents. In retrospect, this arrangement represents a means by
which slave owners may have maintained control over their former female
slaves—by holding their children. Because their children often remained slaves
until the age of twenty-one, black females generally remained tied to the plantation even in freedom.

In Harford, husbands and wives received simultaneous freedom more often
than parents and children. The deed of manumission by James Lee in 1783
recorded that freedom for his slave Jenny

> to commence from the date of these presents, Negro Bob and Grace his
> wife, Bet and Milcah, freedom to commence at finishing the crop now in

the ground, Jack, Jo and Hagar his wife, freedom to commence the eighth day of November 1790, Hagar freedom to commence the eighth day of November 1788, Patience the first day of March (1792) Grace the younger the first day of March (1794) Phillis, the first day of May (1796), Suckey, the first day of September (1798) Tom, the twenty third day of September (1799), Nace the eight day of November (1798) and Simon when he has reached the age of thirty yeas being now about eleven years of age.

The freedom granted to the two sets of couples suggests that planters were cognizant of familial relations among slaves. Yet, the delayed freedom granted to children shows where the sympathies stopped short. While the relationship between adults may have justified simultaneous freedom, children consistently received delayed manumission. Additionally, any children born to women before the women's manumission took place remained in slavery until the age of twenty-one for boys and sixteen for girls.[33]

Harford's pattern delayed the immediate manumissions of children compared to the overall pattern of manumissions in the Chesapeake. In his sampling of Maryland counties, T. Stephen Whitman found that boys and girls equally faced delayed manumission.[34] Likewise, both sexes of children in Harford County equally faced the prospect of delayed freedom (see table 3.5). Planters granted immediate freedom to children much less often than they did to adults, and Whitman found that sixty-three percent of girls, and only thirty-seven percent of boys, received immediate manumissions. In contrast, Harford County slavehold-

Table 3.5. The Manumission of Children in Harford County and other Maryland Counties, 1770–1820

	Maryland Counties 1770–1830	Harford County 1774–1820
Delayed (female child)	991 (40%)	117 (34%)
Immediate (female child)	304 (12%)	41 (12%)
Delayed (male child)	990 (40%)	117 (34%)
Immediate (male child)	177 (.07%)	42 (12%)
Delayed (child sex unknown)		25 (7%)
Immediate (child sex unknown)		1 (.0%)
N (%)	2,462 (99%)	343 (99%)

Sources: Data for Other Maryland Counties from T. Stephen Whitman, *The Price of Freedom: Slavery and Manumission in Baltimore and Early National Maryland.* (New York: Routledge Press, 1997), table 13, 133; data for Harford County from Carolyn Greenfield Adams, *Hunter Sutherland's Slave Manumissions and Sales in Harford County, Maryland 1775–1865.* (Bowie, Md.: Heritage Books, Inc., 1999).

ers granted immediate freedom to young slaves at an equal rate. The gender of the child had no impact on the pattern of freedom in Harford. In addition to delaying manumission at the same rate for both sexes, Harford County planters granted immediate manumission with the same kind of parity. Boys received immediate freedom fifty-one percent of the time while girls received it forty-nine percent of the time.

If Harford owners paid little attention to the sex of the slave child, then freedom often depended on the sex of the owner. Female slave owners elected to delay the manumission of children and retained the services of seventy-eight percent of those promised freedom until they had reached maturity. In contrast with male slave owners, female slave owners showed a reluctance to part with their male slave children and kept forty-three percent of the boys until they had advanced into adulthood. In the event that they released the child immediately, female owners demonstrated no preferential treatment and released both boys and girls at the same rate. In contrast, female slave owners tended to grant immediate freedom to adult males and adult females at a higher rate than male slave owners who tended to delay freedom for both men and women (see table 3.6).

The freedom of children depended upon the immediate manumission of their parents. For instance, in 1782, Mary Presbury freed Negro Lydia and her offspring Pippen, while Ann Lytle in 1792 freed Negro Ester and her one-year-old child. When children received freedom, they found themselves under the supervision of their parents. Likewise, Rachel Price freed Hannah and stipulated, "She keep her children Rueben, George and Rachel until seven years old." Price went a step further and guaranteed, "For this she is to be paid five dollars per year for each child."[35] Without parents, children might have received freedom yet remained powerless to negotiate the conditions. This may have resulted in a less-

Table 3.6.   Manumission of Adult Slaves by Sex of Owner in Harford County, 1774–1820

Type of Manumission	Male Owner		Female Owner	
	N	%	N	%
Delayed (female adult)	40	(12)	8	(13)
Immediate (female adult)	102	(30)	26	(41)
Delayed (male adult)	64	(19)	4	(6)
Immediate (male adult)	104	(31)	24	(39)
Delayed (adult sex unknown)	26	(8)	0	(0)
Immediate (adult sex unknown)	0	(0)	0	(0)
N (% of Sex)	336	100%	62	99%

Source: See note to table 3.5.

than-favorable condition as the case of Margaret Evitt shows. In 1806, Evitt freed
her two slave girls Dorcas (age fourteen) and Nancy (age twelve), "so they might
bind themselves to me as servants until they are twenty-eight."[36]

In some cases, free blacks in Harford purchased the property rights of their
families under slavery and granted them freedom. In 1811, slave owner Nathaniel
Grafton signed a deed that detailed, "in consideration of four dollars paid by Ben
Shaw, Negro Doll, wife of Ben Shaw, is to be and henceforth is free."[37] In 1814,
John McCauley purchased and freed his wife and two daughters. He also set "free
my Negro man Charles, being my grandson whom I purchased from Mary
Hall."[38] As early as 1790, free black Edward Hopkins declared "for natural love
and affection that I bear my son whom I purchased from Richard Robinson, to
be free on August, 28, 1790."[39]

For children, purchase by parents did not always translate into freedom, and
some children simply moved from the control of the planter to the control of the
parent. Legally, the parents owned the child as a slave and could choose to bestow
freedom if they desired. Like planters, some parents delayed their child's manumission. In 1811, Samuel Ruth stipulated that "my daughter Hannah, is hereby
freed, at 10 months of age, but she is to stay with Tudor Cholck until she is 16.[40]
Likewise, in 1815, free black John Durbin stated, "for natural love and affection
for my children, all males are to be free at 21, females at 16: Stephen, Grace,
Mary, Hannah, Harriet, Susan, Isabella Bonaparte, Elizabeth, Christian, and Bennett."[41] The delay of freedom for children may have been a mechanism employed
by black parents to protect their children from white exploitation.[42] While the
reasons for the delay are difficult to determine from manumission records, the
vulnerability of black children, compounded by age, sex, and race, continued
beyond slavery.

Even in freedom, black families faced obstacles. The different degrees of freedom found in Harford reflected the difficulties free blacks confronted in their
efforts to form families. Delayed manumission of a spouse or a child meant that
free blacks still found themselves bound to their old plantations. Although
spouses received more consideration, many children had their freedom delayed.
More often than not, children found themselves tied to the plantation until they
had reached adulthood. If free parents could afford to purchase their children,
this transferal did not guarantee that the child would enjoy freedom. In some
cases, free black parents used the same technique of delayed manumission with
their own children.

Mapping the Free Black Community

It is assumed that once free, blacks left the plantation and struck out on their
own—the American Dream for former slaves.[43] Without a source that identified

household members, it has proven difficult to tell where or with whom the freed slaves lived. Fortunately, the nature of the data from the 1776 census provides a unique opportunity to map the free-black population in Harford. Accounting for one percent of the population, free blacks lived in two types of arrangements— the plantation on which they had already served and independent households. To formulate a hypothesis of why free blacks chose to live on plantations, we will first explore the household composition of those plantations upon which free blacks are found. Second, we will examine the twenty free-black households that existed in Harford for evidence of black families.

In several cases, free blacks stayed on the same plantation that had once owned their services. In the case of free blacks who remained single and unattached, it is not difficult to understand why they stayed on plantations. In 1776, thirty-five-year-old Phill lived and worked for John Penix in Broad Creek Hundred. The Penix household included John, his wife Sarah, four Penix children under the age of ten, one unidentified seventy-year-old woman, and a slave named Pompey who was on loan from James Rigbie. The labor needs of the Penix household would have made Phill a very valuable asset. Since he had already borrowed a slave, to lose Phill would have cut Penix's productive capabilities by one-third.

Labor needs dictated the following household organization in Susquehanna Hundred. Forty-one-year-old Nathaniel Johns and his thirty-three-year-old wife Elizabeth lived in a household that included their six children, ranging in age from one to thirteen; an unidentified eighteen-year-old woman named Mary Touchstone; and eight freed slaves. The ages and sexes of the free blacks are instructive—seventy-year-old Mary, forty-five-year-old Thomas, forty-two-year-old Afee, thirty-six-year-old Margo, thirty-five-year-old William, thirty-three-year-old Gorge, twenty-nine-year-old Pollodore, and twenty-five-year-old Tower. Without this free-black labor force, Johns would have had to operate his plantation with prepubescent children and a teenage servant. In this case, both male and female free blacks were at the height of the productive years. Because one's productive potential served as the basis for taxation, the free blacks in this household would have needed the money to pay the amount due. In this case, Johns, not the freed slave, paid the taxes and dealt with the tax collector. Given this fact, and the fact that the owner no longer could exploit their lives and labor, it is not surprising that some freed blacks remained in the households in which they had worked as slaves.

Beyond the plantation, former slaves found the economic opportunities and freedom to form their own households. In 1776, sixty-nine free blacks lived in twenty independent households. An analysis of the composition of the households contradicts the model of the black family in slavery and freedom that has received the most attention—father/spouse, mother/spouse, and children living together. In Harford, fifty-five percent of the households had a female head. This is not consistent with traditional models of family, which require the presence of an adult male. Upon closer inspection, we find that thirty percent lived in single-parent households, while another thirty-three percent lived in extended households composed of three or more generations. Only ten percent had a simple structure with cohabitating husband/spouse, wife/spouse, and children, with another nine percent living as conjugal couples. Another ten percent faced a solitary existence, while three percent lived with unrelated individuals of the same sex. In Harford, we find that many of the slaves freed by the same person lived together; this finding suggests that either close companionship or familial authority may have dictated their living conditions.

Sixty-four percent of the female households contained children, thus making the households single-parent households. In contrast, twenty-two percent of male-headed households had children and adult females, something that the average female-headed household lacked. Philip Morgan has suggested that women appeared as heads of households more than men did because many women were married to slaves.[44] Yet the patterns of manumission in Harford honored the relationship between spouses above the parent-child connection. The fact that seven out of eleven female-headed households containing children lacked any male presence leads one to conclude that these females did not have spouses. Female-headed households rarely contained adult men. Male-headed households with children tended to have a more simple structure. In the six male-headed households containing other children and other adults, only two had adult females and minor children together.

Among single households where the inhabitant lived alone, males outnumbered females two to one. Additionally, male-headed households tended to have other same-sex individuals living with them, as opposed to females who, if not single parents, lived in extended households. In fact, eighty-two percent of all female-headed households had children, as opposed to twenty-two percent of male-headed households. Since Maryland planters tended to manumit infant children with mothers, we have a better understanding of the living arrangements this freedom produced. If the sample from Harford indicates general trends, free black women generally left plantations and lived with their children. On the other hand, free black males tended to live alone, but on occasion lived with their spouses and children or other adult males. Unlike white women in control of their own households whose headship began with the death of a spouse, headship for free black women began with manumission and therefore depended more on the sympathies of the slave owner.

Finally, we must consider the possibility that not all of the young inmates found in female-headed households were the children of the household head. Linking the census returns to manumission records demonstrates that owners often chose to delay manumission of children in order to minimize the loss of labor on a plantation. Repeatedly, planters in Harford granted immediate freedom to adults and placed term manumission on children.[45] Many black women formed their own households in freedom while they watched their children continue to toil in slavery. Without the capital to purchase their families, despite their freedom, their households continued to exist in the shadow of slavery.

Control over Capital

Once free, Harford County blacks struggled to create stable households. Financial security would have assured that they remained independent. Evidence of property accumulation from the Harford County Court reflected their attitudes as they distinguished themselves as a vital part of the northern Chesapeake economy. Unlike free white servants, free blacks faced the additional pressure to become economically independent since any indication that they were insolvent would have resulted in a fine for their previous owners and a penalty tax. One of the easiest ways free blacks could support themselves and their families was to become part of the seasonal labor force used by Harford planters. In 1773, the following advertisement appeared in *The Pennsylvania Gazette*:

> WANTED, AN honest sober young NEGROE MAN, and a young NEGROE WOMAN, who understand Farming and Country Work. The Woman must understand plain Cooking; Washing, &c. If they are married, and have one or two Children, it will be no Objection.[46]

A search that targeted young adults indicated that planters hoped the free blacks would stay out their productive years on the plantation. The announcement also reflects the gender division of labor that operated on plantations and the types of work required of black women, free or unfree—cooking, washing, and the maintenance of the domestic economy. Finally, the advertisement itself reveals the common expectation that this age cohort would have a family.

Owning one's own labor was the first step toward permanent freedom for newly emancipated blacks. For free blacks, ownership of the means of production served as another vital step toward total independence. Two surviving inventories in Harford reveal the modest amounts of capital some blacks possessed. The inventories attest to the limited social mobility of free blacks in a slave society. The inventory of William Hill, a free black of Harford County, entered probate in 1788. Hills's inventory contained few artifacts, yet he owned a gun. In fact, his estate consisted primarily of a gun and livestock—two distinctive possessions that would have marked him as an independent, free black. Hill's livestock, his plow, and his "bushells and swing of wheat" suggest that he had access to a shelter for his animals and land to cultivate. On July 8, 1803, the inventory of free black Ned Howard entered the probate records of Harford County. His total estate value of fifty-four pounds, two-and-one-half shillings Maryland money placed him firmly in the lower end of the income scale; nonetheless, his inventory provides a glimpse into the lives of free blacks. The first item the enumerator listed was a gun. Howard also owned a cow, a calf, and a yearling. His farm equipment, the bushel of corn, and the rye he had planted just before his death suggest that he supported himself through agriculture, not unlike most of the white males in Harford County. On the surface, the inventory mirrored other Harford inventories of the same time. Yet if we consider the context, it reveals much more. Maryland law prohibited slaves from carrying guns or any weapons. Nor were slaves allowed keep cattle. As free blacks, Hill and Howard possessed both. If their property supplied protection and food, it also provided an important distinction. In a society built upon race, Howard and Hill may have used their property to distance themselves from unfree blacks while they continued to live and work in a slave society. Their guns may have provided not only protection, but also tangible proof that they lived as free men.[47]

The fact that no land appeared in the two estates suggests that the two men leased land instead of owning it. In 1782, the General Assembly ordered the collection of a property-based tax.[48] While the 1782 returns for Harford County did not survive, the 1783 manuscript returns for all fourteen hundreds is extant and reveals the wealth accumulation of northern Chesapeake free blacks. In 1783, a free black named Jehu lived with his wife and children in Susquehanna Hundred. Born in 1711, Jehu had enjoyed freedom since 1775. Instead of moving to Baltimore or Philadelphia, urban centers with large free-black communities, Jehu and his family chose to remain in Harford County. The family had formed important economic and social networks in the local community. One of the wealthiest men in the county, Aquila Hall, kept records of the annual transactions where "free Negro Jehu" rented a "plantation" called "Aquila's Inheritance" for five pounds, Maryland money. The economic transactions between Jehu and Hall did not stop with land. According to Hall's Glen Store accounts from January 1776, Jehu sold to Hall two bushels of beans. In April 1776, Jehu purchased thirteen bushels of wheat and two months later, he returned for another eighteen bushels of wheat.[49] As a result of such transactions, by 1783 Jehu owned fifty acres of land known as West Longs Acre in Susquehanna Hundred, three horses, and five black cows.[50]

The agreement between Hall and Jehu reflected the larger web of black-white networks that benefited both white and free-black communities. While historians have focused on kin networks within the slave and free black community, few works have analyzed economic transactions between free blacks and whites in a slave society.[51] In the land records of Harford County, we find the following conveyance from white planter John Paca to free black Charles.

> This Indenture, made the fourth of November one thousand seven hundred and eighty-two, 1782, between John Paca of Harford County of the one part and Charles, a free negro, of said county of the other. Witness that the said John Paca for and in consideration of five shillings sterling money in hand paid, hath granted bargained and sold and by these presents [sic] doth grant, bargain, and sell unto the said Charles (a free negro) and his heirs, all that lott or parcell of ground in the town of Abingdon, marked and numbered on the platt of the said town ne. sixty two, which s[ai]d plott is hereunto annexed and also right of privileges common with the inhabitants of said town . . . all the streets located on said plott as a common highway, and the remainder and remainders, revision and revisions, rents, issues and profits of the said, property, and demand whatsoever of him, the said John Paca into or of the said Lott or parcell of ground lott the said lott or parcel of ground tight. Privilege and promises unto him the s[ai]d Charles (a free negro) and his heirs . . . forever and to no other is intent or purpose[52]

The agreement benefited both parties. Paca had sold land that he did not need, and Charles had made an investment in his family's future. The land free blacks purchased would be part of an important legacy to their children as it provided them with a means of support.[53]

Black-white economic networks did not exclude women. Two free black females—Rachel and Ruth—appeared in the Assessment of 1783. Rachel lived in the oldest part of the county, Spesutia Lower Hundred, and owned a one-acre tract called Good Neighborhood. The enumerator valued it as "land improved."[54] Ruth lived in Broad Creek Hundred and owned two horses, five black cattle, and various other properties, for a total property value of twenty-seven pounds. While the example of Rachel and Ruth reflects that black women could and did own property independently, the fact remains that free black females proportionately outnumbered free black males as household heads and consistently owned less property. More work that analyzes the lack of social mobility of free black women in the Chesapeake is required.[55]

Conclusion

The 1776 census returns for Harford County have given us an unprecedented opportunity to reexamine the problem of slave-family formation in the colonial Chesapeake. Few studies of Chesapeake plantations have had the benefit of an individual enumeration that can tell us who—white, black, free, unfree—lived in the household and why. The data from Harford suggest that we need to move away from traditional models of slave and free black families in the Chesapeake. As Philip Morgan argued, more subtle categories of analysis that take into account the variety of slave household structure are required. Historians looking for a nuclear household structure—male/spouse, female/spouse, and children— will find very small numbers in Harford.

In the eighteenth century, Harford County contained the largest black population in the northern Chesapeake. Strong demographic indicators improved the chances of slave-family formation. Comparing the sex ratios and child-women ratios with southern counties such as Prince George's, Harford slaves possessed an advantage. From a purely demographic point of view, family formation had become a real possibility for Harford slaves.

However, we found that in Harford improved demographics were not enough to support slave-family formation. Most of the young children tended to live with mothers until they reached age ten. At that point, planters in both Harford and Prince George's removed children, and most children lived without related members of their families. After they reached fifteen years, eighty-five percent of all boys in Harford and seventy-two percent of boys in Prince George's lived without family members. While the majority of girls over the age of fifteen lived without family members, twenty-eight percent in Harford and thirty-five percent in Prince George's County returned to live with their mothers, probably to provide additional care for younger siblings. On Harford plantations with more than ten slaves, senior slave women may have served as primary caregivers to the growing number of children.

The majority of Harford County planters possessed between one and five slaves. Over time, the total number of plantations increased, but the majority of plantations remained small. Slaves on smaller plantations in Harford possessed a better chance of experiencing a balanced sex ratio than slaves who lived on large plantations. Unlike those in Virginia or South Carolina, Harford slaves had fewer chances to find a domestic partner on large plantations. Plantations with more than twenty slaves tended to have extreme patterns of sex distribution. The differences in the numbers of males and females *per plantation* showed that the imbalance in sex ratios affected women disproportionately. The organization of the planter household worked against the formation of slave families, and instead assigned the care of infant children to older female slaves. When one combines this situation with the tendency of owners to separate children from parents and the lack of legal protection for slave marriages, the multiple obstacles that the organization of plantations posed for the formation of slave families become apparent.

Manumission gave blacks the freedom to form their own households. Yet this freedom did not always include spouses and family members. Although they often manumitted spouses, planters in Harford delayed the freedom of children. In many instances, owners continued to control a free black woman who could only watch her children live in slavery. When black adults received freedom, many worked to free their own families. Children often moved from the authority of the planter to the authority of a parent. Their status as a slave remained until a parent officially granted them freedom. In some cases, parents chose to delay manumission for their children.

Once free, some slaves continued to live and work on their former plantation. Several of these slaves were children and their story reflected the fact that many former slaves may not have possessed the knowledge, social authority, or finances to leave the plantation. In some cases, recently freed slaves represented the only adult-labor population living on the plantation. Once free, they could negotiate better conditions with the plantation owner. Some free slaves formed their own households. Most of the households had a single-parent structure. Female heads controlled as many as fifty-five percent of these households, a significantly higher rate than white females. Female household heads often cared for their children; in contrast, male household heads generally lived a solitary existence. Instead of the familiar simple structure identified in the white community, free black households had independent women in control. These patterns are similar to those prevailing under slavery. Historians need to reconceptualize the traditional model of slave and free black families in the Chesapeake to account for these differences.

Free blacks in Harford used black-white economic networks to accumulate property. Selling the product of their own labor in exchange for land or goods, in some instances, they actually increased their holdings. With control over capital, both men and women could ensure their own independence and, in some cases, prepare a legacy for their children. Inventories revealed that free blacks owned specific commodities, such as guns, that would have immediately distinguished them from slaves. Through deliberate steps taken to manumit family members, the cohabitation of mothers and children, and patterns of property accumulation, freed Harford County blacks took calculated risks and moved themselves and their families beyond the bonds of slavery.

Notes

An earlier version of this paper was presented at the Avignon Conference on Slavery and Unfree Labour: Children and Slavery, Avignon, France, May 20–22, 2004. I wish to thank the participants for their remarks and suggestions.

1. For analysis of the demographics of slavery in the Chesapeake, see Russell Menard, "The Maryland Slave Population, 1658 to 1730: A Demographic Profile of Blacks in Four Counties," *William and Mary Quarterly*, 3d ser., 32 (1975): 29–54; Allan Kulikoff, "A 'Prolifick' People: Black Population Growth in the Chesapeake Colonies, 1700–1790," *Southern Studies* 16 (1977): 391–428, idem. *The Development of Southern Cultures in the Chesapeake, 1680–1800.* (Chapel Hill: University of North Carolina Press, 1986). For the slave family and community in the colonial period, see Kulikoff, "The Beginnings of the Afro-American Family in Maryland," in *Law, Society, and Politics in Early Maryland. Proceedings of the First Conference on Maryland History, June 14–15, 1974,* eds. Aubrey C. Land, Lois Green Carr, and Eduard C. Papenfuse (Baltimore: Johns Hopkins University Press, 1977), 171–96; idem. "The Origins of the Afro-American Society in Tidewater Maryland and Virginia, 1700–1790," *William and Mary Quarterly*, 3d ser., 35, (1978): 226–59; Mary Beth Norton, Herbert G. Gutman, and Ira Berlin, "The Afro-American Family in the Age of the Revolution," in *Slavery and Freedom in the Age of the American Revolution*, eds. Ira Berlin and Ronald Hoffman (Charlottesville: University Press of Virginia., 1983), 175–91; Philip D. Morgan, *Slave Counterpoint: Black Culture in the Eighteenth Century Chesapeake and Lowcountry* (Chapel Hill: University of North Carolina Press, 1998). Two very fine examples of the wealth of information from individual plantation records are Herbert Gutman, *The Slave Family in Slavery and Freedom: 1750 and 1925* (New York: Pantheon, 1976), and Cheryll Ann Cody, "Slave Demography and Family Formation" (Ph.D. diss., University of Minnesota, 1982). For gender and slavery in the Chesapeake, see Carole Shammas, "Black Women's Work and the Evolution of Plantation Society in Virginia," *Labor History* 26, (1985): 5–28. For the slave trade into the Chesapeake see Lorena S. Walsh, "The Chesapeake Slave Trade: Regional Patterns, African Origins, and Some Implications," *William and Mary Quarterly*, 3d ser., 58 (2001): 139–70; idem, *From Calabar to Carter's Grove: The History of a Virginia Slave Community* (Charlottesville: University of Virginia Press, 1997). For strategies of slave families in regards to manumissions, see Steve Whitman, *The Price of Freedom: Slavery and Manumission in Baltimore and Early National Maryland* (New York: Routledge Press, 2000), especially chapter 5. For an excellent critique of the manner in which historians have used the slave community argument, see Jean Butenhoff Lee, "The Problem of Slave Community in the Eighteenth-Century Chesapeake," *William and Mary Quarterly*, 3d ser., 43 (1986): 333–61. A notable recent work examining early formation of the slave community in Virginia is Anthony S. Parent, Jr., *Foul Means: The*

Formation of a Slave Society in Virginia 1660–1740 (Chapel Hill: University of North Carolina Press, 2003).

2. John Blassingame, *The Slave Community: Plantation Life in the Ante-Bellum South* (New York: Oxford University Press, 1972), 78–79.

3. Blassingame, *The Slave Community*, 79.

4. Kulikoff, "A 'Prolifick' People," 403.

5. Menard, "The Maryland Slave Population," 44.

6. Menard, "The Maryland Slave Population," 44.

7. Allan Kulikoff, "The Colonial Chesapeake: Seedbed of Antebellum Southern Culture," *Journal of Southern History* 45 (1979): 536.

8. Jean Butenhoff Lee, "The Problem of the Slave Community in the Eighteenth-Century Chesapeake," 343, table 3.

9. Morgan, *Slave Counterpoint*, 504, table 30.

10. Morgan, *Slave Counterpoint*, 506, table 31.

11. Morgan, *Slave Counterpoint*, 502.

12. Morgan, *Slave Counterpoint*, 500, table 29.

13. Morgan, *Slave Counterpoint*, 507.

14. Robert J. Brugger, *Maryland: A Middle Temperament, 1634–1980* repr. ed. (Baltimore: Johns Hopkins University Press, 1996), 6; Phebe Jacobson, "The Census of 1776," *The Archivists' Bulldog* 1, no. 8 (1987), Maryland State Archives, Annapolis. Available online at www.mdarchives.state.md.us/msa/refserv/genealogy/html/census76.html. This series is ongoing and available online at archivesofmaryland.net, where volumes, collectively or individually, can be searched electronically. Modeled on the traditional poll tax used to support the provincial government, this enumeration produced returns of all adult white males over the age of eighteen and all Africans over the age of sixteen. In February 1777, the first legislature in the state of Maryland passed a bill that abolished the poll tax. Manuscript returns for Harford County Courts revealed both parish and countywide taxes lasting until the early nineteenth century. Brugger, 136–37.

15. Outside of the Maryland counties, only Suffolk County, New York, is extant for the 1776 tax. However, these data are not at the individual level. In the tradition of Maryland tax collection, the enumerators organized their returns by hundreds or precincts. The term "hundred" as a measurement related to sixteenth-century traditional English political and geographical subdivisions, wherein "one hundred" men capable of military service resided. Unfortunately, the original boundaries of Harford County can only be estimated, since no maps or physical evidence of their original location remains. By the early nineteenth century, the hundred had fallen out of use, and at the beginning of the twentieth century city planners began to employ precincts based on the number of voting constituents. Jeffrey A. Wyand, "The Hundreds of Washington County," *Maryland Historical Magazine* 67 (1972): 302–6; Louise Joyner Hienten, "The Hundreds of Prince George's County," *Maryland Historical Magazine* 65 (1970): 55–67.

16. All figures for Harford County may be found in the Council of Safety (Census of 1776) MSA S961 1–18, Harford County, Maryland State Archives, Annapolis. Elec-

tronic version provided by the Minnesota Population Center, University of Minnesota. Only Frederick, Prince George's, and Harford Counties included every name, age, sex, and race of household inmates. The other returns listed the first and last name of the head followed by various codes describing the categories of household inhabitants. For instance in Transquaking Hundred, Dorchester County, the following appeared: *Ward, Lousey, 2 ax, 1 az, 1 bx, 1 bz, 1 cx, 1 cz, 1 dx, 1 fz.* Unfortunately, not all counties used Dorchester's code. For household inhabitants, the names and relationships are unknown. The enumerator did not provide first or last names for any of the inmates in the households, and exact identification of the household relationships is nearly impossible.

17. Although the returns for Frederick County are individual-level data, the extant portions include only three hundreds: Sugar Land, North West Hundred, and parts of present-day Montgomery County. Only two parishes—Prince George's and St. Johns—in Prince George's County contained a population comparable to Harford in 1776.

18. Barbara Jeanne Fields, *Slavery and Freedom on the Middle Ground: Maryland during the Nineteenth Century.* (New Haven: Yale University Press, 1985), 11, table 1.5.

19. Charles Steffen, *From Gentlemen to Townsmen: The Gentry of Baltimore County, Maryland, 1660–1776.* (Lexington: University Press of Kentucky, 1993), 49, map 2. In Baltimore County, the largest comparable slave population was in Upper Patapsco River, where they represented thirty-nine percent of the total taxables. In this count, I omitted Upper Gunpowder River Hundred because Steffen included it in his map of Baltimore County without Harford even though several of the taxable slaves lived in what would become Harford. The first list of taxables in Harford appeared in 1774.

20. For the purposes of this calculation alone, I assumed no new immigration and a constant mortality rate. These figures should be used with caution.

21. The ratio in 1776 for ages zero to four was 1.1 and for ages five and under it increased slightly to 1.2.

22. Kulikoff, "A 'Prolifick' People," 410.

23. Jean Butenhoff Lee, "The Problem of Slave Community in the Eighteenth-Century Chesapeake," 340, table 2.

24. Morgan, *Slave Counterpoint*, 505, 506, tables 30 and 31. It is important to distinguish what one intends with the categories "large" or "small" plantations. Table 2 provides a description of the plantations in Harford compared to other Maryland counties. One to five slaves would constitute small and twenty-plus slaves would be categorized as large.

25. These data are consistent with table 3 that includes *all* children even those *over the age of fifteen.*

26. All information for Virginia and South Carolina taken from Morgan, *Slave Counterpoint*, 505, 506, tables 30 and 31.

27. Deborah Gray White, *Ar'N't I A Woman?: Female Slaves in the Plantation South,* (New York: W. W. Norton & Company; Revised edition, 1999), 115. The census lists race, sex, and age. When the enumerator recorded slaves, the pattern is numerical with certain

exceptions. In the case of women misplaced in the census, I categorized them by age and in context of the children recorded after their caregiving roles. I excluded potential mothers. If the female was over forty-five and children who could not possibly be hers followed her in the census, I selected her as a caregiver of the children listed after her. In doing so, I have probably underestimated the number of young and elderly slave women working as caregivers.

28. In Benjamin Osborn's household, the enumerator listed Peter and Moll, both seniors, before the adolescent children too young to be their offspring. Likewise, on George Little's plantation, the location of sixty-year-old Abigail at the end of taxable slaves may have indicated her no-tax status and her position of authority over the following children.

29. *Land Records*, Liber JLG E, i , 1782–1784, Harford County Courthouse, Bel Air, Md., January 12, 1783.

30. Ibid., October 27, 1783.

31. For the laws controlling manumission in Maryland see Thomas Bacon, *Laws Of Maryland At Large, With Proper Indexes: Now First Collected Into One Compleat Body, And Published From The Original Acts And Records, Remaining In The Secretary's-Office Of The Said Province: Together With Notes And Other Matters, Relative To The Constitution Thereof, Extracted From The Provincial Records: To Which Is Prefixed, The Charter, With An English Translation*, eds. Edward C. Papenfuse et al. (Annapolis: Jonas Green, 1765), vol. 75; Archives of Maryland, electronic publication (Baltimore and Annapolis, Md., 1883–), www.archivesofmaryland.net, 1752, chap. I, session 4. Acts 1, 2, 3, and 4, were continued to October 1797, and then allowed to expire. Ibid. 1752, chap. I, sess. 2. Ibid., chap. I, sess. 3. Ibid., sessions 5 and 6. The General Assembly reduced the age of eligibility from fifty to forty-five in 1796, chap. 67, sess. 29.

32. *Land Records*, Liber JLG E, i , 1782–1784, Harford County Courthouse, Bel Air, Md., August 20, 1782.

33. Ibid., November 27, 1783. The following table was included:

Patience was born on	March 1, 1771
Grace	March 1773
Phillis	May 1775
Suckey	September 1776
Pompey	July 1, 1777
Tom	September 23, 1778
Fan	December 10, 1779

34. Whitman, *The Price of Freedom*, 133, table 13.

35. Carolyn Greenfield Adams, *Hunter Sutherlands Slave Manumissions*, (Bowie, Md.: Heritage Books Inc., 1999), Manumission of Rachel Price, 1811, 15.

36. *Harford County Land Records, 1774–1810*. Manumission of slaves Dorcas and Nancy by Margaret Evitt, 1806, Harford County Courthouse, Bel Air, Md.

37. Adams, *Hunter Sutherland's Slave Manumissions*, 1811, Rachel Price, 15.

38. Adams, *Hunter Sutherland's Slave Manumissions*, 1814, John McCauley, 18.

39. Free black Tower Hill wrote, "Elizabeth, my wife, and daughter purchased from Edward C. Tolby are hereby free." Adams, *Hunter Sutherland's Slave Manumissions.*, 1800, Tower Hill, 9. Likewise, Caleb Parsons in 1808 attested that his son Moses Parsons, whom he had purchased in 1803 for twenty-three pounds from Robert Cresswell, was finally free. Adams, *Hunter Sutherland's Slave Manumissions*, 1808, Caleb Parsons, 13, 61.

40. Adams, *Hunter Sutherland's Slave Manumissions*, 1811.

41. Adams, *Hunter Sutherland's Slave Manumissions*, 1811, Samuel Ruth, "a free Negro," 15, 1815.

42. Whitman, *The Price of Freedom*, 138–39.

43. Ira Berlin, *Slaves without Masters: The Free Negro in the Antebellum South*, (New York: Oxford University Press, 1974), 55, table 5. Berlin suggests that newly freed slaves left the plantations on which they had lived in efforts to find lost family members or work in urban sectors.

44. Morgan, *Slave Counterpoint*, 496.

45. For example, prior to 1776, the brothers Nathan and James Rigbie, William Coale Sr., and his nephew, William Coale Jr., all decided to free several female slaves. Once free, the females organized their own households. The census data revealed that both the Coale and the Rigbie plantations retained a number of slaves despite the manumissions. The two families shared a bond since William Coale Jr. was married to Elizabeth Rigbie, the daughter of James Rigbie.

46. *The Pennsylvania Gazette*, September 15, 1773.

47. In comparison to other estates of free blacks found by Philip Morgan, Harford's free possessed much less capital than the free mulatto Azaricum Drighouse, who left an estate in Northhampton County valued at more than a hundred pounds, or South Carolina resident John Goodbe, whose wealth included a house and fourteen cattle bequeathed to his widow. Morgan, *Slave Counterpoint*, 486.

48. *Laws of Maryland Made and Passed at the Session of Assembly . . . Fourth of November 1782* (Annapolis: Frederick Green, 1782), chap. 6. *Archives of Maryland* (SC M 3180), Maryland State Archives, Annapolis. This series is ongoing and available online at archivesofmaryland.net, where volumes, collectively or individually, can be searched electronically.

49. Account and Ledger Book of Colonial James Hall, Aquila Hall, and Jacob Giles, Glen Store. No. 20, located in the Special Collections (MS 1516) at the Maryland State Historical Society, Baltimore, Md. June 25, 1775; December 25, 1776.

50. *Assessment of 1783, Harford County, Maryland*, Susquehanna Hundred, 148 and 148a.

51. Morgan, *Slave Counterpoint*, 486–87. For examinations of black-white economic transactions in the seventeenth century, see T. H. Breen and Stephen Innes, *"Myne Owne Ground": Race and Freedom on Virginia's Eastern Shore, 1640–1676* (New York: Oxford University Press, 1980).

52. *Harford County Land Records*, No. E. 1782–1784. Harford County Courthouse, Bel Air, Md., November 4, 1782.

53. If free blacks owned no real estate, they may have owned other taxable property.

In 1783, Pompey in Broadcreek owned two horses and three black cows. Flip in Gunpowder Upper and Lower Hundred owned one horse and three black cows. Guinea, his neighbor, owned two horses and two black cows. Free London in Spesutia Upper owed tax on one horse and two black cows and Benjamin Brown, a free black previously owned by John Sewell, owned a female slave between the ages of fourteen and thirty-six who was valued at sixty pounds. Ibid., Gunpowder Upper and Gunpowder Lower Hundred 58 and 59a.

54. *Assessment of 1783*, Harford County, Md, Spesutia Lower Hundred, 51 and 51a.

55. One of the most important works to analyze southern black women's control over capital is Suzanne Lebsock, *The Free Women of Petersburg: Status and Culture in a Southern Town, 1784–1860* (New York: W. W. Norton & Co., 1985).

"To Swear Him Free": Ethnic Memory as Social Capital in Eighteenth-Century Freedom Petitions

4

THOMAS F. BROWN AND LEAH C. SIMS

SOMETIME AROUND 1685, an indentured servant in Anne Arundel County named Mary Davis inscribed a remarkable statement in her family Bible:

> Let all Christian people know that I Mary Davis am the daughter of Richard Davis once dwelling in Mark Lane in the City of London. My son Thomas was begotten on my body by a Negro called Dominggoo. This is here Inserted to Satisfy and to whome it May Concern that my said son Thomas Came from a Christian Race by his Mother. I was married to said Negro. I have also a daughter by the same Negro my husband and whose name is Rose.[1]

Mary's inscription is striking because it reveals so much about the concerns of servants who were involved in multiracial unions at the time, and how they thought about racial identity. With clear intent of purpose, Mary Davis is self-consciously creating a paper trail that she hopes will document her children's right to freedom.

Mary's concern for her children's freedom leaps off the page. She acknowledges her multiracial marriage, but her conception of race seems to evoke that of an earlier generation: "my said son Thomas Came from a Christian Race by his Mother." Mary's understanding of race here includes religion as a primary factor. Mary refers to herself and her son not as "white," but as of the "Christian race." Winthrop Jordan observes that in the early colonial era, African heathenism was intrinsically linked with barbarity and blackness: "Heathenism was for Englishmen one inherent characteristic of savage men"—and thus heathenism became part of the ideological justification for enslaving Africans.[2]

But according to Maryland law, Mary's conflation of race and religion was already outdated in 1685. In April 1671, the Maryland Assembly had decreed that notions such as Mary's constituted an "ungrounded apprehension that by becoming Christians they and the Issues of their bodies are actually manumited and made free and discharged from their Servitude and bondage." Thus the assembly explicitly separated race from religion. The act made clear that African heritage alone was the legal and ideological basis for enslavement, regardless of the religious preferences of any given "Negroe."[3]

The title of the 1671 legislation—"An Act for the Encourageing the Importacon of Negros and Slaves into this Province"—makes it clear that the act represents the economic interests of the planter class. But Mary Davis's Bible inscription suggests that poor whites in the Chesapeake may have held diverging ideas about racial-ethnic difference, ideas that still incorporated religion as a component of a free person's identity vis-à-vis slaves. It may have been that the change in law was driven by the economic interests of the elite, moving well in advance of shifting mores on the ground.

An alternate interpretation is that Mary Davis was invoking the older conception of race because current legal doctrine was working against her children's interests, and the argument she made was the best one available to her. Mary Davis's children were doomed to slavery not because of their multiracial ancestry, but because their English mother had married a slave.

On September 19, 1664, Maryland's Upper House asked the Lower House its opinion on what to do with "such weomen of the English or other Christian nacons being free that are now allready marryed to negros or other Slaves." Should these women be considered slaves or free? What was to be the status of their children? Later the same day, the Lower House responded that such women would not "be Constrayned to serve," and that children of such multiracial unions would be bound out as apprentices for thirty years.[4]

However, by the time the act was written into law two days later, on September 21, radical changes had been made. The assembly had in the interim decided to deal much more harshly with those "freeborne English women forgettfull of their free Condicon [who] to the disgrace of our Nation doe intermarry with Negro Slaves."[5] The Act of 1664 now consigned a free woman who married a slave to serve her husband's master as a slave, for the duration of her husband's lifetime. Children born of such unions prior to the act's passage would serve as indentured servants for thirty years. Children born subsequent to the act's passage would be slaves for life.

This feature of the Act of 1664 was repealed by a subsequent "Act Concerning Negroes and Slaves" adopted on September 17, 1681, which manumitted the white wives of slaves and their children, but only for marriages contracted after the last day of that assembly session. A woman who was already married to a slave would remain under the provisions of the original Act of 1664, still enslaved until the death of her husband. So would her children be slaves—even if they were born after the repeal—for any child born to an enslaved mother inherited her slave status.[6]

Thus during the window of seventeen years during which the Act of 1664 was operative, white wives of slaves, and their children, were legally considered to be enslaved. The wife would be freed upon her husband's death; her children and their descendants were slaves for life. So although the Act of 1664 was repealed in 1681, not everyone enslaved by the 1664 act was freed by the repeal.

The Maryland courts would be adjudicating the consequences of the 1664 act into the 1790s and beyond. Many descendants of white female–African male unions who lived as slaves because of the Act of 1664 resisted its decree and would petition for their freedom, persisting even into the early nineteenth century. Some families thus enslaved would repeatedly seek their freedom in the courts, over many generations. The records created as a consequence of these freedom petitions reveal much about ethnic identity in the colonial Chesapeake.

This chapter explores the persistence of historical memories surrounding the ethnic identity of people of color in the Chesapeake region during the colonial and early national periods. Well into the late eighteenth century, slaves and members of the white community alike could remember details about the ethnicity of slaves of previous generations. The community distinguished imported slaves from American–born slaves. It distinguished African slaves from South Asian slaves. It even made ethnic distinctions among slaves from different tribes in Africa. These memories persisted across the subsequent generations. Members of the community, when called into court, could describe ethnically distinctive ancestors and could calculate their genealogical descent into the contemporary, ethnically assimilated population.

Whites and slaves retained memories of slaves' ethnic identity for different reasons. Whites initially made ethnic distinctions among slaves as a component of calculating their human property's economic value. Slaves from certain African tribes were deemed more valuable than others, due to planters' stereotypes about the labor attributes of various ethnic groups. Advertisements for slaves would often describe them in terms of their language abilities and tribal origin in Africa, with the slave being priced accordingly. A slave's ethnic distinctiveness, once perceived, was held in the white community's collective memory for several generations after the slave's importation.

Ethnic Memory as Social Capital

People of color, however, remembered their own ancestors' ethnic distinctiveness for a longer period of time, over more generations, for an instrumental reason—the descendants of a female ancestress who had been free were themselves entitled to freedom. This was a powerful incentive to retain such memories across the generations. For a slave, descent from a white woman in your maternal line was legal evidence of your own right to freedom. Consequently, many slave families cited the white or nonblack ethnic identity of a female ancestor as a legal strategy in the context of a freedom petition. Free people of color were also thus motivated to remember and document their descent from a white (or non-African) ancestress, as a defense against any attempt to illegally enslave them.

Ethnicity thus constituted a significant type of human capital, and consequently motivated persistence of memory. Petitioners for freedom would argue that since their ancestress was so ethnically different from the African-American slave population, she must have been enslaved illegally, and thus her descendants were entitled to freedom. For example, Madagascarians and other South Asians stood out from sub-Saharan slaves in both culture and appearance. Since South Asians were a minority among the slave population, the community's perception of their distinctiveness persisted for a longer period of time.

Some slaves pursuing this legal strategy would even fabricate a false ethnic identity for their ancestor as an attempt to justify a claim to freedom. Other families remembered only that their ancestress was different, but forgot the details of her difference. When you trace their claims over the generations, occasionally the ancestor's identity mutates in the family memory. For example, there was a significant contingent of "East Indian" slaves in the colonial Chesapeake. Over subsequent generations, the community would sometimes mistakenly remember East Indian ancestors as American Indian ancestors—often because American Indian ancestors provided more capital than East Indian ancestors for a slave pursuing a freedom petition.

In general, ethnic distinctiveness on the part of slave ancestors was remembered in terms of symbolic ethnicity, by their descendents who were otherwise acculturated into Chesapeake society. The ethnic distinctiveness of an ancestor was most likely to be remembered when there was a benefit to claiming that distinctive identity for yourself, in the context of a freedom petition.

While ethnic memory was a form of human capital inhering in the individual, it was accessible only by means of *social capital*. Alejandro Portes defines social capital as "the capacity of individuals to command scarce resources by virtue of their membership in networks, or broader social structures . . . The ability to obtain [social capital] does not inhere in the individual . . . but instead is a property of the individual's set of relationships with others." For slaves pursuing freedom petitions, it was crucial to have a "set of relationships" with sympathetic white members of the community. As a petitioner you needed credible witnesses who would testify as to your ancestress's reputation as a free woman, or testify that she was a member of an ethnic group that was generally thought to have been free. Petitioners who lacked relationships with witnesses who had a credible reputation were far less likely to win their freedom. Thus ethnic identity inhered not just in the individual, but also in the memory of the broader community, as a form of social capital.[7]

Methodology and Historiographic Context

Historians of slavery have for almost a century been addressing issues of slaves' agency, identity, and culture. In the past half-century, the historiography of slavery has moved away from U. B. Phillips's "plantation school" model of slave socialization. Recent work has offered a more complex and nuanced analysis of how North American slaves created a social and cultural space for themselves.[8]

This chapter draws on primary data sources that record the slaves' own voices and the voices of those who knew them. The court cases discussed in this chapter provide us with firsthand testimony that was recorded in eighteenth-century freedom petitions entered by slaves in the county courts of southern Maryland during the colonial era. Other petitions are drawn from the region's appellate court of the early national period, the General Court of the Western Shore. Some petitions were appealed to the General Court from the county court. Others originated in the General Court when the petitioner could argue that the decision in a case heard at the county level would have been biased.

Few of these records have been employed by previous researchers. A handful of the appellate decisions that were published by the Maryland court reporters have been cited by such historians as Philip D. Morgan, David Brion Davis, and Martha Hodes.[9] In general, scholars citing freedom petitions have been more focused on the legal construction of boundaries on race and freedom, and less concerned with the ongoing construction and persistence of ethnic identity.

The case of Eleanor Butler is well known to Chesapeake historians. "Irish Nell" Butler was an English servant of Lord Baltimore who in 1681 married Charles, a "saltwater Negro" slave man, and whose children fell into slavery as a consequence. Lord Baltimore was so disturbed that a white woman would willingly marry a slave—and thus consign herself to slavery—that he seems to have been a major force in getting the Act of 1664 repealed in the fall of 1681, a month after Nell's wedding to Charles.

In 1763, two of Charles and Nell's descendants petitioned for their freedom. The community's memory was recorded in the court proceedings. Edward Edelen recounted how Baltimore himself had attempted to talk Nell out of the marriage:

> What a pity so likely a young girl as you are should fling herself away so as to marry a Negro . . . you'll make slaves of your children and their posterity.[10]

Nell repudiated Baltimore's counsel. Benjamin Jameson recalled that Baltimore had asked Nell "how she would like to go to bed with a Negro," to which Nell replied that she "would rather go to bed with Charles than His Lordship."

This remarkable statement is undoubtedly the major reason why details of Nell Butler's marriage to Charles were remembered by white members of the Western Shore community, and passed down for several generations. It also may be why the Butler case is so commonly cited by historians, although the legal precedent set by the court in the Butler family's proceeding is far more significant.

The Provincial Court decided in the Butler descendants' favor in 1770, but the appellate court overturned the ruling on the grounds that Eleanor Butler had been legally enslaved under the Act of 1664. The next Butler generation tried again, petitioning once more in 1787. This time the court granted them freedom.

The 1787 opinion was a landmark decision. It represented a major shift in doctrine, one that would affect petitioning slaves and their masters for more than a decade. The court in *Butler* held that the burden of proof fell on the slave owner to show that his slave's white ancestress in the maternal line had been married to her African-American consort. This was a major departure from previous decisions in similar freedom petitions. Having to prove that a marriage took place a century before imposed a nearly insurmountable burden on the slave owner. Plenty of hearsay evidence had been offered in the previous Butler petition in 1765, showing that Nell and Charles had been legally married. The court in 1787 discounted that hearsay, instead giving credence to contradicting hearsay testimony, which held that Nell had never been enslaved as a consequence of her marriage to Charles.[11]

As a consequence of the court's liberalizing decision in 1787, hundreds of slaves filed new freedom petitions and won on the same grounds that the Butlers had. In subsequent cases, the courts granted significant weight to hearsay evidence, generally leaning in favor of the petitioner. Although the legal logic of *Butler* and consequent decisions is arguable, the practical results were that hundreds of people were released from the bondage that had been imposed on them by the Act of 1664. Furthermore, hundreds of pages of depositions and testimony were recorded, giving historians a remarkable window into colonial slave life.

While the Butler case is well known because of its human interest and its significant legal precedence, there is a host of similarly evocative cases that have scarcely been analyzed in print. Furthermore, the original records reveal far more detail than the published appellate decisions do. As in the ubiquitous Butler case, we find preserved in these original records the voices of the participants in the court proceedings. Testimony was recorded, both in court and in deposition, which reveals striking detail about how the people of the Chesapeake understood and thought about ethnic distinctiveness. Such testimony illuminates the nature and extent of community memories of ethnic identity in the Chesapeake, and the function of ethnic memory as social capital.

Some of the most enlightening freedom-petition documents emerge from the early national period. The political arguments of the Revolutionary era were heard by black Americans as well as white. In 1776, the first Maryland state constitution permitted male property owners—including free black men—to vote, although blacks gradually lost that right, with none voting after 1810. Furthermore, the war caused disruptions in work routines and reductions in standards of living. Combined with the decline in the Chesapeake tobacco economy, these changes led to increasing expense in maintaining a slave, and hence decreasing economic incentive to fight a freedom petition or chase down a runaway.[12]

During this brief window of opportunity in the early national period, popular ideology supporting political egalitarianism and autonomy was readily extended to other aspects of freedom. Slaves began to voice appeals to universal natural rights by filing freedom petitions. In 1803, a Maryland plantation overseer named James Eagle described the development of freedom ideology among slaves:

> I am now drawing towards 50 years of age. I have spent 21 of that time on this place, the first part of it more agreeable than the latter.

Eagle's complaint was about the slaves he supervised:

> They Get much more Dissatisfied Every year & troublesome for they say that they all ought to be at there liberty & they think that I am the Cause that they are not . . . By that means [they] Gaves me all the trouble that they can which keeps me one half of my time in hot blood & when that is the Case I Cannot Conduct my business as I ought to do.[13]

Many of the families petitioning in the early national period had parents or grandparents who had tried and failed to get free in colonial-era court actions. But in the last two decades of the eighteenth century, freedom petitions would be upheld by the courts with far more frequency than they ever had been before or would be after, mainly because of a temporary relaxation in the rules of evidence.

Beginning in 1787 with petitions by the descendants of Nell Butler and her slave husband Charles, the Western Shore courts began to give more credence to hearsay evidence regarding an ancestor's community reputation as a slave or free. Although the hearsay in the Butler case indicated that Charles and Nell had been married, the community memory was divided on whether Nell had been enslaved by that marriage or not. In earlier times, the crux of Eleanor Butler's ethnic identity had been "Irish Nell," indicating that she was ethnically distinguished as an Irish woman. But by the 1787 petition, the deponents were more focused on Nell's whiteness than her Irishness, and seem to have found her marriage to an African slave more of a curiosity than such unions had been a century before. By 1787, the community sensibility was disturbed by the notion of a white woman's being enslaved. The contradiction posed by white slavery seems to have been driving the court's willingness to bend over backward to ignore evidence of the marriage between Nell and Charles—the marriage that had made Nell's enslavement legal.[14]

As a consequence of this shift in the ideological winds and its ramifications in legal doctrine, slaves suing for freedom were remarkably successful over the next decade or so. But the window of opportunity was already beginning to close by the turn of the century. In 1797, Maryland's attorney general complained to the court about freedom petitioners:

> Our courts have determined that general reputation, that such persons are descended from white women, or that they have exercised the right of freedom, is evidence to the jury. It is giving the power to ignorant persons to judge of rights . . . Hundreds of negroes have been let loose upon the community by the hearsay testimony of an obscure illiterate individual.[15]

The Maryland courts would eventually exclude hearsay evidence in freedom proceedings. However, during the brief period when hearsay evidence was allowed, numerous depositions and testimony were recorded that shed much light on the ethnic identity of ancestors in the colonial era.

Mary Queen's Fine Clothing

Ethnic distinctiveness manifested itself in language and customs, as well as racial appearance. For example, in testimony taken for freedom petitions filed by the Queen family in 1796, the petitioners' ancestress Mary Queen was well remembered by the people of the Western Shore. Eighty-three-year-old Benjamin Duval described Mary's arrival in Charles County circa 1721, on a slave ship entering via the West River. The locals were struck by Mary's unusual clothing and her regal bearing. She was nicknamed "the Pappow Queen" by her new master. This nickname was a reference to her Popo tribal origins, in the present-day country of Benin. From this nickname came the family surname Queen, which remains even today the surname of Mary's progeny, many of whom still reside on the Western Shore. Duval testified that Mary "wore beads on her arms and had her head dressed with them and twisted round her hair which was near a yard long. And on the top she had a knot of beads."[16]

Benjamin Duval also recalled that at the same slave sale, his father purchased a slave woman named Sarah who was a "Mundingo," and arrived "almost naked, having only a shirt around her shoulders and another around her waist, and that she likewise wore some blue beads." Duval noted that the ship had carried slaves of several different West African ethnic groups. Duval described Mary, the Pappow Queen, as a "very yellow" woman, as opposed to Sarah, whom he remembered as a "black" woman. Benjamin remembered another slave on the ship as "Golden Coast Tom." Duval recounted that Sarah and the Pappow Queen had told him that many of the slaves had died during the voyage and were thrown overboard.[17]

Mary Queen seems to have made quite an impression with her West African clothing, jewelry, and hairstyles, and for continuing to speak her native "country language" with coethnic slaves she knew on the Western Shore. Her ethnic identity was so striking that it was vividly recalled several generations later by the elders who had known her or known of her.

The ethnicity of other slaves is inscribed in the evocative names by which the community recalled them, such as "Malaga Moll," "Golden Coast Tom," "Indian Sawony," and "Thomas India." The court records also document the community memory of white servants' ethnicity over several generations, as in the examples of the slave descendants of "Welsh Moll" and "Irish Nell" Butler. Irish and Welsh servant women in particular were remembered for their national origin, whereas ancestresses from England were not distinguished by nationality, but described merely as "white," "free," or "Christian."

Mary Davis's Bible

Mary Davis—the white servant woman who attempted to circumvent the Act of 1664 by documenting her children's ancestry in her Bible inscription—was born in London, England. She married Dominggoo, the "Negroe man," who was a slave belonging to Joseph Tilley of Calvert County, Maryland. Their first child, Thomas, was born in 1677; their second child, Rose, was born in 1684. Mary and Dominggoo were living together on Lord Baltimore's plantation when she wrote in a Bible the details of her marriage to Dominggoo, and the birth and baptism of her children, probably shortly after the Rose's birth in 1684. Although the whereabouts of that Bible are unknown today, Mary's daughter Rose produced it for the Anne Arundel County Court in August 1715. The court transcribed the passage quoted at the beginning of this chapter into the record as evidence in Rose's freedom petition.[18]

Rose Davis was among those challenging the courts' evolving interpretation of the 1664 act. Mary Davis's fears for her children, as expressed in her Bible inscription, had turned out to be well founded. Mary's daughter Rose had her thirty-first birthday on August 11, 1715. This was the age at which the indenture expired for bastard children of mixed-race unions. The same month, Rose petitioned for her freedom from her master, Henry Darnall, in Anne Arundel County Court. Rose's theory seems to have been that since she was born in 1684—after the repeal of the Act of 1664—she was legally entitled to her freedom after having served thirty years.

The court appears to have interpreted the repeal act of 1681 more literally. Rose lost her case, and was ordered to "serve Dureing Life as a slave." Since Rose's mother Mary had been a slave at the time of Rose's birth, under the Act of 1664, Rose was a slave for life under the matrilineal rule—regardless of the fact that Rose's mother was once a free Englishwoman of "a Christian race."[19]

Mary Davis's paper trail, in the form of a Bible inscription, had failed to accomplish its purpose. But our examination of Maryland law as it pertained for a seventeen-year period in the late seventeenth century makes clear why Mary Davis was so desperate to document her children's free ancestry as best she could.

The Davis family did not give up its quest for freedom. In March 1779, Rose Davis's granddaughter Rosamond Bentley and her siblings sued Anthony Addison in the Prince George's County Court, petitioning for their freedom. The case concluded two years later, in August 1781, with Rosamond and her siblings William, Mary, Eleanor, and Margaret Bentley winning their case and being set free.

According to the doctrine in place at the time, the court erred in setting the Bentleys free. The Bentleys were the descendants of a woman who was legally enslaved when their ancestress was born, and thus the Bentleys were legally enslaved themselves. The court's error was due in part to evidentiary misrepresentation by the Bentley petitioners and their witnesses.

What is especially notable about the Bentleys' petition is their reworking of their racial-ethnic heritage. They claimed that:

> Your petitioners great grand mother was an English woman and came into
> this province with Lord Baltimore. The said Mary Davis had the misfor-

tune of having an Indian Native of this Country for her husband and by him had your petitioners' mother.

This misrepresentation of Dominggoo's identity was embellished by the Bentleys' witnesses. William Dove testified that:

Mary Davis came into this Country with Lord Baltimore about seventy years ago . . . her husband was an East Indian.

Catherine Harley testified that:

The said Rose Davis was free born and that Rose Davis was the daughter of Mary Davis begotten by an East India Indian who came into this country with Lord Baltimore.[20]

Although Mary Davis identified her husband Dominggoo as a "Negro" in her Bible inscription, four generations later her descendants found it convenient to alter Dominggoo's identity. The petitioners label Dominggoo as "an Indian Native of this Country," apparently meaning an American Indian. Their witnesses, perhaps not adequately prepared, identified Dominggoo instead as an "East India Indian." Rose Davis's daughter was described by the petitioners as "Indian Polly."

The Bentleys' motive for misrepresenting Domingoo's identity is clear. Whereas African ancestry was prima facie evidence of slave status in the late eighteenth century, the same was not true for Indian ancestors. By misrepresenting Dominggoo as an American or East Indian, the Bentleys were establishing prima facie evidence of Dominggoo's freedom on the basis of his race. If Dominggoo had been free when he and Mary married, then Mary would have been free, and hence her descendants would be free.

William Dove's testimony adds another legal tack when he claimed that "Mary Davis came into this Country with Lord Baltimore about seventy years ago." If Mary had arrived in North America in 1709, as Dove argued, then the Act of 1664 that had enslaved Mary for the lifetime of her husband—and that had enslaved Mary's descendants in perpetuity—would have been irrelevant, having been repealed in 1681. Thus in his testimony, William Dove is manipulating the Davis family's timeline in order to help them sidestep the consequences of the Act of 1664.

The Prince George's County Court does not seem to have had access to the records of Rose Davis's earlier Anne Arundel County petition from 1715, which contained the evidentiary details that would have undermined Rose's grandchildren's case in 1779. Thus it becomes apparent why Mary Davis's Bible may have gone missing. Mary Davis's Bible would have provided proof of her marriage to an African slave, and thus fatally undercut the Bentleys' case, instead of helping it as Mary had originally hoped when she made her inscription. No wonder the Bible does not make another appearance in this petition.

The Davis/Bentley family is fascinating on many dimensions. It demonstrates how knowledgeable laypeople were about slave law. Mary Davis knew that her children faced the possibility of slavery due to their "Negro" paternity. Rose Davis knew to the precise day when her indenture would have expired, had she not been held to the most conservative reading of the Act of 1664 by the Anne Arundel court. The Bentleys and their witnesses seem not only to have been well aware of the legal utility of a white ancestress, but were able to make the crucial distinction between the legal utility of a white ancestress with an African husband, and a white ancestress with an Indian husband, under the Act of 1664. Their understanding of this long-defunct law persisted in 1779, when the Bentleys initiated their petition. The Bentley petitioners seem to have still been well aware of every implication of the Act of 1664 for their case, even though it had been repealed nearly a century before.

The Bentley case shows the mutability of racial-ethnic identity in the early national period, as the family instrumentally manipulated the ethnic identity of their colonial ancestor in response to the contemporary legal environment. It also shows how community memory functioned as a form of social capital, as the Bentleys were able to procure witnesses who would testify to their most favorable—albeit false—interpretation of their family's history.

"To Swear Him Free"—John Bartley's Imposture

The Bentleys were not the only petitioners who deliberately misrepresented their family history in an attempt to win freedom. John Bartley (who also called himself John Barton during the court proceedings) filed a freedom petition in 1793, claiming descent from an ancestress of the surname Savoy.[21]

There was a free African-American Savoy family on the Western Shore, but John Bartley was not descended from them. Mingo Savoy, his wife, and several children had been freed in 1704 in the will left by their mistress. However, one of their daughters remained indentured under the terms of the will. Her master illegally retained her in bondage even after her indenture was completed, so she was never able to get free during her lifetime. During the window of Revolutionary liberalism, her descendants successfully petitioned for freedom.[22]

The Savoys were mainly tenant farmers, and they had a good deal of visibility within the white community. The Savoys were exceptional because of their dark skin. One elderly white witness recalled entertaining a guest who inquired, after the Savoy man had left the room, whose slave he was. In a community where most free people of color were descended from multiracial unions, the dark-skinned Savoys stood out, and were hence more memorable. This visibility made it more likely that during the post-Revolutionary window of opportunity for free-dom petitions, elderly whites would recall the Savoys as having been free.

A similar process can be observed with such families as the Butlers, Bentleys, and others who petitioned the Western Shore courts for freedom multiple times, one generation after the next. Although petitions by earlier generations may have failed, even unsuccessful petitions increased the likelihood that white community members would have heard about the family's claims to freedom. When hearsay evidence became admissible during the brief window of liberalism, the families that had publicly articulated their right to freedom in earlier generations—whether successfully or not—thus had a better chance of garnering supporting testimony from white members of the community.

During the window of liberalism, once one member of a family won freedom, most owners dropped their opposition to petitions from relatives, and the courts most often simply upheld related petitions without bothering to retry the case. John Bartley saw an opportunity in this trend. His freedom petition was an attempt to piggyback on the Savoy family's success by falsely claiming his own female Savoy ancestress.

John Bartley's ruse was not successful, due to his lack of the necessary social capital. The community remembered the Savoys well, and also knew John Bart-ley's ancestry. It is interesting that Gabriel Duvall defended Bartley's master. Duvall more often served as the plaintiff's lawyer in freedom petitions. Duvall was probably well aware that Bartley's was a losing cause (and a fraudulent peti-tion), and hence was unwilling to align himself with the plaintiff as was his custom.

John Bartley's first cousin was descended from a free female Savoy, because Bartley's uncle William, a slave, had married the daughter of a Savoy woman and a Barton man. So Bartley did have a distant family connection with the Savoy line, but it was by marriage, not by blood, and it was not in his own maternal line. John Bartley presented himself to the court as "John Barton"—apparently trying to create a halo effect of closer relations to the Savoy women by slightly altering his surname to that of his uncle's wife.

John Bartley's primary claim was that his own female ancestress Priss was a sister of the free Savoy family. Two damaging lines of testimony challenged this argument. First, one witness remembered observing Mingo Savoy attempting to have sex with Bartley's ancestress Priss. This cast doubt on Bartley's claims that

Mingo and Priss were brother and sister. Second, another witness testified that John Bartley had tried to bribe him, offering to remunerate the potential perjurer with two "half Joes" if he would agree "to swear him free."

John Bartley had no legal right to freedom according to the laws in place at that time. But the Butlers and Davises—and several other families that won their petitions—also lacked a clear legal entitlement to freedom. The difference was that the successful petitioners were able to draw on social capital, garnering support from reputable members of the white community who would support their cause by testifying about ancestors' reputations—as white or not, free or not—in the petitioner's favor. John Bartley's frustration in his search for sympathetic witnesses led him to attempt to bribe one potential witness. Furthermore, Bartley was not only unable to engage the most prominent plaintiff's lawyer in the region, but he found that same lawyer representing the opposing side. John Bartley's case was fraudulent, although not much more fraudulent than the Bentleys' case. But lacking social capital, Bartley's petition was doomed to failure.

William Creek's "Love Powder"

In 1736, William Creek petitioned the Anne Arundel County court for his freedom. Creek was "born in the East Indies & Carryed into England very young where he was Christined, bound to and serve an apothecary for some time." Testifying on behalf of Will Creek was Samuel Chew, a relative of Will Creek's master. Chew recalled the practical joke that led Creek to be sold overseas to Maryland around 1717:

> I have frequently heard my uncle old Mr. Samuel Chew & my cousin the late Mr. Samuel Chew Senr. say that Will Creek lived with Harris an Appothecary in the City of London and that he served the said Harris in his shop. That for some unluckey Prank that he played which was the giving some person a Dose of Cantharides for a Love Powder. Harris' wife & daughter were so offended at it that they would not suffer the said Creek to live in the Family which occasioned Harris to send him over to this Province by one Capt. John Burton and either consigned him to my uncle for sale or left him to be disposed by Burton of whom my uncle bought him. Signed Samuel Chew.[23]

Samuel Chew's testimony was instrumental to Will Creek's case. Creek was also able to bring to court another white man, Peter Galloway, to testify on his behalf.

Creek claimed that after his prank, he had been sold overseas by his London master—"most unjustly & clandestinely sent & consigned"—for a seven-year indenture, but that he had by now already served the Chew family for nineteen years. Although Creek sought his freedom, he does not seem confident in his prospects, plaintively noting that "your petr. should be sett free altho your petitioner would be very willing to serve Mr. Chew if he should be pleased to hire your petr."[24]

William Creek won his case and was set free. Once again, this case demonstrates the importance of the white community memory for nonwhite petitioners. Creek's claim was upheld because he was supported by white witnesses who recalled his ethnic origins, and who also recalled the circumstances under which he came to America.

It is notable that Creek's main witness was Samuel Chew, a member of the same family that stood to gain by keeping Creek in their service, unremunerated. In fact, it was not uncommon for members of the same white family to testify on opposite sides of a freedom case. In some cases, this seems to indicate a sense of moral obligation on the part of many Western Shore planters to testify accurately on behalf of people who were unjustly enslaved. In other cases, petty family feuding better explains such divisions.

Will Creek formed a union with a slave woman, and so his descendants lived as slaves. During the rush of freedom petitions in the early national period several generations later, Creek's descendants petitioned for freedom. They brought forward William Creek's ethnic distinctiveness to bolster their claim. However, by this time they remembered Will Creek as a native American Indian, having forgotten that he was of South Asian origin from the "East Indies." They lost their case because under slave law, freedom was inherited matrilineally, and not through the paternal line. William Creek's descendants are today most likely part of the African-American population, with no idea of their South Asian heritage.

The experience of Will Creek exemplifies that of other South Asian servants on the Western Shore during the colonial era. Many were imported to the colonies by way of England, arriving already Christianized and fluent in English. Others arrived as slaves who had been captured and sold in Madagascar. It is impossible to confidently estimate the size of the South Asian population in the Western Shore counties, but "East Indians" outnumber "Indians" in the extant colonial records after 1710 or so. Thus it would seem that during the eighteenth century either native American Indians were fewer in number than South Asians on the Western Shore, or that they were more assimilated and thus less noticeable to the record makers as ethnically distinct. It is probable that some people recorded as "Indian" were actually of South Asian descent. Such errors can occasionally be traced across generations, as demonstrated by Will Creek's descendants' misidentification of their forebear as a native American Indian.

Will Creek's union with a slave woman meant that his descendants assimilated into the African-American population. Meanwhile, Peter, an "East Indian" servant who lived on Lord Baltimore's plantation in St. Mary's County, formed a union with a servant woman from Ireland named Mary Molloyd, resulting in the birth of an illegitimate daughter circa 1680. After completing his indenture, Peter became "a free molato."[25]

Peter and Mary Molloyd's daughter was also named Mary Molloyd. Under the operative laws regulating interracial bastardy, Mary Jr. should have been a servant only until age thirty-one. However, she was illegally held as a slave past her thirty-first birthday by her master, John Beale. While in servitude, Mary Jr. married Francis Fisher, a "Negro slave" of Beale's, in a ceremony performed by a Roman Catholic priest.

Their daughter Ann Fisher was born circa 1702. She was about thirty-two years old when she petitioned for her freedom from John Beale in the Anne Arundel County court in August 1734. Ann Fisher lost that case. She was sold to Thomas Gassaway of Baltimore County, and in June 1743 she and her siblings brought another unsuccessful freedom petition in Anne Arundel County court.[26]

In 1783, Ann Fisher's daughter Eleanor Toogood petitioned yet again, arguing as the family always had—that they were free by virtue of their descent from a free white woman, Mary Molloyd of Ireland. In the new post-Revolutionary legal climate, Eleanor Toogood won her case. Her master appealed, but the court of appeals affirmed the judgment in Eleanor's favor on the grounds that Eleanor's grandmother Mary Fisher should have been free after serving her indenture for interracial bastardy.[27]

While the descendants of the East Indian, Peter, and his consort Mary Molloyd based their claim to freedom on Mary's free white identity, they still retained their memory of Peter's own ethnic distinctiveness. This multiethnic family had Irish, East Indian, and African heritage, all of which was remembered by the family and the community well into the early national period when Eleanor Toogood filed her petition. Another remarkable thing about this family is their persistence in insisting on their right to freedom in the face of repeated rejections by the Anne Arundel court. Not until the brief window of liberalism in the early national era were they successful.

It should be noted that a successful freedom petition was good news for many members of the petitioning family, but freedom was not automatic for all. During the rash of petitioning in the late eighteenth century following the Butler decision, many petitions resulted in release from slavery for multiple members of the same family. Once one member of a family won a case, the court would generally uphold all related petitions extant in the same court. Many owners of relatives would drop their opposition after the first case had been won.

However, freedom was heritable only in the maternal line. Family members who descended from a free woman in a male line were out of luck. Furthermore, family members who lived at a distance had to petition in a different court, and were thus subject to varying decisions. The farther away you had been sold, the less likely it was that you had social connections with white elders who remembered your ancestors and who could "swear you free." As a consequence, it was common among many families on the Western Shore to have some relatives who were free, and others who were legally enslaved.

The Mingo-Thomas Family

The importance of living in a community in which the white elders knew you were free must have been a disincentive to emigrate. The experience of the Thomas family exemplifies the potentially disastrous consequences of being removed from local access to your social capital. The Thomas' long-running battle to win freedom lasted over a century, with but temporary success for some family members. Tracing the Thomas family's bittersweet fight for freedom through the generations demonstrates the importance of social capital for winning and keeping freedom.[28]

The male progenitor of the Thomas family was an African slave named Joseph Mingo who arrived in Charles County prior to 1680. Joseph Mingo appears to have married his white consort—Elizabeth Thomas, a Welsh woman—prior to repeal of the Act of 1664. Had they postponed their marriage until after the act's repeal, she would have been allowed to live as a free woman during their marriage.

In 1702, Joseph Mingo petitioned the Charles County court for freedom. According to the petition, Mingo's owner Joshua Doyne had promised Mingo his freedom after Mingo served Joshua's son Dennis for seven more years. However, after Dennis Doyne died, his brother William Doyne inherited Mingo and claimed him as a slave. When Mingo began to ask for his freedom from William Doyne, Doyne sold him to William Stone. Mingo could offer no proof to support his assertion to the court's satisfaction. He lost his case and was ordered to return to William Stone's household and serve as a "servant" during his life.[29]

Eleven years later, Joseph Mingo's son Lewis sued for his freedom. Lewis Mingo argued in his petition that he was the thirty-one-year-old son of a white woman, and thus his indenture was completed and he deserved to be freed. The Act of 1664 that had enslaved the children of a marriage between a white female and slave male had been repealed in 1681. If Lewis was thirty-one in 1713, then he would have been born in 1682—*after* the law was repealed. This was crucial to Lewis's case. Interracial children born to a couple who formed a union after the repeal of the 1664 act would not be enslaved, but would only be indentured for thirty-one years.

Lewis was attempting to deceive the court by altering his age. According to the birth records entered in the Charles County court three decades prior, Lewis had been born in 1681—not 1682 as he claimed—and was thus a slave for life under the Act of 1664, according to the doctrinal interpretation operative at that time. Lewis won his case in the Charles County court, but Henry Wharton appealed the case to the provincial court. Wharton argued that Lewis was the son of a white woman and a black man lawfully wed in the Church of England, and was a slave because of the law in effect at his birth. The provincial court accepted Wharton's argument and ruled that Lewis would remain in slavery.[30]

In spite of these denials, the descendants of Joseph Mingo and Elizabeth Thomas refused give up their quest for freedom. Since freedom was heritable only in the maternal line, the only strategy for a male slave who wanted free children was to establish a union with a free woman. Charles Mingo began an illicit relationship with a white servant woman named Mary Curtis, resulting in the birth of their illegitimate child, Jonathan.[31]

In the early 1750s, Charles Mingo's sister, Betty Mingo, filed her own freedom petition. The planter Leonard Boarman testified that had heard that "some of the family of the petitioner claimed their freedom upwards of forty years ago and while I lived with Mr. Pile Betty Mingo sold a horse belonging to her and gave a Hhd. Of Tobacco to a lawer [*sic*] who visited at Mr. Piles to plead for her freedom."[32] Boarman's testimony indicates that even as a slave, Betty was allowed to own and trade livestock. Slaves who could not marshal court costs were at a serious disadvantage in filing a freedom petition. But Betty's hopes for freedom were in vain. She sold her horse to pay the lawyer for naught. Betty died around 1772, when she was over eighty years old. She was still a slave.[33]

In the more liberal era following the Revolution, the Mingo-Thomas family finally began to realize some success in freedom petitions they initiated in 1793. The family's descent from a white woman seems to have remained common knowledge in the local community. One deponent stated that she had heard about their ancestry "as often from the negroes as from white people," which indicates that similar lines of gossip circulated throughout the community, regardless of people's status.[34]

Several people who owned Elizabeth Mingo or her descendants clearly knew of her descent from a white woman and they told others in the community. In the 1750s, Elizabeth Pile, who owned Betty Mingo and several of Betty's relatives, told Leonard Boarman that Betty's mother was a white woman who had married a slave.[35] Elizabeth Pile's knowledge of Betty's ancestry appears to have come not from direct personal knowledge, but from Betty herself. When Elizabeth Pile was asked if Betty Mingo was descended from a white woman, she replied, "Betty says so."[36] About ten years prior to the Thomas family's freedom petition, Harriet Wheeler heard Dorthea Boarman, wife of Raphael Boarman, talk about how the family of Nanny Cooper (another Mingo descendant) "came of a free white woman, and that they would be entitled to be free, but that the white woman aforesaid married a negro, and in them days the marriage of a free white woman with a negro enslaved her posterity."[37] According to Harriett Wheeler, Dorthea Boarman also told this information to her husband, asking his opinion on whether he thought the Thomas family was free, and whether they should still be enslaved. Raphael Boarman replied that he favored their continued enslavement because "as their ancestor had married a negro, the law enslaved them."[38] Other deponents claimed that they had never heard that the Thomas family had any right to freedom, but "that they up any claim to it until the Butlers were free."[39]

The Mingo-Thomas family's case now followed the pattern set in the seminal Butler case. The issue in dispute was whether Elizabeth Thomas had actually been married to a slave. One petitioner, Nanny Cooper, claimed that Elizabeth, her grandmother, had not been married to a slave. Nanny's owner rejoined with the claim that "Nanny knew nothing about it for they were married."[40]

After the Butlers obtained their freedom, Wilfred Neale recounted that neighborhood gossip was that the Shorters and Mingoes (who were by now surnamed Thomas) would also petition, because those two families had a similar right to their freedom.[41] According to Basil Smith, "If the Butler breed got free the Mingos would of course, as they were upon the same footing."[42]

Most of the Mingo-Thomas descendants had been known by the surname Mingo or Cooper during their enslavement. They seem to have decided during their freedom petition to use the surname Thomas, rather than Mingo. By naming themselves Thomas, they emphasized their connection to their claimed white ancestress, Elizabeth Thomas. Meanwhile, eschewing the Mingo surname served to obscure their descent from Elizabeth's slave husband Joseph Mingo. In this, the Thomas family emulated the successful freedom petitions of the Butler and Shorter families, both of whom also used the original surname of their white ancestress.

The Thomas women had a reputation as "brisk lively and active people, and remarked for being valuable House Servants and cooks."[43] Betty Mingo had worked both as a housekeeper and cook, rather than in the tobacco fields like many other enslaved women.[44] Betty and her relations may have been favored for household work because of their light skin color.

Elizabeth Mingo's daughter Peg, on the other hand, was described in testimony as black with "woolly" hair. Peg worked in a tavern in Port Tobacco, where she was remembered as a talkative woman who conversed freely with everyone.[45] Thomas Webster, a free mulatto, described Peg as a "woman of high spirit," who often did not agree with her master David Stone.[46] Peg's inability to agree with her master resulted in his trading her to a new owner.

Peg's disputes with her master were characteristic. Many of the deponents in the freedom case described the Thomas family members as "forward." The Thomas family's strong sense of its right to freedom may have led the Thomases to be more "impudent" than other slaves. The community memory that supported the Thomases' claims to freedom may have provided some shield against reprisals from offended masters. The master's response to an unruly Thomas seems to have been to trade her rather than punish her. Better to foist the problem on someone else than to risk losing the price of a valuable slave altogether if she decided to petition for freedom.[47]

But Peg Mingo's position in her master's tavern in Port Tobacco seems to have worked in the family's favor. At that time, Port Tobacco was the economic center of the Western Shore. This position thus ensured for Peg a high visibility among whites who were doing business in the region.[48] By working positions within the household and tavern, the Thomas women had more intimate encounters with the master's white guests than would a field hand. The Thomas women's outspokenness, and their constant public articulation of their right to freedom in the context of white society, increased the likelihood that white members of the community would some day be able to recall the hearsay gossip that eventually supported the Thomas descendants' freedom petitions.

However, the court transcripts also reveal the limitations of the community memory. While most individuals remembered Betty Mingo herself, or had heard the common knowledge of Betty's descent from a white woman, most were vague about who Betty's parents were.[49] One deponent thought he had heard Elizabeth Pile tell who owned the slave who married Betty's mother, but could not remember any name.[50] William Swann testified that he had heard in the neighborhood that Charles Mingo's father was a "Mingoe Indian."[51]

Because the community memory was unreliable, some members of the Thomas family took steps to solidify their position by getting it in writing. Once the first Thomas petitioner, Robert Thomas, had won his case, other Thomas family members were required to prove that they were also descended from Elizabeth Thomas. While some owners acquiesced after the first member of a family won, other owners put up a fight and tried to prevent their slaves from receiving freedom.

A paper trail would be necessary to protect a hard-won freedom. Violette Thomas, a great-granddaughter of Betty Mingo, took such steps to record her family history. In 1797, John M. Daniel agreed to manumit Violette Thomas after two years of additional "faithful service," stating that he did not free her "from any belief that she is entitled to liberty by being descended of a free woman" but because of "her humility and obliging conduct."[52] Perhaps Violette believed that serving an additional two years would be a safer strategy than taking her master to court, since he clearly did not believe that she was entitled to her freedom.

On the same day that Violette had her deed of manumission recorded, she also had entered a statement into the Charles County deed book, to document her descent from Elizabeth Thomas. Violette was described in this document as "a lusty woman above the common sire and about twenty nine years of age formerly the property of Miss Peggy Stone." While Violette had not received her freedom because of her descent from Elizabeth Thomas, she must have believed that her relationship with the Thomas family was worth having recorded. In creating a paper trail to document her freedom, Violette Thomas was following in Mary Davis's footsteps.

For some members of the Thomas family, the importance of social capital continued to be crucial even after they were set free. In 1822, Phillis Thomas and her children petitioned for their freedom in Jefferson County, Kentucky. Phillis claimed that she and her children were free people of color, and that James Burk had kidnapped the family in St. Mary's County, Maryland. Burk then transported the Thomases—"by a circuitous route to avoid pursuit and detection"—to Kentucky, where he kept them as slaves.[53]

The Thomas petition indicates that the family had "great reason to fear and do in fact believe" that once James Burk learned of their petition, "immediately on discovery of their intention to appeal to this Honorable Court [Burk would] send them by force out of this Commonwealth . . . sell them as slaves where their rights and their sufferings will be unknown and disregarded."

The Thomas' freedom petition in Kentucky appears to have been instigated by Phillis's brother, Seaman Thomas, who had been searching for his lost relatives since their kidnapping. He appeared before the Jefferson County justice of the peace on March 27, 1822, and testified as to the Thomas family's successful freedom suit in Maryland years earlier. Seaman Thomas related that Phillis and her children had been living at the time of their kidnapping on a small tract of land that he had rented for them in St. Mary's County. Seaman Thomas had been in England when the kidnapping occurred (this fact suggests that "Seaman" was probably his occupational title, not his given name.)

When Seaman Thomas returned from England a few months after the kidnapping, he began a search for his missing relatives. The rumor was that they had been stolen and taken to Georgia. Despite his "incessant enquiries for near eight years no tidings obtained of his unfortunate family until a few months since— when this Affidant was residing in New Orleans—He made all dispatch in his power and has now taken at Louisville in pursuit of the justice which is due to his much injured relations. Several of the children of his Sister are grown up—but most if not all of them are minors."

In Kentucky, far from home on the Western Shore, the Thomas family lacked social capital. There were no whites who could testify as to the family's free status. In a place where the Thomases found themselves "poor frendless and forlorn," their petition was dismissed by the court, and the Thomases remained in bondage.

Conclusion

The Western Shore freedom petitions of the late eighteenth century reveal that many slaves were distinguished within Chesapeake communities according to their ethnic origins. Slave families remembered their ancestors' ethnic distinctiveness to the extent that it formed the basis for their claim to freedom. Memories of a white ancestress in the maternal line were especially valuable, in that they formed the legal basis for a freedom petition. The slave owning class also remembered ethnically distinct slaves. Ethnic memories constituted a form of capital for slaves. Slaves who could mobilize the community's memories in their favor possessed social capital that could win them freedom—if only during the brief window of post-Revolutionary liberalism.

Notes

1. See records regarding the freedom petition of Rose Davis in the Anne Arundel County Court Judgments, August 1715, 93, 178, 244–46.

2. Winthrop Jordan, *White over Black: American Attitudes Toward the Negro, 1550–1812* (Chapel Hill: University of North Carolina Press, 1968), 24.

3. Maryland Assembly Proceedings, vol. 2, Liber W H&L, March–April 1671, 272. Electronic copy downloaded August 2003 from Maryland State Archives website at: www.mdarchives.state.md.us/megafile/msa/speccol/sc2900/sc2908/000001/000002/html/am2—272.html.

4. Maryland Assembly Proceedings, vol. 1, September 1664, 527. Electronic copy

downloaded August 2003 from: www.mdarchives.state.md.us/megafile/msa/speccol/sc2900/sc2908/000001/000001/html/am1—527.html.

5. Maryland Assembly Proceedings, vol. 1, September 1664, 533–534. Electronic copy downloaded August 2003 from: www.mdarchives.state.md.us/megafile/msa/spec col/sc2900/sc2908/000001/000001/html/am1—533.html.

6. Maryland Archives, vol. 7, 204, electronic version downloaded August 2003 from: www.mdarchives.state.md.us/megafile/msa/speccol/sc2900/sc2908/000001/000 007/html/am7—204.html.

7. Alejandro Portes, "Economic Sociology and the Sociology of Immigration: A Conceptual Overview," in *The Economic Sociology of Immigration: Essays on Networks, Ethnicity, and Entrepreneurship*, ed. Alejandro Portes. New York: Russell Sage Foundation 1995), 12–13; Thomas F. Brown, "Consumer Demand and the Social Construction of Industry," in *Working Paper Series, Program in Comparative and International Development* (Baltimore: Johns Hopkins University Press, 1997).

8. For the process of change in slave historiography, see: Sylvia R. Frey, *Water from the Rock* (Princeton, N.J.: Princeton University Press, 1991); Eugene D. Genovese, *Roll Jordan Roll* (New York: Pantheon, 1972); Gwendolyn M. Hall, *Africans in Colonial Louisiana* (Baton Rouge: Louisiana State University Press, 1992); Michael A. Gomez, *Exchanging Our Country Marks* (Chapel Hill: University of North Carolina Press, 1998); Daniel C. Littlefield, *Rice and Slaves* (Baton Rouge: Louisiana State University Press, 1981); Phillip D. Morgan, *Slave Counterpoint: Black Culture in the Eighteenth Century Chesapeake and Lowcountry* (Chapel Hill: University of North Carolina Press, 1998); Gerald W. Mullin, *Flight and Rebellion* (New York: Oxford University Press, 1972); Gerald W. Mullin, *Africa in America* (Urbana: University of Ilinois Press, 1992); James Sidbury, *Ploughshares Into Swords* (Cambridge: Cambridge University Press, 1997); Mechal Sobel. *The World They Made Together* (Princeton, N.J.: Princeton University Press, 1987); Kenneth M. Stampp, *The Peculiar Institution* (New York: Knopf, 1956); John Thornton, *Africa and Africans in the Making of the Atlantic World, 1400–1860* (Cambridge: Cambridge University Press, 1992); and Peter Wood, *Black Majority* (New York: Knopf, 1974).

9. Morgan, *Slave Counterpoint*; David Brion Davis, *The Problem of Slavery in the Age of Revolution, 1770–1823*, (Oxford: Oxford University Press, 1999); Martha Hodes, *White Women, Black Men: Illicit Sex in the Nineteenth-Century South*. (New Haven: Yale University Press, 1997);

10. Deposition of Edward Edelen in *Butler v. Boarman*, Provincial Court Judgments 1770–1771, 233–44.

11. William Boarman's estate record provides corroborating evidence of Nell's enslavement, although no one in the court proceedings appears to have thought to consult this document.

12. Lorena S. Walsh, "Slave Life, Slave Society, and Tobacco Production in the Tidewater Chesapeake, 1630–1820," in *Cultivation and Culture: Labor and the Shaping of Slave Life in the Americas*, eds. Ira Berlin and Philip D. Morgan (Charlottesville: University of Virginia Press 1993), 189.

13. Quoted in Walsh, *Slave Life*, 189.

14. *Mary Butler v. Adam Craig in the General Court for the Western Shore in October 1787* [*Cases in the General Court*, 214–36].

15. Helen T. Catterall, *Judicial Cases Concerning American Slavery and the Negro, Vol. IV* (New York: Negro Universities Press, 1968), 54.

16. Petition of Nancy Queen, Charles County Judgments, 1796.

17. Nancy Queen petition.

18. Rose Davis petition.

19. Rose Davis petition.

20. Rose Davis petition.

21. See Bartley petition, General Court of the Western Shore, May 1795, 50ff.

22. *Negro Nanny v. Ormond Hammond*, May term 1790, Western Court Liber JG fol. 253.

23. Anne Arundel County Judgments 1736–1738, Liber IB, no. 2, March 8, 1736/7, p.126.

24. Ibid.

25. Anne Arundel County Judgment Record 1734–1736, 83; 1743–1744, 11.

26. Ibid.

27. *Cases in the General Court and Court of Appeals of Maryland*, 26–31; Catterall, *Judicial Cases*, vol. 4:49–50.

28. See the Thomas petitions in General Court of the Western Shore, October term 1795.

29. Charles County Court Records, 1701–1704, Liber A, no. 2, 132–33.

30. Lewis Mingo's birthdate recorded in Charles County Register of Births, Marriages and Burials, 8.

31. John Swann testified that Mary Curtis had a mulatto bastard child that was sold by St. Mary's County Court to its father James Swann. St. Mary's County Court records do not survive from this period to confirm this testimony. However, there was an individual named Jonathan Curtis identified as a free negro in the Charles County Court records in 1749/1750.

32. Thomas petitions, deposition of Leonard Boarman.

33. Thomas petitions. Depositions of Leonard Boarman and Sophia Leigh made in 1792 stated that Betty had died about twenty years earlier.

34. Thomas petitions, deposition of Harriet Wheeler.

35. Thomas petitions, deposition of Leonard Boarman. The deposition occurred on 22 May 1792. Boarman stated that Mrs. Elizabeth Pile had told him about Betty's family forty years prior, circa 1752.

36. Thomas petitions, deposition of Sarah Boarman.

37. Thomas petitions, deposition of Harriet Wheeler.

38. Thomas petitions, deposition of Harriet Wheeler.

39. Thomas petitions, depositions of Mrs. Mary McKay, Richard Barnes.

40. Thomas petitions, depositions of Harriet Wheeler and Mrs. Ann Thompson.

41. Thomas petitions, deposition of Wilfred Neale.

42. Thomas petitions, deposition of Henry Smith.

43. Thomas petitions, deposition of Sophia Leigh.

44. Thomas petitions, depositions of Sophia Leigh and Sarah Doyne.

45. Thomas petitions, deposition of Sarah Fowke, Miss Mary Stone, Mrs. McLaran, Charles Ray.

46. Thomas petitions, deposition of Thomas Webster.

47. Thomas petitions, deposition of Harriet Wheeler.

48. Thomas petitions.

49. Thomas petitions, deposition of Leonard Boarman.

50. Thomas petitions, deposition of Leonard Boarman.

51. Thomas petitions, deposition of William Swann.

52. Charles County, Maryland, Deeds, Liber IB 3 (1799–1801): 76–77, Maryland State Archives, Annapolis, Md.

53. Records of the Circuit Court, Jefferson Co., Kentucky, Phillis Thomas, Mary Thomas, *Sarah Thomas et al., Free Persons of Color v. James Burks,* 27 March 1822, Case Files, Box 1–25, Case #1842, KDLA. Dismissed. Race and Slavery Petitions Project, PAR #20782204.

CLASS: REBEL REFORMERS AND SICK SAILORS

3

ART 3 ADDRESSES the broader implications of class in the Anglo-American world with essays by Angelo Angelis and James Alsop. Angelis's essay, "'By Consent of the People': Bacon's Rebellion and Political Reform," focuses on a significant group of frontier farmers and their conflict with established ruling elites that led to important reforms, not revolutions. Angelis places Bacon's Rebellion in seventeenth-century Virginia within the larger context of similar British colonial reform movements. Bacon's Rebellion in 1676 was not just a glimpse into America's future battle for independence. Rather, Angelis believes we should understand its significance as a marker of change in Virginia's colonial maturation process and as a harbinger of more extensive changes throughout the British American colonies over the next century. Bacon's Rebellion was the first in a chain of American regulator movements, and these popular rebellions appear at critical political, economic, and social moments, and the laboring men involved forced colonial governments to make significant reforms, even when their rebellions were suppressed.

Alsop's essay "Royal Navy Morbidity in Early Eighteenth-Century Virginia" is a close examination of previously unexplored Admiralty documents that shed light on common sailors' "fevers and fluxes." Moving beyond the anecdotal evidence supplied by naval surgeons in their reports to the Commissioners for Sick and Wounded Seamen, Alsop uses ships' musters, logbooks, and pay books to provide an invaluable quantitative study of eighteenth-century morbidity and the treatment of illness within the naval convoys. This study of male pattern diseases—within a culture of liquor and sex—offers, from a transatlantic perspective, new insights into the lives of working-class men while it also explores the impact this phenomenon had on the Chesapeake region as well as Anglo-American trade.

Angelo Angelis's "'By Consent of the People': Riot and Regulation in Seventeenth-Century Virginia" utilizes traditional political history documents in new ways to argue that the rebel leaders were not wild-eyed crazies bent on revolution, but were true reformers chosen by the people. We have included Nathaniel Bacon's "Declaration of the People, against Sir William Berkeley, and Present Governors of Virginia" in this section to better understand Angelis's interpretation of Bacon's Rebellion. James Alsop's "Royal Navy Morbidity in Early Eighteenth-Century Virginia," on the other hand, uses new sources to uncover information about seamen who experienced increased morbidity upon arriving in the Chesapeake—a problem that would follow them after leaving the contagious port of York Town. His primary sources, however, can best be understood in the aggregate. Thus, Alsop has provided the reader with a peek into his analysis of vast amounts of minuscule data with a short narrative and data table.

The Declaration of the People against Sir William Berkeley and Present Governors of Virginia (1676)

NATHANIEL BACON

OR HAVING upon specious Pretences of public Works raised unjust Taxes, upon the Commonalty, For advancing of Private favorites. And other sinister Ends, but no visible Effect, in any Measure adequate.

For not having during the Long time of his Government, In any Measure advanced, this hopeful colony, either by Fortifications, Towns, or Trade.

For having abused, and rendered contemptible, his Ma[jesty's] Justice, by advancing to Places of Judicature, scandalous and ignorant favorites.

For having wronged his Ma[jesty's] Prerogative, and Interest, by assuming the monopoly of the beaver Trade.

For having in that unjust gain, betrayed and sold, His Ma[jesty's] country, and the Liberties of his loyal Subjects to the Barbarous Heathen.

For having, Protected, favored, and emboldened the Indians against his Ma[jesty's] most loyal Subjects; never Contriving, requiring, or appointing any due or proper means of Satisfaction; for their many Incursions, murders, and Robberies, Committed upon Us.

For having when the army of the English, was upon the Tract of the Indians, which now in all Places, burn spoil, and Murder, And when we might with ease, have destroyed them, who were in open hostility.

For having expressly, countermanded, and sent back, our army, by Passing his word, for the Peaceable demeanors of the said Indians, who immediately prosecuted their evil Intentions—Committing horrid Murders and Robberies, in all Places, being Protected by the said Engagement, and word passed by Him the said Sr. Wm. Berkeley having Ruined and made Desolate, a great Part of his Ma[jesty's] country, having now drawn themselves into such obscure and remote places, and are by their success so emboldened, and Confirmed, and by their Confederates strengthened. That the cries of Blood, are in all Places, and the Terror, and Consternation of the People so great, That They are not only become difficult, but a very formidable enemy Who might with Ease have been destroyed.

When upon the loud outcries of Blood, the Assembly had with all Care, raised and framed an army, for the Prevention of future mischief, and safe guard of his Ma[jesty's] colony.

For having only with the privacy of a few favorites, without the acquainting of the People, only by Alteration of a Figure forged a Commission, by I know not what hand, not only without, but against the Consent of the People, for the Raising and Effecting of civil war, and Destruction, which being happily and without Bloodshed prevented.

For having the second time attempted the same, thereby calling down our forces from the defense of the frontiers, and most weakened and Exposed Places, for the prevention of civil mischief, and ruin amongst our selves; while the barbarous enemy in all places did Invade Murder and spoil us, his Ma[jesty's] loyal Subjects.

Of these the aforesaid Articles we accuse Sr. Wm: Berkeley as guilty of Each and every of the same. As one who hath traitorously attempted, violated and Injured his Ma[jesty's] Interest here, by the loss of a great Part of his Ma[jesty's] colony, and many of his faithful and loyal Subjects, by Him betrayed in a Barbarous and shameful Manner Exposed to the Incursion, and murder of the Heathen. And We further declare the Ensuing Persons in this List to have been his wicked and Pernicious counselors and Confederates, Aiders, and Assistants against the Commonalty in these our civil Commotions . . . [Sir Henry Chichely, Colonel Chistopher Wormly, Philip Ludwell, Robert Beverly, Richard Lee, Thomas Ballard, William Sherwood, William Cole, Richard Whitecar, Richard Spencer, Joseph Bridges, William Claiborne, Thomas Hawkins, Mathew Kemp, Jonathan Page (Clerk), Jonathan Cuffe (Clerk), Habbard Farrill, John West, Thomas Readmuch]

And we further Command that the said Sir William Berkeley with all the Persons in this List be forthwith delivered up, or Surrender Themselves, within four days after the notice hereof, or otherwise we declare as follows.

That in whatsoever place, House, or ship, any of the said Persons shall Reside, be hid, or protected, we do declare the Owners, Masters and Inhabitants of the said Parties, to be Confederates, traitors to the People and the Estates, of them; as also of all the aforesaid Persons, to be Confiscated, this we the Commons of Virginia do declare.

Desiring a firm union amongst our Selves, that we may jointly and with one accord defend our selves against the Common enemy, and let not the faults of the guilty, be the Reproach of the Innocent, or the faults and Crimes of the oppressors, divide and separate us who have suffered, by their oppressions.

These are therefore in his Ma[jesty's] name to command you: forthwith to seize the Persons above mentioned, as traitors to the King, and country, and Them to bring to the Middle Plantations, and there to secure them till further Order and in Case of opposition, if you want any further Assistance, you are forthwith to demand It. In the name of the People, in all the Counties of Virginia.

NATHANIELL BACON
General, by Consent of the People.

Navy Morbidity Data (1740–1741)

THE EXAMINATION OF health patterns described for the early eighteenth century can be extended to other decades, and to the lived experiences of other ship complements. In particular, it may be valuable to study the theme during the next period of eighteenth-century warfare, 1739–1748. The following tables provide information from the muster books of the HMS *Winchester* for a voyage that began in September 1740 and concluded in September 1741, during which time the *Winchester* served on convoy duty to and from Virginia. The first table is a replication of the general muster book for the ship's complement. Unfortunately, the general muster records between July and October 1740, which cover the end of prevoyage preparations and the early outward voyage, have been lost. The second table, compiled by this author from the individual musters, lists all deaths in chronological sequence. The musterbooks are: P.R.O., ADM 36/4572, 4574, and 4580. The *Winchester* had a normal complement of 300 officers and crew. She sailed from England in convoy with a fleet of merchantmen and alongside the HMS *Southsea Castle* from Torbay on September 19, 1740.

Explanation of terms. Musters normally took place approximately once a week. The number borne was the total included in the accounts (as opposed to the ship's complement, which was notional). The number mustered was expected to be a head count. The "chequed" were the members of the company whose pay had been stopped. The category "sick ashore" covers personnel who were borne but were not mustered because they had been formally placed in the custody of another set of officials (for example, at a naval hospital). The total of the "mustered," "chequed," and "sick ashore" should equal the number "borne," because there was no other administrative category into which seamen could fall. Those "mustered" included everybody aboard in receipt of wages as a member of the ship's complement, regardless of their health status. The ship's surgeon kept a "sick list" of those who were aboard and incapacitated, but this information does not appear in the musters because all seamen, whether ill or not, were entitled to their wages (eventually). Sick lists rarely survive, and there are none for the *Winchester*. The number of men "borne" fluctuated for the following reasons: formal transfer of individuals onto, or out of, the ship's books; death; desertion.

General Musters: HMS *Winchester*

Date		Place	Borne	Mustered	Chequed	Sick ashore
1740						
June	18	Spithead	294	254	13	27
	25	"	291	256	5	30
[In July the ship was in Plymouth Sound but no musters survive. Departure was from Torbay on Sept. 19]						
Nov.	4	At sea	276	271	5	—
	12	"	273	268	5	—
	19	"	272	267	5	—
	26	Virginia	268	263	5	—
Dec.	4	"	270	264	5	1
	11	"	265	259	4	2
	18	"	266	258	4	4
	26	"	266	239	4	23
1741						
Jan.	3	"	264	220	4	40
	10	"	264	220	4	40
	19	"	263	247	4	32
	26	"	284	260	4	20
Feb.	2	"	284	261	4	19
	10	"	285	265	4	16
	17	"	288	270	4	14
	25	"	289	281	4	4
Mar.	5	"	291	284	4	3
	12	"	292	285	4	3
	19	"	298	291	4	3
	27	At sea	300	297	3	—
Apr.	4	"	300	297	3	—
	11	Virginia	300	296	3	1
	18	"	299	291	3	5
	25	"	300	297	3	—
May	4	At sea	300	297	3	—
	12	"	300	297	3	—
	19	"	300	297	3	—
	26	Nantucket	300	297	3	—
June	3	At sea	294	291	3	—
	11	"	294	291	3	—
	19	"	293	290	3	—

June	26	"	291	288	3	—
July	4	"	289	286	3	—
	13	Spithead	282	276	6	—
	18	At sea	280	259	4	17
	24	Plymouth	282	259	6	17
Aug.	1	"	280	165	11	104
	6	"	277	128	43	106
	14	"	269	167	13	89
	21	"	268	191	33	44
	29	"	257	214	17	26
Sept.	3	"	300	238	25	37
	9	"	295	244	21	30
	18	"	309	284	5	20
	30	The Downes	293	236	46	11

Deaths on HMS *Winchester*

	Month	No. of deaths
1740	July	3
	Aug.	6
	Sept.	6
	Oct.	10
	Nov.	10
	Dec.	15
1741	Jan.	1
	Feb.	0
	Mar.	3
	Apr.	1
	May	1
	June	5
	July	10
	Aug.	0
	Sept.	0
	Total	71

"By Consent of the People": Riot and Regulation in Seventeenth-Century Virginia

5

ANGELO T. ANGELIS

"**B**ACON'S DEAD," William Berkeley mused. "I am sorry at my heart/ That lice and flux should act the hangman's part." These two strands of verse summarize Governor Berkeley's position on the civil uprising that gripped Virginia in 1676 and 1677. It was Nathaniel Bacon's Rebellion: the treason of an ambitious man who had managed to stir the passions of the worst elements in the colony. Berkeley's original interpretation has had a lasting influence on the historiography of Bacon's Rebellion. Historians revisit causation, but no one questions Berkeley's fundamental assertion that Nathaniel Bacon was at the center of an effort to overthrow government. Some historians join Berkeley in blaming the rebellion on "temporarily enraged frontiersmen." Others point to "a gouging government." Some accounts view the uprising as a clash between two dominant personalities; some as emblematic of a colony in chaos. Bacon's Rebellion has been described as an early flowering of democracy in America. One historian dismisses the rebellion itself, finding singular importance in the discovery that race could be used to ameliorate class conflict. In this way, Bacon's Rebellion initiated what would become the enduring contradiction in the American understanding of freedom.[1]

Bacon's Rebellion cannot be reduced to a personal clash between two notable men; much more was at stake than the men's individual status in the colony. Nor can the rebellion—or Virginia's experience in the seventeenth century as a whole—be described in terms of race alone. The uprising was not symptomatic of endemic chaos in Virginia. It was much more than a sudden uprising of self-interested farmers and servants, but it was not a dress rehearsal for the American Revolution.

If they took up arms with Nathaniel Bacon—and most did not—or joined the rising chorus demanding redress, Virginians were not intent on revolution. The men who supported the uprising in Virginia, the planters, freeholders, and freedmen, held a generally positive view of government as a necessary agent of order and progress. But they held a dim view of William Berkeley, his administration, and his policies. These men found an immediate cause in the recurring crusade against the Indians and a ready leader in Nathaniel Bacon. From that point forward the rebellion transcended the original demands of the frontier settlements, assuming a new dimension as local issues blended with longstanding grievances. But the larger uprising that followed was not a call for revolution or a denunciation of government as a whole. It was a demand for reform.

Viewed from this perspective and placed in its political and economic context, Bacon's Rebellion emerges as the first regulation in America. It was not that the men who rallied around Nathaniel Bacon identified themselves as regulators, but they did act in a manner that anticipated the regulations that would unfold a century later. Like Bacon's Rebellion, the Regulators in North Carolina and the Shays's Rebels in Massachusetts never aimed at revolution; they sought reform within the existing political system. And they demanded more, not less, involvement with government along with increased incorporation into the growing market economy.

To an outside observer, little reason existed in the 1670s for civil discontent in Virginia. Tobacco cultivation was thriving and William Berkeley appeared well placed as the governor of a growing colony that was arguably the most important English outpost in mainland America. Governor Berkeley could justifiably claim a share of the credit for Virginia's economic success, in particular for his efforts to manage Indian relations, both as a military leader and as a diplomat. His policies had resulted in an extended period of "surface peace," or détente, that encouraged Virginians to push outward into the frontier. Berkeley was richly compensated for his success, both politically and materially. Praise flowed from the crown in England, allowing Berkeley to hold the governor's seat for more than two decades. Material rewards flowed from the colonial assembly in the form of an annual supplement to Berkeley's salary and a generous grant of land that added handsomely to his estate in Green Spring. The governor reciprocated with key appointments for his supporters, including choice council seats that came with valuable tax exemptions.[2]

Given the outward appearance of the colony, it is not surprising that the events surrounding Bacon's Rebellion have been consistently described as a human storm that was tied to the arrival in Virginia of Nathaniel Bacon, a young, educated scion of an important family. Bacon's arrival in 1674 was indeed notable. But it did not initiate unrest in the colony. Bacon brought with him no design for glory or revolution. Instead, he came with his wife to participate in the economic windfall of the Chesapeake. And he found a warm welcome from the colonial elite, who included his cousins, Governor William Berkeley and Nathaniel Bacon Sr., a wealthy landowner and member of the colonial Council. Nathaniel Bacon also found a thriving economy. Encouraged by the promise of tobacco, Virginians had broken out of their contained position on the James River, pushing upriver and inland with a vehemence that was unequaled in the other English colonies. Bacon entered this phase of the colonial experience, joining the ranks of enterprising tobacco planters who were settling on land in the outer fringes of Virginia.[3]

If it were likened to the experience in Massachusetts, where the distribution of land and the creation of towns were closely controlled, expansion in seventeenth-century Virginia would appear chaotic—a field of weeds against New England's closely cultivated garden. In contrast to New England's practice of incremental growth through the creation of small farms and careful management of townships, Virginia's expansion was fueled by *head rights*: a system of property distribution that granted sizable portions of land to new arrivals and to newly freed servants.[4]

Rapid expansion into the interior had an indelible influence on Virginia's politics and economy in the seventeenth century. Ready access to land, an experience that was for the most part unimaginable in England, shaped the political environment in Virginia, contributing to a growing base of men who were qualified to participate in colonial government. But the rate of settlement outpaced the development of government, creating real and imagined distance between government on the seaboard and voters in the interior. Virginia was not unique in this respect: North Carolina, Massachusetts, and Pennsylvania would experience similar dynamics a century later, with strikingly similar results.

In 1674, government in Virginia rested firmly in the hands of William Berkeley and the established planters from the coastal region. This was clearly evident in the actions of Virginia's representative assembly, the House of Burgesses. While the colony expanded outward, Burgesses, prompted by the governor, focused inward on the development of Jamestown, or James City, as the inhabitants now saw it. Berkeley's plans for Jamestown envisioned it as a center of colonial government and economy and, perhaps, as the leading entrepôt of the English empire in the Americas. Encouraged by Berkeley, the General Court ordered construction of a statehouse that would equal the governor's ambitions for James City. Funds for this particular project were secured through voluntary subscriptions, beginning with generous pledges from the governor, the council, and the

Burgesses. The assembly followed with a more ambitious program for thirty-two brick houses to be built according to a town plan developed by the governor. In mandating the use of brick, Burgesses was responding, in part, to the constant threat of fire in Jamestown, a consequence of urban growth. The plan also revealed a second facet of the governor's vision. The cluster of brick homes encircling a statehouse and church would serve as the core of an expanding commercial center.[5]

To ensure that the newly developed center would function as the principal market for the colony, Burgesses ordered that all tobacco produced in the three coastal counties (James City, Charles City, and Surry) be shipped to storehouses that would be built in Jamestown. Burgesses also mandated the building of roads along with the development of secondary town centers and county courts to guarantee a steady flow of business from the interior to the coast. But the new infrastructure and much of the commercial center would be constructed at the expense of taxpayers and landowners. Each county would be responsible for building one of the brick houses in Jamestown, impressing the necessary labor and supplies for the project and incurring stiff penalties if it failed to meet deadlines. Individual planters, in turn, would be responsible for constructing a road to connect their plantations with the main route.[6]

While it envisioned a prosperous future, the town plan did little for the larger economy of the colony. Costs were passed down through the counties to ordinary planters and taxpayers at a time when tobacco growers were suffering economically. Although the consumer market for tobacco remained robust, planters faced steadily declining prices at the wholesale level. This was due, in part, to the annual cycle of tobacco. It was also the result of English mercantile policy, which encouraged constant expansion but limited sales of tobacco to English merchants. One bounty crop after another filled English ships and warehouses, creating downward pressure on prices at the point of supply. Added to this were ongoing efforts on the part of English merchants to monopolize trade in Virginia. The results were beneficial to the English economy as a whole, but they had a negative effect on Virginia's planters. William Berkeley saw it as an economy trapped by the "vicious weed"—tobacco. The colony, he argued, "can neither subsist with it, nor without it."[7]

Governor Berkeley responded by lobbying in his reports and in a personal appearance in London in 1663 for more liberal trading policies and encouragement of economic alternatives in Virginia. Berkeley's vision of diversification called for transfer of known technology, including shipbuilding, silk making, and the manufacture of leather and leather goods, along with adaptation of Indian crops and techniques that remained to be discovered. The end result anticipated a more diversified economy centered in James City, similar to the economies that would develop around Boston and New York. And Berkeley's trial efforts did show some limited success: prizes were awarded for experimental efforts at making silk and building ships. But the new industries and crops never took hold. Berkeley received much of the blame for this. The governor, Robert Beverley remembered, "was full of Projects, so he was always very fickle, and set them on Foot, only to shew us what might be done, and not out of Hopes of any Gain to himself; so never minded to bring them to perfection."[8]

The plan had little chance of success whatever Berkeley did. Virginia was about tobacco. It had become an important colony for England not because of its potential for diversification, but for its singular contribution to the imperial system. London might issue instructions for increased diversification, but English colonial policy was headed in the opposite direction. Virginia's planters were headed in this direction as well and they were unwilling to exchange safe but declining profits in tobacco for any of the governor's new ventures. Placed in the larger context of the colonial economy, Berkeley's plan for a budding English port on the west coast of the Atlantic—a colonial Bristol—was poorly timed and extravagant. More importantly, the plan for James City failed to secure the harbor from external attack. Burgesses did assess a series of fees to build forts and supply them with cannon and ammunition. Lack of initiative took hold, however. This, coupled with limited funds and poor management, left the colony unprepared. Berkeley looked instead to England for direct military aid, supporting his argument with an unflattering comparison of English and Dutch colonial policies. "Had the *Dutch Virginia*," Berkeley wrote, "they would make it the Fortresse; Mart and Magazin of all the *West Indies*."[9]

Berkeley's argument was timely, even if it was somewhat self-serving. England was at war with the Dutch; it was a war that would have a significant effect on each nation's colonial aspirations. Crown and Parliament, Berkeley argued, should shoulder some, if not most, of the cost for harbor defense as part of their larger plan for securing the empire. The argument was reasonable, but it failed to win support, leaving the colony exposed at its most strategic point on the coast. The vulnerability of the port became painfully apparent in 1667, when the Dutch mounted an attack on several English ships anchored on the James River. Berkeley responded with a belated plan for upgraded forts at strategic points on the various rivers, with the costs being divided among the responsible counties. Little progress was actually made and the town and colony were vulnerable six years later, when the Dutch attacked shipping on the James River for a second time. The English put up dogged resistance, but eleven ships were lost along with a significant portion of the cargo "wherein the Inhabitants of James River bore A very Great Share."[10]

Government came under fierce criticism following the attack. Among the leading issues was the failure to construct suitable fortifications, even though government had collected significant fees for this purpose. The council quickly dismissed criticism of government in its report to London, blaming dissatisfaction in Virginia on "Some ill affected Persons Who are vexed with their losse in this Unhappy Accident." The report was disingenuous. Dissatisfaction spiked following the second loss to the Dutch. But the causes of public discontent were more enduring and more widespread than the Council or Governor Berkeley would admit.[11]

Three years earlier, in 1670, the council reversed a liberalizing trend in Virginia by revoking suffrage for freedmen who were taxpayers but not landowners. The change, government argued, was justified by the need to conform to English laws and by the need to avoid public conflict during elections. The first reason offered legal justification for the change; the second seemed to strike more directly at the cause. Civil quarrels at the polls suggested growing tensions that were not readily evident in the reports to London or the surviving records of the council and Burgesses. Silent records and limited petitions to government did not testify to colonial harmony; quite the opposite was true. Virginians were uniformly reluctant to file petitions with a government that had a notoriously low threshold of tolerance, especially for grievances that were critical of Berkeley and his supporters.[12]

The threat of excessive fines, physical punishment, and public humiliation kept individual protests to a limit. This did not, however, dissuade a group of dissidents from rising up at the close of 1673 to protest unfair taxation and misappropriation of public funds. The protest was inspired more immediately by the recent loss to the Dutch. It was founded, however, on longstanding grievances over taxes and government expenditures. Polls in Virginia were assessed at a flat rate on all males over fifteen years of age and, beginning in the 1670s, on women who were employed in tobacco production. Grievances about fairness were further enflamed by suspicions of collusion. Decisions concerning taxes were routinely hidden from public view, with assessments and tax rates determined at the county level by justices of the peace meeting in closed sessions with leading planters. And there was no formal method of accountancy, either for taxes collected or for funds expended on government projects. More importantly, taxpayers had little hope of redress, either locally or at the colonial level.[13]

Frustrated by years of unjust taxation, the dissidents met at the Lawnes Creek church, where they agreed to "not pay theire publiq taxes" until their grievances were given a fair hearing by government. The decision to meet at Lawnes Creek was itself a bold step in Berkeley's Virginia. The dissidents' subsequent actions were more extreme. They scheduled a second meeting to secure broad support for their boycott and to organize direct action against government. One target for this dissent loomed above all others in rural Virginia. By 1673, the county court had become the primary extension of government in the more remote areas, acting not only as the principal institution of law, but also as the economic and social focal point of the region. The Lawnes Creek plan called for men armed with clubs who would intimidate local magistrates and interfere with the court's operation. It was a desperate plan that was sure to bring reprisal. But the dissidents agreed to stand united no matter how government responded. "If one suffers," Roger Delke announced defiantly, "they would burne all."[14]

Meetings and actions like this would become more commonplace a century later in North Carolina and Massachusetts, where men who identified themselves as Regulators filed petitions, formed committees and conventions, withheld taxes, and, finally, obstructed county courts to secure much-needed reforms. These later protests drew actively on the Anglo-American tradition of careful riots that allowed crowds to take direct action in support of their protests, as long as every other avenue had been exhausted and as long as violence was limited to logical symbols of the underlying grievance. Dissidents in seventeenth-century Virginia were even closer to the English roots of this tradition. But in challenging government they were also breaking new ground in Berkeley's Virginia. And they were unprepared for the response.[15]

Government moved quickly to suppress dissent, using advance intelligence from men who had attended the first meeting. Fourteen dissidents were arrested and charged with contempt, breach of peace, and riot. Most of them apologized and were released on bonds against good behavior. Two of the dissidents remained resolute—Roger Delke and Mathew Swan. Delke continued to insist that the taxes were unjust and the people would not pay them. Swan, who was identified by government as the "ringleader," argued that no laws had been broken, since the meeting was a lawful exercise of the right of redress. Neither argument had any influence on the court. Delke and Swan were placed in custody until they paid their fines and posted bond. Both men held out for some time, possibly out of conviction or, more likely, for want of funds (the fines were excessive). In any case, Governor Berkeley agreed eight months later to cancel the fines, provided the dissidents acknowledged their culpability and paid the court fees.[16]

Berkeley's generosity reflected good politics: swift suppression of the protest might dissuade other dissenters and clemency might restore his public appeal. But no changes were made to taxes and no effort was made to account for government expenditures. Grievances related to both of these issues continued to simmer along with a second strain of discontent that was equally flammable: The governor's Indian policies had created significant resentment among small planters and freedmen in the frontier regions of the colony.

Berkeley had gained popularity earlier in his career as an Indian fighter. More recently, he had replaced warfare with diplomacy. The governor's current strategy focused on the development of a buffer zone of friendly and cooperative Indians, who, Berkeley believed, would protect the colony from attack by unfriendly Indians in the interior. This strategy was, in turn, based on a policy of protecting Indian rights. Friendly Indian groups were given ready access to the General Court, where they could expect relatively evenhanded hearings in disputes with settlers. Operating under these guidelines, the General Court ruled against three settlers in a suit they had filed against the chief of the Potomac Indians. The court acquitted the chief of all charges, including murder and treason. But the court did not stop there. Finding the plaintiffs guilty of libel and contempt, the court disqualified the settlers from office and ordered them to pay all court fees.[17]

Berkeley's policy of détente with local Indians also encouraged protection of Indian land. Accordingly, the General Court used its judicial powers to restrain unauthorized expansion of English settlers into the interior. In 1673, the General Court ruled in favor of the Chingoskin Indians in a suit that charged Thomas Harmonson with trespass amounting to 650 acres of land. The ruling ordered Harmonson's eviction if a survey proved that he had, in fact, encroached on Chingoskin land. A year later, the General Court upheld a suit by the Notoway Indians in a dispute with settlers over land that spread across multiple counties. The resulting decision ordered the eviction, forcible if necessary, of numerous English settlers "that have Seated within bounds of the Said Indians Land."[18]

Expansion of the tobacco economy and related demands for new land forced the General Court to enact more sweeping legislation aimed at protecting Indian rights. In April 1674, Burgesses passed legislation prohibiting Indians from selling or leasing any land assigned to them by the colonial government. This, the assembly argued, was for the Indians' protection: to shield them from avid planters and from their own culpability. The court was also concerned with the "mischiefs and Inconveniences as are like to follow Such illegal Disturbances." Conflict between settlers and Indians seemed inevitable, if forced settlement were allowed. And the colony was not prepared to deal with the consequences of this conflict, either militarily or diplomatically.[19]

Berkeley's policies had merit, but his authority was tainted by contradictory legislation. In 1675, the court, having restricted English settlement and planting, authorized the Appomattuck Indians to plant and clear any land in their region not already settled by Englishmen. More misguided, at least from a public relations perspective, was the 10,000-acre grant Berkeley received that same year in New Kent County—a gift from a grateful assembly. Berkeley was not the only beneficiary of legislative largesse: the General Court granted a sizable tract of land during the same session to Nathaniel Bacon Sr., a trusted member of the governor's Council.[20]

Viewed from the perspective of small landowners and freedmen, these policies and actions smacked of unjustified restraint and favoritism. They also ignored the general trend of colonial expansion, which was underwritten by the Crown and council in England. Current English policy encouraged rapid expansion of tobacco crops, not stabilization of Indian relations. Berkeley's Indian policies also failed to reduce tensions on the frontier, where the pressure for land was at its greatest. Faced with a crucial decision—continued peace with the Indians or continued expansion—the governor chose to do nothing until actual conflict had begun.[21]

The closing months of 1675 witnessed a tense and brittle stalemate on the frontier. "[N]o man stirr'd out of door unarm'd, Indians were (ever and anon) espied, three 4, 5, 6 in a party lurking throughout the whole land." The situation took a dramatic turn in January 1676, when thirty-six English settlers were killed in a major Indian raid. An atmosphere of siege quickly settled over the region. Many settlements hunkered down in defensive posture, but Englishmen on the frontier continued to lose lives, fields, livestock, and homes in subsequent Indian raids over the next few months. Defense eventually yielded to demands for an offensive campaign against the Indians, with the frontier settlers petitioning government for authorization and support.[22]

Berkeley responded to the petitions in March 1676 by activating 500 militiamen from the "most secure parts" of the colony. The choice of troops made good political sense, if the goal was to preserve détente with the Indians. Men from the coastal counties who had less at stake in an Indian war would have a pacifying effect on the frontier, particularly if they were stationed at the crucial points of conflict. Accordingly, troops were sent to reinforce forts; others were deployed at the heads of rivers and other fixed positions in the interior, where they faced Indian settlements and strategic entry points into the colony. The rules of engagement were simple: no attack could be made without orders from the governor, except in an emergency and only then on the order of the chief commander, who would be appointed by the governor.[23]

It was a defensive plan aimed at avoiding further escalation and it depended heavily on Berkeley's buffer zone of friendly Indians. But it did not meet the demands of the frontier settlers. Instead it corresponded to the governor's under-standing of the situation. The conflict, Berkeley concluded, was the fault of English planters in the interior, who "covet more land than they are safely able to hold or defend." These men seized on any excuse to rally planters, freedmen, and servants against the Indians, including inflated reports about King Philip's War in the north. By pursuing the Indians without authorization, Berkeley argued, the settlers had placed themselves in direct opposition to government. The settlers understood events in strikingly different terms. Government support of an Indian campaign was not only a matter of continued prosperity for the settlers; it was also viewed as necessary for basic survival.[24]

Both sides appeared sure of their position, although Berkeley's interpretation has survived the test of time. It is difficult, however, to gauge the validity of the Indian threat. King Philip's War to the north may have inspired unnecessary levels of fear among the settlers, or it may have inspired aggression among local Indians, who were facing constant competition for land. To accept the first interpretation solely on the strength of Berkeley's interpretation is to deny the possibility of Indian organization. Settlers, on the other hand, may have misread—or, perhaps, properly read—a growing desire among local Indians to hold and work land on a more permanent basis, as evidenced in recent actions by the General Court. Whether or not their fears were justified, settlers in the frontier pressed their demand for a campaign against the Indians, petitioning the General Court for authorization to elect commissioned officers who would lead a force of local men—"now redy to take armes"—in retaliatory and preventative raids against the Indians.[25]

Berkeley viewed to the petitions as affronts to his authority, even though requests of this type were thoroughly in keeping with English political tradition. They would continue to play an important role in popular politics into and beyond the American Revolution. With varying degrees of success regulators in South and North Carolina, land rioters in New York and New Jersey, and the men who supported Shays's Rebellion in Massachusetts employed petitions to express grievances and demand reforms. Formal presentations of grievances and demands for redress were necessary first steps to protest and direct action. They served as due warning to government that redress or, at the very least, careful consideration was necessary. Nevertheless, the petitions had little effect in Berke-ley's Virginia. The General Court remained resolutely in favor of the governor's strategy of fixed defensive positions, a decision that met with widespread disap-pointment in the frontier settlements. "If you had been here," Nathaniel Bacon's wife, Elizabeth, wrote to her sister, "it would have grieved your heart to hear the pitiful complaints of the people, The Indians killing the people daily the Govern[or]: not taking any notice of it for to hinder them."[26]

The court's decision also met with resistance from the local militia, who took matters into their own hands, electing Nathaniel Bacon to lead them in a retaliatory raid against the Indians. Born in England to an aristocratic family and educated at university, Bacon stood out among his contemporaries on the frontier. He was tall and slender and between thirty and thirty-five years old when the rebellion began. Surviving descriptions are generally unflattering. Read critically they describe an ambitious man with an arrogance that suited his status. They also describe a thinker not given to rash decisions: a man who pondered matters carefully before offering a position. When he spoke, Bacon was eloquent and, as one critic put it, "in every way qualified to head a giddy and unthinking multitude." Bacon fit the profile of a preindustrial popular leader in chief who acts as a rallying point for a crowd filled with men from the ordinary and middling ranks. Bacon also had personal incentive to participate in the vigilante raid and in the protests that would follow. He had already lost his overseer along with livestock and crops to Indian raids. And the governor had summarily dismissed his request for a formal commission to lead the campaign against the Indians.[27]

Bacon responded by agreeing to lead a vigilante force of 211 men, hoping to capture or kill those who were responsible for the attacks on the frontier. The campaign bore mostly bitter fruit. In May 1676, Bacon's force located a small group of Susquehannock Indians in Occaneechee territory. Bacon secured the support of the Occaneechees, one of the friendly Indian groups that comprised Berkeley's buffer zone. Together they attacked the Susquehannocks. Bacon's forces then turned on their allies, inflicting heavy losses on the Occaneechees. The attack on the Occaneechees may not have been justified; they had indeed lived up to Berkeley's expectations. But the account from the field said otherwise, trumpeting the militia's success against the Indians while it leveled direct criticism at the governor and his program of détente. Allegedly cooperative Indians had been "in all places unwilling to assist us against the common enemy, they having received orders to ye contrary from the Right Honourable the Governor."[28]

In the end, Bacon's campaign did little to settle matters on the frontier. It did succeed, however, in tapping a wellspring of suspicion against government. Rumors spread that the governor had warned hostile Indians that an attack was imminent. Bacon did his share of damage as well, tying Berkeley's Indian policies to widespread corruption in government. It was the governor and his supporters, Bacon argued, who benefited most from land grants and government-sponsored trading monopolies with so-called peaceful Indians. The accusations fell on welcoming ears throughout the colony, merging easily with widespread grievances concerning taxes, government expenditures, and the security of the Jamestown harbor. Similar patterns would emerge a century later in the North Carolina and Massachusetts Regulations, when local grievances assumed colonial proportions and dissent spread geographically, escalating from petitions to civil actions, all aimed at gaining the attention of the governor and the assembly.[29]

Berkeley and the court remained sanguine in the face of growing dissent, treating Bacon's actions as an isolated incident. Bacon was suspended from his civil appointments, pending further review by the General Court, and a general pardon was offered for any man who would immediately quit the vigilante force and return home. Berkeley followed these actions by leading a highly visible expedition to the James River falls, where he expected to confront and defeat what he saw as the primary Indian threat, the Susquehannock Indians. Berkeley's response was good politics, if the immediate goal was restoration of order and continuation of the policy of détente. But the campaign to the falls was an utter failure militarily—one officer believed it was ill advised from the beginning.[30]

The strategy was also a failure politically. On his return to Jamestown, the governor found a government besieged by petitions and a colony disrupted by sporadic protests. Civil unrest had spread in his absence. Once again, Berkeley pointed to Nathaniel Bacon as the primary culprit, but his accusation was disingenuous. "Perhaps," the governor confessed in a later appeal to the public, "I have Erred in things I know not of." It was late May 1676. Less than a week later, Berkeley dispatched a letter to London requesting that he be relieved of his duties. "This Rebellion," Berkeley argued, "is the more formidible because it has no ground and is not against any particular Person but the whole Assembly." Given his past behavior, Governor Berkeley would not have been so quick to concede defeat had the main threat been limited to Bacon and his small army of Indian fighters.[31]

The governor's actions admitted to a different course of events. For years government had successfully closed off all avenues for grievance, with the notable exception of an unflattering report that had made its way from Virginia to London. The report was the product of Giles Bland, who had come to Virginia in the 1670s to settle a sizable estate for his father. Bland had also arrived with a commission as the royal collector of customs. Both of these duties placed him in a precarious position with the governor. The issue of the estate involved a property dispute with two of the governor's staunchest supporters, Thomas Ludwell, councilor and secretary of the General Court, and his brother Philip, who was also a councilor. The commission also left Bland in a unique relationship with Berkeley. As collector of customs, Bland was responsible directly to the commissioners in England, a line of authority that placed him outside the control of the governor.[32]

Bland's training as an attorney and his combative personality made conflict with the governor and his supporters more likely than not. He quickly became a leading critic of government, earning arrest, bail, and fines for his efforts. Bland countered with a report to his superiors in London accusing Berkeley and his administration of corruption and gross mismanagement, including misspent fees, misdirected duties, and smuggling by colonial officials that had cost the Crown £100,000 per year in income. Called to appear before the General Court, Bland refused to retract his statements or to give an account of his findings. The information, he insisted, was privileged and protected by his royal commission. Bland's defiance was more than the governor could stand. Berkeley demanded immediate vindication and the court dutifully found Bland guilty of "scandalous and mutinous" behavior. Given no chance to defend himself, Bland was suspended from his office as customs inspector "until his Majesties Pleasure shall be further Knowne."[33]

Neither the General Court nor the governor had the authority to suspend Bland from his post as collector of customs. It was, however, a necessary action, if the goal was to deny Bland an opportunity to extend or publicize his investigation. Berkeley could not stop the report from reaching London. He could and did suppress publication of the report in Virginia, where it would have lent credence to a host of local grievances against government. But one report quashed and one critic silenced had little effect on growing dissent in Virginia. Dissent underwritten by resistance to the governor's Indian policy gained momentum, spreading from the frontier settlements to the seaboard.

The civil unrest that followed in Virginia was neither isolated nor unexpected. Two attempted mutinies and an uprising in 1674 that failed in its early stages had already placed the government on edge. The General Court responded in March 1675 by ordering a standing guard for the governor consisting of twenty-four men whose expenses were paid out of the public coffers. It was a timely precaution, even if it admitted to a certain level of official paranoia. Tensions remained high into 1676, forcing Berkeley to call for elections for a new assembly, something he had avoided doing for the prior fifteen years. In his election address, Berkeley charged the new House of Burgesses with responsibility for a "Redresse of all just Grievances." But the governor envisioned a limited agenda that would quiet growing unrest without altering the basic operations of government.[34]

The elections revealed a different set of expectations among ordinary voters. The new assembly that gathered in Jamestown in June 1676 was stocked with fresh faces. Among them was Nathaniel Bacon, who arrived as a representative for Henrico County. The assembly that followed took his name in the historical record, becoming Bacon's Assembly. It is doubtful, however, that Bacon played a leading role in the deliberations. Some accounts depict Bacon as quite active. Others have him quitting Jamestown at an early date to escape the governor's vengeance. Bacon did leave suddenly, but he left to lead the militia against the Indians, having secured three important concessions from the governor: the promise of a commission as general of the militia; a personal pardon (granted in exchange for Bacon's apology); and restoration to his position on the council.[35]

The June assembly surged forward without Bacon, encouraged by the public vote and by the governor's charge to redress the colony's grievances. Burgesses responded first to the governor's order to "Consider of Meanes for Security from th' Indian Insults and to Defray the Charge." But the assembly had a more ambitious agenda in mind. All Indians were identified as potential enemies of the colony. Forts prized by the governor were to be closed; their garrisons, supplies, and budgets transferred to newly formed "marching" armies, an action that would satisfy a principal demand from the frontier. Seizure and sale of all land deserted by the Indians was authorized to offset the cost of the campaign against the Indians. To encourage thorough and complete prosecution of the war, the assembly offered generous salaries and pensions to officers and enlisted men, along with the right to plunder the enemy at will and seize Indian prisoners as slaves.[36]

The revised Indian policy was not merely a concession to the frontier or to Bacon's leadership; the Indian war had become a public cause. It had also unleashed a wave of resentment against government from every corner of the colony. Accordingly, the June assembly pressed forward, exceeding the limits of its authority, as defined by Governor Berkeley, by assuming responsibility for "the redressing of severall Grievances the Country then Labour'd under." Ad hoc meetings and unauthorized musters of militia regiments were suspended to quiet the countryside. This was offset by a general pardon for any action involving the Indians, with the notable exception of those men who had been indicted for illegal trade with the natives. These measures were followed by a series of general reforms: limits were placed on office holding; open meetings were ordered for assessment of taxes; tax exemptions for government officials were eliminated; and suffrage was restored to all freedmen. This last action would remain in place until 1684. The assembly also authorized audits of taxes and public revenues, including funds associated with the building of a fort at Point Comfort. Finally, Burgesses placed strict limits on the outer boundaries of James City. The governor's vision of a colonial center, it appears, had become a major grievance in itself.[37]

The program of reform addressed directly the majority of grievances, those from the frontier and those from the more established portions of the colony.

But the new assembly, having met for three weeks of deliberation, failed to publish any interim reports. Ordinary voters were left to wonder if Berkeley had reasserted his authority over Burgesses, stymieing any hope of constructive reform. Acting on this assumption, Bacon returned to Jamestown on June 22 with a force of 500 men to confront the governor and the assembly. He was met by Berkeley and an equally determined force of supporters from Jamestown. The governor treated the confrontation as a personal issue, offering to settle the matter with a duel between himself and Bacon. Bacon saw the situation in different terms, insisting that he had not come to Jamestown to settle a personal score with the governor. Nor would he take any man's blood. He had marched for a greater purpose: to secure "redress of ye peoples grievances."[38]

In that moment, the movement for reform of government so recently in the hands of the new assembly shifted from Burgesses to Bacon and his militia. But it was not Bacon's movement alone. Leading members of the opposition faction, sensing an opportunity to dislodge Berkeley, rushed to join forces with Bacon. Among them were Giles Bland, Richard Lawrence, and William Drummond. These men, and a handful of others, would reshape Bacon's campaign against the Indians into a larger movement for reform and for a change in executive leadership.

Giles Bland was still seething from his recent confrontation with Berkeley over lines of authority and the accountability of colonial funds, a confrontation that had cost him heavily. Berkeley had fined Bland and stripped him of his royal appointment in seeming opposition to the will of the crown. Richard Lawrence, a wealthy landowner and merchant, was the unofficial leader of the opposition in Virginia. The Lawrence home, which served as the largest and most elegant public house in the capital, hosted many important visitors to Jamestown when the General Court was in session, including Nathaniel Bacon. Accordingly, Lawrence had significant influence in Burgesses and in his counsels with Bacon. Nathaniel Bacon, one contemporary argued, was "too precipitate, to Manage things to that length those were carried, had not thoughtfull Mr. Laurence been at the Bottom." Bacon had a third influence in William Drummond, an immigrant from Scotland by way of the Carolinas, where Drummond had served as governor from 1664 to 1667. Drummond's term in the Carolinas had been marked by a bitter dispute with Berkeley over land grants in that region. And time had not diminished the dislike each man held for the other.[39]

Opposition to the governor united Bland, Lawrence, and Drummond. The three men openly supported Bacon in his earlier negotiations with Berkeley, and together in the June assembly they organized support for the reforms. All three men arrived in Bacon's camp at the end of June 1676 prepared to accelerate the political phase of the uprising. Their influence was indelible. Indian war remained the primary issue for Bacon at this point, as reflected in his *Manifesto*, with its focus on frontier issues and demand for a forthright campaign against the Indians. Bacon's *Declaration in the Name of the People*, issued no more than a month later, was the first product of Bacon's collaboration with Bland, Lawrence, and Drummond. Accordingly, the *Declaration* revealed a concerted shift from frontier to colonial issues: from war against the Indians to a larger campaign to reform government as a whole.[40]

It was still not rebellion, at least as Bland, Lawrence, Drummond, and Bacon understood it. Tremendous pressure had been brought to bear on the governor for a series of concessions, but no direct action had been taken to overthrow government. And given the opportunity, Bacon had rejected bloodshed; this approach was in keeping with the English tradition of the careful riot. The situation could have stabilized at this point, at least from the English perspective, with Bacon's pursuing the Indians and Berkeley's supporting the assembly's reforms. Subsequent actions on both sides prevented this outcome, yielding instead to steady escalation that altered the substance and, more thoroughly, the perception of the uprising.

Governor Berkeley initiated this process by refusing to engage in the Indian war. Richard Lawrence, for one, doubted that the governor would honor the commission he had granted to Bacon or the reforms the assembly had recently passed. The governor's intentions became clear when he ordered the withdrawal of forces from a fort at York, leaving the settlers to face possible Indian attack without powder or shot. Berkeley followed his retreat by revoking Bacon's commission and by calling for active suppression of the uprising. This action, coupled with rumors that the governor would offer no quarter to those who joined the uprising, placed Bacon, Lawrence, Drummond, Bland, and their supporters in a defensive posture.[41]

The final phase of the uprising reflected this turn of events. It also colored the entire uprising as a rebellion or insurrection, a coloration that has persisted into the historical record. Lost in many accounts is the fact that Bacon and his supporters withheld fire until Berkeley went on the offensive. And Berkeley's actions were indeed threatening. The governor withdrew to the safety of Accomack, where he gathered his army, which included 500 newly recruited Indians. He returned with this force to retake Jamestown, setting the stage for a direct engagement with Bacon. It was the first incident of Englishmen's using Indians to combat other whites, and it signaled the worst intentions. Bacon's march on Jamestown was a direct response to this threat, but Bacon found a lightly garrisoned city. Once again, Berkeley had withdrawn rather than confront the enemy. The easy victory cost the Baconites heavily in terms of support when Jamestown was set on fire during their occupation. The fire was the work of Richard Lawrence and William Drummond, who kindled it by torching their own homes. The intention was to deny Berkeley his prized town center. But the troops followed suit, laying waste to the whole town.[42]

Berkeley could be faulted for recruiting Indians to fight Englishmen. But Bacon's forces also contained their own mix of irregulars in the form of servants and slaves. It is unclear, however, when and how these servants and slaves found their way to Bacon's camp. There is no direct evidence pointing to an active program of recruitment. They may have arrived as runaways or were possibly brought along with masters who supported the campaign. However they arrived, they were, at the very least, allowed to remain. This was not surprising, given Berkeley's recruitment of Indians. And the servants and slaves did play a role in the uprising, particularly at its conclusion when many regular militiamen had abandoned the campaign.[43]

The presence of bonded and enslaved men in Bacon's militia lent an air of revolution to the uprising. And some of them may have had expectations of freedom. In the end, however, their presence is of little importance to the larger understanding of the uprising, except to historians who are intent on proving that Nathaniel Bacon was indeed at the head of a nascent revolution. Contemporary reports, on the other hand, were strikingly silent on the issue of servants and slaves. This is particularly significant in negative treatments of Nathaniel Bacon; the arguments of these treatments would have been strengthened if Bacon had been at the head of a servant/slave rebellion. But most reports issued after the uprising had been quelled, including the official report by the royal commissioners, and they made no specific mention of bonded or enslaved men in Bacon's forces; they referred only to volunteers, men pressed into service, and "Reformadoes."[44]

The identification of reformers in Bacon's camp was consistent with the reformist direction of the enlarged uprising, as was the convention at Middle Plantation (the future site of Williamsburg). The convention, held in the aftermath of Jamestown, operated as an ad hoc legislature in place of the June assembly that had been dismissed by Berkeley. The presence of the clerk of Burgesses attested to this perception, as did the initial actions of the convention. Resolutions were issued that were in complete accord with the pronouncements of the June assembly: the convention agreed to a forthright campaign against the Indians and continued attention to grievances against government. But the nature of the uprising had changed in the short time since the June assembly had been in session. Berkeley's campaign to suppress every aspect of the movement—from the war against the Indians to the most basic reforms of government—had placed

Bacon and the leaders in a desperate position. Public support was tenuous, men switched sides, and spies were suspected.

The leadership of the uprising responded with an oath of loyalty that called for sustained resistance until the king had been properly acquainted with the "state of this Country." Convinced that a fair accounting would justify their actions and clear them of treason, Bacon, Bland, Lawrence, and Drummond set as their ultimate goal a royal commission that would be authorized to conduct a thorough investigation of all grievances against government. The oath went one step further, however, demanding resistance to any troops from England who might come to the aid of the governor. This final condition proved to be, as one critic put it, the "bugbeare" that undermined public support for the uprising. It was meant to secure safety from the governor until a royal commission arrived. But it turned the uprising from a reform movement into an "Al-a-mode Rebellion."[45]

The royal commissioners did arrive in February 1677 with broad authority from the Crown to suppress the uprising and remedy its causes. Nathaniel Bacon was not there to meet them. He had died of disease, leaving the movement without its charismatic leader. The commissioners were greeted instead by Governor Berkeley, who was once more in control of the colony. Berkeley had thoroughly suppressed the remaining Baconites once their numbers had dwindled through desertion and disenchantment. The governor followed with a program of reprisal. Property was seized without warrant as compensation for the rebellion and distributed without due process to "injured" friends of the governor. A number of rebels were summarily hanged without the benefit of formal trial, including Giles Bland and William Drummond. Richard Lawrence escaped the hangman's noose, running into the frontier with four other men, never to be heard from again. But the swift suppression of the uprising actually worked against Berkeley.[46]

With the rebellion at an end, the royal commission proceeded with the second phase of their mission: an investigation into the "true grounds and originall occasion of these late troubles and disorders among you." Berkeley did his best to influence, delay, and distract the commissioners, insisting that the colony had returned to its original harmony. But he was unable to derail the investigation. The commissioners had arrived well informed, drawing in all probability on Berkeley's panicked reports to the crown and on the damning report from Giles Bland. Giving little credence to Berkeley, they launched an exhaustive county-by-county assessment of grievances. Many of the grievances collected by the royal commission were products of the uprising, focusing primarily on losses resulting from destruction or seizure of property by both parties—the rebels and government. But a second and more telling set of grievances reflected long-standing demands for redress that were not related to the Indian war or to Nathaniel Bacon.[47]

In meeting after meeting voters complained about unequal and unnecessary taxes and fees; misuse of public funds; unnecessary expenditures; lack of access to government; the high cost of government; and multiple-office holding. These were longstanding grievances that predated the rebellion. Residents of Gloucester County, for example, pointed specifically to the two-pence-per-hogshead tax on exported tobacco. Nansemond County generalized their grievances as "the great Taxes imposed these 3 or 4 years last past, and they know not for what." Multiple counties criticized Berkeley's failure to provide adequate security for the harbor, a grievance that dated back to 1673. Isle of Wight County specified the high cost of developing Jamestown; other counties concurred, demanding relocation of the capital to a more central site. Multiple counties complained about longstanding abuses in the county court system. The list went on, forcing the commissioners to resort to shorthand in recording the grievances of additional counties.[48]

Berkeley rejected the results, denouncing the accumulated grievances of the people as "libelous scandalous and Rebellious." Instead the governor and his supporters laid the blame entirely on Bacon and other "persons of mean and desperate fortunes," who had seduced the "giddy multitude" into rebellion. Philip Ludwell, a member of Berkeley's council, painted a rosy image for the commission of an all-caring government. "Nor do I think it can, or will appear," Ludwell insisted, "that any ever came with a complaint, and went away without a remedy fit-for-it." But government's actions had already proven otherwise. The governor had summarily dissolved the June meeting of Burgesses, forming his own unelected assembly at his estate in Green Spring. Operating under this edict, Berkeley nullified the June reforms and embarked on a program of retribution that reeked of personal vengeance and personal profit.[49]

Berkeley did not win and neither did Bacon in the final report. The commissioners ruled with disfavor in both cases. Berkeley was recalled to England, replaced by one of the commissioners who had arrived in Virginia with his own appointment as governor in hand. A broken man, Berkeley died, mercifully perhaps, soon after his arrival in England. Bacon had already perished, but the commission condemned him in the historic record as the author and principal leader of the rebellion. Bacon's Rebellion: the nomenclature served the purposes of government in 1677, suggesting an unwarranted and unjustified attack by an irrational mob under the direct control of an ambitious ringleader. The label has persisted, obscuring grievances and demands that had simmered for years and obscuring as well the reform movement that erupted in their name in 1676. The attempt to regulate government did succeed to a limited extent, however, even though it failed to make its mark in the historical record. Over time the new administration in Virginia enacted many of the reforms championed by the June session of Burgesses.

The reforms enacted in the wake of the uprising were not connected to the demands of racial politics or to the original issue that had motivated Nathaniel Bacon and his supporters. Instead they reflected the same grievances that had broadened the uprising from a vigilante action against the Indians into a colony-wide movement for reform. The uprising was never intended, however, as a rebellion. And Nathaniel Bacon never sought a revolution against government, as many of his detractors claimed. Bacon made only one assertion: that he was "Generall by Consent of the People." Bacon's pronouncement can be tossed off as the product of overbearing ambition. This would be a historical injustice to the ordinary men and women who had called Bacon to lead the campaign against the Indians and who supported him as the visible leader of the reform movement.[50]

It would also be an injustice to overstate Bacon's role. The political foundation for the larger movement was the work of a second set of men—men like Giles Bland, Richard Lawrence, and William Drummond. These men were not revolutionaries. They had a stake in orderly government. But they could no longer profit, at least from their perspective, under the rule of Governor William Berkeley. They could, however, benefit from the public attention that Nathaniel Bacon claimed with his campaign against the Indians. In their hands, Bacon's Rebellion became the fulcrum for a wide-ranging reform of government. Efforts to secure these reforms through the usual channels of petition and appeal had consistently failed. New actions were needed: the forming of militia, manifestos and declarations, resistance to government force, and oaths of allegiance.

It is easy from our twenty-first-century perspective to misinterpret as rebellion, and possibly as terrorism, seventeenth- (and eighteenth-) century attempts to use force or the threat of force to gain government's attention. Perceptions were different in the seventeenth and eighteenth centuries. Careful riots had a place in English and Anglo-American tradition as long as acceptable limits were not exceeded and neither side—the rioters or government—took steps to escalate them. Collective popular violence of this type, one historian concludes, was, paradoxically, a search for order. A variety of movements fit this model of careful riot or regulation, beginning with Bacon's Rebellion in 1676 and continuing to the Whiskey Rebellion in 1794.[51]

Notes

The author would like to thank the "Sunday Salon" for their assistance in the preparation of this essay: Carol Berkin, Cindy Lobel, Kathy Feeley, Phil Papas, and Iris Towers.

1. William Berkeley, "A History of Our Miseries," ed. Washburn, *William and Mary Quarterly* [*WMQ*] 14 (June 1957): 412; Wilcomb E. Washburn, *The Governor and the Rebel: A History of Bacon's Rebellion in Virginia* (Chapel Hill: University of North Carolina Press, 1957); Stephen Saunders Webb, *1676: The End of American Independence* (New York: Alfred A. Knopf, 1984); Bernard Bailyn, "Politics and Social Structure in Virginia," *Seventeenth-Century America: Essays in Colonial History*, ed. James Morton Smith (Chapel Hill: University of North Carolina Press, 1959), 90–115; Jefferson Wertenbaker, *Torchbearer of the Revolution: The Story of Bacon's Rebellion and Its Leader* (Princeton, N.J.: Princeton University Press, 1941); Lamar Middleton, *Revolt U.S.A.* (Freeport, N.Y.: Books for Libraries Press, 1968); Edmund S. Morgan, *American Slavery, American Freedom: The Ordeal of Colonial Virginia* (New York: W. W. Norton & Co., 1975).

2. Act XXXVIII, March 1661 and Acts II and IX, September 1674, in *The Statutes at Large: Being a Collection of All Laws of Virginia from . . . 1619*, ed. William Waller Hening, 3 vols. (Richmond: 1810–1813), 2:32, 314, 319–21; William Berkeley to John, Lord Berkeley, of Stratton, 18 March 1675, in *Virginia Magazine of History and Biography* [*VMHB*] 16 (December 1908): 199; H. Coventry to William Berkeley, 12 May 1675; Order of the King's Council, 12 October 1675, *Papers of the Colonial Office* [*CO*] [microform], Virginia State Library, 92:154, 238; Council [Virginia] to King and Council, 7 November 1673, in *The Old Dominion in the Seventeenth Century: A Documentary History of Virginia, 1606–1689*, ed. Warren M. Billings (Chapel Hill: University of North Carolina Press, 1975). See also: Middleton, 30; Wertenbaker, *Torchbearer of the Revolution*, 14–15.

3. Lois Green Carr and Russell R. Menard, "Immigration and Opportunity: The Freedman in Early Colonial Maryland," in *The Chesapeake in the Seventeenth Century: Essays on Anglo-American Society*, ed. Thad W. Tate and David L. Ammerman (New York: W. W. Norton & Company, 1979), 235–36; Washburn, 17–18.

4. Thomas J. Wertenbaker, *The Planters of Colonial Virginia* (New York: Russell & Russell, 1959), 31–32, 40–41; John C. Rainbolt, "The Alteration in the Relationship between Leadership and Constituents in Virginia, 1660–1720," *William and Mary Quarterly* 27 (July 1970): 411–434.

5. Orders, March 1661; Act XVI, December 1662, in Hening, 2:38, 172–76.

6. Order of the Assembly, 24 September 1672, *Journals of the House of Burgesses of Virginia*, ed. H. R. McIlwaine (Richmond: E. Waddey Co., 1905–15), 6:55; Acts XIX, XXXI, March 1662; Act V, December 1662, in Hening, 2:58–60, 69–70, 261.

7. William Berkeley, *A Discourse and View of Virginia* (London: 1663; reprint, Norwalk, Conn.: William H. Smith, 1914), 4.

8. Berkeley, 6–7; Acts CIX–CXI, March 1662, in Hening, 2:121–23; Wertenbaker, *Torchbearer of the Revolution*, 17–19; Beverley, *The History and Present State of Virginia*, ed. Louis B. Wright (London: 1705; reprint, Chapel Hill: University of North Carolina Press, 1947); 72, 135. See also: Warren M. Billings, "Sir William Berkeley and the Diversification of the Virginia Economy," *VMHB* 104 (Autumn 1996): 433–54.

9. Berkeley, *Discourse*, 4.

10. William Berkeley to King and Council, July 1673, in *The Old Dominion*, 258–61.

11. Council [Virginia] to King and Council, 7 November 1673, in *Old Dominion*, 262–63.

12. 21 October 1673; 9 April 1674, *Minutes of the Council*, 348, 371; Middleton, 26; Wertenbaker, *Torchbearer of the Revolution*, 24–26; Morgan, 209, 400–401; Wilcomb, 49–50; Warren M. Billings, "The Growth of Political Institutions in Virginia, 1634 to 1676," *William and Mary Quarterly* [*WMQ*] 31 (April 1974): 225–42.

13. Warrant for Arrest of the Dissidents, 3 January 1674; Testimony of Lawrence Baker and Robert Spencer, 3 January 1674, in *Old Dominion*, 263–64; Testimony of Lawrence Baker and Robert Spencer, 3 January 1674, "Papers from the Records of Surry County, *WMQ* 3 (October 1894): 122–23.

14. Testimony of Francis Taylor, 3 January 1674; Verdict of the Surry County Court, 6 January 1674, in *Old Dominion*, 264–66; Billings, "The Growth of Political Institutions": 225–42.

15. For careful riots, see: Wayne E. Lee, *Crowds and Soldiers in Revolutionary North Carolina: The Culture of Violence in Riot and War* (Gainesville: University Press of Florida, 2001).

16. Testimony of William Edwards, 13 January 1673, "Papers from the Records of Surry County," 123–25; 6 April 1674, *Minutes of the Council*, 367; Verdict of the Surry County Court, 6 January 1674; William Berkeley, Order, 23 September 1674, in *Old Dominion*, 265–67.

17. Council [Virginia] to King and Council, 7 November 1673, in *Old Dominion*, 262; Orders, March 1662, in Hening, 2:149–51.

18. 24 October 1673; 4 April 1674, *Minutes of the Council*, 353, 365.

19. Minutes, 8 April 1674, *Minutes of the Council*, 365.

20. Orders, 7 March 1675, *Journals of the House of Burgesses*, 6:64; William Berkeley to John, Lord Berkeley, 18 March 1675, "Letters of Governor Berkeley," in *VMHB* 16 (December 1908): 199.

21. King and Council to Moryson, Ludwell and Smith, 12 October 1675, *CO*, 92.

22. Thomas Mathew, "The Beginning, Progress, and Conclusion of Bacon's Rebellion in Virginia, In the Years 1675 and 1676," in *Narratives of the Insurrections, 1675–1690*, ed. Charles M. Andrews (New York: Barnes & Noble, Inc., 1967), 20; William L. Shea, *The Virginia Militia in the Seventeenth Century* (Baton Rouge: Louisiana State University Press, 1983), 99–100.

23. Act I, March 1676, in Hening, 2:326–33.

24. Berkeley to Secretary [Coventry], 1 April 1676, *Virginia Papers*, George Bancroft Collection, Special Collections and Rare Books, New York Public Library, N.Y., 13–20; Berkeley, "A History of Our Miseries," 406.

25. Petition to Berkeley [10 May 1676], *CO*, 92.

26. Elizabeth Bacon to [sister], 29 June 1676, "Bacon's Rebellion," *WMQ* 9 (July 1900): 4–5; Virginians Plea for Opposing ye Indians, [May 1676], *CO*, 92.

27. "Narrative of Bacon's Rebellion," *VMHB* 4:2 (1896): 122; Beverley, 78; George Rudé, *Paris and London in the Eighteenth Century: Studies in Popular Protest* (New York: The Viking Press, 1952), 17–34; Elizabeth Bacon to [sister], 29 June 1676, "Bacon's Rebellion," *WMQ*, 9 (July 1900): 4–5.

28. "A Description of the Fight between the English and the Indians in Virginia in May 1676, *CO*, 92.; "Mrs. Bird's [Mary Byrd's] relation . . . ," *WMQ* 9 (July 1900): 10; Shea, 103.

29. Elizabeth Bacon to [sister], 29 June 1676; "Mr. Bacon's acct of their troubles in Virginia by ye Indians, 18 June 1676," *WMQ* 9 (July 1900): 6–9.

30. Berkeley, Election Proclamation, 10 May 1676, in *Old Dominion*, 269–70; Berkeley, Orders, 10 May 1676; William Travers to Giles Cole, 13 May 1676, *Virginia Papers*, 7:49–61, 73–74.

31. Berkeley, "Declaration and Remonstrance," 28 May 1676, in *Old Dominion*, 271–72; Berkeley to Coventry, 3 June 1676, in *Old Dominion*, 272–73.

32. Wertenbaker, *Torchbearer*, 63–64; Washburn, 92–93; Webb, 50–52.

33. Minutes, 5 October; 21 November 1674, 3 March 1675; 7 October 1675, *Minutes of the Council*, 390, 399, 423; Report of the General Court, 17 October 1675, *CO*, 92; Webb, 50–52.

34. Orders, 7 March 1675, *Journals of the House of Burgesses*, 6:64; Berkeley's Election Proclamation, 10 May 1676, in *Old Dominion*, 269–70.; Richard L. Morton, *Colonial Virginia*, 2 vols. (Chapel Hill: University of North Carolina Press, 1960), 1:225–26.

35. Henry Chicheley to Nathaniel Bacon Sr., 2 June 1676; Nathaniel Bacon Jr., Submission, 9 June 1676, in *Old Dominion*, 273–74; Act LXXXVII, March 1662, in Hening, 2:107; Mr. Bacon's acct of their troubles: 8; Bacon's Account with Thomas Ballard, October 1674–1676, *CO*, 609; Berkeley, "A History of Our Miseries," 408; Wertenbaker, *Torchbearer*, 24–25, 109; William Sherwood to Joseph Williamson, 28 June 1676; Wertenbaker, *Bacon's Rebellion, 1676* (Williamsburg: Virginia 350th Anniversary Celebration Corporation, 1957), 25; Washburn, 49–51; Mathew, 27–28.

36. Mathew, 23; Acts I, II and III, June 1676, in Hening, 2:341–52.

37. Mathew, 24; Acts IV–XX, June 1676, in Hening, 356–365; 5 June 1676, *Journals of the House of Burgesses*, 6:65; Bailyn, 102; Wertenbaker, "Richard Lawrence: A Sketch," *WMQ* 16 (April 1959): 244; Alexander Brown, *English Politics in Early Virginia History* (New York: Russell & Russell, 1968), 235.

38. Mathew, 28–29; William Sherwood to Joseph Williamson, 28 June 1676; Philip Ludwell to Joseph Williamson, 28 June 1676, *VMHB* 1 (July 1893): 178–86; Alexander Culpepper, "An Answer to the Objections raised against Sir William Berkeley in Justification of his proceedings," *Bacon's Rebellion: Miscellaneous Papers*, Special Collections, Colonial Williamsburg Foundation Library, Williamsburg, Va., 146–54.

39. Berkeley, "A History of Our Miseries," 409; Wertenbaker, "Richard Lawrence," 244–46.

40. Bacon, *His manifesto concerning the Present troubles in Virginia*, [June 1676], *CO*, 92; Bacon, *The Declaration of the People against Wm Berkeley and Present Governors of Virginia*, [July 1676], [microform] Special Collections, Colonial Williamsburg Foundation Library, Williamsburg, Va.; Giles Bland to Thomas Povey, 8 July 1676, *CO*, 92; Mr. Bacon's acct of their troubles: 9; Giles Bland to Thomas Povey, 8 July 1676, *CO*, 92.

41. Mathew, 30, 34; Morton, 262–63; Anne Cotton, *An Account of Our Late Troubles in*

Virginia (1676; Washington: Peter Force, 1835); Herbert R. Pascal, ed., "George Bancroft's 'Lost Notes'" on the General Court Records of Seventeenth-Century Virginia, *VMHB* 91 (July 1983): 358.

42. Pascal, 355–59; Mathew, 35.

43. Webb, 6–7; Shea, 114–15.

44. *Reformado* had a number of meanings in the seventeenth century. Reformer applies most directly to Berry and Moryson's description of Bacon's forces and to the context in which it was written. See: John Berry and Frances Moryson, "A True Narrative of the Rebellion by the Royal Commissioners, 1677," in *Narratives of the Insurrections*, 118.

45. Bacon, *The Oaths that Bacon administered to ye People in Virginia*, [?]; Anonymous, "The History of Bacon's and Ingram's Rebellion," in *Narratives of the Insurrections*, 61, 64.

46. Charles I to Herbert Jeffrys, John Berry, and Francis Morrison, 9 November 1676, *CO*, 578; Berry and Moryson to Williamson, 2 February 1677, *CO*, 93; Berry and Moryson to Secretary [Henry Coventry], 2 February 1677, *Virginia Papers*, 8:5–13; Mathew, 39.

47. Berry and Morryson, Declaration to H[is] M[ajesties] Subjects of Virginia, 6 February 1677, *Virginia Papers*, 8:29–36; Charles I to Berkeley, 5 November 1676, *Bacon's Rebellion: Miscellaneous Papers*, 43–44.

48. "A Repertory of the General County Grievances of Virginia . . . ," 15 October 1677, *CO*, 32.

49. Orders [issued at Green Spring], 20 February 1677, *Journals of the House of Burgesses*, 6:68–69, 87–89; Commissioners to Berkeley, 8 February 1677; Moryson to Berkeley, 11 February 1677; Commissioners to Berkeley, 13 February 1677; Commissioners to Coventry, 14 February 1677, *Virginia Papers*, 8:45–53, 93–96, 113–16, 125–30; Berkeley, Proclamation, [February 1677], *CO*, 92; Philip Ludwell to Coventry, [undated], *Bacon's Rebellion: Miscellaneous Papers*, 68–72.

50. Bacon, *The Declaration of the People*.

51. Lee, 3, 14–18.

Royal Navy Morbidity In Early Eighteenth-Century Virginia

6

JAMES D. ALSOP

O N 12 June 1747 Walter McClurg wrote to the Commissioners of the British Admiralty from Hampton, Virginia, lamenting,

> the miserable Condition of the sick, and Wounded Seamen, belonging to his Majesties Ships on the Virginia Station, And Certainly the Surgeons Journals Belonging to those ships, will Convince you of the fatall Conse-quences That attends Epidemicall Distempers, Sweeping off the Choisest and Ablest Seamen, Which att this Juncture is a very great Loss to the Service in generall, and the Trade of this Coloney in Particular. . . .[1]

As a former surgeon's mate on the HMS *Rose*, stationed in the Carolinas, McClurg knew well of what he wrote. In particular, he stressed in this 1747 communication the slowness in the recovery of incapacitated seamen and high mortality levels, occasioned by the lack of effective nursing care and "good Lodgings," "they [the seamen] being, when Labouring under the most Dangerous Distempers, Expos'd to the Inclemences of the most surprising Changeable Climate in the Universe."[2]

As we shall observe, McClurg's observations were apt, but he was, as he noted, simply "a young man, Just setting out in the World." He was, in the parlance of the time, a "projector": a person who hoped to capitalize upon timely knowledge or opportunity for career advantage. In McClurg's case, he requested appointment as surgeon for a permanent royal naval hospital in Virginia. This new institution, he argued, would provide effective health care to the sick and diseased seamen and marines. Projectors who petitioned Whitehall with unsolicited proposals and without high-level patronage rarely succeeded, no matter how astute in their recommendations.[3] McClurg's initiative on its own produced no noteworthy result. There was no revolution in health care. McClung would eventually become superintendent of the Hampton smallpox hospital, be enrolled as a naval surgeon for the Commonwealth of Virginia in the Revolutionary War, and acquire lasting notice as the father of the distinguished physician James McClurg, but neither Great Britain nor (for all it efforts after 1780) the Commonwealth would establish a marine hospital in Virginia. That achievement, constituting the first institution of its kind in America, awaited the year 1800 and concerted joint initiatives of Virginia and the U.S. government.[4] The scale of warfare during the 1740s produced breathtaking challenges to the British state in its administration of nutritional and medical care to its servicemen. Faced with quantitatively far more substantial mortality in the West Indies,[5] and closer to home,[6] health provision in the mid-Atlantic colonies was in good measure left to traditional practice.

To date, this traditional practice remains obscure and largely unstudied. This is not a consequence of an absence of scholarly interest. The extent of ill health, and Royal Navy arrangements for health care in the plantation colonies possess dual significance. On the one hand, naval ships brought infection and contamination to the populations. This was especially the case during the late seventeenth and early eighteenth centuries when the navy depended largely upon the quartering system whereby some ill servicemen were placed for recuperation in private homes of the inhabitants willing to sell this service. On the other, the presence of either substantial mortality or long-term morbidity (together with the other recurring problems of undermanning and desertion) led naval commanders to extend controversial impressment activities and discouraged British authorities from increasing the quota of seamen allotted to the tobacco, sugar, and other staple trades. The adverse economic consequences for the colonies are indicated by increased freight rates and by the repeated frequent complaints forwarded from North America, especially Virginia, to the Commissioners for Trade and Plantations, Secretaries of State, and the Admiralty.[7] In view of these consequences, the theme is not lacking in significance; it is lacking in documentation. McClurg referred the readers of his 1747 communication to the journals of medical practice kept by Royal Navy surgeons for substantiation of the long-term crisis he was witnessing in Virginia. Readily available to the authorities in London, these case records would (one suspects) have soon established his case. From 1703 all naval surgeons were required to produce journals of their treatment of diseases and "wounds" before the Commissioners for Sick and Wounded Seamen and deposit these records with the Barber-Surgeons' Company of London (the body that certified naval surgeons).[8] Penalty for noncompliance was loss of pay, and we know that the case records were turned over to the Barber-Surgeons'

Company in large numbers.[9] Unfortunately, with one lone exception, none of the journals survive.[10] Prior to the better-documented period of the latter eighteenth century after the American Revolution, we are thrown back on largely anecdotal evidence.[11] Anecdotal evidence has its value, but it is also biased towards the spectacular and the special interests of the narrator.[12] To date, relatively little has been accomplished for the theme of maritime morbidity and medicine in colonial Virginia or adjacent areas.[13] This present study attempts to develop this topic as it relates to the navy, but the objective must be to comprehend in time the diverse experiences of the maritime world overall.

Movement beyond anecdote requires innovative use of surviving, dispersed archival sources. Early-eighteenth-century imperial and naval administrators saw little reason to multiply documentation on naval morbidity and mortality; apparently the detailed coverage of health care then present in the case records of sea surgeons, hospital ships, and naval hospitals sufficed to meet the occasional, haphazard demands for quantitative information. Summary statistics or detailed overviews were extremely rare. The long period of almost continuous warfare between 1689 and 1713 created the new phenomenon of a British navy of unprecedented size and worldwide responsibilities,[14] but little of the surviving documentation bears directly upon the issues of health and illness, not least in the colonial context. The records of the early-eighteenth-century Commission for Sick and Wounded Seamen have suffered greatly from the ravages of time.[15] One expansive source alone survives in the records of British central government: the abundant, albeit incomplete, ships' muster and pay books. The use of these complementary records provides invaluable quantitative evidence on shipboard mortality.[16] Only infrequently, however, do muster and pay books (or ships' logbooks) explain the causes of the mortality that they document. Moreover, these records are less than satisfactory for the investigation of morbidity at sea. They identify the ill, diseased, or incapacitated seaman principally in instances where he ceased to draw victuals or pay, as in the case of removal to a shore hospital or hospital ship. Medical care on board the vessel under the direction of the sea surgeon and mates is virtually invisible.[17] Morbidity, however, is of crucial historical importance: as N. A. M. Rodger has observed, sickness and disease were problems for the eighteenth-century British navy, overall, not so much in terms of absolute losses through death of seamen, as in terms of the wholesale temporary incapacitation of its workforce.[18] The limitation is particularly severe for Virginia (and, indeed, for all the early mainland colonies) because in the absence of a naval hospital the movement of invalids ashore is also generally invisible: upon arrival in the colony the sick left the ship but they never left the ship's books. Only occasionally, as we shall see below, does the veil of obscurity lift, permitting informative glimpses of the quantitative incidence and treatment of illness within the naval convoys that helped maintain the colonial lifeline of maritime trade during wartime.

The wars of 1689 to 1713 brought Royal Navy warships to Virginia for the first time on a regular, extended schedule.[19] Health-care provision, however, remained ad hoc and largely the responsibility of individual commanders. Queen Anne's War saw the creation and staffing of an important naval hospital in the West Indies, at Kingston, Jamaica, but not complementary measures for the less mortality-ridden mainland colonies.[20] At New York in 1706, for example, the distant British Commissioners for Sick and Wounded Seamen paid for the temporary assistance rendered to incapacitated seamen by a surgeon, one Philip Rockby, and on at least one occasion, in the financial year beginning 30 June 1706, the commissioners issued the modest sum of £3. 5s. for the cost of renting two houses in Virginia (precise location unspecified) used to receive and hold sick naval seamen (for an unspecified period).[21] These were one-off initiatives, designed to provide immediate remedy for specific problems deemed to be beyond the capabilities of the individual ship surgeons. The regulations governing the Commission for Sick and Wounded Seamen and Prisoners of War recognized that in locations overseas devoid of a naval hospital or commission agent, arrangements for the care of injured or diseased seamen were left largely in the hands of the individual ship captain or squadron commander.[22] There was no routine provision of systematic health care.

In comparison to the British West Indies, Virginia and the colonies to the north were considered relatively healthy destinations for the navy, or at least ones not requiring exceptional measures.[23] Nonetheless, early-eighteenth-century Virginia suffered regular outbreaks of contagious disease. In September 1708 Lieutenant Governor Edmund Jenings commented upon "the severe and extraordinary fevers and other sicknesses with which almost all parts of the country have been afflicted for near two months past." In April 1709 a general fast day was proclaimed for divine intercession against "the dangerous pestilential distemper which has already swept away great numbers . . . to the great terror and consternation of all." Once again, in January and April 1710, Jenings reported on a contagious "distemper" killing many of the inhabitants and creating sickly conditions in divers parts of the colony.[24] The study of disease in the colonial Chesapeake reveals two seasonal peaks for European mortality: one in the relatively cold and damp winter and early-spring months and another in September and October, as a consequence of the fevers later linked to endemic malaria.[25] The Reverend John Clayton observed in 1688 that during July and August the Virginian air became stagnant, with the heat "violent and troublesome," followed by September rains, "when the weather breaks [and] many fall sick, this being the time of an endemical Sickness, for Seasonings, Cachexes, Fluxes, Scorbutical Dropsies, Gripes, or the like."[26] The health risks for incoming shipping, especially the late summer/autumn tobacco fleet, were considerable. At the same time, maritime trade and travel presumably were the sources for some outbreaks; certainly, illness was a routine feature aboard the vessels calling at Virginia, not least within the Royal Navy itself.

The wars of 1689 to 1713 produced heightened problems of morbidity and mortality within the navy, defying administrative reforms intended to assuage the crisis.[27] To the time-honored difficulties created by defective provisions; exposure; crowded, damp, or overheated quarters; and limited medical facilities were added the challenges of rapid manpower expansion and long-term shipboard service. The extended seasonality of naval operations combined with contemporary efforts to resolve the "manning problem" produced the first sustained attempt in Britain to maintain year-round crewing of vessels. Traditionally, large numbers of naval seamen were released into the maritime economy each winter, not least to reduce government expenditure. The medical consequences inherent within the movement toward year-long retention of crews quickly became all too apparent. One of the earliest commentators was the naval chaplain William Hodges, who in 1695 condemned the practice of keeping crews aboard ship for extended periods. He advocated the creation of a minimum one-month period ashore each year for every seaman, free from the press gang, for sailors to "Recruit their Healths."[28] Hodges (who would himself die in service at sea in 1703) resorted to hyperbole and unsupported assertions to clinch his argument,[29] but the basic point is clear. Moreover, reduced opportunity for seamen to recover their health ashore was compounded by the increased circulation of disease aboard ship through the extended intermingling of crews and the resort to secure holding stations, on stationary vessels in harbor or elsewhere, for mariners not on active service. Frequently crowded and sometimes disease ridden, some holding stations were particularly inappropriate from a health perspective. In 1706 the commander of one HMS warship received permission to place his entire crew in the Deal naval hospital during the refitting of the vessel, for the sole reason that the hospital was a secure site from which desertion was difficult.[30] Clearly, isolation for the purpose of containment of disease took a backseat to isolation for the benefit of crew retention. In some instances it is possible to trace the spread of infection out of secure holding quarters into different theaters of conflict, as human carriers moved from ship to ship and garrison to garrison, creating a spiral of sickness and death.[31]

The Atlantic was a well-known and well-traveled connector for the English-speaking populations on its periphery,[32] but transatlantic travel was not free of risk. The newspapers of Queen Anne's England considered it a newsworthy event when a vessel voyaged to or from the plantation colonies *without* significant mortality.[33] Shipboard morbidity, on the other hand, appears to have been taken for granted, requiring little public comment. In these circumstances, it may be expected that Royal Navy ships arriving in American ports would bring with them a morbidity problem, composed of longstanding medical complaints within the crews combined with the incidence of aliments and diseases arising, or coming to notice, during the passage of eleven or twelve weeks.

Charting the incidence of naval morbidity for colonial Virginia depends in part upon utilization of haphazard observations in ships' logbooks. Because incapacitated crewmen remained on the ship's books, the muster and pay accounts normally reveal only mortality. High mortality in the absence of naval engagements or life-endangering storms is in itself an indication of high morbidity, although the converse is not always true. Some loquacious ships' officers upon arrival in American ports noted the removal of sick seamen into land quarters; others, apparently under no obligation to record the information, did not.[34] A standard observation of "sent our sick ashore"[35] establishes the presence of morbidity, but not its extent. Certainly, the prevailing orthodoxy on the unwholesome character of shipboard vapors suggests that ships were routinely emptied of all incapacitated seamen whenever conditions on land and the sailing schedule of the ship permitted the recovery of health on land.[36] One illustration for Virginia arises out of the efforts at the turn of the century to reduce piracy in the Chesapeake region. On 23 August 1700 British captain William Passenger reported that upon taking a prize into Elizabeth Town, New Jersey, he was experiencing sustained illness aboard his ship, with one death and "above forty of the best of my men sick & some very dangerously." He petitioned Lieutenant Governor Francis Nicholson to have his sick cared for ashore at Hampton, on credit, "otherwise they must lye aboard & perish for want of refreshment for they Infect one another, that I have ten in one night [newly] taken sick."[37] The observations in logbooks establish that naval vessels on convoy duty to Virginia and other colonies availed themselves of every opportunity to land ill seamen, but in the absence of additional information on numbers and provisions for care the practice remains nebulous. Moreover, without information on the nature of health problems confronting the navy in North American waters, we are, perforce, thrown back upon general statements for the nature of ill health in the eighteenth-century British navy overall, or even merely the health problems identified within particular English naval hospitals whose records happen to survive.[38]

Occasionally the records of the expanding British state throw up more serviceable evidence. Such is the case with one Henry Heart, ship's surgeon in April

1706 aboard HMS *Ruby*, formerly surgeon of HMS *Kingston*. Heart was an Englishman with a grievance: he had not been paid for his care of the ship's company of the *Kingston* at York Town, Virginia, in the previous summer of 1705. By customary practice, extraordinary care of sick seamen on shore was rewarded by the Commissioners of Sick and Wounded Seamen by way of an allowance of six shillings and eight pence per head, for the duration of the "cure." Payment of these allowances occasionally appears in the financial records of the commissioners, but always, it seems, in exceptional circumstances wherein the service was provided by off-ship medical personnel, not by the sea surgeons who possessed their normal pay and allowances. Heart's argument was that he was entitled to the extraordinary payment, and he provided a detailed account of his medical practice to establish his point. The unusual event of a sea surgeon's requesting additional remuneration for the care of his men who remained on the ship's books appears to have caught the Commissioners of Sick and Wounded Seamen unprepared, for they declined to act without express order from the Lord Admiral of England. It is relevant to observe here that a petition for the increase of the pay rates for all navy surgeons in January 1704 had been rejected by the authorities.[39] Heart was perhaps attempting to gain through the back door what had not been secured by way of a frontal assault. In any case, Heart's appeal to the Admiralty, complete with records, met with a predictable bureaucratic response: the board wrote to the Commissioners for Sick and Wounded Seamen requesting information on whether Heart's request adhered to customary practices, enclosing the original documentation. Thus, we find—within the context of the general loss of the commissioners' archive—a surgeon's case records amidst the out-letters of the Admiralty.[40] Heart's request was unusual; we have, however, no reason to believe that his record of treatments for the Virginia convoy vessel HMS *Kingston* was out of the ordinary. The commissioners did not authorize an extraordinary payment, believing, it would seem, that Heart's service in Virginia during the summer of 1705 was routine and unexceptional.[41]

HMS *Kingston*, a 64-gun warship with a regular complement of 365 men, sailed from the Downes on 9 May 1705 in company with HMS *Falkland*, a fourth-rate of 54 guns and 240 men, on convoy duty bound for Virginia. Initially, they, and other R.N. ships, escorted 100 merchantmen, bound for Virginia, the West Indies, and New England, but the fleets eventually parted company, with 41 merchantmen continuing under naval protection to Virginia. Aboard the *Kingston* was one distinguished passenger: Lieutenant Governor Edward Nott, sent to Virginia to replace the controversial Francis Nicholson. Soon, Nicholson would himself journey to England aboard the *Kingston* on its return passage. In all, the round trip occupied some eight months. The naval vessels sighted the North Carolina coast on the morning of 9 August and anchored in the York River, hard against York Town, at 7:00 p.m. on 11 August. There they remained for over one month. Preparations for departure began on 13 September, and they set out for England with the homeward fleet of 33 merchantmen on 4 October. Arrival at the Downes on 27 November was followed by mooring in late December of the *Kingston* at Upnor Castle and the *Falkland* at Woolwich.[42]

The outward voyage had been uneventful, with one major exception that presumably would have affected the health of the seamen. The fleet failed, due to rough weather, to anchor at Funchal, Portuguese Madeira, and the *Kingston*'s captain, George Clements, decided to push on with the fleet across the Atlantic without watering. At the end of the log entries for 2 August the *Kingston*'s master noted cursorily, "drank all water."[43] More routine problems also arose toward the midpoint in the outward journey. The two ship's masters began condemning sizeable quantities of corrupt cheese and smaller amounts of butter on 20 June. Five days earlier the *Kingston* reduced the daily beer ration by one-half due to shortages, and on 11 July short allowance for provisions was begun, reducing caloric intake by one-third.[44] The first beer noted condemned as "sour & stinking" was not until 3 September, but the ships' companies had begun drinking rum on 22 August.[45] In his first communication with the British authorities, Lieutenant Governor Nott referred to his ocean travel as a "tedious passage," but made no other observation.[46] The duration of the voyage from the final departure from Plymouth Sound on 18 May to disembarkment at York Town on 12 August had lasted twelve weeks and two days, only slightly above average.[47] Possessing few navigational problems or natural hazards, the route was considered "as easy a voyage as any [in the empire]."[48] Both naval captains were experienced seamen: Clements had been promoted to captain in 1694, and would be killed in action in May 1707; John Underdown on the *Falkland* achieved the rank of commander in 1695 and captain in 1696.[49] Convoy duty regularly produced slow Atlantic passages because of problems of coordination. In this case there were problems with the Royal Navy ships as well. On the return passage the *Falkland* sprang leaks in the breadroom. The *Kingston* arrived home in a dilapidated state: "She Wanted soe muche repair," in the words of the Navy's master builder on 29 December, that all the crew was transferred to the *St. George* on 17 February 1706 and on 4 April the ship as put out of commission.[50]

Mortality losses for the duration of the voyage were: the *Kingston*, 24 (6.6 percent of the complement of 365); the *Falkland*, 20 (8.3 percent of 240).[51] These figures can be compared to surviving information for HMS *Guernsey*, a fourth-rate on convoy duty to Virginia in 1703, when 27 died (11.2 percent of 240).[52] Moreover, the chronology of mortality in 1705 differed from that of 1703. Aboard the *Guernsey* the mortality began in Virginia, with deaths on 17 August and 27, 29, and 30 September; six crewmen died on the return voyage, most in late November, and seventeen more died in port at Chatham between 2 December and 28 February 1704. This mortality pattern suggests the presence of one or more contagious diseases picked up in Virginia, either from the host population or from the crews of other vessels, although without information on morbidity this remains speculative. The mortality pattern in 1705 was distinct, with some differences between the incidence aboard the *Kingston* and the *Falkland* (see table 6.1).

On board the *Falkland*, the first death, in July, was a drowning. Mortality began early upon arrival at York Town, with the deaths of the boatswain and an able seaman on 22 August, followed by pronounced mortality between 11 September and 4 October (the day of departure); in all 10 died in Virginia. Deaths continued in rapid succession immediately following departure—indicative of ill seamen being carried homeward rather than left behind to recuperate—with a total of seven deaths at sea up to 17 November. Thereafter the ship was mortality free with the exception of the isolated death of an able seaman while the vessel lay off Queensborough, Kent, on 22 December. Seventeen men were taken ashore at Deal between 9 and 24 December, and at least some of them were sick. The only known death from this group was that of Joseph Dyson, an able seaman who died in quarters at Woolwich on 6 March. While some of the incapacitated may well have died at a later date in the hospital or sick quarters, the evidence suggests that immediate postvoyage mortality was very limited. At least three of the incapacitated able seamen who departed immediately following the ship's return were later discharged from the service as infirm. The designation was generally used in

Table 6.1.   Naval Mortality in Virginia Convoy of 1705

Month	Kingston	Falkland
May	0	0
June	0	0
July	2	1
August	5	2
September	2	7
October	3	5
November	2	3
December	8	1
January	2	0
February	0	0
March	—	1
	24	20

the period for those disabled through age, rupture, tumors, or the like, rather than for sufferers of contagious disease. The *Falkland* also carried homeward a company of Lord Shannon's regiment, commanded by Captain Gustavus Bellford, listed in the ship's books as marines and therefore paid and provisioned on the establishment. Of the total of thirty-nine men and officers, four (10.3 percent) died on the homeward journey beginning, as with the mariners, within days of departure. The fact that eight of the remainder were put ashore at Deal on 23 December suggested the presence of substantial illness. Although speculative, scurvy appears to be a likely explanation for the sizable end-of-voyage morbidity that produced several service discharges but few deaths.

The *Kingston* had wintered in England for 1704–1705 following service in the Iberian theater of the war. This service included naval action at the siege of Gibraltar in the summer of 1704, when the crew suffered substantial mortality and injuries. In consequence, the months immediately prior to departure with the Virginia convoy of 1705 witnessed extensive crew alterations. A sizable number of seamen—at least twenty-nine—were discharged as either unserviceable or infirm. Over half of these discharges were, in fact, for pressed men placed on the ship's strength earlier in the winter and now, on the point of departure, judged to be infirm, or "aged." Clearly, the *Kingston* was experiencing difficulties in filling its complement, and the quality of those retained may have been compromised. A substantial majority of the crew had seen long-term service aboard the vessel, including recent participation in the unhealthy Mediterranean theater. Nonetheless, few seamen were discharged sick from the vessel during the first four months of 1705, and deaths in this period numbered only four (the same as for the *Falkland*). On both ships, April, May, and June were free from mortalities. However, deaths unlikely to have been the consequence of accident began earlier than on the *Falkland*, and at an elevated level within the ship hierarchy: on 24 and 25 July the ship lost in succession its chaplain and quartermaster. The latter had been a member of the ship's original crew whereas the former, Patrick Crosby, entered into wages on 24 February of that year. The first two deaths below decks, of an able and an ordinary seaman on 5 and 8 August, repeat this division between the established crew and the recent recruits. The same was true of the string of deaths at York Town of ordinary or able seamen, on 14, 16, 22 August and 24 and 27 September.

The chronology of mortality for the *Kingston* clearly peaked earlier than with the *Falkland*, but the two deaths in late September should be associated with the higher death rate on the sister ship in this period, for the *Kingston* also experienced immediate postdeparture deaths, on 4, 6, and 10 October. The remaining losses at sea were experienced on 6 and 11 November, and 3 and 6 December. However, mortality rose in the weeks following arrival in England, with seven deaths between 11 December (when three died) and 16 January, followed by a final case of drowning on 24 January. One possible explanation for the continuing mortality aboard ship was that the crew was kept together as much as was possible while decisions were made on removing the ship from commission and transferring the crew intact to another vessel. It is true that twenty men were sent ashore at Deal or Chatham during December, and at least some of them ended up in Deal Hospital. However, the entry in the master's logbook for the desertion on 10 January by five pressed men who broke out of locked confinement in the ship's powder room indicates significant discipline problems on the *Kingston*. Moreover, whereas the *Falkland* was provided immediately with fresh beer on 26 November and new provisions on 12 December, the logbook for the *Kingston* is wholly silent, except for continuing disposal of condemned victuals.[53] These end-of-voyage deaths, therefore, could be consistent with unrelieved scurvy, although other explanations are certainly possible.

The mortality aboard the *Kingston* and *Falkland* was spread generally among the ships' complements, with perhaps higher mortality among the petty officers and officers than might have been expected: four marines, thirteen ordinary seamen, nineteen able seamen, three captain's servants, two cook's mates, and one steward's mate, lieutenant's steward, quarter gunner, quartermaster, boatswain, midshipman, and chaplain. Apart from the two drownings, no information is provided in the logbooks or pay records on causes of death. The early demises of the chaplain, quartermaster, and boatswain suggest that, at least in these instances, the explanation lies neither in deficient provisioning nor in preexisting medical complaints. Early deaths of senior members of the complement suggest the presence of contagious disease on board at least the *Kingston*.

The preceding mortality statistics imply, but do nothing to describe, the presence of significant morbidity among the ships' crews, both upon arrival and during their sojourn in Virginia, and on the return voyage. The captain's logbook for the *Falkland* provides more information than most when he reported how, on 13 August at York Town, "this day blowing fresh, we put Summ of our Men on shore that was trubled with the Scurvey."[54] The ship's master informs us how on the preceding day, the first at anchor in the river, "we raised a Tent a shore In order for sick men."[55] The implied urgency in these actions might indicate the extent of the problem, but it is only from surgeon Henry Heart's information, provided for the *Kingston* alone, that we can, for the first time, secure a quantitative appraisal of naval morbidity following a fairly routine ocean crossing. The master of the *Kingston* noted on 13 August, "We got 90 of our Men a shoar sicke."[56] This action was undertaken even in advance of initiating watering for the ship, which began on 14 August. There clearly was a perception of urgency. Under the title of "An Account of such seamen as were sett sick on shore from her Majestys ship ye Kingston, at York Town in Virginia by Order of Capt. G. Clements Commander," Heart provided for the Lords of the Admiralty the names of 119 members of the *Kingston's* company under his care on land during August and September 1705, with individual dates of reception on shore, a brief description of the ailment, the eventual disposition of the men (either returned to the ship or dead), and the date of these dispositions.[57]

Heart's information may be arranged under two classifications: the nature of incapacitation at the time of arrival, as revealed in the diseases of the eighty-five crewmen (not ninety) taken ashore on 13 August, together with individual additions of one sailor each on 14 and 16 August (dysentery and quotidian ague, respectively); and the nature of incapacitation for the thirty-two crewmen received ashore in the second period of removal, 1–10 September. Apparently, all those placed on land remained in Heart's care there until 27 September, when, in the midst of preparations for final departure, they returned to the *Kingston.* The following begins by utilizing Heart's descriptions of the ailments (table 6.2).

It may be wondered whether the 119 patients treated on shore by Heart constituted the total extent of sickness among the *Kingston's* crew, or only those seamen deemed to be fully incapacitated and for whom shore rest was thought to be beneficial. Would Heart's now missing medical journal (from which this evidence is clearly extracted) include on-ship care for other seamen? To judge from the sole surviving sea surgeon's medical journal of this period, where relatively minor ailments were treated over brief durations,[58] the answer is likely affirmative. We have, then, a record of extended care for incapacitated members of the crew;

Table 6.2.   Naval Mortality, the *Kingston*, 12 August–27 September 1705

Ailment	Removed 12–16 Aug.	Removed 1–10 Sept.	Total
scurvy	41	–	41
dysentery	18	4	22
fever	10	3	13
quotidian ague	5	11	16
tertian ague	4	8	12
intermittent fever	3	6	9
confusion	2	–	2
ulcerous leg	2	–	2
diabetes	1	–	1
unlisted	1	–	1
	87	32	119

herein, morbidity stood at 24.1 percent upon arrival on 12 August, and rose to 33.0 percent prior to departure. We have no reason to consider this to have been an exceptional morbidity rate; if anything, the available evidence suggests that the experience of the *Kingston* was at the lower end of the scale of human suffering for the time and locale. Upon the arrival of HMS *Oxford* from England in June 1708, for example, the Reverend William Black, a passenger, reported that nearly 100 were "dangerously" sick, but what distinguished this episode, and called for Black's comment, was the high outward mortality of 30 dead. The *Oxford* was fourth-rate crewed at a level of 275; although some of the incapacitated were presumably passengers, this evidence suggests morbidity upon arrival of approximately one-third of the complement.[59] In 1734 while on service in Virginia, a total of 98 crewmen were set ashore sick from HMS *Winchelsea*, a sixth-rate vessel of only 130 men.[60]

The severity of the afflictions on the *Kingston* presumably varied over time, but Heart's evidence, composed to assert the strongest case for additional remuneration rather than to chart individual patient progress, obscures this issue. We may recall McClurg's statement in 1747 that seamen housed out of doors in Virginia recuperated slowly. Later in the century, medical-reform advocates repeatedly commented upon the problem of *keeping* men healthy in tents in hot climates, in view of problems with heat, air circulation, and overcrowding, and James Lind would comment adversely on the health risks for strangers produced by Virginia's hot, moist climate.[61] In 1755, the Virginia surgeon Robert Bell, then serving the Royal Navy Squadron in the Chesapeake as ad hoc surgeon and agent for the Commissioners for Sick and Wounded Seamen, lamented that the seamen under his care ashore at Hampton scarcely began to recover from one ailment when they fell into others; he could only offer hope of recovery through a long continuance of his dietary regimen, nursing care, and the eventual arrival of more temperate autumnal weather.[62] Treatment of army and naval dysentery in the eighteenth century required a fairly lengthy convalescence, and at least some of the so-called intermittent fevers (malaria) were notoriously difficult to "cure."[63] Once seafarers were removed from the ship (and provided with a fresh diet), contemporaries invariably remarked upon the rapid speed of recovery from scurvy, although they also emphasized the difficulty in treating the numerous and frequent complications.[64] Heart's information, therefore, probably simplifies a rather more complex pattern of illness, complications, recovery, relapse, and perhaps malingering on shore. The early deaths following reembarkation, though, point to at least some sustained illness. This level of incapacitation may well have been sufficiently severe to delay the homeward departure of the convoy. Lieutenant Governor Nicholson noted that the HMS convoy ships were under orders not to tarry in Virginia longer than one month;[65] in the event, they stayed almost seven weeks.

For the *Kingston* in 1705, scurvy accounted for 34.5 percent of long-term illness, fevers for 42 percent, and dysentery for 18.5 percent. Experienced medical practitioners invariably noted that these were the three great challenges confronting ship surgeons of the period. External injuries, although commented upon extensively in the specialist literature, were, in the absence of battle, far less common. Heart's practice was no exception, although minor injuries were likely under-reported in this instance.[66] Through cross-reference with the pay books, we can determine that those afflicted covered the range of occupations and ranks aboard the vessel, from swabber through yeoman of the sheets, quartermaster's mate and quartermaster, to two midshipmen, with a preponderance of ordinary and able seamen. Muster records prior to 1764, unfortunately, do not specify ages for individual members of the crew. For the later eighteenth century, it has been calculated that 82 percent of ordinary seamen were aged 16–25, and 71 percent of able seamen were aged 16–30; petty officers were somewhat older— only 2 percent were under 21, 45 percent were aged 21–30, and 31 percent were 31–40.[67]

The crew of the *Kingston* shared a potent cocktail of all the major epidemic diseases found in the general early-eighteenth-century naval population. Presumably this condition was not limited to the one ship. In specifying the presence of scurvy on the *Falkland* on 12 August, the ship's captain probably was indicating only the most widespread, urgent illness at that time. The increase in mortality in September and October can not be ascribed to scurvy; it likely had a common origin in some of the fevers or dysentery arising among the *Kingston*'s crew in the same period. The merchantmen of the Virginia tobacco fleet would not have been immune: one week out of York Town on the return passage both the *Kingston* and the *Falkland* came to the aid of one merchant ship in the convoy which, having sprung leaks, was in extreme difficulty due to the number of crewmen sick in the vessel.[68] Lieutenant Governor Nott was himself afflicted by either an unspecified disease acquired aboard ship, or by the "seasoning" experienced by new arrivals to Virginia's endemic environment. On 22 September he noted from Williamsburg how two members of the colony's council had taken sick, "and myself very much indisposed."[69] He would die at Williamsburg in August 1706.

With the two ships anchored hard by York Town, the incapacitated of both crews were likely placed under canvas in the immediate vicinity of the settlement. York Town, founded in 1691, was a busy port but a diminutive settlement. The local impact of perhaps several hundred sick from the naval and some of the merchant vessels could have been considerable, and almost an annual occurrence.

ROYAL NAVY MORBIDITY   155

Opportunities for social interaction between crew members and inhabitants were sufficient to enable two men from the *Falkland* and four from the *Kingston* to desert while the ships were at anchor.[70] If the tent city was established on the bluff, as appears likely,[71] contamination of the drinking water was a possibility. Sanitation was primitive: the fact that later medical personnel repeatedly called for the digging of deeper privies and, during an outbreak of dysentery, the daily covering over of excrement with earth is indicative of the limitations of earlier and ongoing practices.[72] Aboard ship, the "head" was simply above the grate at the bow, with the discharge being moved around by the actions of wind and waves. Because of the belief in the miasmatic theory of disease, sanitation measures were focused upon making the air "sweet" in ships, tents, or other enclosed spaces. Aboard ship the only action endorsed by the navy in this period was the occasional washing of the decks with a vinegar solution, thought to purify the air. The recording of this action in the ship's log informs us of the times when a general removal of accumulated filth above the level of the bilge might have had beneficial effects. But for neither the *Kingston* nor the *Falkland* is there evidence that this action was taken during the course of this voyage.

As an active port, York Town was an open environment where measures to prevent the spread of disease in and out were largely ineffectual. These early years of the eighteenth century saw the first movement to enact quarantine laws in some of the American colonies; between 1698 and 1714 four jurisdictions did so, but Virginia was not among their number.[73] Neither the naval warships nor the merchantmen of 1705 were quarantined; the merchantmen immediately dispersed on their way to multiple destinations in the Chesapeake. The *Kingston*'s logs record much of the traffic into and out of the York River during the ship's period at anchor, and within a week of their arrival the navy was joined by several slavers from West Africa. Others would follow.[74]

What was the relationship between the morbidity pattern and the incidence of mortality? Heart announced that a mere two of the 119 servicemen under his care ashore died of their ailments. This understates the truth, for the *Kingston* lost five men while in Virginia and they all appear in Heart's records: the first two deaths in August were from dysentery, followed by one from fever on 22 August; two crewmen initially diagnosed with cases of tertian fever and scurvy died in late September. Presumably the scurvy sufferer, at least, died of something else. Of the fifteen men of the *Kingston* who died after 27 September, only two names appear among the 119 earlier sent ashore: William Fletcher, the lieutenant's steward, and Stephen Pantry, the ordinary seaman, who died together on 11 December while the ship lay before Deal, had been among the original forty-one scurvy patients of 12 August. Their cause(s) of death, of course, remains undetermined.

Apparently, the twenty-four deaths aboard the *Kingston* were almost as varied in origin as the disparate causes of morbidity.

Medical care of the incapacitated from both ships was limited in good measure to the individual sea surgeons and their staff. Heart himself was typical of the most experienced naval surgeons of the period.[75] He began service as a surgeon's mate during the Nine Year's War, on 17 January 1696. Discharged following the peace, on 22 June 1698, he disappeared from view, only to surface again with the increase in naval preparedness that preceded England's entry into Queen Anne's War. On 5 June 1701 Heart passed his examination for the post of master surgeon on any available fourth-rate, but on the next day he was warranted surgeon of the modest *Carcase* bomb vessel. This was followed by promotion to the *Kingston* on 26 January 1703. On 27 February 1706 he transferred to the *Ruby*, and then on 12 July 1708 to the *Sunderland*. In November of the same year Heart moved to the *Suffolk Hagboat*, then in service as a hospital ship. The experience and backgrounds of his mates aboard the *Kingston* were varied but their inexperience stands out. William Larwood served on board as an ordinary seaman, volunteer, before becoming mate on 20 January 1705. He was one of the original scurvy sufferers moved onto land on 12 August. One second mate, Samuel Hull, was an able seaman who reentered the ship's company in November 1704 as a pensioner and then was promoted to surgeon's mate at the outset of this voyage, 19 May 1705. He had only recently, on 6 March 1705, passed his examination at Barber-Surgeons' Hall, qualifying as second mate for a fourth-rate warship. In June 1706 he transferred to the HMS *Chatham*, qualified on 16 July 1706 as a first mate on a third-rate, and on the next day was promoted to first mate on the *Chatham*. Subsequent promotion proved to be slow: by the time he qualified as surgeon on a fifth-rate in 1719 Hull had seen service as first mate on five vessels. The other second mate on the *Kingston* was Michael Masterson, and this was also his first appointment. Masterson qualified on 6 April 1704 as second mate on any third-rate and within the week was posted to the *Kingston*, where he saw service at the siege of Gibraltar. He left ship on 13 February 1706 for the *Jefferies* hospital ship, having passed the examination as first mate on a fourth-rate.

On the *Falkland*, the master surgeon was James Kerr (or Carr). Kerr served ten years on HMS *Dispatch*, a brigantine, first as surgeon's mate and then, following his successful examination in January 1702 as surgeon on any fifth-rate, as ship's surgeon. Two commanders in succession observed that "he behaved himself very carefully & dilligent in his business; being very well affected to her Majestie and Government: A Person of a Sober Life and Conversation, and in my opinion is very deserving of preferment." Although Kerr passed his examination for surgeon of a fourth-rate in February 1704, he remained without preferment until warranted to the *Falkland* on 7 May 1705, on the eve of its departure for Virginia. He would remain in service on the ship until at least 1711, seeking in vain for advancement in the wake of qualifying in January 1709 as surgeon of a second-rate ship.[76]

In the absence of the medical journals, the particulars of the treatment provided for the incapacitated remain obscure. Heart informed the admiralty that he supplied certain "eatables" for the 119 men, "where I found the ships provisions might be prejudicial."[77] Presumably this followed the contemporary theory, as enunciated by Dr. William Cockburn, physician to the Blue Squadron of the fleet, that a ship's salt provisions required "exercise, work and fatigue" to be digested properly and thus were unsuitable for invalids or those in recovery.[78] The consequence, of course, was the reversal of the vitamin C deficiency. Heart apparently limited his medicinal contribution to the contents of his medical chest, and complained that a considerable store was expended. Treatments, therefore, can be expected to have followed standard sea practice, either as outlined in the principal medical treatises for maritime medicine of the period,[79] or as reduced to their basic applications in practice.[80] Naval surgeons had limited opportunity to build up a particular expertise within any one geographical region or disease environment. Neither Heart nor Kerr, for example, appears to have served in the Virginia convoys prior to 1705, nor did they return. Thus, although the disease environment of the Chesapeake differed significantly from that of southern Britain,[81] medical emphasis was placed upon common, basic actions.

Military and naval medicine in this war, as presumably in others, attempted to establish universally applicable, empirical remedies that would return the men to service as quickly, efficiently, and cheaply as possible.[82] Cockburn, who played a leading role in promoting this philosophy, has left on record examples of his individual treatments for scurvy, dysentery, and fever in the navy during the 1690s, and these are suggestive of at least some practices. For scurvy he used a far less intrusive course than many practitioners, arguing that seamen taken ashore recovered speedily on their own when living upon the "Green-Trade," defined as "Coleworts, Carrots, Cabbages, Turnips, etc." He recommended clearing the body of vicious matter by way of a vomit and purge, followed by an antiscorbutic electuary and a diet that included as little beef or pork as possible and plenty of "burgoo" (oatmeal porridge) or water gruel.[83] Various combinations of purging and bleeding for dysentery, and purging, bleeding, and vomiting for fevers were adhered to, subject to the needs of the individual case. Cockburn commented upon how hard it was to cure a young adult of a fever in a hot season or warm climate, for when sweating was either induced or allowed to proceed naturally, patients regularly caught cold and suffered relapses. The recommended course was a range of cooling drinks and plasters and a diet of burgoo or water gruel.[84] Textbook advice, and presumably actual practice, varied for all three diseases, but Heart, Kerr, and their mates almost certainly followed a regimen steady in the use of purgatives and bleeding with efforts to keep the incapacitated comfortable, cool, and nourished on a thin diet that contained little meat, none of it (if possible) salted or dried. This was all standard advice and—for what we know of it—practice. Certainly, naval captains on the Virginia station recognized that "Fresh provisions and a Good Nurse in All Disorders Contribute much to the Recovery of a sick person."[85] Nursing was the responsibility of the mates and of the recovering sick. In those instances when the incapacitated were removed from the care of the ship's surgeon into lodgings ashore, the fragmentary surviving accounts acknowledge the nursing care provided by landladies or other women, although the only detail of care even casually noted is the bathing of the sick.[86]

Ship surgeons had no difficulty in identifying scurvy. Dysentery (the bloody flux) was likewise a term normally (but not always) used in distinction from diarrhea. Practitioners, however, did not distinguish until the late nineteenth century between bacillary dysentery, spread through water and food and characterized by a short incubation period, and amoebic dysentery, caused by a protozoal parasite and generally endemic and chronic.[87] Fevers were far more problematic. Heart's use of the term "intermittent fever" alongside the standard categories of tertian and quotidian probably indicated fevers so irregular in the repetition of high temperature as to defy classification. Given his care to identify intermittent fevers, his recourse to the unqualified word "fever," used in particular for seamen removed from the *Kingston* on 12 August, presumably stood for what contemporaries designated continual fever. Although of necessity speculative, this interpretation does match with what is known concerning contagious disease in Virginia. The intermittent fevers are tied by medical historians to the fever spikes of malaria, which struck the colony routinely in late summer and autumn. *Plasmodium vivax* malaria was endemic in Virginia by the mid-seventeenth century, and *plasmodium falciparum* malaria produced epidemics in the late seventeenth and early eighteenth centuries.[88] If this diagnosis is correct, the crew of the *Kingston* carried home with it one strand of this disease, although *plasmodium vivax* malaria was already endemic to parts of southern Britain. The suggestion that malaria proved to be so difficult to eradicate from the ports and coastal areas of the Thames and Medway estuaries in the eighteenth century in part as a consequence of periodic "refueling" from overseas, appears thus to be eminently reasonable.[89] These were the geographic destinations for the great majority of naval and merchant vessels, and the sick from both sectors of the maritime workforce continued in the main to be cared for in private lodgings in the ports. The continual fever was possibly either typhus or typhoid fever, both present in the eighteenth-century navy, in Britain, and in Virginia.[90]

Disease in this context was "the great debilitator," which weakened resistance rather than killed outright in the majority of infections.[91] It is, therefore, impossible to assume that causes of mortality followed closely the morbidity patterns. Typhoid fever, typhus, dysentery, and sometimes malaria tended to run concurrently through the maritime community.[92] Dysentery in this instance, although statistically less in evidence than other diseases, was the reported cause of the first two deaths in Virginia, on 14 and 16 August, aboard a ship that had already lost two senior members to an unknown killer (both of whom died in late July while the ship was becalmed and experiencing what was described as very hot weather). Thereafter, at least for the *Kingston*, new cases of dysentery while at anchor totaled only four. Those already known to be infected were of course removed, and one-third of the crew was now absent. In view of the scanty reporting of new cases of continual fever in late summer, the second, far larger, wave of mortality that began in the tent camp in mid-September and continued on board both ships during the early weeks of the return voyage might be attributed either to a resurgence of the dysentery never eliminated from the tent camps and carried back to the ships, or to the malaria found in the increasing intermittent fevers of early September.[93]

Regrettably, so much must remain speculative in respect to the causes of death. We are on firmer ground in identifying the morbidity problem as multi-faceted, where any improvements in one area were offset by setbacks elsewhere. What is also certain is that schedules for the annual tobacco convoys that produced late-summer or autumn departures from Virginia exposed crews of all ships to the height of the fever season. Nonetheless, this departure schedule was increasingly the trend in the early eighteenth century.[94] Before the end of the century, medical opinion would determine that the very worst time of year for strangers to arrive in South Carolina, an area that experienced a similar pattern of seasonal malaria, was the summer or early autumn because of the annual fever season, particularly deadly for "the labouring part of the community."[95] However, the ships kept coming.

Whether as a result of the stamina of the men, the surgeon's work, or the land rest and fresh victuals, the morbidity problem of 1705 failed to escalate into a mortality crisis. This was unexceptional: in the absence of virulent epidemics, some 95 percent of adult patients in the eighteenth century recovered following medical treatment, thanks to the human body's reparative abilities.[96] A death to morbidity ratio of 5:119, or 4.2 percent (for the traced morbidity of 12 August—27 September), was not unpromising. Fragmentary information suggests that this experience was typical for early-eighteenth-century Virginia. For example, the captain of the HMS *Seahorse*, a sixth-rate warship with a complement of 120, described his crew as being very sickly during its stay in the colony in the summer of 1736, but noted in total only six deaths over that period.[97] As noted above, morbidity was the crucial long-term problem. The ratio for the *Kingston* was, however, considerably higher than the death-to-illness ratio of 5:209 (2.4 percent) experienced by the HMS *Tiger*, a fourth-rate ship of forty-eight guns and a complement of 230 men on active service in the Mediterranean over a ten-month period in 1706.[98] It is true that much routine, nonincapacitative morbidity aboard the *Kingston* (unlike for the *Tiger*) probably is not captured in the documentation. None the less, it is striking that, in all, the death-to-manning ratio aboard the *Kingston* of 24:365 (6.6 percent) over ten months far exceeded the ratio of approximately 5:246 (2.0 percent) aboard the *Tiger* for an identical period. The principal contagious diseases experienced by the *Tiger* were fever and dysentery. In contrast to the *Kingston*, merely two cases of scurvy were present. The *Tiger* was never far from a port, and it had regular recourse to fresh water and to some fresh victualing. On the other hand, virtually all its sick remained shipboard for the duration of the voyage. The removal of the *Kingston*'s incapacitated to shore, as was common practice for the Virginia convoys, had notable positive consequences, including more spacious accommodations and the separation of the crew. These measures may have aided in recovery, and almost certainly limited the spread of some infectious disease, especially dysentery. To the fact that only two of the 114 survivors of the tent camp died on the homeward journey, in December, we may add that, of the twenty seamen discharged into Deal or Chatham in December 1705 from the *Kingston*, only two had been among their numbers, one diagnosed with scurvy on 12 August and the other with dysentery on the same date. Apparently, the substantial majority of the former invalids were in satisfactory condition upon their return; most were transferred to the *St. George* in February 1706 as a matter of course.

Death and incapacitation depleted Royal Navy crews. The *Kingston*, having lost nine men to death and three to desertion by the date of its departure from York Town, took on at least seventeen fresh men while in this colony. Some, such as William Rudd who signed on as ship's chaplain, along with his servant William Henry Rudd, came on board willingly, eventually to depart the service on 16 February at Chatham. Others were taken from merchantmen. The experience of Andrew Langrishouse of Virginia indicates another pattern: enlisted on 15 August as a volunteer, he "Ran" on 1 September.[99] In total, the *Kingston* and the *Falkland* buried fifteen men in Virginia in 1705, but higher mortality—and morbidity—was experienced by naval ships that journeyed to the Chesapeake after cruises in the West Indies. HMS *Ruby*, another fourth-rate with a complement of

260 men, buried nineteen crewmen in August 1697 after arriving with Vice Admiral John Nevell's ill-fated squadron.[100]

In respect to mortality, though, the one identified case of the early eighteenth century that stands out is the 1708 voyage of the fourth-rate warship on convoy duty, HMS *Oxford* (table 6.3). As noted previously, William Black reported life-threatening morbidity for nearly 100 individuals upon arrival in Virgina, and the accumulated deaths of another thirty. The ship departed from Portsmouth on 7 March with a complement of 248 crew members, twenty-seven marines, and an unknown number of passengers. By the time the ship anchored at Point Comfort on 18 June, the ship's books recorded the deaths of twenty-eight men. Fourteen more died in Virginia prior to departure on 4 October, followed by twelve on the return voyage and three in immediate postvoyage mortality after arrival at Spithead on 3 December.[101]

The difference in outward morbidity between Black's figure of thirty and the twenty-eight identified in the musterbooks may, perhaps, represent the death of two passengers; certainly, for the return passage the captain's log recorded one death of an individual on 2 November who is not in the muster records and therefore was likely a passenger.[102] In any case, the death of fifty-seven seamen and marines over eleven months constitutes the highest level of mortality at present known for any direct England-Virginia-England naval voyage of the early eighteenth century. Most existing scholarship on mortality in the eighteenth-century Royal Navy has not been presented in ways that permit the calculation of crude death rates, but the loss experienced by the *Oxford* is considerably higher

Table 6.3. Naval Mortality, the *Oxford*, 1 January 1708–15 January 1709

Month	prevoyage	Outward	Virginia	return	postvoyage
January	0				
February	1				
March	0	0			
April		6			
May		14			
June		8	5		
July			4		
August			3		
September			2		
October			0	3	
November				8	
December				1	2
January					1
Totals	1	28	14	12	3

Table 6.4.   Royal Navy Mortality, Selected Fourth-Rates

Ship	Location	Year	Population at risk[i]	Deaths	CDR per month per thousand[ii]
Tiger	Mediterranean	1706	243.5	5	2.05
Guernsey	Virginia	1703	227.5	27	14.65
Kingston	Virginia	1705	360	24	5.60
Falkland	Virginia	1705	247.5	24	8.68
Oxford	Virginia	1708	264	57	19.23

i. The average population at risk is defined as the population at the beginning of the voyage, minus one-half the voyage deaths, plus one-half of any additions to the ship's complement. See the method described in: Robin Haines, R. Shlomowitz, and L. Brennan, "Maritime Mortality Revisited," International Journal of Maritime History 8 (1996): 136. Because the number of passengers and their losses are both uncertain, this information is excluded.

ii. The crude death is the number of voyage deaths per thousand of the population at risk, per month of 30 days. See Raymond L. Cohn, "Maritime Mortality in the Eighteenth and Nineteenth Centuries: A Survey," International Journal of Maritime History 1 (1989): 160–64.

than the average death rate of 9.15 suffered by the navy in the West Indies during the campaign of 1758.[103] Crude death rates have been established for some oceanic travel of the eighteenth century, and this research produces rates of, for example, 15.8 for adult male German migrants to Pennsylvania, 1727–1805; 15.3 for Dutch voyages to Batavia, 1620–1780; and 11.8 for the European crews of French slave ships, 1714–1778.[104] The Virginia evidence certainly reinforces the conclusion that maritime death rates were highly variable for individual voyages.[105] However, the case of the Kingston also demonstrates that it was not the mere presence of infectious disease on board a vessel that substantially raised the likelihood of death. A great deal depended upon the precise nature of the disease and the characteristics of the populations at risk. Mortality, therefore, cannot fruitfully be studied in isolation from an analysis of morbidity (see table 6.4).

It remains unclear why the voyage of 1708 was so deadly. For all of 1706, in spite of the Oxford's service on the African coast, total mortality on that ship was thirteen, three of these deaths being drownings; in 1707 the figure was also thirteen, with five of these deaths resulting from an engagement with a French vessel.[106] Once again, the mortality pattern of 1708 is different from that experienced by the Guernsey in 1703, or by the Kingston in 1705 and by the Falkland in the same year. The Oxford lost far more on the outward voyage, and as many as the Kingston and Falkland combined in Virginia (during a stay twice as long), but far less than the Guernsey and the Kingston at the conclusion of service. Most certainly, the Oxford brought contagious disease to Virginia in 1708. Could this have been why Lieutenant Governor Jennings identified the August and September 1708 fevers as exceptionally severe and "extraordinary," or was it connected to the "pestilential distemper" which ravaged Virginia's population by April 1709? And what was its nature? The deaths—beginning with three ordinary seamen on 3, 5, and 12 April—began too early in the voyage to be the consequence of scurvy; the ship was taking on some fresh foodstuffs as late as 3 March.[107] By the time of the last two deaths at sea on 17 June, shortly after reaching Lynnhaven Bay, the ship had lost fourteen able seamen, nine ordinary seamen, two marines, a captain's servant, a member of the carpenter's crew, and a quarter gunner. Over the next week another four ordinary seamen died, as the ship's officers speedily watered the vessel and then used the sails and several booms to construct on shore, at Hampton, tents for the ill. A total of ninety-two sick were sent to the camp on 22 June, one dying while being transported ashore; that day alone saw the funerals of three crewmen, followed by a night of heavy rain.[108] This outward voyage had been—at fourteen weeks and six days—considerably longer in duration than the average convoy crossing. The *Oxford* experienced difficulty in locating a southerly current following watering at Madeira on 6–8 April. However, even a voyage of average duration would have seen exceptional mortality, for early May was the deadliest period aboard ships that year, with eight deaths in the week of 7 to 13 May alone.

The continuation of deaths in the weeks following arrival of the *Oxford* indicates that scurvy could not have been the only health challenge confronting the crew. Although precise figures are lacking, the men remained sickly, and/or fell into fresh distempers, for some time. The *Oxford* had to borrow forty sailors from the *Burlington* on 3 August to permit a two-week cruise off the capes. Even then, the cruise was cut short for health reasons: on 15 August the master noted, "The weather Excessive hot[.] ye Capt & Severall of our people very ill."[109] Following steady rain in early July, the weather had turned hot and sultry. Fresh removals to the tents are a certainty, but presumably so mundane that the logs refer only to the unusual circumstance of the erection of a new tent on 3 September for the cooper; as a petty officer he warranted separate accommodation. Incapacitated sailors remained in the camp until at least 23 September when, in the midst of watering and preparations for departure, they began to return to the ship. The master's log in this instance clearly states that sick men, not recovered crewmen, were being brought aboard.[110] This year, the *Oxford* took on thirty-five new men while in Virginia, of whom thirty-two were impressed from the assembling merchantmen as the tobacco fleet prepared to sail. Several of these men would die before arrival in England. Disease, of unknown nature, clearly followed the men aboard the ship, and it struck down a quartermaster on 31 October and a second quarter gunner on 11 November. Contagion is also suggested by the dismissal on 6 January 1709 from naval service of the surgeon's mate, Hugh Montgomery, due to sickness, and the death of the surgeon, William Leake, on 14 January.[111] Apart from three drownings, no causes for the fifty-eight deaths are specified in the records. The dispersed chronology of mortality, the increase in life-threatening distempers during the hot August weather, and the evidence from 1705 all suggest another complex mixture of health problems on board the *Oxford*, although one differing from that experienced on the *Kingston* three years earlier. The increased mortality while at Virginia apparently resulted from three factors: the presence of a particularly virulent contagious disease during the outward voyage; the long duration of the stay; and the presence of the crew in the Chesapeake during the fever season of late summer. The one truly exceptional feature is the unexplained outward contagion.[112]

For Virginia and the Royal Navy, mortality and morbidity held several consequences. If the case of the *Guernsey* in 1703 suggests that its crew suffered from contagious disease picked up at York Town, the *Kingston* in 1705 and the *Oxford* in 1708 brought more than a modest share of health risks in their wake. Certainly, further study of the relationship between shipboard and port and settlement epidemics is warranted. Morbidity, overall, incapacitated Royal Navy ships, delaying departures, preventing or restricting cruising, and creating work environments at sea where overworked crews were susceptible to fatigue and human error. Perhaps most importantly, the navy's experience with disease is suggestive of wider problems within the far larger, ill-documented merchant marine engaged in transatlantic commerce. Here, all that we possess at the present is anecdotal evidence. Nonetheless, this can reveal features of complex patterns, as in the case of the British sailor Nathaniel Uring. In Virginia from late autumn 1698 to June 1699, Uring soon after arrival contracted smallpox on board a vessel recently arrived from Bristol, went ashore ill to convalesce in the care of hard-up planters, subsequently developed a spring fever, and finally ventured himself sick aboard another merchant ship for the return trip to England.[113] Uring was ill or convalescing for his entire time in the colony, caught up in an intricate web of morbidity, impossible to trace but suggestive in its implications.

The Atlantic basin in the early modern period was uniquely susceptible to the widespread transmission of disease, as individuals and populations moved from one disease environment to another.[114] To date, attention has focused largely upon the experiences, perceptions, and life expectancies of the migrants.[115] However, the itinerant sailor also had forsaken the disease environment of his childhood, and he became both victim and villain in the spread of transatlantic disease to an extent at present unknown. The evidence presented above implies that the Royal Navy workforce, more restricted in freedom of movement and social interaction than merchant seamen, quickly fell into the disease pattern of their temporary environment in Virginia, not least because the convoys were present during the malarial outbreaks. Containment on board ship or in tent camps offered no protection. The "seasoning," then, had a direct impact upon this itinerant workforce. But the ships' complements also carried with them their own unique disease microenvironments. These were, it seems, different from (although no doubt influenced by) the British patterns of their origins,[116] and were presumably in constant flux as personnel and locations altered. In these conditions, seafarers could be carriers of some infections, and victims of many.

All aspects of the British naval presence affected the economy of Virginia, and morbidity was no exception. Opportunities for employment in nursing care, and attendent epidemiological risks, were left in part to the private initiatives or desires of individual captains. Although on some other occasions the authorities arranged this service, the documentation is silent for 1705. The rental of houses to accommodate the sick in 1706–1707 was seemingly a restricted action not repeated during the war, but practiced on occasions in the second and third decades of the century.[117] The official sale of fresh victuals and drink for the incapacitated alongside private sales of useful dietary supplments and dehabilitating liquors to sick and healthy seamen alike were possibly the greatest direct economic advantages. In October 1701 Captain James Moody of the coastal guardship, the fourth-rate HMS *Southampton*, requested that the Council of Virginia arrange for credit for his purchase of provisions and for the care of his sick. A jaded council replied that Royal Navy sick had been looked after upon credit before, not least for the former guardship of 1697–1700, the sixth-rate *Essex Prize*, and no reimbursement had been forthcoming to date. Nonetheless, rather than the royal service should suffer, credit would be advanced once again.[118] In the same period, across the Atlantic, wholesale failure to pay the quarterers contracted with the care of English seamen in private sick quarters led to outright refusals to take in additional men without cash in hand.[119] It may be that Heart was left largely on his own in 1705, and the Commissioners of Sick and Wounded rented sick accommodation briefly in the following fiscal year because of recalcitrance in Virginia over unpaid obligations. Certainly, in April 1708 the Virginia Council seized the initiative: it ordered that a house be rented to accommodate the sick from the HMS *Garland* (which had arrived in the preceding February to serve briefly as guardship prior to sailing in convoy with the homeward summer tobacco fleet), with the rent to be paid out of the queen's standing tax of two shillings per hogshead of tobacco. This practice of coordinated care of the incapacitated in lodgings ashore was repeated in the following year for 106 seamen from two Royal Navy convoy vessels.[120]

The continuing problem of delayed, haphazard reimbursements may have helped to inspire the request in August 1710 by Lieutenant Governor Spottis-wood for construction of sick barracks as part of a proposed fortification and naval careening facility at Port Comfort, for the use of sailors requiring medical attention and rest. This appeal, more modest than McClurg's later recommenda-tion, would nonetheless have placed the financial obligation for care firmly on the British central government. Although unsuccessful in his effort, Spottiswood was sufficiently aware of British priorities, so he couched his argument exclusively in terms of the prevention of desertion, "which now frequently happens as soon as they [seamen] begin to recover," rather than mention superior health care for the incapacitated.[121] However, the preferred, less expensive, response to desertion remained actions to improve enforcement of the law, and ministerial support in England for Spottiswood's proposed sick quarters appears to have been nonexis-tent. Certainly the Board of Trade and Plantations took no action.[122] In view of the ad hoc measures current on both sides of the Atlantic, each convoy continued to bring with it both sick and diseased seamen and administrative variations on the same themes of ad hoc measures and uncertain consequences.

Following Queen Anne's War, the navy moved very slowly to implement a practice in Virginia whereby at least some of the incapacitated were placed under the care of local surgeons, usually ones resident at Hampton, who provided care and medicines, and arranged with private householders for quarters, subsistence, nursing, and funerals.[123] However, in an age of fiscal retrenchment at Whitehall, the Navy Board routinely balked at the relatively substantial associated costs. Care ashore in tent camps or onboard ship involved minimal additional expenses. By way of comparison, the charges of quartering 106 seamen ashore in 1709 for up to five weeks amounted to 97.1.0, inclusive of nursing but excluding medical care (apparently in this instance provided by the ship surgeons), and the only saving was on ship's victuals. Indeed, the strenuous attempts by the Commissioners for Sick and Wounded Seamen and their successors on the Navy Board to hold exter-nal medical personnel to an unrealistic flat fee of six shillings and eight pence per cure, including the cost of medicines, is one reason why surgeons and physicians, in Virginia and elsewhere, were more than willing to take responsibility for a "total care package" in which their own extra remuneration could be hidden from direct view.[124]

The move toward external medical treatment in lodgings appears to have orig-inated in the individual actions of ship captains (possibly encouraged by the Vir-ginia authorities), presumably as a consequence of concerns for shipboard morale or effective manning, or in order to retain the ship's medical personnel for onboard care. It was routinely challenged and criticized by naval administrators, who sought to limit the practice to emergencies and life-threatening disorders.

When Captain Mayne of the HMS *Biddeford* made extensive use of Alexander Mackenzie, surgeon of Hampton, between April 1727 and March 1730, producing a charge of 285.18.0 sterling, the Navy Board instituted a wide-ranging, protracted investigation, complete with allegations of corruption, collusion, and malfeasance, even though the employment appeared to have been beneficial to the men and the ship's surgeon testified in support of Mackenzie and Mayne.[125] Other, more cautious, commanders used external shore care very sparingly: the two-month visit to Virginia by the HMS *Lyme* in 1719 saw only a single crewman going into quarters, and even he was removed from thence too soon and had to return for a second period of convalescence; presumably the other sick found their places in the customary tent camps.[126] Thus McClurg's comment of 1747 on the needless exposure of incapacitated seamen to an inclement climate was but one more voice raised against the frugality of the British central administration. Benevolent paternalism from a distance was not Whitehall's strength; those on the spot were better placed to view the individual suffering, and to observe the social and economic consequences of ill health.

Space does not permit a full discussion as to whether the eighteenth century witnessed changes to the underlying human and environmental challenges to health for the Royal Navy's workforce in Virginian waters. It is, however, instructive to draw attention to some of the documentation that arose out of the next period of warfare. Early in the War of Jenkin's Ear, HMS *Winchester* (complement 300) and HMS *Southsea Castle* (complement 250) were dispatched on convoy duty to Virginia. The documentation for the *Winchester* is provided in the introduction to Part 3 of this volume. Both warships experienced substantial morbidity and mortality.[127] Indeed, the sixty-two deaths over eleven months on the *Winchester*, between September 1740 and July 1741, provide a crude death rate very close to that for the *Oxford* in 1708. It is noteworthy, however, that these vessels arrived in the late autumn, and wintered in Virginia. Both warships experienced mortality spikes early in their stay at Virginia, and later near to the conclusion of the return voyage. Both experienced significant morbidity spikes, the first close to the timing of the heaviest mortality in Virginia, and the second on the homeward passage. In this instance, a temporary naval hospital had been established at Hampton, Virginia, to which at least some of the incapacitated sailors were transferred. This evidence provides an approximation of the chronology of morbidity (while in port): for the *Winchester*, illness peaked at forty "sick ashore" in each of two musters of 3 and 10 January 1741; for the *Southsea Castle*, documented illness peaked at fifty-four and fifty-five "sick ashore," respectively, at the musters of 15 and 22 December 1740.[128] While it cannot be known whether any incapacitated seamen remained on board the vessels, and officers were never admitted to a general hospital, the levels of documented illness (which peaked in the *Southsea Castle* at 33.1 percent) point to the ongoing importance of the theme of morbidity for the Royal Navy in Virginia well into the eighteenth century.

In the absence of documentation similar to the evidence provided by Henry Heart, it is difficult to evaluate the typicality of the 1705 experience. Certainly, the evidence indicates that Royal Navy vessels habitually arrived in Atlantic seaboard ports with their share of sick, that the incapacitated were speedily moved ashore, either with or without the assistance of the local community, and that morbidity was generally a more significant problem than mortality. The year 1705 was typical in respect to both customary health-care provision and administrative inertia. Well might McClurg call, forty years later, for the establishment of a naval hospital in Virginia, although the evidence to date gives us reason to subject to further scrutiny his claim that distempers routinely carried off "the Choisest and Ablest Seamen." The essential problem appears to have been incapacitation, not fatality. When the Italian academic Bernardino Ramazzini in 1700 initiated the systematic study of occupational illness, mariners were an afterthought and—when included—were studied in the abstract.[129] Many, even in Britain, were content to follow his example, providing general, often superficial, assessments of the maritime susceptibility to ill health.[130] Although knowledge has improved since that age, the study of the incidence of death and illness within this Royal Navy manual workforce is of interest in enlarging upon our all-too-limited understanding of the health risks and health care within the expanding Anglo-American world.

Notes

1. Public Record Office [P.R.O.], London, ADM 97/85 (unnumbered).

2. P.R.O., ADM 97/85 (unnumbered)

3. For a discussion of projecting for the early eighteenth-century British colonies, see: J. D. Alsop, "The Age of the Projectors: British Imperial Strategy in the North Atlantic in the War of Spanish Succession," *Acadiensis*, XXI (1991), 30–53.

4. Wyndham B. Blanton, *Medicine in Virginia in the Eighteenth Century* (Richmond, 1931), p. 328; Martin Kaufman et. al., *Dictionary of American Medical Biography* (Westport, 1984), 2: 472; Harold D. Langley, *A History of Medicine in the Early U.S. Navy* (Baltimore, 1995), pp. 8–17.

5. D. Crewe, *Yellow Jack and the Worm: British Naval Administration in the West Indies 1739–1748* (Liverpool, 1993). Christian Buchet, *La Lutte pour L'Espace Caraibe et la Facade Atlantique de L'Amérique Centrale et du sud (1672–1763)*, Paris, 1991), pp. 693–818. For the French experience of mortality in the most aggressive colonial campaign of this war, see: James Pritchard, *Anatomy of a Naval Disaster: The 1746 French Expedition to North America* (Montreal, 1995).

6. J. D. Alsop, "The Health Care of Army Recruits for the Eighteenth-Century Mediterranean," *Journal of the Society for Army Historical Research* 76 (1998): 5–10.

7. For example: *Calendar of State Papers, Colonial Series, America and the West Indies*, eds. J. W. Fortescue, C. Headlam, and K. Davies (London, 1901–69), 20: 221, 251, 21: 79–80; *Royal Instructions to British Colonial Governors 1670–1776*, ed. Leonard W. Labaree (New York, 1967) 1: 442–43. A. P. Middleton, "The Chesapeake Convoy System, 1662–1763," *William and Mary Quarterly*, 3d ser., 3 (1946): 183–207; Patrick Crowhurst, *The Defense of British Trade, 1689–1815* (Folkestone, 1977), pp. 140–48; D. W. Jones, *War and Economy in the Age of William III and Marlborough* (Oxford, 1988), pp. 104–5, 154–62; S. O. Margolin, "Guardships on the Virginia Station, 1667–1767," *American Neptune*, 55 (1995): pp. 24, 32–33. The competition for seamen in mid-eighteenth-century American ports is outlined in: Carl E. Swanson, *Predators and Prizes: American Privateering and Imperial Warfare, 1739–1748* (Columbia, S.C., 1991), pp. 76–112.

8. John J. Keevil, *Medicine and the Navy, 1649–1714* (London, 1958), pp. 244–45, 260.

9. R. D. Merriman, ed., *Queen Anne's Navy: Documents Concerning the Administration of the Navy of Queen Anne, 1702–1714* (London, 1961), p. 221; Guildhall Library, London, MS 5264 (list of case records delivered to Barber-Surgeons' Company).

10. Keevil, *Medicine and the Navy*, p. 247; Christopher Lloyd and J. L. Coulter, *Medicine and the Navy, 1715–1815* (London, 1961), p. 23. For the only known survival: J. D. Alsop, "Sickness in the British Mediterranean Fleet: The *Tiger's* Journal of 1706," *War and Society* 11 (1993): 57–76. The extant sea-surgeons' journals in P.R.O., ADM 101 begin with the 1790s.

11. Merriman, *Queen Anne's Navy*, p. 221.

12. Alsop, "Sickness in Mediterranean Fleet," 57–76.

13. The lack of quantitative information on early American naval and maritime morbidity is particularly striking: Maurice B. Gordon, *Naval and Maritime Medicine during the American Revolution* (Ventnor, N.J., 1978), pp. 93–105, and passim. The best study remains the overview provided by John Duffy, "The Passage to the Colonies," *Mississippi Valley Historical Review* 38 (1951): 21–38. Most studies of colonial medicine pay scant attention to maritime themes: Maurice B. Gordon, "Medicine in Colonial New Jersey and Adjacent Areas," *Bulletin of the History of Medicine* 17 (1945): 38–60; idem., *Aesculapius Comes to the Colonies: The Story of the Early Days of Medicine in the Thirteen Original Colonies* (Ventnor, N.J., 1949; repr. 1970); Wyndham B. Blanton, *Medicine in Virginia in the Seventeenth Century* (Richmond, 1930); Blanton, *Eighteenth Century*; W. J. Bell Jr. "Medical Practice in Colonial America," *Bulletin of the History of Medicine* 31 (1957): 442–53; Larry L. Burkhart, *The Good Fight: Medicine in Colonial Pennsylvania* (New York, 1989), pp. 34–38, 185–87.

14. John Brewer, *The Sinews of War: War, Money and the English State, 1688–1783* (New York, 1989); Michael Duffy, "The Foundations of British Naval Power," in M. Duffy, ed., *The Military Revolution and the State* (Exeter, 1980), pp. 49–85.

15. Christopher Lloyd, "The Evolution of Naval Medicine," in *A Guide to the Sources of British Military History*, ed. Robin Higham (Berkeley, 1971), p. 607.

16. P.R.O., ADM 31–33, 36, 39. By this period the admiralty had in place a complex system of checks to prevent fraud, especially for the muster records used to establish victualling entitlements. Pay and muster books were independently created and, for our purposes, include identical information. When both records are extant for a ship, research has demonstrated that they invariably agree.

17. In spite of the limitations of muster records, published research on morbidity in the early-eighteenth-century British Navy is derived exclusively from this source. This scholarship paradoxically produces statistics for the unhealthy Caribbean theatre of operations far lower than those presented here for Virginia, because the musters reveal only some aspects of shipboard incapacitation. Crewe, *Yellow Jack*, pp. 65–98; Buchet, *La Lutte*, pp. 709–13.

18. N. A. M. Rodger, *The Wooden World: An Anatomy of the Georgian Navy* (London, 1986), p. 104. For confirmation of Rodger's conclusion for the early eighteenth century: Alsop, "Sickness in Mediterranean Fleet," p. 66 and passim.

19. The allocation of vessels, and their monthly locations, are recorded in: P.R.O., ADM 8/2–12. Trade protection is covered in: Crowhunt, *Defense of Trade*, pp. 140–48, and Middleton, "Chesapeake Convoy System," pp. 183–207.

20. P.R.O., E 351/2561–5 (financial accounts for the Commissioners for Sick and Wounded Seamen and Prisoners of War 1700–1708), passim.

21. P.R.O. E 351/2563, 2564.

22. For example, the Admiralty instructions for the guidance and government of the Commissioners of the Register, and the Commissioners for Sick and Wounded Seamen, 9 July 1698 and 20 June 1702: National Maritime Museum, ADM/E/5, 1–22, p. 18, ADM/E/1 (unpaginated).

23. For example: *Calendar of State Papers, Domestic Series, Of the Reign of William III*, ed. William J. Hardy and Edward Bateson (London, 1895–1937), 8: 423; Newton D. Mereness, ed., *Travels in the American Colonies* (New York, 1916), p. 38; R. B. [Nathaniel Crouch], *The English Empire in America* (London, 1685), pp. 125, 136–37.

24. Blanton, *Eighteenth Century*, p. 51; *Calendar of State Papers, Colonial*, 24: 96, 481, 25: 5, 83, 411. See also: Thomas P. Hughes, *Medicine in Virginia, 1607–1699* (Williamsburg, 1957), pp. 31–36, 43.

25. Darret B. Rutman, Charles Wetherell, and Anita H. Rutman, "Rhythms of Life: Black and White Seasonality in the Early Chesapeake," *Journal of Interdisciplinary History* (1980): 36, 43–46. See also the eighteenth-century description of these sickness cycles in: William Curry, *An Historical Account of the Climates and Disease of the United States of America* (Philadelphia, 1792), pp. 271–72, 274–76, 283, 289, 302, 308–21.

26. "A Letter from Mr. John Clayton Rector of Croston at Wakefield in Yorkshire, to the Royal Society, May 12, 1688," in *Miscellanea Curiosa*, ed. William Denhan (London, 1726), 3: 386–87.

27. John P. Ehrman, *The Navy in the Wars of William III, 1689–1697* (Cambridge, 1953); Merriman, ed., *Queen Anne's Navy*, passim.

28. William Hodges, *Humble Proposals for the Relief, Encouragement, Security and Happiness of*

the Loyal, Courageous Seamen of England (London, 1695), pp. 5, 22, 30. See also the argument advanced in 1747 by the physician John Huxham in his "A method for preserving the health of seamen in long cruises and voyages," printed in Huxham, *An Essay on Fevers* (2d ed., London, 1750), pp. 264–65.

29. P.R.O., ADM 36/3088; Alsop, "Sickness in Mediterranean Fleet," pp. 62–63.

30. National Maritime Museum, Greenwich, ADM/E/3, fol. 2.

31. Alsop, "Health Care of Army Recruits," pp. 5–10.

32. Ian K. Steele, *The English Atlantic 1675–1740* (Oxford, 1986).

33. *The London Gazette*, nos. 3730 (28 Aug.–1 Sept. 1701), 3862 (12–16 Nov. 1702); *The Post-Boy*, no. 1108 (20–22 June 1702); *The Flying Post*, no. 531 (4–6 Oct. 1698).

34. This point is established through comparison of the logs kept by different officers aboard the same ships, and from the silence of some logs in cases where it is known that seamen were sent ashore.

35. P.R.O., ADM 51/4171/9 (Captain's log, HMS *Dreadnought*, on convoy duty to Virginia, 1704).

36. See, for example: James Christie, *An Abstract of Some Years Observations Concerning such General and Unperceived Occasions of Sickliness in Fleets and Ships of War* ([London,] 1709), pp. 3–8; William Cockburn, *A Continuation of the Account of the Nature, Causes, Symptoms and Cure of the Distempers that are Incident to Seafaring People* (London, 1697), p. 86.

37. W. Passenger to F. Nicholson, 23 August 1700: Huntington Library, San Marino, MS. EL 9786.

38. For the limitations of this approach, see: Gordon, *Medicine during the American Revolution*, pp. 102–5.

39. Merriman, ed., *Queen Anne's Navy*, p. 220.

40. National Maritime Museum, ADM/E/3, fol. 43 (and attachments).

41. P.R.O., E 351/2563, 2564.

42. P.R.O., ADM 51/338/2–3 (captain's logbooks, the *Falkland*), 52/166/5 (master's logbook, the *Falkland*), 52/200/14 (master's logbook, the *Kingston*), passim.

43. P.R.O., ADM 52/200/14, fol. 28.

44. Ibid., fols. 25, 27.

45. Ibid., fol. 30; P.R.O. ADM 51/338/2, unfoliated.

46. Note to Secretary of State Hedges and the Commissioners for Trade and Plantations: *Calendar of State Papers, Colonial*, 22: 623–28.

47. P.R.O., ADM 52/200/14, fols. 22, 28–29. The average duration of the outward voyage for Royal Navy warships between 1676 and 1715 was eleven and one-half weeks, with a range from a low of seven weeks up to twenty-five weeks. The average duration of the homeward voyage (to the Lizard) was six and one-half weeks. Steele, *English Atlantic*, pp. 45–51. It has been demonstrated that the British route to the West Indies which, as in the case of these Virginia convoys, went via Madeira produced an ocean passage approximately two weeks longer than that experienced by the French navy, and consequently provided higher mortality levels. Christian Buchet, "Des Routes Maritimes Europe-Antilles et de Leurs Incidences sur la Rivalit Franco-Britannique," *Histoire, Economie et Société*, 13 (1994): 563–82.

48. Hugh Jones, *The Present State of Virginia*, ed. R. L. Morton (Chapel Hill, 1956), p. 72.

49. David Syrett and R. L. DiNardo, eds. *Commissioned Sea Officers of the Royal Navy, 1660–1815* (London, 1994), pp. 85, 448.

50. P.R.O., ADM 51/338/2, 52/200/14, fols. 40, 43–44.

51. The following information on mortality aboard these vessels is extracted from: P.R.O., ADM 33/248 (pay books, the *Kingston*, 1 July 1704–19 April 1706), 33/239, 253 (pay books, the *Falkland*, 1 July 1704–30 June 1706). The calculations for the *Falkland* exclude the company of marines, examined below. There exists no consistent method of determining mortality among passengers carried aboard Royal Navy vessels (in this case of the *Kingston*, for example, among Lieutenant Governor Nott's entourage) when they were in receipt of neither wages nor victuals.

52. P.R.O., ADM 33/248.

53. P.R.O., ADM 51/338/2, 52/200/14, fol. 40.

54. P.R.O., ADM 51/338/2.

55. P.R.O., ADM 52/166/5, fol. 19.

56. P.R.O., ADM 52/200/14, fol. 29.

57. National Maritime Museum, ADM/E/3, attachments beside folio 43. All subsequent information is drawn from this record, or from Heart's accompanying petition of 20 April 1706. Partway through the listing, Heart left the final two columns of his evidence incomplete, apparently because (apart from several deaths) the information was identical: the incapacitated seamen were all returned to the vessel on 27 September.

58. Alsop, "Sickness in Mediterranean Fleet," p. 70. The mortality on board the *Oxford* is examined below.

59. Duffy, "Passage," p. 22.

60. Captain V. Pearse to the Commissioners for Sick and Wounded Seamen, Virginia, 1 July 1734: P.R.O., ADM 97/85.

61. John Pringle, *Observations on the Diseases of the Army, in Camp and Garrison* (2d ed., London, 1753), p. 79; Donald Monro, *An Account of the Diseases which were most frequent in the British Military Hospitals* (London, 1764), p. 381; John Jones, *Plain Concise Practical Remarks, on the Treatment of Wounds and Fractures, to which is added an appendix, on camp and military hospitals; principally designed, for the use of young military and naval surgeons, in North America* (Philadelphia, 1776), p. 106; James Lind, *An Essay on Diseases Incidental to Europeans in Hot Climates* (3d ed., London, 1777), p. 34. See also: Karen O. Kupperman, "Fear of Hot Climates in the Anglo-American Colonial Experience," *William and Mary Quarterly*, 3d ser., 41 (1984): 213–40.

62. R. Bell to the Commissioners for Sick and Wounded Seamen, Hampton, Virginia, 21 June 1755: P.R.O., ADM 97/85. Similar problems at another important location in tidewater Virginia are outlined in Marianne Bagley, "The History of the Public Health of Norfolk, Virginia, up to 1860," (M.A. thesis, Duke University, 1939), pp. 5–20.

63. Thomas Willis, *The London Practice of Physick* (London, 1692), pp. 531–47; John Astruc, *Academical Lectures on Fevers* (London, 1747), pp. 41–79.

64. William Cockburn, *Sea Diseases* (London, 1706), pp. 6, 206. Willis, *London Practice*, pp. 353–69; Walter Charleton, *De Scorbuto* (London, 1672), pp. 220–27.

65. *Calendar of State Papers, Colonial*, 22: 594.

66. Cockburn, *Sea Diseases*, p. 4; Alsop, "Sickness in the Mediterranean Fleet," pp. 69–70.

67. Rodger, *Wooden World*, pp. 360–63.

68. P.R.O., ADM 52/166/5, fol. 23.

69. *Calendar of State Papers, Colonial*, 22: 624–25. For the "seasoning," see Darret B. Rutman and A. H. Rutman, "Of Agues and Fevers: Malaria in the Early Chesapeake," *William and Mary Quarterly*, 3d ser., 33 (1976): 31–60.

70. The *Falkland*: John Sheller, armorer; Edward Ferguson, ordinary seaman. The *Kingston*: John Hayward and Edward Feveryeare, able seamen; Andrew Langrishouse, ordinary seaman; Issac Preston, master's mate. P.R.O., ADM 33/253, 248. The deserters from the *Kingston* were from the ship, not the tents.

71. Eighteenth-century advice for tent camps was to locate them on high, breezy ground away from immediate seawater (sea air in the early years of the century was considered noxious by some): Monro, *Diseases*, p. 338; Jones, *Practical Remarks*, p. 108. The alternative location for the tents, the beach, would have placed the sick directly adjacent to the port's commerce. Although presumably tents were erected in the same location year after year, this site has not been identified from local lore or documentation.

72. Monro, *Diseases*, pp. 344–45; Jones, *Practical Remarks*, p. 109.

73. Robert Straus, *Medical Care for Seamen: The Origin of Public Medical Service in the United States* (New Haven, 1950), pp. 89–90. Virginia's first quarantine legislation was enacted in 1722, in reaction to the outbreak of plague at Marseilles. Not until 1767 was quarantine extended to include Europeans suspected of carrying typhus or smallpox; slavers were first included in 1772: *Journals of the House of Burgess of Virginia*, ed. Henry R. McIlwaine and J. P. Kennedy (Richmond, 1905–15), 5: pp. 340–3, 345, 353; Blanton, *Eighteenth Century*, pp. 397–98.

74. P.R.O., ADM 52/200/14, fols. 29–32.

75. This statement is based upon an examination of the surviving surgeon's certificates and postings in P.R.O., ADM 106. The information for Heart (or Hart) is found in P.R.O., ADM 106/2958.

76. P.R.O., ADM 33/248, ADM 106/2957 (Hull), 2959 (Kerr), 2960 (Masterson).

77. National Maritime Museum, ADM/E/3, fol. 43.

78. Cockburn, *Continuation*, p.114; J. Worth Estes, "The Medical Properties of Food in the Eighteenth Century," *Journal of the History of Medicine and Allied Sciences*, LI (1996), 127–54.

79. John Moyle, *Chirurgus Marinus: Or the Sea—Chirurgion* (London, 4th ed., 1702) pp. 226–38 (fevers), 238–47 (dysentery), 247–58 (scurvy), 258–66 (agues); William Cockburn, *An Account of the Nature, Causes, Symptoms and Cure of the Distempers that are Incident to Seafaring People* (London, 1696), p. 152 (scurvy), and passim.

80. Alsop, "Sickness in Mediterranean Fleet," pp. 70–71. Surgeon John Atkins, who began his naval service by 1703, later commented that not one-twentieth of the medicines listed in the standard pharmacopoeia were carried to sea, and this proportion could be reduced still further with no adverse effects: John Atkins, *The Navy-Surgeon* (London, 1734), pp. iii–iv.

81. Mary J. Dobson, "Mortality Gradients and Disease Exchanges: Comparisons from Old England and Colonial America," *Social History of Medicine* 2 (1989): 259–97.

82. Harold J. Cook, "Practical Medicine and the British Armed Forces after the Glorious Revolution," *Medical History* 34 (1990): 1–26.

83. Cockburn, *Sea Diseases* (3d ed., London, 1736), pp. 204–8. Although all cases noted here date from the 1690s, not all were included in the edition of 1696; those that were included possibly influenced (not simply reflected) practice. For a more intrusive course of treatment, see the highly regarded recommendations of Thomas Willis, *London Practice*, pp. 326–79. For Cockburn's influence on policy decisions relating to health care, see Cook, "Practical Medicine," pp. 21–25.

84. Cockburn, *Sea Diseases*, pp. 71–72, 117–86, 208–23.

85. Captain J. Compton to the Commissioners for Sick and Wounded Seamen, York River, 20 February 1737: P.R.O., ADM 97/85.

86. P.R.O., ADM 97/85, passim.

87. Allen Richman, "The Development of Medical Services in the United States Navy in the Age of Sail: 1815–1850" (Ph.D. dissertation, University of Minnesota, 1973), pp. 198–99.

88. Rutman and Rutman, "Fevers and Agues," pp. 31–60; Dobson, "Mortality Gradients," pp. 270–72; Todd L. Savitt, *Fevers, Agues, and Cures: Medical Life in Old Virginia* (Richmond, 1990); Edmund Berkeley and D. S. Berkeley, eds., *The Reverend John Clayton: A Parson with a Scientific Mind* (Charlottesville, 1965), p. 26.

89. Mary J. Dobson, *Contours of Death and Disease in Early Modern England* (Cambridge, 1997), p. 348.

90. Dobson, *Contours of Death*, p. 468; Dobson, "Mortality Gradients," pp. 266, 272, 280, 285; John Post, *Food Shortage, Climate Variability, and Epidemic Disease in Pre-Industrial Europe* (Ithaca, 1985) passim; C. V. Earle, "Environment, Disease, and Mortality in Early Virginia," in *Chesapeake in the Seventeenth Century*, eds. Thad W. Tate and D. L. Ammerman (Charlotte, 1979), pp. 96–127; Blanton, *Eighteenth Century*, p. 50; Todd L. Savitt, *Medicine and Slavery: The Diseases and Health Care of Blacks in Antebellum Virginia* (Urbana, 1978), p. 61.

91. Rutman and Rutman, "Fevers and Agues," p. 50.

92. Duffy, "Passage," pp. 27–28.

93. All the deaths for the *Kingston's* crew in Virginia took place in the tent camp. It seems likely, therefore, that (violent deaths apart) the mortality among the *Falkland's* crew, beginning on 11 September and totaling eight deaths by the day of departure, also occurred largely in the camp, to which location we know their incapacitated were sent. This being the case, the two deaths in camp for the *Kingston*, on 24 and 27 September, were apparently part of this wider trend, connected to the mortality on the early return voyage.

94. Steele, *English Atlantic*, pp. 43–44, 291–92.

95. David Ramsay, *A Sketch of the Soil, Climate, Weather, and Diseases of South-Carolina* (Charleston, 1796), pp. 14, 20–21; H. R. Merrens and G. O. Terry, "Dying in Paradise: Malaria, Mortality, and the Perceptual Environment in Colonial South Carolina," *Journal of Southern History* 50 (1984): 549.

96. J. Worth Estes, *Naval Surgeon: Life and Death at Sea in the Age of Sail* (Canton, Mass., 1998), pp. 180, 187; idem, "Medical Properties," p. 148.

97. J. Compton to the Commissioners for Sick and Wounded Seamen, York River, 20 February 1737: P.R.O., ADM 97/85.

98. Alsop, "Sickness in the Mediterranean Fleet," p. 66.

99. P.R.O., ADM 33/248.

100. Karen R. Dick, "Health Care and the British Navy, 1689–1713" (M.A. thesis, McMaster University, 1997), p. 96.

101. P.R.O., ADM 36/2343, 2344 (musterbooks, the *Oxford*, July 1707–March 1709).

102. P.R.O., ADM 51/4282/4 (unfoliated). In total, the captain's logbook recorded the deaths of twenty-two individuals, all unnamed; the master's logbook (ADM 52/249/7) recorded the deaths of twenty-two (mostly different) individuals, all but two identified by name. Clearly, neither officer considered the notation of death as mandatory material for their logs; repeatedly on days when crewmembers died the terse captain's log reads as in the entry for 12 April (when the third death took place): "Fair & Cleare Weather. Small winds: nothing Remarkable."

103. Rodger, *Wooden World.*, pp. 98–105; Crewe, *Yellow Jack*, pp. 68, 73–74; Buchet, *La Lutte*, pp. 704, 708.

104. James C. Riley, "Mortality on Long-Distance Voyages in the Eighteenth Century," *Journal of Economic History* 41 (1981): 655; Cohn, "Maritime Mortality," pp. 159–91; Haines, et al., "Mortality Revisited," p. 135. It should be noted that most published research is on mortality at sea, frequently on one-way voyages. The present study assesses round-trip voyage mortality, including time in port and the immediate postvoyage period.

105. Cohn, "Maritime Mortality," p. 175.

106. P.R.O., ADM 36/2344, fols. 145–92, 51/4282/2.

107. P.R.O., ADM 52/249/7, fols. 1–3.

108. P.R.O., ADM 51/4282/4, 52/249/7, fols. 11–12.

109. P.R.O., ADM 52/249/7. fol. 15.

110. Ibid., fols. 16, 17.

111. P.R.O., ADM 36/2344, fols. 54, 62v.

112. The virulence of the distemper rules out the likelihood of the *plasmodium vivax* malaria found in Britain, and the concentration of deaths among the lowest members of the ship's company perhaps speaks against dysentery, which was difficult to restrict so exactly in shipboard conditions. Typhus and typhoid fever were the most virulent contagious diseases routinely found within eighteenth-century European navies, and the onset

of death twenty-seven days after departure is consistent with the incubation period for typhoid fever. Interestingly, with one exception all the early deaths arose among the established crew, not from the ranks of the 129 recruits taken on board in December 1707 and January 1708 to compensate for earlier losses and removals. The *Oxford* had anchored in November and December of 1707 in the Portsmouth harbor, in January and February 1708 at Plymouth, and then at Portsmouth until departure. Large numbers of the crew were discharged from the service, sick, in November and December, and others were eventually discharged sick from both Plymouth and Gosport hospitals (P.R.O., ADM 36/2344, fos. 145–92). It may well be that the navy's preference for maintaining manning levels and restricting the issuing of sick tickets may have permitted the continuance of contagious disease aboard ship in this instance. We may note, as well, that during the outward voyage in May and June the *Oxford* made three exchanges, of two men each, with merchant ships in the convoy (presumably to acquire more serviceable seamen), with unknown consequences for the spread of disease.

113. *A History of the Voyages and Travels of Nathaniel Uring* (London, 1726), pp. 8–20.

114. Philip D. Curtin, "Epidemiology and the Slave Trade," Political Science Quarterly 83 (1968): 196–99; idem, *Disease and Imperialism Before the Nineteenth Century* (Minneapolis, 1990), pp. 1–14.

115. For example: Kupperman, "Hot Climates," pp. 213–14, 239–40; Lorena S. Walsh and Russell R. Menard, "Death in the Chesapeake: Two Life Tables for Men in Early Colonial Maryland," *Maryland Historical Magazine* 69 (1974): 211–27; Dobson, "Mortality Gradients," 259–97.

116. Dobson, *Contours of Death*, passim; Dobson, "Mortality Gradients," pp. 270–71, 279, 285, 287; Lucinda M. Beier, *Sufferers and Healers: The Experience of Illness in Seventeenth-Century England* (London, 1987), passim.

117. P.R.O., ADM 97/85, passim.

118. *Calendar of State Papers, Colonial,* XIX, 743, XXI, 79.

119. *Calendar of Treasury Papers, 1697–1702,* ed. Joseph Redington (London, 1871), pp. 6, 28, 55, 61, 70, 89, 109; *Calendar of Treasury Papers, 1702–1707,* ed. Joseph Redington (London: 1874), pp. 173–74, 176–77, 198.

120. *Executive Journals of the Council of Colonial Virginia,* ed. Henry R. McIlwaine et al., (Richmond, 1925–1966), III, 170; P.R.O., ADM 97/85; Blanton, *Eighteenth Century,* p. 289.

121. Alexander Spottiswood to the Commissioners of Trade and Plantations, 18 August 1710: *Calendar of State Papers, Colonial* 25: 171–72. Although Blanton (*Eighteenth Century,* p. 289) does not provide a reference, and misdates the proposal to "before 1705" (five years before Spottiswood arrived in Virginia), he apparently based his comments upon this same source. If so, he exaggerated the scope of Spottiswood's when he termed the facility a "hospital" and referred to surgical care. The Lieutenant Governor seemingly had in mind merely secure, isolated, and sanitary accommodation for the navy's incapacitated. The absence of any request for medical personnel implies that health care would remain the responsibility of the individual ship surgeons.

122. *Journal of the Commissioners for Trade and Plantations*, eds. E. G. Atkinson and K. H. Ledward (London, 1920–38), 2: 188, 191, 194.

123. Deposition by William Williamson, merchant of London and former Virginia resident, 11 August 1719: P.R.O., ADM 97/85.

124. P.R.O., ADM 97/85, passim, 99/11–16, passim; National Maritime Museum, ADM/E/4/34, 37, 94.

125. P.R.O., ADM 97/85.

126. P.R.O., ADM 97/85.

127. P.R.O., ADM 36/3889, 3890, 3894, 4572, 4574, 4580.

128. P.R.O., ADM 33/366, 36/3894.

129. Bernardino Ramazzini, *Diseases of Workers*, trans. W. C. Wright, ed. G. Rosen (New York, 1964), pp. vii, 353–57, 459–69. First published in English as *A Treatise of the Diseases of Tradesmen, shewing the various influences of particular trades upon the state of health* (London, 1705), pp. 181–84.

130. For example, Archibald Pitcairne, *The Works* (London, 1715), pp. 239, 252–57, and passim; Thomas Price, *An Authentic Narrative of the Success of Tar-Water* (London, 1746), pp. 63–65, 157, and passim; Stephen Hales, *Philosophical Experiments: Containing useful and necessary instructions for such as undertake long voyages at sea* (London, 1739).

GENDER: WOMEN'S WORK, RELIGION, AND SEXUALITY   **4**

A S ESSENTIAL AS RACE, ethnicity, and class are for understanding early modern Chesapeake power relationships and identity politics, Sarah Hand Meacham, Debra Meyers, and Catherine Cardno demonstrate in the essays of part 4 the importance of gender, religion, and sexuality in shaping the lives of colonists. By using alcoholic beverage production as a lens, Meacham reveals some of the gendered social conventions of the Chesapeake. She describes how labor was divided and exposes a little-known facet of women's lives: that making alcohol was women's work. Alcohol consumption was an essential part of life in the Chesapeake, partly because of the English tradition and partly because of the brackish water in the Chesapeake. The introduction of new technologies had led men in Western Europe, Latin America, New England, and the Middle Colonies to assume control of alcoholic beverage production in the early modern period. In contrast, seventeenth-century Chesapeake men returned to relying on women's cider, rather than men's beer. Unlike women in other countries, however, women in the Chesapeake did not enjoy any economic control or status because of their alcoholic beverage production. And just as the production of alcohol was a gendered activity, Meacham shows, so too was its consumption.

Debra Meyers points to another gendered arena. In "Reconstructing Gender" she describes the social change for women in the eighteenth century and argues for a tenable connection between politics and the reconstruction of social norms based on the religious ideals of ruling elites. She argues that while the Roman Catholics controlled Maryland, women had more rights, responsibilities, and freedoms. After the Calvinists took control of the province in 1689, women's place in society as well as in their families declined. Meyers asserts that the new Calvinist ruling class struggled to establish a decidedly patriarchal value system using the provincial legislature, as they legally redefined what it meant to be a family, a woman, an orphan, a guardian, a criminal, and a sinner.

In "The Fruit of Nine, Sue kindly brought," Cardno's examination of bastardy cases uncovers the eighteenth-century shift in the enforcement of sexual
norms. Charting changes in sexual mores, she notes the movement from public
shaming to punitive fines in law and satiric jesting in print. By integrating legal
and cultural history with a traditional social history approach, Cardno uses
county court records to understand the relative importance of colonial-defined
sexual "deviance" as a crime. In her close reading of the language used in such
cases, she uncovers what it meant to be part of an illicit sexual relationship, and
this draws a fuller picture of the increasing move toward social reinforcement of
moral behavior, as opposed to legal reinforcement. In other words, as bastardy
became a less serious offense that no longer required court action, there was an
increase in the permissibility of print culture to lambaste characters that did not
behave in sexually appropriate ways. This transition was paralleled by the community's focus on status and race as key defining components of sexual requirements.

Sarah Hand Meacham's "'They Will be Adjudged by Their Drinke, What
Kind of Housewives They Are': Gender, Technology, and Household Cidering in
England and the Chesapeake, 1690 to 1760" uses such nontraditional sources as
cookbooks and kitchen probate records, as well as such traditional sources such
as the promotional literature presented here. Keeping in mind its principal purpose as promotional literature aimed at increased immigration from England to
the Chesapeake, John Hammond's "Leah and Rachel, or, The Two Fruitfull Sisters, Virginia and Mary-Land" sheds light on a number of colonial Chesapeake
issues. Debra Meyers's "Reconstructing Gender: Early Modern English Politics
and Religion in the Chesapeake" employs probate records, city planning, and legislation to underscore the differences in the application of law and moral codes
based on the religious ideals of ruling elites. We have chosen some of that legislation—available online—to present here. And it seems appropriate to include
some extensive reproductions of the poetry used in Catherine Cardno's "'The
Fruit of Nine, Sue kindly brought': Colonial Enforcement of Sexual Norms in
Eighteenth-Century Maryland" for a better understanding of her close reading of
the primary sources in her literary analysis that raise themes about race and class
shared with other essays in this volume.

Leah and Rachel, or, The Two Fruitfull Sisters, Virginia and Mary-Land (1656)

JOHN HAMMOND

THE COUNTRY IS AS I SAID of a temperate nature . . . here seldom hard-weather keep men from labour, yet there no work is done all winter except dressing their own victuals and making of fires.

The labour servants are put to, is not so hard nor of such continuance as Husbandmen, nor Handecraftmen are kept at in England, as I said little or nothing is done in winter time, none ever work before sun rising nor after sun set, in the summer they rest, sleep or exercise themselves five houres in the heat of the day, Saturdayes afternoon is always their own, the old Holidayes are observed and the Sabboath spent in good exercises.

The Women are not (as is reported) put into the ground to worke, but occupie such domestique imployments and houswifery as in England, that is dressing victuals, righting up the house, milking, imployed about dayries, washing, sowing, etc. and both men and women have times of recreations, as much or more than in any part of the world besides, yet som wenches that are nasty, beastly and not fit to be so imployed are put into the ground, for reason tells us, they must not at charge be transported and then mantained for nothing, but those that prove so aukward are rather burthensome then servants desirable or usefull.

The Country is fruitfull, apt for all and more then England can or does produce. The usuall diet is such as in England, for the rivers afford innumerable sortes of choyce fish, (if they will take the paines to make wyers or hier the Natives, who for a small matter will undertake it), winter and summer, and that

John Hammond, "Leah and Rachel, or, The Two Fruitfull Sisters, Virginia and Mary-Land," in *Narratives of Early Maryland, 1633–1684,* ed. Clayton Colman Hall (1656; reprint, New York: Charles Scribner's Sons, 1910) 290–94.

in many places sufficient to serve the use of man, and to fatten hoggs. Water-fowle of all sortes are (with admiration to be spoken of) plentiful and easie to be killed, yet by many degrees more plentifull in some places then in othersome. Deare all over the Country, and in many places so many that venison is accounted a tiresom meat; wilde Turkeys are frequent, and so large that I have seen some weight neer threescore pounds; other beasts there are whose flesh is wholsom and savourie, such are unknowne to us; and therefore I will not stuffe my book with superfluous relation of their names; huge Oysters and store in all parts where the salt-water comes.

The Country is exceedingly replenished with Neat cattle, Hoggs, Goats and Tame-fowle, but not many sheep; so that mutton is somwhat scarce, but that defect is supplied with store of Venison, other flesh and fowle. The Country is full of gallant Orchards, and the fruit generally more luscious and delightfull then here, witnesse the Peach and Quince, the latter may be eaten raw savourily, the former differs and as much exceeds ours as the best relished apple we have doth the crabb, and of both most excellent and comfortable drinks are made. Grapes in infinite manners grow wilde, so do Walnuts, Smalnuts, Chesnuts and abundance of excellent fruits, Plums and Berries, not growing or known in England; graine we have, both English and Indian for bread and Bear, and Pease besides English of ten several sorts, all exceeding ours in England; the gallant root of Potatoes are common, and so are all sorts of rootes, herbes and Garden stuffe. . . .

Beare is indeed in some place constantly drunken, in other some, nothing but Water or Milk and Water or Beverige; and that is where the goodwives (if I may so call them) are negligent and idle; for it is not for want of Corn to make Malt with (for the Country affords enough) but because they are sloathfull and carelesse: but I hope this Item will shame them out of those humours, that they will be adjudged by their drink, what Kinde of Housewives they are.

Those Servants that will be industrious may in their time of service gain a competent estate before their Freedomes, which is usally done by many, and they gaine esteeme and assistance that appear so industrious. . . .

And whereas it is rumoured that Servants have no lodging other then on boards, or by the Fire side, it is contrary to reason to believe it: First, as we are Christians; next as people living under a law, which compels as well the Master as the Servant to perform his duty; nor can true labour be either expected or extracted without sufficient cloathing, diet, and lodging; all which both their Indentures (which must inviolably be observed) and the Justice of the Country requires.

But if any go thirther, not in a condition of a Servant, but pay his or her passage, which is some six pounds: Let them not doubt but it it is money well layd out; yet however let them not fail, although they carry little else, to take a Bed along with them, and then few Houses will give them entertainment, either out of curtesie, or on reasonable tearms; and I think it better for any that goes over free, and but in a mean condition, to hire himself for reasonable wages of Tobacco and Provision, the first year, provided he happen in an honest house, and where the Mistresse is noted for a good Husewife, of which there are very many (notwithstanding the cry to the contrary) for by that means he will live free of disbursment, have something to help him the next year, and be carefully looked to in his sicknesse (if he chance to fall sick) and let him so covenant that exceptions may be made, that he work not much in the hot weather, a course we alwayes take with our new hands (as they call them) the first year they come in.

If they are women that go after this manner, that is paying their own passages, I advise them to sojourn in a house of honest repute, for by their good carriage, they may advance themselves in marriage, by their ill, overthrow their fortunes; and although lose persons seldome live long unmarried if free, yet they match with as desolute as themselves, and never live handsomly or are ever respected. . . .

Yet are the Inhabitants generally affable, courteous and very assistant to strangers (for what but plenty makes hospitality and good neighbourhood) and no sooner are they settled, but they will be visiting, presenting and advicing the stranger how to improve what they have, how to better their way of livelihood.

An Act Concearning Servants That Haue Bastards (1658)

WHEREAS DIVERS women Servants w^{th}in this Province not haveing Husbands living with them, have bene gotten with Child in the tyme of their Servitude to the Great dishonnor of God and the apparant damage to the Masters, or Owners of such Servants, and no lawe yet provided where that damage shalbe recoverable. For remedy whereof Bee it Enacted by the Lord Proprietary, by and with the consent of this present Gennerall Assembly, That Every such Mother of a Bastard Child not able sufficiently to proue the party charged to be the begetter of such child, in every such case The mother of such Child shall onely be lyable to satisfie the damages soe sustained by Servitude, or other wayes as the Court before whom such matter is brought shall see convenient Provided that where the mother of any such child as aforesaid shalbe able to prove her charge either by sufficient testimony of wittnesses or confession Then the party charged, if a Servant to satisfie halfe the said damages, if a freeman then the whole damages by Servitude or otherwise as aforesaid. And if any such mother as aforesaid be able to prove by such testimony or confession as aforesaid that the party Charged (being a single person and a ffreeman) did before the begitting of such Child promise her Marriage, That then hee shall performe his promise to her, or recompense her abuse, as the Court before whom such matter is brought shall see Convenient, the quallity and condition of the persons considered. This Act to continue for three yeares or to the End of the next Gennerall Assembly and noe longer

The Burgesses haue The Vpper howse haue assented assented

THOMAS TURNER CLER. PHILIP CALVERT

[An act passed under the Free Will Christian government]

Proceedings and Acts of the General Assembly, January 1637/8–September 1664, vol. 1, p. 373 (1658).

An Act for the Publication of Marriages (1658)

B E IT ENACTED by the Lord Proprietary by and with the Consent of this present Generall Assembly, That all persons who shall desire Marriage haue liberty to apply themselves either to a Magistral or Minister for the Contracting thereof. It is further Enacted by the authority aforesaid that all Persons within this Province intending marriage shall make publication thereof, either at the county court Church Chappie next where they dwell, or meeting Howse, and that at such tyme as such Court Church Chappell or meeting be full and thereby capable to take cognisance thereof, from which Court Church Chappell or meeting Certificat being given forth, it shalbe lawfull for such Magistral or Minister to marry such persons as aforesaid. And if any person shall presume to contract Marriage without such publication and certificat as aforesaid, Every such person soe Contracted or marryed shalbe lyable to a fine of one Thousand Pounds of Tobacco. And every such Magistral or Minister contracting or marrying without such publication and certificat as aforesaid shalbe lyable to a fine of five thousand Pounds of Tobacco the one halfe of the said fine to the Lord Proprietary, the other halfe to the Informer. This Act to continue for three yeares or to the end of the next Gennerall Assembly and no longer

The Burgesses haue The Vpper howse haue
assented

THOMAS TURNER CLER. PHILLIP CALVERT

[An act passed under the Free Will Christian Government]
Proceedings and Acts of the General Assembly, January 1637/8–September 1664. Volume I, 374 (1658).

An Act for Punishment of Blasphemy, Fornication, Adultery, Prophane Swearing, and Cursing (1699)

B E IT ENACTED by the Kings most Excellent Ma'y by and with the Advice and Consent of this Present Generall Assembly and the Authority of the Same That from and after the publication hereof if any Person or Persons whatsoever Inhabiting or being within this Province shall Blasphem God (That is to say) Curse him or deny our Saviour Jesus Christ to be the Son of God or shall Deny the Holy Trinity the father Son and holy Ghost or the God head of any of the said Three persons or the Unity of the Godhead or shall utter any reproach-full Speeches words or Language Concerning the holy Trinity or any of the three Persons thereof for his her or their first Offence Shall be bored through the Tongue and fined the Sume of Twenty pounds Sterling to his Sacred Ma'y towards the defraying the County Charge where the said Offence shall be Comit-ted to be leavied upon his or her Goods and Chattells Lands and Tenements (if any they have) but if Such Offender or Offenders have not goods and Chattells Lands and Tenements to the Value aforesaid then Such Offender or Offenders shall Suffer Six months Imprisonment without Baile or Mainprize and for every Second Offence whereof every such Offender or Offenders shall be Legally Con-vict he she or they so offending as aforesaid shall be stigmatized in the forehead with the Letter B: and to be fined fourty Pounds Sterling to the uses aforesaid and in Case he she or they so Offending as aforesaid shall not have goods & Chattells Lands and Tenements to the Value aforesaid every such Offendr or Offenders shall Suffer Imprisonment for the Space of one whole Year without Baile or Mainprize as aforesaid and for every third offence whereof any Such Offender or Offenders Legally Convicted as aforesaid he she or they so Offend-ing shall Suffer Death with Confiscation of all his her or their Goods & Chattells

[An act passed under the Calvinist government]
Proceedings and Acts of the General Assembly, June 29–July 22, 1699. Volume 22, 523–25.

to his Ma'y his heires and Successors And be it further Enacted by the Authority advice and Consent aforesaid That Every person or persons Comitting fornication and being thereof Convicted shall for every time so Offending be fined (by the Court before whom such Matter shall be brought) to his Sacred Ma'y in the Sume of Twenty Shillings Sterl or four hundred pounds of Tobbacco to be leavied &c. for and Towards the defraying the County leavy where Such fact shall be Comitted or receive Corporall punishment by whipping att the discretion of the said Court not Exceeding thirty nine lashes and that every Person or Persons Comitting Adultery and being thereof Legally Convict shall be fined as aforesaid for the uses afd in the Sume of fourty Shillings Sterl or Eight hundred Pounds of Tobbacco to be leavied as aforesd or to receive Corporall Punishment as aforesaid And be it further Enacted by the Authority aforesd by and with the Advice and Consent aforesaid that every person or persons who shall harbour Enterteine and Provide for the Maintenance of any Lewd woman or women or frequent her to their Companys or the Company of any Lewd woman or women after Publick Admonition to avoyd the same given by the Ministers or Church Wardens or Vestry of the Parish or Parishes where Such person or psons Dwell and in Case there be no Ministers by the Church wardens of the Same or Vestry aforesaid shall for every time it shall be proved that he she or they shall Cohabit together or frequent the Company of Each other after such admonition Given as aforesaid undergo Such pains and Penaltys as is by this Act Provided for such who are Legally Convicted of fornication or Adultery And Whereas those horrid and Detestable Sinns of Prophane Swearing and Cursing are Notwithstanding Severall Good Laws heretofore made grown so Ripe that it is to be feared they provoke the Divine Vengeance to Inflict many and terrible Punishments upon us to prevent Such Wickedness for the future Be it Enacted by the Kings most Excellent Majesty by and with the Advice and Consent of this Present Generall Assembly and the Authority of the Same That if any person or Persons whatsoever within this Province after the publication of this Act Prophanely Swear or Curse in the presence or hearing of any one Iustice of the Peace or head Officer of any Town City or Burrough within this Province or that shall be thereof Convicted by the oath of one Wittness before any one Justice or other head Officer or by the Confession of the Party Offending shall forfeitt and pay for Such Offence the Sume of five Shills. Sterling to our Sovereigne Lord the King for the use of the poor of County where the offence shall be Comitted to be leavied upon Such Offender or Offenders Imediatly by Comand or Warrant from the Justice of the Peace or head Officer of any Town City or Burrough before whom Such Offender or Offenders shall be Convicted to the Constable or other Person whom Such Justice or head Officer shall Comand or Appoint by distress or Sale of his her or their Goods or Chattells rendering to them the overplus and in Case any person should refuse to obey to Execute the Comand or Warrant of any Justice of the Peace head Officer as aforesaid in this Case Such person or persons shall forfeitt and pay the Sume of five Shillings to be leavied as aforesaid to the use aforesaid And be it further Enacted by the Authority aforesaid that for every time any person or persons shall prophanely Swear or Curse in any Court house dureing the Sitting of any Court within this Province and be thereof Convict as aforesaid he she or they so Offending shall Imediatly forfeitt and pay the Sume of Tenn Shillings as aforesaid to the uses aforesaid or Sett in the Stocks for the Space of one houre by Order or Comand of any Such Justice of the Peace or head Officer as aforesaid Provided allways and it is hereby Enacted that no Person shall be prosecuted or troubled for any such prophane Cursing and Swearing unless the same be proved or Prosecuted within Ten days next after the Offence Comitted and lately be it Enacted by the Authority aforesaid by and with the Advice and Consent aforesaid that every Such Justice of the Peace or head Officer afd are hereby obliged to receive all Such forfeitures as afd that are leavyed as aforesaid and render a Just Accompt thereof to the Justice of each respective County Yearly att the time of laying the County to be by them disposed of to the uses aforesaid.

Poetry from the Maryland *Almanack*

From the 1758 Maryland *Almanack*

The Poetic Couple

As *Richie* and *Pattie* Sat up very late,
Each a Pen in the Hand, and a Muse in the Pate,
The Design was to finish a Piece on *Enjoyment*,
O ye Gods! For the Author's how fit the *Employment*!
Dick cry'd, Dearest, find me a Crambo to Bliss.
Patt stretch'd out her Neck, and answer'd, *A-kiss*.
The Prologue begun, no more to be said;
They stripped, and soon finishe'd the Poem in Bed.

The Undecided Case

Dick join'd in nuptial Conjugation
    With *Susan*, whom he long had sought:
But four Months after Cultivation,
    The Fruit of Nine, Sue kindly brought.
Dick scolded: She was in a Swoon:
    About their Case the Neighbours varied:
Some urged that Susan came too soon;
    Others—that Dick too late was married.

From the 1762 Maryland *Almanack*

The **FEMALE CAUTION**, *Or*, **Pair of Stockings.**

MOTHER *Breedwell* presented her Husband each Year
With a chopping brave Boy, and sometimes with a Pair;
'Till the primitive Blessing of Multiplication

Had fill'd the whole House with a young Generation.
But as they increas'd, so Sorrow and Care,
Those primitive Curses, put in for a Share;
And the toilsome Employment of Mother and Wife,
Had hag'd the poor Woman half out of her Life.

    To the Doctor she goes with a pitiful Face,
And begs he wou'd give his Advice in her Case.
She tells him her Husband was wretchedly poor,
And prays he'd consider her chargeable Store,
And prevent for the future her having of more.

As for that, quoth the Sage, *I've a Cure never failing,*
Which neither Hippocrates *thought of, nor* Galen.
Look here—I present you this wonderful Hose,
Into which ev'ry Night when you Bed with your Spouse,
Thrust both Legs; nor pull off the magical Fetters,
Till you rise in the Morn about Family Matters.
Observe but this Rule, which I give you in Charge,
And your Stock may diminish, but never enlarge.
    Many Thanks for your Kindness, dear Sir, *quoth the Dame,*
(*Here she drop'd him a Curt'sie*)—if it were not for Shame,
And for fear you wou'd think me too bold, I'd fain beg
T'other *Stocking*—and so have a *Hose* to each Leg;
For if such rare Virtue contain'd is in one,
How safe shou'd I be, had I both of them on.

From the 1763 Maryland *Almanack*

On a *CIVILIAN*.

A WEALTHY, old, grave, and grey-headed Sire,
Stole to a Wench, to quench his Lust's desire:
She ask'd, "Of what Profession he might be;"
I am a Civil-Lawyer, Girl, quoth he:
"A Civil Lawyer, Sir, you make me muse,
"Your Talk's too Broad for *civil Men* to use:
"If *Civil Lawyers* are such bawdy Men,
"Oh! What, (quoth she) are *other* Lawyers then?"

A Case to the CIVILIAN.

NOKES went, he thought, to *Style's* Wife to bed,
Nor knew his own was laid there in her stead:
Civilian, Is the Child he then begot
To be allow'd Legitimate, or Not?

From the 1764 Maryland *Almanack*

The MAD-DOG.
A TALE.

A PRUDE, at Morn and Evening Prayer,
Had worn her Velvet cushion bare;
Upwards she taught her Eyes to roll,
As if she watch'd her soaring Soul;
And when Devotion warm'd the Croud,
None sung, or smote their Breast so loud:
Pale Penitence had mark'd her Face
With all the meager Signs of Grace,
Her Mass-book was completely lin'd
With painted Saints of various Kind:

But when in ev'ry Page she view'd
Fine Ladies who the Flesh subdu'd;
As quick her Beads she counted o'er,
She cry'd—such Wonders are no more!
She chose not to delay Confession,
To bear at once a Year's Transgression,
But ev'ry Week set all Things even,
And balanc'd her Accounts with Heav'n,
     Behold her now in humble Guise,
Upon her Knees with downcast Eyes
Before the Priest: She thus begins,
And sobbing, Blubbers forth her Sins.

Who could that tempting Man resist?
My Virtue languish'd, as he kiss'd;
I strove,— till I could strive no longer?
How can the Weak subdue the Stronger?

The Father ask'd her where and when?
How many? and what Sort of Men?
By what Degrees her Blood was heated?
How oft' the Frailty was repeated?
Thus have I seen a pregnant Wench
All flush'd with Guilt before the Bench,
The Judges (wak'd by wanton Thought)
Dive to the Bottom of her Fault,

They leer, they simper at her Shame,
And make her call all Things by Name.
        And now to Sentence he proceeds,
Prescribes how oft' to tell her Beads;
Shows her what Saints could do her good,
Doubles her Fasts to cool her Blood.
Eas'd of her Sins, and light as Air,
Away she Trips; perhaps to Prayer.
'Twas no such Thing. Why then this haste?
The Clock has struck, the Hour is past,
And on the Spur of Inclination,
She scorn'd to Bilk her Assignation.

Whate'er she did, next Week she came,
And piously confest the same;
The Priest, who Female Frailties pity'd,
First chid her, then her Sins remitted.
        But did she now her Crime bemoan
In penitential Sheets alone?
And was no bold, no beastly Fellow
The nightly Partner of her Pillow?
No, none; for next Time in the Grove,
A Bank was conscious of her Love.
        Confession Day was come about,
And now again it all must out,

She seems to wipe her twinkling Eyes,
What now my Child, the Father cries.
Again, says she!— with threatening Looks,
He thus the prostrate Dame rebukes.

Madam, I grant there's something in it,
That Virtue has the unguarded Minute;
But pray now tell me what are Whores,
But Women of unguarded Hours?
Then you must sure have lost all Shame,
What ev'ry Day and still the same,
And no Fault else! 'tis strange to find
A Woman to one Sin confin'd!

Pride is this Day her darling Passion,
The next Day slander is in Fashion;
Gaming succeeds; if Fortune crosses,
Then Virtue's mortgag'd for her Losses;
By Use her Fav'rite Vice she loaths,
And Loves new Follies like new Cloaths:
But you, beyond all Thought, unchaste,
Have all Sin center'd near your Waste!
Whence is this Appetite so strong?
Say, madam, did your Mother long?
Or is it Lux'ry and high Diet
That won't let Virtue sleep in Quiet?

She tells him now with meekest Voice,
That she had never err'd by Choice,
Nor was there known a Virgin chaster,
Till ruin'd by a sad Disaster.
That she a fav'rite Lap-dog had,
Which, (as she stroak'd and kiss'd) grew mad;
And on her Lip a Wound indented,
First set her youthful Blood fermenting.
The Priest reply'd with zealous Fury,
You should have sought the Means to cure ye.
Doctors by various Ways we find,
Treat these Distempers of the Mind.

Let gaudy Ribbands be deny'd
To her, who Raves with scornful Pride;
And if Religion crack her Notions,
Lock up her volumes of Devotions;

But if for Man her Rage prevail,
Bar her the sight of Creatures Male.
Or else to cure such venom'd Bites,
And set the shatter'd Thoughts arights;
They send you to the Ocean's Shore,
And plunge the Patient o'er and o'er.
  The Dame reply'd; alas! In vain
My kindred forc'd me to the Main;

Naked and in the Face of Day:
Look not, ye Fishermen, this Way!
What Virgin had not done as I did?
My modest Hand, by Nature guided,
Debarr'd at once from human Eyes
The Seat where Female Honour lies,
And though thrice Dipt from Top to Toe,
I still secur'd the Post below,
And guarded it with Grasp so fast
Not one Drop through my Fingers Past;
Thus owe I to my bashful Care
That all the Rage is settled there.

  Weigh well the Projects of Mankind;
Then tell me, Reader, canst thou find
The Man from Madness wholly free?
They all are mad—save you and me.
Do not the Statesmen, Fop and Wit,
By daily Follies prove they're Bit?
And when the briny Cure they try'd,
Some Part still kept above the Tide?
  Some Men (when drench'd beneath the Wave)
High o'er their Heads their Fingers save:
Those Hands by mean Extortion thrive,
Or in the Pocket lightly Dive;

Or more expert in pilf'ring Vice,
They burn and itch to Cog the Dice.
  Plunge in a Courtier; straight his Fears
Direct his Hands to stop his Ears.

And now Truth seems a grating Noise,
He Loves the Sland'rer's whisp'ring Voice;
And hangs on Flatt'ry with Delight,
And thinks all fulsome Praise is right.
    All Women dread a watry Death:
They shut their Lips to hold their Breath,
And though you Duck them ne'er so long,
Not one salt Drop e'er wets their Tongue;
'Tis hence they Scandal have at Will,
And that this Member ne'er lies still.

"They Will Be Adjudged by Their Drinke, What Kind of Housewives They Are": Gender, Technology, and Household Cidering in England and the Chesapeake, 1690 to 1760

7

SARAH HAND MEACHAM

"Beer is indeed in some place constantly drunken, in other some, nothing but water or Milk and water or beverage; and that is where the goodwives (if I may so call them) are negligent and idle; for it is not for want of corn to make malt with (for the country affords enough) but because they are slothful and careless: but I hope this item will shame them out of those humors, that they will be adjudged by their drink, what kind of housewives they are."

—JOHN HAMMOND, "LEAH AND RACHEL, OR, THE TWO FRUITFUL SISTERS, VIRGINIA AND MARY-LAND."1656[1]

"Whereas Thomas Phillips . . . was brought before this Court on suspicion of Picking open the Lock of George Sissons Chamber and taking out the Keg of his Syder house and Disposing of his Syder and on Examination of Several Evidences Touching the Same, It is the Opinion of this Court that the said Thomas Phillips is Guilty of the Crime Laid to his Charge. It is therefore Ordered that the Sherrif take him and Carry him to the Common whipping post and give him Tenn Lashes on his bare back well laid on."

—RICHMOND COUNTY COURT, JANUARY 3, 1721/2[2]

IN 1656 JOHN HAMMOND denounced Chesapeake women for making insufficient quantities of alcohol, particularly beer, for their households. Hammond informed Chesapeake women that they were "negligent and idle . . .
slothful and careless," and warned them that their housewifery would be judged
"by their drink." Sixty-five years later a Richmond County court sentenced
Thomas Phillips to ten lashes for stealing George Sisson's cider, stating repeatedly
that the cider was male property. Although the two passages do not appear at
first to be related, in fact they share a close connection. By the late seventeenth
century, when women in the Chesapeake were fulfilling Hammond's challenge
and regularly making the alcohol so necessary for early Chesapeake households,
men and women in England were concluding that alcohol production was men's
work. Over the course of the seventeenth and eighteenth centuries, Chesapeake
men and women came to depend on women's cider rather than the men's beer
that was popular in England. So, when the Richmond court called the cider that
Thomas Phillips stole George Sisson's property, the court unintentionally dis-
guised the fact that the cider was probably made by Sisson's wife and daughters.

In addition to adding to our knowledge about women's work and lives in
early American, this essay reveals the anomalous nature of the early Chesapeake.
Eighteenth-century alcoholic beverage production in the Chesapeake increasingly
resembled that of sixteenth-century England, where women made unhopped ale
and cider. Despite the contentions of such scholars as Jack Greene that the southern colonies were normative, the case study of alcohol illustrates how unique the
early Chesapeake was. While men and women in the rest of western Europe made
and enjoyed beer (made with hops) and distilled liquors, like gin, Chesapeake
colonists made only ciders from apples, peaches, and persimmons, concoctions of
molasses and water, a little ale (made without hops, and in the Chesapeake from
corn and molasses rather than from oats and barley), and some apple brandy
(distilled cider). The Chesapeake did not follow the masculinization trajectory of
alcohol production in Europe, New England, and the Middle Colonies because
of the Chesapeake's immigration patterns, scattered population, and tobacco
monoculture.[3]

Small planter households in the Chesapeake made much of the alcoholic
drink that they consumed. Small planters were those men who owned 100 to 200
acres. Their households on average included six members, two or three of whom
were tithable, meaning that they were indentured servants, or increasingly slaves,
for whom their masters paid a property tax.[4] Small planters, just as the term
meant in the eighteenth century, raised crops for a living and often worked their
land themselves. Their households made up about one-half of the Chesapeake
households from the late seventeenth century on. In these households women

made enough raw alcoholic beverages, meaning ciders of apples, peaches, and persimmons that had not been distilled, to meet their needs from July to December. When small planters' alcoholic beverage supplies ran out, they depended on large planters to sell their surplus distilled liquors, which is the subject of another essay. From the seventeenth until the latter half of the eighteenth century, alcoholic beverage production in small planter households (the subject of this essay) often fell under women's province. Smaller households could not afford the wealthy planters' expensive distilling equipment that permitted the production of longer-lasting alcoholic beverages that men claimed as their domain, nor could they afford to import alcohol. So they depended on women's cidering.

Alcohol was a necessary part of early modern life, and Chesapeake colonists came from a tradition of heavy alcohol consumption. Most early modern English adults drank at least one gallon of ale a day. The early modern English drank for religious and secular celebrations, weddings, childbirths, funerals, medicine, beauty, and with meals. Men drank the most, but women and children drank heartily as well. English children, like their parents, drank alcohol at every meal. The 1512 account books for the Percy family of Northumberland reveal that the lord and lady of the manor shared a quart of ale and a quart of wine each day at breakfast; their two children, ages eight and ten, shared a quart of ale at breakfast as well. Dinner and supper included ale, mead, cider, or wine. The accompanying food was steeped in alcohol. Cookbook writers listed alcohol recipes first in their cookbooks, signifying that they viewed them as the most important or popular part of the book. For example, Sir Kenelme Digbie devoted the first one-third of his very popular English cookbook to alcohol recipes; of 337 recipes, 138 were for alcoholic beverages.[5]

The English believed that alcohol was salubrious, and that belief partly explains their constant consumption of alcoholic beverages. English physician Andrew Boorde expressed a typical attitude when he praised wine in 1542 because it "it doth rejuice all the powers of man, and doth nourish them; it doth ingender good blood, it doth nourish the brain and all the body." Health providers sold alcohol to their patients, like a surgeon in 1633 who "obtained a license [to sell alcohol] with a limitation to sell ale to none but his patients." Breastfeeding women drank extra beer to help their milk flow. Forty-three of the medicinal recipes in the first English gynecological handbook contained alcohol. Physicians prescribed alcohol mixed with marigolds to cure depression, and alcohol with cowslips to cure memory loss and headaches. Wives gave white wine with hops to their husbands to invigorate them. In England and America bathing in alcohol was thought to promote health. Until at least the mid-nineteenth century most women bathed babies in spirits rather than water, thinking it better for the infants. Ill or consumptive adults similarly bathed in warm white rum.[6]

Women used alcohol as cosmetic treatments. Women applied wines stewed with thyme, sage, winter-savory, sweet marjoram, and rosemary to their faces to maintain fairness. They patted their bodies with mead mixed with rose juice and petals. Authors suggested washing with white wine mixed with flower blossoms to reduce freckles and spots. Women bleached their hair blonde by shampooing their hair with white wine cooked with rhubarb, or dyed their hair red with wine tinted from radishes.[7]

Alcoholic drinks also served as cleaning agents. Prescriptive literature recommended washing plated items in wine, and then boiling them in spent mash, aqua-vitae, and vinegar. Silver was scrubbed with gin. Servants cleaned fireplace grates with gin and cleaned the inner hearths with sour beer. They then blackened the grates with sour beer mixed with molasses and sugar. Metal was scrubbed with rum; mirrors with gin. Beer and distilled wine gave hats and boots a "brilliant jet lustre." There was little that alcohol could not accomplish inside the household. When household items broke, alcohol glued them back together. Slugs or isinglass (from sturgeon) mixed with gin repaired broken china; mixed with brandy the concoction cemented broken glass. Candle wicks were dipped in sprits of wine to make them easier to light.[8]

Chesapeake colonists depended on alcohol as much as, or even more than, their English counterparts did. Alcohol provided much-needed calories, was thought to prevent scurvy, offered respite from water infected by disease and mosquito larvae, gave some relief from illness, and fostered community. Moreover, colonists did not have a choice about whether to drink alcohol; nonfermented drinks did not yet exist. Before refrigeration and pasteurization there was no way to prevent apple, pear, persimmon, and other fruit juices from fermenting. Naturally occurring airborne yeasts entered any fruit juice and caused fermentation. Coffee was unfamiliar to most colonists until the late eighteenth century. Tea remained an expensive luxury until the tea duties were lowered in 1745. Colonists could not simply drink milk because cows were expensive items of property. Milk was more expensive than even *imported* ale and cider. "Ale [is] 15 [pence] per bottle and English cyder the same . . . milk [is] 3d per quart," recorded one traveler.[9]

Moreover, the water in the Tidewater was, at best, unhealthy. The shallow wells that the colonists dug contaminated easily and bred typhoid fever. Water could not provide the calories and nutrition of ale or cider, and it was filled with refuse, excrement, and insects. As early as 1625 George Percy described the water in Virginia as "at a flood verily salt, at a low tide full of slime and filth, which was the destruction of many of our men." The warm climate of the Chesapeake meant that much of the water was contaminated with pathogenic bacteria. The water-bred disease, causing malaria pandemics in 1657–1659 and from 1677 to 1695. During the summer months a salt bloc caused the Jamestown River to stagnate, and gave the colonists salt poisoning.[10]

Some areas of the Chesapeake were fortunate, and enjoyed relatively safe drinking water. Southern Marylanders enjoyed clean water in their early years. Areas that began with better water, though, quickly destroyed it by using it for their refuse; it was only, for example, in 1874 that Baltimore made it illegal to throw dead animals and other substances into the river. Most areas had foul water. In Baltimore, citizens complained that the water was a "muddy substitute for the pure element." In Norfolk the water was brackish, and the public spring was filled with domestic pollution. In Williamsburg, colonists warned newcomers that the water "is very bad . . . which, with the Heat of the Weather is sufficient to keep a Man in a continual Fever."

Illnesses and death were often blamed, perhaps correctly, on drinking water. For example, when William Coone sold a slave who died soon after the purchase, the new owner sought to be excused from paying for the now-dead slave. Coone refused to excuse the payment, arguing that the slave's death was the new master's fault, since he had allowed the slave to "drink much cold water." In another example, when Nicholas Cresswell, a teacher in Virginia, became ill, his doctor advised him "to drink a little more rum than I [Cresswell] did before I was sick," and concluded that "in short, I believe it was being too abstemious that brought this sickness upon me at first, by drinking water." Cautions against drinking water were published widely. As *The Virginia Almanack* for 1766 humorously warned:

> Now we advise that you would not
> Drink water when you're very hot;
> For doing so, the blood congeals,
> And throws the grease into your heels.[11]

So when colonists had a choice, they drank alcohol. Much of this consumption was gendered, with white men drinking in male groups often out of doors at public festivities, church services, court days, and militia musters and elections, while white women drank in indoor groups at sewing circles and birthings. For instance, male colonists drank at such outdoor celebrations as Royal holidays. When King James II died, the royal governor of Virginia celebrated the ascendancy of the new queen with cannon salutes and the distribution of glasses of rum and brandy to all who attended the celebration in Williamsburg. Similar celebrations caused William Byrd to remark that "there was a great noise of people drunk in the street [a] good part of the night." Not drinking on a royal holiday was so unusual that Byrd recorded it in his diary. "The Governor had made a bargain with his servants," he reported, "that if they would forbear to drink upon the Queen's birthday, they might be drunk this [the next] day. They observed their contract, and did their business very well and got very drunk today."[12]

Male colonists routinely drank at church, and they drank at court. Drinking at church became so problematic that in 1710 the governor signed a law to restrain drinking in churchyards. However, the habit of drinking in churchyards was too ingrained for the law to be effective. When "My brother Custis and I [William Byrd] and Mr. Dunn walked into the churchyard," Byrd described, "we saw several people drunk, notwithstanding the late law." "A southern planter was considered temperate enough to belong to the Methodist Church," notes W. J. Rorabough, an authority on alcohol in early America, "if he restricted his daily intake of alcohol to a quart of peach brandy." It was customary for juries and judges (which were all-male) to drink during court sessions. For example, one desperate judge informed jurors who had been unable to reach a decision that "they would not be permitted to eat or drink until reaching a verdict." The quarterly court days in Williamsburg were opportunities to drink wildly. Byrd recorded that when he "walked to the courthouse . . . the people were most of them drunk."[13]

Male colonists gathered to drink on militia days and election days, at horse races and at auctions. Militia officers were expected to treat their men to alcohol. Byrd "caused a hogshead of punch to be made for the people when they should come to muster" for one such occasion. Candidates standing for election similarly provided alcoholic beverages for men at polling sites. George Washington, for instance, spent over £37 for "brandy, rum, etc." Horse races provided another social opportunity for men to drink together. One visitor recorded such a gathering as "a number of people collected there to see quarter races . . . Grog as usual had great effect upon them and created much noise." Men who bid at auctions found themselves plied with drinks. Merchant James Robinson, for instance, told employees to provide "all good usage and drink in abundance" for customers.[14]

Women had their own gatherings that included imbibing. When women collected to sew or quilt, there was alcohol. Soon-to-be-mothers drank during labor, to help manage the pain of childbirth. Their female neighbors gathered before, during, and after childbirth, in what was called the "lying in" period. The pregnant woman was expected to have prepared for women's visits by having cakes and alcoholic beverages on hand. "I sent Mr. Harvey a bottle of wine," noted Byrd, "for his wife who was ready to lie in."[15]

Men and women drank together as well, particularly at mealtimes and indoor events. Colonists often had a drink before going to sleep: "a good hearty cup to precede a bed of down," as one traveler described. And they woke to a breakfast with "the cold remains of the former day, hash'd or fricasseed; coffee, tea, chocolate, venison-pasty, punch, and beer, or cyder, upon one board." Funerals were an indoor occasion where both men and women drank. It was the deceased's responsibility to have provided the mourners with alcohol before dying, or the cost of the alcohol was subtracted from the estate. "We walked to Mrs. Harrison's to the funeral," recorded William Byrd, "where we found abundance of company of all sorts. Wine and cake were served very plentifully." Funerals were, however, an exception. Most alcohol consumption outside of the home occurred in same-sex groups.[16]

Historians do not know yet if slaves' alcohol consumption was similarly gendered, but we do know that slaves consumed alcohol, as their predecessors, indentured servants, had done. Indentured servants were guaranteed alcohol; the contracts they signed stipulated that planters provide them with shelter, clothing, food, and drink in exchange for the servants' seven years of labor. As planters moved from servants to slaves after 1680, they continued some of the traditions of providing alcohol, and slaves worked to enforce these traditions. Planters provided slaves and laborers with alcohol on special occasions and for particularly onerous labor. It was customary to give slaves whiskey at harvest time; planters often purchased the whiskey expressly for this purpose. Thomas Jefferson bought thirty gallons of whiskey per year for his slaves to consume during harvest. Other Virginia planters such as Richard Eppes and William Jerdone similarly gave their slaves whiskey during harvest. Rorabaugh has estimated that during harvest a laborer received a half-pint to a pint of rum per day. In addition, slaves were given alcohol for weddings, childbirths, funerals, and illness. Peter Jefferson allotted his pregnant slaves a quart of brandy for use during childbirth. Joseph Ball instructed his nephew who was managing his plantation that "you must give the negroes at each plantation a bottle pretty often in the winter; and when they are sick." Planters also gave slaves alcohol as a reward for extra or unusual work. When an "abundance of snow fell in the night," Byrd recorded, "my people made paths for which I gave them cider." "I gave all the people a dram," he noted on another occasion, "after planting in the rain." Planters distributed alcohol at other times to curry slaves' loyalty. "At night talked with my people," wrote Byrd, "gave them cider, and prayed."[17]

Since the early Chesapeake had no towns, marketplaces, or shops, colonists had to import or produce whatever goods they needed, including alcohol. Only the very wealthy could afford to import alcohol, and importing held frustrations.

Bottles, kegs, and barrels consistently broke or leaked during transportation. "Your convict ship arrived safe with the goods, if one may call that safe where everything is damaged and broke to pieces," fumed William Byrd. "Opened Mr. Lee's claret," wrote Landon Carter, "and had 5 bottles broke in it out of the 6 dozen, entirely by the loose careless way of packing it up." "The corks were so thick and rotted," wrote John Custis, "they all came off," and the liquid spilled. "We unpacked the beer that came from England," noted Byrd on another occasion, "and a great deal was run out." "Much of my wine was run out," again sighed a resigned Byrd, "God's will be done."[18]

Small planter families could not afford to import alcohol given its costs and risks, and so they had to make their own. Traditionally, alcoholic beverage production had fallen to women as part of cookery. English women had been responsible for producing alcoholic drinks since at least the third century. While English women's brewing tasks differed by class, with the countess of Shrewsbury directing her female servants in brewing while the shepherd's wife brewed her own, English women were responsible for cidering, brewing, infused wines (flavoring wines with berries and fruits), mead, and simple distillations of garden fruits and berries. Sixteenth- and seventeenth-century prescriptive literature agreed that alcohol production was women's work. Anthony Fitzherbert's popular *Book of Husbandry* stated in his "Prologue for the wives occupation" that "what works a wife should do in general . . . to order corn and malt to the mill, to bake and brew." Thomas Tusser's popular *The Good Huswife* told housewives that at "dawn" they should "set some [female servants] to grind malt" and that "where brewer is needed be brewer thyself, what filleth the roof will help furnish the shelf." Tusser reminded women that "well brewed, worth cost: one bushel well brewed, out lasts some twaine, two troubles to one thing is cost no gain," and warned that in making ale "too new is no profit, too stale is as bad: drink sour or dead makes husband half mad." Gervase Markham was writing of the malthouse when he reminded men that "this office of place of knowledge belongs particularly to the housewife; and though we have many excellent men—malsters, yet it is properly the work and care of the woman, for it is a house-work, and done altogether within doors, where generally lies her charge." "The art of making the malt," Markham continued, "is only the work of the housewife, and the maid-servants to her appertaining." The word "brew" is a distant etymological relation of words such as "broth" and "boil," because brewing was women's work as part of cookery.[19]

English cookbooks encouraged and reflected women's alcoholic beverage production activities by instructing women specifically on methods of brewing, distilling, and cidering. Richard Bradley, author of the popular *The Country Housewife and Lady's Director,* subtitled his book as "Containing Instructions for Managing the Brew House, and Malt Liquors in the Cellar; the Making of Wines of all sorts." Bradley included in his cookbooks lengthy discussions on brewing, recommending the types of water, corks, vessels, and cellars to be used for the best brewing. Bradley urged women to keep bees so that they could make mead from the honey. He also exhorted them to cultivate gooseberries, elderberries, and currants for home winemaking. He explained that alcoholic beverage production belonged to women's province because "the fair sex" should "have [the] care and management of every business within doors, and to see after the good ordering of whatever is belonging to the house." Gervase Markham's *Country Contentments and The English Huswife* likewise offered explicit advice to women on brewing. Mary Cole, author of *The Lady's Complete Guide,* reminded women that "the house-keeper cannot be said to be complete in her business, without a competent knowledge in the art of brewing." Sir Kenelme Digby advised women on how to cider, suggesting that they "take a peck [eight quarts] of Apples, and slice them, and boil them in a barrel of water . . . draw forth the water . . . three or four times a day . . . then press out the liquor, and tun it up; when it has done working, then stop it up close." His instructions indicate that the women reading his recipe were already familiar with cidering. He never described how to "tun" or "draw" the cider, nor what it would look, smell, or taste like when it was finished. Instead, he assumed that women already had this knowledge.[20]

Yet over the course of the sixteenth and seventeenth centuries, men increasingly assumed control of alcoholic beverage production in western Europe, Latin America, New England, and the Middle Colonies. By the eighteenth century alcohol production in these areas was a mostly male pursuit. In large part this regendering of alcohol production, at least in England, was due to rising population and urbanization during the sixteenth and seventeenth centuries. According to Judith Bennet, an expert on gender and brewing in medieval England, in London and other densely populated areas, women who did not have the space for, or the desire, to brew found that they could purchase their beer. For example, Lady Margaret Hoby brewed her own ale and cider when she lived in rural Hackness, England, but bought her beer when she resided in London. To summarize Bennet's analysis, the brewers' guild had begun in London in the fourteenth century with both male and female members. But during the sixteenth century the brewers' guild became all-male, giving men the control of the trade. Several factors coincided to transform the brewers' guild into an all-male guild. The first of these was the king's desire to increase revenues. In 1552 the king decreed that ale could be sold only from alehouses that were licensed for a fee intended to line the king's coffers. If this act had been enforced, it would have prevented women from selling in the streets or out of their homes. As it stood, the act was not enforced, and women continued to sell their ale out of doors. The act did, however, set a precedent. Particularly in urban areas where surveillance was easier, alehouses were increasingly required to purchase their ale from licensed wholesalers. Over time, women who could not afford the licenses, or who brewed only a little extra on the side, found themselves removed from selling to the alehouses, on the streets, or out of their homes.[21]

The brewers' guild, as Bennet shows, supported the king's decrees for its own reasons. Those who belonged to the guild wanted to limit the number of ale producers and sellers in order to maintain profits. They limited those who could join the guild by policing the licensing requirements, brewing apprenticeships, and apprenticeship fees. Over time these actions removed women from the guild since women, who were expected to marry, raise children, and maintain households, could not spend three to seven years training, as was required to become a professional brewer.

The king's and the brewers' guild's desires for revenues alone, however, could not have caused the transition from female to male brewers in England. The brewing fees were unpopular. At St. Edmund's a great number of poor people "presented a petition to the Justices of Assize against the new licensed common brewers' monopoly," who "under pretense of doing good to the commonwealth, have for their own lucre and gain privately combined themselves, and procured orders from the Privy Council." The male and female petitioners thanked female brewers who "at the several times of their brewing (being moved with pity and compassion, knowing our great extremities and necessities) with such quantities of their small beer as has been a continual help and comfort to us." Such people were unlikely to report those who resisted the new licenses, fees, and regulations. Without an additional element, the king and the brewers' guild would have continued to attempt to enforce the new regulations, but most likely with only erratic success. The English were accustomed to women brewing and selling their production. There was no reason to change.[22]

Or so was the case before the introduction of hops. As Bennet has explained, Dutch aliens, men who were brewers in the highly masculinized Dutch brewing industry, began to brew and market their *hopped* beer in southeast England during the fifteenth century. Beer brewed with hops will keep significantly longer than ale (which in early modern lexicon was, by definition, unhopped, a distinction in the language that lasted until the early nineteenth century), which spoils in about three days. The hopped beer would eventually dominate the market. But its acceptance was slow. Instead, the English continued to prefer the sweeter unhopped ale until at least the end of the fifteenth century. More conservative English people continued to view beer with xenophobia throughout the seventeenth century. "Beer is a Dutch boorish liquor," wrote John Taylor in 1651, "a thing not known in England, till of late days an alien to our nation, till such times hops and heresies came among us." By the end of the seventeenth century, however, most English men and women were drinking hopped beer and this drink increasingly dominated the alcohol trade.[23]

The transition to hopped beer held long-term gender implications, as Bennet has shown. The production of hopped beer required more fuel, more labor, and more capital, than unhopped ale. Imported hops were expensive, and since hopped beer needed to mature before sale, the producer had to have the capital to maintain larger stocks. The majority of women lacked the capital to brew beer on the commercial scale. Bennet has also suggested that women lost control of the brewing industry in England because English misogyny limited women's managerial authority, access to distant markets, and participation with the wholesale distribution market that requires business relations of mutual trust and obligation. Accordingly, writes Bennet, "In the sixteenth century the civic face of brewing became a male face." Ultimately, women lost control over alcoholic beverage production, Bennet argues, because "public anxieties about the drink trade—its resistance to effective regulation, its encouragement of vice, its manipulation of the public—were displaced from all brewers onto female brewers alone." Bennet's history ends in sixteenth-century England with urban alcohol production, which was mostly beer, having become men's domain. For our purposes it is useful to add that English men had also assumed control of cidering. Authors wrote books for men to aid them in both brewing and cidering. For example, Thomas Chapman's *The Cyder-Maker's Instructor* advised men "to make his cyder in the manner foreign wines are made . . . directs the brewer to fine his beer and ale in a short time." Chapman, like other authors, offered cider, beer, yeast, and wine recipes for men.[24]

While English alcohol production became masculinized in the seventeenth century, it became feminized in the Chesapeake. Readers may be wondering at this point how Chesapeake colonists obtained alcohol before the eighteenth century. The scarcity of extant documents makes it difficult to know. It appears likely that, just as colonists vociferously complained, they were indeed "a colony by water drinkers" in large part because they had so few women.[25]

Around 1680, Chesapeake colonists began to enjoy greater demographic gender parity. From the 1650s to the 1680s the Chesapeake had about three men to every woman. After 1680, more women immigrated to the Chesapeake. Lorena Walsh and Lois Carr found, for example, that while male London immigrants to Maryland from 1634 to 1635 outnumbered women by six to one, from 1697 to

1707 that ratio dropped to two and one-half men to each woman. At the same time the population began to grow through reproductive increase. As a result of immigration and natural increase, the gender imbalance declined and more men could find wives. Until the 1680s men who managed to marry often used their wives to grow tobacco. The increasing importation of slaves and the decline in tobacco prices in the 1670s and 1680s released white women from raising tobacco. Women then had more time to perform household work, part of which was cidering.[26]

So in the latter half of the seventeenth century while English women were decreasing their alcohol production activities, women in the Chesapeake were increasing theirs. For example, when the Accomack County court awarded land to John Cole in 1690, Mary, "the wife of the said Cole, was to have the privilege during her life to make use of the old orchard [for] making liquor." When Edward Pitway sold his land to George Corke in 1668, he stipulated that half of the fruit the orchard produced each year was to be given to Pitway's wife Elizabeth for her cidering. Henry Baker left his wife Sarah "half my land, orchards, etc. during her natural life," for her cidering. Elizabeth Middleton was presented to the court for selling alcohol that she made out of her house without a license in 1723. And in 1734 Elizabeth Harrison of Berkely, Virginia, ordered "1 great cooling tub" for her brewing and cidering.[27]

Wills and inventories indicate that women of a wide variety of economic standings cidered in the Chesapeake. Well-off Elizabeth Ballard of Charles City County owned three cider casks, three cider hogsheads, three cider barrels, and seven dozen bottles as well as two slaves, a feather bed, a mirror, pewter cutlery, some fine cloth, a cow, a horse, and five pounds in gold. Middling-class Sabra Crew had two "old cows," one "old horse," an "old gun" without a lock, one "old rug," and one "old blanket," as well as "old pots," "old pot hooks," and "two old tubs" for cidering. Mary Tye, who was of lower-middling status, also owned the tools necessary to cider although she had little else: a "parcel of old iron," an "old pot with hook," and two "pots with racks."[28]

The room-by-room inventories compiled by researchers at Colonial Williamsburg reveal that cidering equipment was housed in the same "women's spaces" where women performed their other household labors. When men assumed control of alcoholic beverage production in the latter half of the eighteenth century, the necessary equipment moved to "men's spaces," particularly the barn. Until then such equipment stayed in the kitchen, dairy, or where women made textiles, in places where women could check on its contents frequently. For example, Nathaniel Bradford's 1690 estate maintained two cider casks and three cider pipes in the kitchen. John Thompson's 1700 Surry County household also kept "old casks" and "old tubs" for alcohol production in the kitchen. James Burwell's household stored four tubs for cidering in the kitchen. In 1704, Joseph Ring's household in York County maintained one "old still" in the same chamber as the buttering equipment, including a "stone butter pot," thus combining women's alcohol production and dairying in one room. Joseph Frith's household similarly stored dairying and alcohol-production equipment together, with cider casks and dairying tools in the dairy. Madam Katherine Gwyn kept her syllabub pots in the dairy with her milk pans, decanter, and butter pots. Arthur Allen's household kept sixteen cider casks and other cidering and molasses-beer brewing equipment including thirty-five gallons of molasses, four pot racks, two cider clothes, and six yards of hair cloth (used for straining cider) in the still house with the spinning wheel.[29]

Cookbooks that were popular in seventeenth- and eighteenth-century America, and recipe books written by early American women themselves presumed or asserted that it was women who produced alcoholic beverages. The cookbooks that colonial women wrote themselves reveal their brewing, cidering, and winemaking activities. Hannah Huthwaite either concocted or copied recipes for quince wine and raspberry wine in her *Recipe Book*. As a newlywed, Harriott Horry copied recipes for eleven alcoholic beverages, including recipes for spruce beer (fermented molasses) and shrub. Martha Washington compiled and created recipes in a recipe book that she presented to her granddaughter, Eleanor Parke Custis, when Custis married. Washington's presentation of her recipes, including how "to make cider," to Custis as a gift suggests that alcohol recipes were valuable property.[30]

Chesapeake women made perry (a cider of pears), peach "brandy," (a cider of peaches), and persimmon "beer" (a cider of persimmons) as well as apple cider through a straightforward, if laborious, procedure when orchard fruits were in season from July to December. Men occasionally helped with cidering, particularly with beating the apples. Few households had cider presses because carpenters charged upwards of £2,000 to build them. So, in the majority of households women and men first beat the apples (or pears, or peaches, or persimmons) in a wooden trough. Then the women transferred the pulp to bags of woven hair that would let the juices run through. Next, they pressed the remaining pulp with sieves, and collected all the juice into a tub where it sat covered with cloths or boards for at least twenty-four hours. Then the women decanted the liquid into another container to leave the lees behind, a time-consuming process that was repeated several times. The cider was then bottled or tunned into cider casks.[31]

Colonial writers celebrated women's alcoholic beverage production activities. "What a useful acquisition a good wife is to an American farmer," exclaimed St.

John De Crevecoeur, "and how small is his chance of prosperity if he draws a blank in that lottery! [Without wives] *what should we do with our fruit*, our fowls, our eggs? There is no market for these articles but in the neighborhood of the great towns" [emphasis added]. Colonists, Crevecoeur stressed, depended on women's skills in food and drink preparation. "There lies the 'aurum potabile' of an American farmer," he concluded, the farmer "may work and gather the choicest fruits of his farm, but if female economy fails, he loses the comfort of good victuals . . . if we are blessed with a good wife, we may boast of living better than any people of the same rank on the globe." Similarly, Benjamin Franklin rhymed in his popular 1746 *Almanack*:

> Thanks to kind readers and a careful wife,
> With plenty blessed, I lead an easy life;
> My business writing; her's to drain the Mead,
> . . . Press nectarous cider from my loaded trees,
> Print the sweet butter, turn the drying cheese.[32]

The reference in Franklin's 1746 poem to his wife's making mead in Pennsylvania may be confusing since alcohol production in New England and the Middle Colonies followed England's trajectory and was increasingly masculinized in the seventeenth and eighteenth centuries. Alcoholic beverage production in those colonies, as in England, was masculinized because those areas were drinking ever larger amounts of alcoholic beverages like beer and distilled liquors that involved technology, namely hops and stills, which led to their masculinization. Mead, however, was a raw alcohol, requiring only water and honey. While mead was not a common drink in the colonies, making it before the latter half of the eighteenth century was women's work. Women likewise made molasses "beer," which was a fermented mixture of water and molasses.[33]

Why did Chesapeake colonists turn to women to make alcoholic beverages during the late seventeenth and early eighteenth centuries when the rest of the Western world was turning to men? This question is particularly puzzling because immigrants to the Chesapeake in the seventeenth and eighteenth centuries knew that alcoholic beverage production was increasingly men's domain. The answer is in part demographic. While people from many parts of Europe and Africa emigrated to the Chesapeake, both freely and unfreely, the Chesapeake remained an overwhelmingly English society in the late seventeenth and early eighteenth centuries. "The two colonies," writes James Horn, a leading authority on the seventeenth-century Chesapeake immigration, "depended on large-scale immigration from English provinces to maintain their populations and allow economic growth." As Horn found, the majority of these English immigrants left for the

New World from urban areas of England, most commonly from London and Bristol where men controlled the alcohol trade. Nearly one-third of the free immigrants to the Chesapeake in the seventeenth century came from London; when immigrants from the metropolis and southeastern counties surrounding London are included that number rises to just under one-half. Another twenty percent were from the Bristol Channel area and the counties from there to the Thames Valley. So, almost sixty percent of the free immigrants to the Chesapeake left from urban regions. Indentured servants sailed from urban areas even more frequently. Eighty to ninety percent of the servants who went to the Chesapeake during the first four decades of colonization left from London. During the rest of the century, sixty percent of indentured servants left from London, and the rest came from Bristol and Liverpool. Immigrants from other areas of western Europe were accustomed to male alcohol production as well. The situation was similar in Holland, for example, where alcohol production was increasingly restricted to men. In fact, the Amsterdam Brewer's guild declared in 1682 that women could no longer practice the trade. Chesapeake immigrants knew that it was increasingly men who made alcohol.[34]

While Chesapeake immigrants had spent time in the English cities, and thus encountered male-brewed hopped beer, most had grown up in less-urban areas. Horn concluded that almost sixty percent of the immigrants "were from urban backgrounds [which] strongly suggests that aspiring colonial merchants and planters first moved from their own county town or parish to one of the two major colonial ports before eventually taking ship to America." In other words, many servants who immigrated to the New World had first left their home parishes to try their luck in England's cities. When they were unable to find work in London or Bristol, they decided to move on to the New World. When Horn analyzed the background of servants who ostensibly came from Bristol, he found that they were really from county towns and provincial capitals. "Servants traveled to Bristol," Horn has concluded, "in ones and twos from hundreds of parishes scattered throughout the West."[35]

Despite the urban experiences of the Chesapeake's white immigrants, most of these immigrants had rural origins. This fact is important because it means that they were familiar with both men and women making alcohol. In parishes, villages, and small towns throughout England women continued to make cider and ale until the eighteenth century. Just when the role of women in rural English alcohol production declined during the end of the seventeenth century, English immigration to the Chesapeake slowed. In fact, English immigration slowed so much that by the second decade of the eighteenth century, the white population of the Chesapeake formed a Creole society. English immigration to the Chesapeake thus reduced to a trickle, just as English alcohol production rushed toward complete masculinization. Immigrants to the New World had become familiar with men making their beer and spirits when they lived in London, Bristol, and other urban areas, but retained a memory of women making alcohol, particularly ale and cider in their home parishes.

Chesapeake colonists drew on this memory, and before the latter half of the eighteenth century, Chesapeake households depended on women's cider production because the requirements of the tobacco crop left them little time to develop the crops and technology, namely hops, oats, barley, and stills, necessary for other forms of (male) alcohol production. Lois Carr, Russell Menard, and Lorena Walsh have shown that the labor necessary to raise tobacco prevented Chesapeake colonists from growing much else. Raising tobacco required an extraordinary amount of labor. Planters raising tobacco had to clear the land, burn the underbrush, mix ashes into the earth for fertility, prepare and plant the seedbeds, and cover the beds with leaves and boughs to protect them from frost. On warm days, planters removed the coverings and laid them again at night. Planters had to water the plants twice a day if it was dry, weed and thin the plants, transplant the seedlings to hills made with hoes as the seedlings grew, replace the plants that had died, crush the hornworms that infested the plants, top and sucker the plant, and then cut, cure, pack, and transport the leaf for sale. If colonists wanted to eat, they also had to shell corn, haul water, slaughter hogs and cattle, salt and smoke meat, replace damaged fruit trees, and chop thirty cords of firewood per cooking hearth. Women had to card, spin, and weave the wool, sew the clothes, grind the corn, nurse their babies, tend their children and, if they could read themselves, teach the children to read, make the food, preserve the fruits, vegetables, and meats, dip the candles, press the butter and cheese, clean the home, plant, weed, thin and hoe the gardens, wash the laundry, and, of course, make the cider.[36]

Men and women in the Chesapeake did not have time to grow the hops, barley, or oats necessary for English-style beer; these crops were labor intensive and time-consuming at a time when colonists wanted to use their land, labor, and time for tobacco. It was more labor effective for Chesapeake colonists to make cider, just as in order to save labor they grew corn rather than wheat. Hops were extraordinarily time consuming and expensive to grow. In order to grow hops, planters had to remove the rocks from the ground, plant the hops in deep, mellow soil, shelter them, space them evenly, groom them frequently to prevent mold, lice, and insects, water them often, and protect them from hogs, cattle, and fowl. The vines of the hops had to be twisted, laid with dung, covered, and placed on tall poles. Then the hops had to be picked, cleaned, and turned constantly while drying in bags. For replanting the following year to be possible, the poles had to be stripped, and the land manured. Moreover, as the Royal Dublin Society warned, growing hops was expensive and risky. "It is not proper for poor farmers, or men of small fortunes, to engage far in this improvement, for it requires a considerable stock," the society cautioned. "The expenses will be great, and the undertaker must expect to lay out his money for two or three years, before he can have any return of profit, and even when his hops come to their bearing state, and he is in hopes of making good the charges he has been at, he may be disappointed by a bad season." Furthermore, "the hop is a very tender plant, and an uncertain commodity to deal in, that it is very apt to suffer by winds, blights, mildews, rains, droughts, and insects, and when it wholly fails, the loss is intolerable, and if there be a general good crop, the price will be so low, that it will hardly answer the charge." The Virginia Assembly offered repeatedly to pay any Virginia colonist who raised "so much silk, flax, hops or any other staple commodity (except tobacco) as is worth two hundred pounds sterling," a credit for ten thousand pounds of tobacco. (Such credits circulated like money.) But hops production in the Chesapeake remained insignificant. The amount of labor and the expense of growing hops explains why Chesapeake colonists chose not to plant them. Colonists decided to focus on the production of the profitable tobacco crop rather than waste their land and their time on a crop that might not succeed.[37]

Not only did Chesapeake colonists not grow the hops necessary to make beer, most of them could not purchase hops. Because of the Chesapeake's emphasis on tobacco, it remained overwhelmingly rural; in contrast, New England and the Middle Colonies developed towns. Even small planters needed 100 to 200 acres. In contrast, much of New England was laid out in towns that required all colonists to live within five miles of a church. As a result of New England's and the Middle Colonies' towns and mixed farming economies, these areas developed markets where colonists could purchase malt, hops, barley, and oats if they did not grow them themselves. But with a few exceptions, before 1760 Chesapeake colonists could not purchase hops, malt, barley, or oats, in part because they did not have markets or towns in which to purchase these items. The lack of coastwide shipping meant that residents could not import these items from the northern colonies. The importation of hops from England was negligible because they were expensive and because, given the requirements of growing tobacco, few people had time to experiment with them anyway.

The Chesapeake was anomalous. It was not only families in England that increasingly relied on male-produced beer; New England and Middle Colony colonists who did not wish to brew or cider could also purchase male-produced beer. By 1637 Massachusetts had to restrict the number of brewing licenses because the colony had so many men brewing. By 1800 New York had forty male-operated breweries and Pennsylvania had forty-eight. When Ellen Cary married in Boston, her Virginia mother, Martha Randolph, wrote to her that "I have not sent you those 'receipes' [*sic*] which as a town lady would be useless to you. For example you need not know how to make soap or blackening or yeast or ley and rennet &c &c, nor do I presume you will ever brew your own beer or make your own candles, therefore I sent you nothing of that sort." Unlike New England town women, Chesapeake women could not purchase locally made beer, yeast, or malt. In Jean Russo's study of craftsmen in one Chesapeake county from 1690 to 1760, she found over 800 craftsmen, but no brewers. Indeed the first advertisement for beer in either the *Virginia Gazette* or the *Maryland Gazette* did not appear until 1746.[38]

Chesapeake colonists quickly discovered that even English ale (made without hops) was impracticable in the Chesapeake because it required malt. In England, New England, and the Middle Colonies, well-off women could purchase malt, and poor women at least had the ingredients, namely oats and barley, to make malt. To make malt the brewer needed a large vessel for soaking the grain, a ladle to draw off the water, a shovel or fork to turn the grain, and a device for drying the grain, or access to a malt kiln, as well as yeast and oats, or a mixture of oats and barley called dredge. Once the grain began to produce sugars it was dried, at which point it became malt. The brewer then ground the malt and mixed it with boiling water in a mash tun or other vessel until the mash reached a pudding-like consistency. Then the brewer slowly percolated hot water through the mixture. Next, the brewer drew off the wort or liquor and mixed it with yeast and herbs, which produced a strong beer ready for drinking in a day or less. To brew small ale, the brewer made a second brewing from the spent mash of the first brewing.[39]

Chesapeake women could not make even this simple, unhopped ale because they did not sow oats and barley, which were more labor intensive than corn, for malt. "The richer sort generally brew their small-beer with malt, which they have from England," wrote Robert Beverley in his early-eighteenth-century history of Virginia, "but for want of the convenience of malt-houses, the inhabitants take no care to sow it," and so small planter households had no malt from which to brew. The lack of oats and barley was not the only reason that Chesapeake women did not make ale from malt. Malting itself, as explained above, required a good deal of work, even when the ingredients were easy to come by. "Few of them are come to malting their corn, of any kind, at which I was much surprized," commented one traveler, "as even the Indian grain, as I have found experimentally will produce an wholesome and generous liquor." Chesapeake colonists found it less labor intensive to rely on cider than to make ale from either dredge or corn.[40]

It was not only with alcoholic beverages that the early Chesapeake was a most unusual English province. Indeed, alcoholic beverage production was only one realm in which Chesapeake colonists reduced unnecessary labor. For example, colonists quickly learned to fence their vegetables rather than their animals, a practice that reduced the amount of necessary fencing and labor. In another instance, despite numerous attempts on the part of the Chesapeake legislatures to create English-style capitals and towns, Chesapeake colonists did not succumb. With the vast majority of colonists growing tobacco and obtaining their goods through home-production or imports dispersed by the great planters along the rivers, what were they going to do in towns? Colonists kept English laws and governance, but simplified them to meet their needs. In England, provincial assemblies and courts of appeals were separate affairs, but in the Chesapeake they were frequently the same. Colonists continued to celebrate traditional English holidays, but also added celebrations for the anniversaries of successes in battles with Native Americans.[41]

Chesapeake colonists "adapted to the New World" with their alcoholic drinks as well, making beverages that were unfamiliar to men and women in England. Persimmon "beer," in particular, was not an English tradition. In fact, Europeans were unfamiliar with persimmons. A Frenchman touring Virginia in 1686 commented upon seeing a persimmon that "there are quantities of a kind of tree that bears fruit as large as apples. Its flavor is excellent & it is pleasant to see." In 1736 an English traveler in the Chesapeake recorded that "we gather'd a fruite [while traveling in Maryland] , in our route, called a parsimon, of a very delicious taste, not unlike a medlar, tho' somewhat larger: I take it to be a very cooling fruit, and the settlers make use of prodigious quantities to sweeten a beer . . . which is vastly wholesome." In 1735, Virginian John Custis sent his friend in England, Peter Collinson, some persimmon seeds because the famous English horticulturalist had never seen persimmons despite his travels. Even as late as 1777, British travelers in the Chesapeake remained unfamiliar with persimmon beer. One noted that "there are amazing quantities of persimons [sic] all along the road. The Virginians make beer of them."[42]

Chesapeake households supplemented their fruit alcohols with corn-based alcohols that were, again, unfamiliar to the English. One was an ale made of coarsely crushed corn and mixed with water, making a sour, fermented beverage. Another was a mix of water and whole corn kernels that formed a sharp, sweet, fermented drink. Sometimes honey was added to these mixtures for a type of mead. "We had a hodge podge of breakfast," griped one traveler of a meal in Virginia, which included "only one gallon of corn toddie," although it cost him two dollars. "The poorer sort brew their beer with molasses and bran," commented Robert Beverley, "with *Indian* corn malted by drying in a stove; with persimmons dried in cakes, and baked; with potatoes; with the green stalks of *Indian corn* cut small, and bruised; [and] with pompions [pumpkins]."[43]

While authors appreciated women's skills in making traditional and New World drinks, alcoholic beverage production did not give women any special status or power in the seventeenth- or early-eighteenth-century Chesapeake. This is striking because Bennet found that ale production gave women economic and social power in medieval England. In the fourteenth and fifteenth centuries, Bennet has shown, women took turns producing ale and selling it to their neighbors and local markets; this practice gave women significant business experience and profits. In the Chesapeake the situation was different. Although Chesapeake women sold their alcohol occasionally, this activity was not common. In the Chesapeake there were no markets for women to sell their cider to, and few neighbors close by. Besides, women could not make enough cider to keep their households in drink year-round, so they had little surplus to sell. Women did often manage "taverns," usually in the front room or kitchen of their houses. These operations, as I explain in more detail elsewhere, were family endeavors. There is no evidence that this public housewifery gave the majority of tavern-keeping women economic or social power. Like alcoholic beverage production, tavern keeping was simply something that women did as part of their share of the household labor.[44]

Why have we forgotten that alcoholic beverage production used to be women's work? The answer is in part because until quite recently neither the study of alcohol, nor the study of women, was viewed as legitimate. The general illiteracy of Chesapeake men and women meant that they left few records behind from which to study women's work. It is only delving into documents that previous generations of historians discounted, such as cookbooks and the probate records of kitchens, that reveals that women made alcohol as well as food. Court records have made it appear that women did not engage in alcoholic beverage production, or much else, because they appear so infrequently. Cornelia Dayton has shown that while women may have had equal access to courts in the seventeenth century, a growing "legal fraternity" of judges, justices of the peace, professional attorneys, trial jurors, and grand jurors in the eighteenth century meant that increasingly court cases "were filtered through several layers of men." The resulting eighteenth-century court records, like the case of George Sisson's cider cited at the beginning of this essay, therefore portray only men's perceptions. Finally we have forgotten that alcoholic beverage production was women's work for the same reasons that women's other labors became invisible or denigrated. Kathleen Brown has argued that planters' desire for complete control over women and slaves led them to discount women's labor in eighteenth-century Virginia. Deborah Rosen has demonstrated that laws of coverture and inheritance "worked to marginalize women from the growing [eighteenth-century] economy." And Jeanne Boydson has shown that the value placed on women's domestic labor in general declined during the eighteenth century. So that while "the colonial goodwife [was] valued for her contribution to household prosperity," by the mid-eighteenth century "the denigration of women's household labor was becoming an established cultural practice." I would add that women's acceptance of men's assumption of women's labor has further hidden women's alcohol production from view. When men began producing rum and other distilled beverages in the second half of the eighteenth century, women supported their activities by purchasing the rum. It is possible that early American women—and not just early American men—wanted the regendering of alcoholic beverage production. Since women gained little by making alcoholic beverages in the early Chesapeake, perhaps they were just as happy to forget that making alcohol was women's work.[45]

Notes

1. Fellowships from The Library Company of Pennsylvania, Virginia Historical Society, Winterthur Library, Museum & Gardens, and a Beveridge grant from the American Historical Association supported the research for this article. John Hammond, "Leah and Rachel, or, The Two Fruitfull Sisters, Virginia and Mary-land," in *Narratives of Early Maryland 1633–1684*, ed. Clayton Colman Hall (New York, 1910), p. 292.

2. *Criminal Proceedings in Colonial Virginia: [Records of] Fines, Examination of Criminals, Trials of Slaves, etc., from March 1710 [1711] to [1754] [Richmond County, Virginia]*, eds. Peter Charles Hoffer and William B. Scott (Athens, Ga., 1984), p. 43.

3. Greene argues that "far from having been a peripheral, much less a deviant, area, the southern colonies and states were before 1800 in the mainstream of British-American development," in Jack P. Greene, *Pursuits of Happiness: The Social Development of Early Modern British Colonies and the Formation of American Culture* (Chapel Hill, 1988), p. 5.

4. Rhys Isaac, *The Transformation of Virginia 1740–1790* (New York, 1982), p. 21. For further discussion about the definition of a small planter see Lois Green Carr and Lorena S. Walsh, "Economic Diversification and Labor Organization in the Chesapeake, 1650–1820," in *Work and Labor in Early America*, ed. Stephen Innes (Chapel Hill, 1988), p. 148.

5. A. Lynn Martin, "How Much Did They Drink? The Consumption of Alcohol in Traditional Europe," Alcohol History and Temperance Society Listserv, 3 Jan. 2001. See also A. Lynn Martin, *Alcohol, Sex, and Gender in Late Medieval and Early Modern Europe* (New York, 2001), pp. 28–32, and Judith M. Bennet, *Ale, Beer, and Brewsters in England: Women's Work in a Changing World, 1300–1600* (Oxford, 1996), p. 17. Kenelme Digbie, *The Closet of the Eminently Learned Sir Kenelme Digbie Kt. Opened*, ed. Jane Stevenson and Peter Davidson (1669; reprint, Devon, 1997), p. xxx.

6. Martin, "How Much Did They Drink?" *Gervase Markham, Country Contentments, or The English Huswife* (London, 1623), p. 11. Microfilm. Peter Clark, *The English Alehouse: A Social History 1200–1830* (New York, 1983), pp. 101–2. Elspeth Graham, "Diary," in *"Capacious Hold-All": An Anthology of Englishwomen's Diary Writings*, ed. Harriet Blodgett (Charlottesville, 1991), p. 85. Brian Harrison, *Drink and the Victorians, The Temperance Question in England 1815–1871* (Pittsburgh, 1971), p. 39. *The Servants' Guide and Family Manual*, 2d ed. (London, 1831), p. 118. Microfilm. Lydia Maria Child, *The Family Nurse; or, Companion of the Frugal Housewife* (Boston, 1837), p. 118. Microfilm.

7. Christina Hole, *The English Housewife in the Seventeenth Century* (London, 1953), pp. 71–72.

8. See *The Servants' Guide*, pp. 53, 56, and Robert Roberts, *The House-Servant's Directory; or, a Monitor for Private Families*, 2d ed. (Boston, 1828), pp. 20–21, 24. Microfilm. Roberts, *The House-Servant's Directory*, pp. 80, 87, 92, 33, 108. Lydia Maria Child, *The Frugal Housewife* (Boston,1831), p. 19. Microfilm. Roberts, *The House-Servant's Directory*, p. 27.

9. Gregory A. Stiverson and Patrick H. Butler III, eds., "Virginia in 1732: The Travel Journal of William Hugh Grove," *Virginia Magazine of History and Biography* 85: 1 (1977), p. 24.

10. Gloria Main, *Tobacco Colony: Life in Early Maryland 1650–1720* (Princeton, 1982), p. 197. Wyndham B. Blanton, *Medicine in Virginia in the Seventeenth Century* (Richmond, 1930), p. 72. George Percy quoted in Steven G. Davison, Jay G. Merwin, Jr., John Capper, Garrett Power, and Frank R. Shivers, Jr., *Chesapeake Waters: Four Centuries of Controversy, Concern and Legislation*, 2d ed. (Centreville, Md., 1997), p. 3. Andrew Barr, *Drink: A Social History of America* (New York, 1999), p. 32. Blanton, *Medicine in Virginia in the Seventeenth Century*, pp. 54, 55.

11. Davison et al., *Chesapeake Waters*, p. 35. See also Moses N. Baker, *The Quest for Pure Water: The History of Water Purification from the Earliest Records to the Twentieth Century* (New York, 1948), pp. 35–36. The first attempt at water filtration in the United States was not until 1832, in Richmond, Virginia, and the attempt quickly failed. It would take another century before the city made its next attempt at water purification. Increasing industrialization in the nineteenth century only made the water pollution worse. Colonists, visitors, servants, and slaves drank the filthy and disease-ridden water when they had to; this practice led, among hundreds of other illnesses, to cholera outbreaks in 1832, 1843, 1849, 1854, 1865, and 1873 from the mosquitoes that bred in the stagnant water in the Chesapeake. Gloria Main, *Tobacco Colony*, p. 197. Blanton, *Medicine in Virginia in the Seventeenth Century*, p. 72. George Percy quoted in Davison et al., *Chesapeake Waters*, p. 3. Blanton, *Medicine in Virginia*, pp. 54–55. Ebenezer Hazard, "The Journal of Ebenezer Hazard in Virginia, 1777," ed. Fred Shelley, *Virginia Magazine History and Biography* 62:4, p. 410. John Frederick Dorman, *Caroline County, Virginia Order Book 1759–1763: part 1 1759–1760* (n.p., 1982), 15 June 1759. Nicholas Cresswell, *The Journal of Nicholas Cresswell 1774–1777*, ed. Lincoln MacVeagh (New York, 1924), p. 22. Theophilus Wreg, *The Virginia Almanck for the Year of our Lord God 1766* (Williamsburg, 1765), n.p., LCP.

12. Francis Louis Michel, "Report of the Journey of Francis Louis Michel from

Berne, Switzerland, to Virginia October 2, 1701–December 1, 1702," trans. and ed. William J. Hinke, *Virginia Magazine of History and Biography* 24: 2 (April 1916), p. 127. William Byrd, *The Secret Diary of William Byrd of Westover 1709–1712*, eds. Louis B. Wright and Marion Tinling (Richmond, 1941), p. 270. Byrd, *Secret Diary*, p. 298.

13. Byrd, *Secret Diary*, p. 324, law signed 9 Dec. 1710. W. J. Rorabaugh, *The Alcoholic Republic: An American Tradition* (Oxford, 1979), p. 15. Alice Granbery Walter, *Lower Norfolk County, Virginia, Court Records: Book "A" 1637 to 1746 and Book "B" 1646–1652* (Baltimore, 1994), 16 Dec. 1647, p. 58. Byrd, *Secret Diary*, p. 218.

14. Byrd, *Secret Diary*, p. 232. Thomas R. Pegram, *Battling Demon Rum: The Struggle for a Dry America, 1800–1933* (Chicago, 1998), p. ix. Rorabaugh, *The Alcoholic Republic*, p. 20. Grog was a mixture of rum and water. "Trade and Travel in Post-Revolutionary Virginia: A Diary of an Itinerant Peddler, 1807–1808," ed. Richard R. Beeman, *Virginia Magazine of History & Biography* 87:2 (April 1976): p. 183. Robinson quoted in Ann Smart Martin, "Buying into the World of Goods: Eighteenth-Century Consumerism and the Retail Trade from London to the Virginia Frontier," (Ph.D. diss., College of William & Mary, 1993), p. 202.

15. Byrd, *Secret Diary*, p. 60.

16. "Observations in Several Voyages and Travels in America," *William and Mary Quarterly*, 2d ser., 16: 1 (Jan. 1907): p. 4. Byrd, *Secret Diary*, p. 165.

17. See, for example, Thomas Jefferson, *Jefferson's Memorandum Books: Accounts, with Legal Records and Miscellany, 1767–1826*, ed. James A. Bear and Lucia C. Stanton (Princeton, 1997), 25 June 1813 when Jefferson furnished his overseer with whiskey for Jefferson's slaves. Lawrence William McKee, "Plantation Food Supply in Nineteenth-Century Tidewater Virginia," (Ph.D. diss., University California, Berkeley, 1988), p. 128. John Harvie, *Account Book of John Harvie, 26 July 1759 and 30 Aug. 1759*, photostat, UVA. Joseph Ball, *Joseph Ball Letterbook 1743–1780*, letter to Joseph Chinn, 25 March 1742/43, LC. See also Edward Ayres, "Fruit Culture in Colonial Virginia," *Colonial Williamsburg Research Report*, April 1773, 142. Microfilm. William Byrd, *Another Secret Diary of William Byrd of Westover 1739–1741*, ed. Maude H. Woodfin (Richmond, 1942), p. 32. Byrd, *Secret Diary*, p. 528. Byrd, *Another Secret Diary*, p. 119.

18. "Letters of the Byrd Family," *Virginia Magazine of History and Biography* 37: 2 (April 1929): p. 109. John Custis, letter to Mr. Loyd or Mr. Boyd (name is difficult to read) 1733, *John Custis Letterbook 1717–1744*, vol. 2, p. 131. Byrd, *Secret Diary*, pp. 315, 211.

19. Continental winemaking was generally men's domain, although widows sometimes continued their husband's winemaking trade. English women made household "wines," which did not necessarily ferment, from a variety of garden berries and fruits. Susan Cahn, *Industry of Devotion: The Transformation of Women's Work in England 1500–1660* (New York, 1987), p. 33. Clark, *The English Alehouse*, p. 47. Thomas Tusser, *Thomas Tusser 1557 Floruit: His Good Points of Husbandry*, ed. Dorothy Hartley (New York, 1970), pp. 166, 169, 171 quoted in Hole, *The English Housewife in the Seventeenth Century*, pp. 108–9. Stanley Baron, *Brewed in America: A History of Beer and Ale in the United States* (Boston, 1962), p. 14.

20. Richard Bradley, *The Country Housewife and Lady's Director* (1727; reprint, London

1732) pp. vii, 51–52, LCP. Mary Cole, *The Lady's Complete Guide; or, Cookery in all its Branches*, 2d. ed. (1788; London, 1791), p. 361, LCP. Kenelme Digbie, *The Closet of the Eminently Learned Sir Kenelme Digbie Kt. Opened*, p. 81.

21. See Bennet, *Ale, Beer, and Brewsters in England.*

22. Quotes protesting fees are from Clark, *The English Alehouse*, p. 227.

23. By 1400 Holland and Germany already had highly masculinized beer-brewing industries with breweries of size that England would not reach for another 100 years. German lager would not become popular in England or America until the nineteenth century. See Judith M. Bennet, *Ale, Beer, and Brewsters in England*, p. 82, and Hole, *The English Housewife*, p. 58–59. See also Richard W. Unger, *A History of Brewing in Holland 900–1900: Economy, Technology and the State* (Leiden, 2001).

24. Bennet, *Ale, Beer, and Brewsters*, pp. 11, 12. Thomas Chapman, *The Cyder-Maker's Instructor, Sweet-Makers Assistant, and Victualler's and Housekeeper's Director* (London, 1762), p. 9, LCP.

25. Francis Wyatt, letter dated 3 April 1623, quoted in Baron, *Brewed in America*, p. 6.

26. Lois Green Carr and Lorena S. Walsh, "The Planter's Wife: The Experience of White Women in Seventeenth-Century Maryland," in Nancy F. Cott and Elizabeth H. Pleck, *A Heritage of Her Own: Toward a New Social History of American Women* (New York, 1979), pp. 26–29.

27. Stratton Nottingham, *Land Causes of Accomack County Virginia, 1727–1826* (1930; Baltimore, 1999), p. 5. Weynette Parks Haun, Surry County, *Virginia Court Records, 1664 thru 1671, vol. 2* (Durham, N.C., 1987), pp. 44. Eliza Timberlake Davis, *Wills and Administrations of Surry County, Virginia 1671–1750* (Baltimore, 1995), p. 9. Charles City County, Virginia, Order Book August 1722 to February 1722/3, pp. 143, 151, ViHi; John Banister, *John Banister Account Book 1731–1734*, (n.p), ViHi.

28. Room-by-room inventories 1646–1824, Rockefeller Library, Williamsburg. Inventory of the Estate of Nathaniel Bradford, Accomac County, deceased 1690 (no further date); Inventory of John Thompson, Surry County, 18 June 1700; Inventory of James Burwell, York County, 10 May 1718; Inventory of Joseph Ring, York County, 1704 (no further date); Inventory of Joseph Frith, York County, 16 June 1712; Inventory of Madam Katherine Gwyn, Richmond County, 6 Nov. 1728; Inventory of Arthur Allen, Surry County, May and June 1711 (no further date).

29. Charles City County Deeds, Wills, etc., 1724/25–1731, 87, 131–33, 260, VHS.

30. Hannah Huthwaite, *Hannah Huthwaite Recipe Book* (ca. 1720), Winterthur Library. Harriott Pinckney Horry, *A Colonial Plantation Cookbook: The Receipt Book of Harriott Pinckney Horry*, ed. Richard J. Hooker (1770; reprint, Columbia, S.C., 1984), pp. 28–29; 96, 98. Martha Washington, *Martha Washington's Booke of Cookery and Booke of Sweetmeats: Being a Family Manuscript*, trans. Karen Hess (New York, 1981).

31. Lois Green Carr, Russell R. Menard, and Lorena S. Walsh, *Robert Cole's World: Agriculture and Society in Early Maryland* (Chapel Hill, 1991), pp. 72–74.

32. St. John De Crevecoeur, *Sketches of Eighteenth Century America*, ed. Henri L. Bourdin, Ralph H. Gabriel, and Stanley T. Williams (New Haven, 1925), pp. 124, 40. Benjamin

Franklin, *Poor Richard's Almanack for the Year of Our Lord 1746* (1745; reprint, New York, 1976), p. 81.

33. Mead fell under women's province in part because it was a raw alcohol that did not require any new technology (stills or hops). Mead also fell to women it was women's province to keep bees. Bees provided honey for cookery and alcoholic beverage production, and pollinated gardens. It had traditionally been women's work to keep bees in England. Lady Margaret Hobby, discussed earlier, kept bees. Beekeeping became a male pursuit in England during the late seventeenth century. Like alcohol production, bee keeping was masculinized in the New England and Middle Colonies. For example, when Isaac Stephens of Pennsylvania died, his creditors advertised that they were selling his cider casks and "several stocks of bees." In areas like Pennsylvania where alcoholic beverage production had been masculinized, men kept the bees to propagate their orchards for distilled fruit brandies. When men assumed control of alcohol production in the Tidewater in the latter half of the eighteenth century, they also took over beekeeping. We thus see that when technology caused the regendering of one form of labor, it could also cause the regendering of related forms of labor.

34. James Horn, *Adapting to a New World: English Society in the Seventeenth-Century Chesapeake* (Chapel Hill, 1994), pp. 25, 39–41.

35. Horn, *Adapting to a New World*, pp. 39, 41.

36. Carr, Menard, and Walsh, *Robert Cole's World*, pp. 55–76.

37. Baron, *Brewed in America*, p. 32. See Royal Dublin Society, *Instructions for Planting & Managing Hops & for Raising Hop-Poles* (Dublin, 1733), Winterthur Library, especially pp. 8–9, 12. For laws encouraging men to grow hops see, for example, W. W. Hening, *The Statutes at Large: Being a Collection of all the Laws of Virginia from the First Session of the Legislature in the Year 1619* (Richmond, 1809), vol. I, March 1657–8, Act LXXVI, p. 469.

38. H. S. Corran, *A History of Brewing* (Newton Abbot, UK, 1975), pp. 273–74. Martha J. Randolph to Ellen Wayles Cary, Jefferson Papers, 26 Nov. 1825, UVA. Jean B. Russo "Self-sufficiency and Local Exchange: Free Craftsmen in the Rural Chesapeake Economy," in Lois Green Carr, Philip D. Morgan, and Jean B. Russo, eds. *Colonial Chesapeake Society* (Chapel Hill, 1988), pp. 388–432, 394. In the February 18, 1746, issue of the *Maryland Gazette*, Mark Gibson advertised that he sold beer.

39. Bennet, *Ale, Beer, and Brewsters*, p. 17.

40. Robert Beverley, *The History and Present State of Virginia*, ed. Louis B. Wright (Charlottesville, 1947), p. 293. "Observations," p. 3.

41. Horn, *Adapting to a New World*, p. 434.

42. Durand de Dauphine, *A Huguenot Exile in Virginia: or Voyages of a Frenchman Exiled for his Religion with a Description of Virginia & Maryland*, ed. Gilbert Chinard (1687; reprint, New York, 1934). "Observations," p. 2. Peter Collinson to John Custis, believed to be 3 July 1735, *Brothers of the Spade: Correspondence of Peter Collinson of London, and of John Custis, of Williamsburg, Virginia, 1736–1746*, ed. E. G. Swem (Barre, MA, 1957), p. 28. Hazard, "The Journal of Ebenezer Hazard in Virginia, 1777," p. 420.

43. "Trade and Travel in Post-Revolutionary Virginia," p. 178. Robert Beverley, *The History and Present State of Virginia*, ed. Louis B. Wright (Chapel Hill, 1947), p. 293.

44. See chapter 4 of my dissertation for a discussion on Chesapeake women and tavern keeping. Linda Sturz offers an alternative interpretation in *Within Her Power: Propertied Women in Colonial Virginia* (New York, 2002), chapter 4.

45. Cornelia Hughes Dayton, *Women Before the Bar: Gender, Law, & Society in Connecticut, 1639–1789* (Chapel Hill, 1995), p. 5. Kathleen M. Brown, *Good Wives, Nasty Wenches, & Anxious Patriarchs: Gender, Race, and Power in Colonial Virginia* (Chapel Hill, 1996). Deborah A. Rosen, *Courts and Commerce: Gender, Law, and the Market Economy in Colonial New York* (Columbus, 1997), p. 111. Jeanne Boydston, *Home & Work: Housework, Wages, and the Ideology of Labor in the Early Republic* (New York, 1990), pp. xi, 18.

Reconstructing Gender: Early Modern English Politics and Religion in the Chesapeake

8

DEBRA MEYERS

IN THE EARLY MODERN Atlantic world many believed that governance and organization of the family mirrored or informed proper governance and organization of the state. This chapter explores the changing nature of this reciprocal relationship by asking several crucial questions. To what extent did patriarchy in the family reflect the needs and beliefs of the polity? How did the structure and ambitions of the state shape, reinforce, or limit patriarchy in the household? How did the willingness to treat family decisions as public and legal rather than private and spiritual facilitate state building? And in what ways did legislation about such decisions encourage the civic responsibility of the general public? In this essay, by emphasizing the importance of politics in social/cultural history, I address these questions by comparing the last wills of political figures for two early modern Chesapeake governments in addition to their city planning, architecture, education policies, philosophies, and morality legislation.

Historians of early modern Europe have already established a strong connection, albeit a negative one, between governance and organization of the family and that of the state.[1] Principally, European historians' assumptions rest on the possibility that governments attempted to regulate gendered issues—especially marriage, clothing, and prostitution—by imposing precise gender boundaries based on the ruling elite's notion of masculinity and femininity.[2] As an example, in response to cultural change, the various Renaissance governments in Italy aspired to enforce patriarchy to protect their positions of authority in an effort to restore order.[3] Stanley Chojnacki writes, "The roles and relationships of all the age and gender groups in patrician society were reconstituted on the basis of officially enhanced paternal authority over wives and children."[4] For our purposes then, the work of European historians suggests that social change—particularly the construction of restrictive gender codes—can be fostered by the empowered elites for political purposes. Still, couldn't ruling elites enforce positive, perhaps even progressive, messages through traditional political devices to inculcate less restrictive gender relationships that in turn influenced the less oppressive power relationships within the entire community? I argue that this was the case for early modern Maryland while the Arminian Anglicans, Quakers, and Roman Catholics controlled the government.

The Calverts, Cornwaleys, Gerards, Greenes, and Wintours formed the nucleus of the Maryland gentry when they established the province in 1634. Those settlers unable to form alliances with these reigning families died without heirs, emigrated to other colonies, returned to England, or, in some cases, were excluded from holding lucrative positions of power. Suffering from decreasing numbers, the gentry yearned for an influx of faithful, new blood, and chose to incorporate others of modest backgrounds into the ruling class (as long as they were loyal to the proprietor) during the second half of the seventeenth century. Subsequent generations of elites came to seek their fortunes, as in the case of Charles Carroll, and accumulated wealth, married into the gentry families, and became both rich and prominent.[5] Much like their feudal ancestors, wealthy Free Will Christian families—primarily the Arminian Anglicans, Quakers, and Roman Catholics—in the seventeenth century sought to secure their fortunes by consciously aligning themselves with the rich and powerful proprietor. Thus, nearly all of the ruling families of Maryland by 1689—when the Associators wrestled control away from the proprietor—could claim some familial relationship to Lord Baltimore.

Initially, Maryland's proprietary government was a feudal holdover in both structure and mindset. Thus the Stuart monarch bestowed upon Lord Baltimore and his descendants palatine status as autonomous proprietors invested with royal privileges and rights equivalent to the Crown's. Some of these included: naming magistrates and judges; presiding over any judicial proceedings; initiating all legislation; the right to establish a nobility; and the privilege of trading in foreign markets.[6] In keeping with this ancient feudalism, Lord Baltimore required each colonist to swear an oath of fealty to him directly, rather than to the Crown or provincial government. Moreover, Baltimore encouraged immigration to his new province by offering two thousand acres of land—coupled with feudal land rights—in Maryland to every English gentry man or woman who brought five others with them to settle the new land. Owning a thousand acres entitled a lord or lady to preside over courts baron and courts leet in order to settle disputes among their tenants.[7] The headright system soon replaced this introductory offer, allowing one hundred acres for a man or woman, one hundred additional acres for transporting a wife, fifty for each child under sixteen years of age, and fifty for each servant.

It seems likely that these early Free Will Christian ruling elites—bound together through blood and marriage—sought colonists who shared similar values, rituals, and associational formats. These Arminian Anglicans, Quakers, and Roman Catholics valued female family members and believed women had a duty to their families to be active partners in marriage, authority figures in the home, to act on the family's behalf in commerce or in court when necessary, and to serve their religious communities according to their means.[8] And these settlers' last wills and testaments attest to this belief. A statistical analysis of 3,190 Maryland wills reveals two distinctive family strategies for estate distribution in the wills of married males. Free Will Christian men left their wives large tracts of land to manage during their lifetime and they enjoyed the rights and responsibilities of a marital partnership. Indicative of their firm belief in patriarchy, Predestinarian men (that is to say, Calvinists, primarily the Particular Baptists, Presbyterians, and Puritans) preferred to give land to sons.[9] It might be logical to assume that the leading Free Will Christian men in the courts, legislature, and other positions of authority imposed their notions of womanhood upon the laws, courts, and common practices at the local and provincial levels. Unable, or unwilling, to align themselves with the ruling families through intermarriage, wealthy Calvinists sought to gain control of the province to free themselves from the influence of the Free Will Christians. As some of the Free Will Christian ruling class lost its political power beginning with the Associators' Revolution in July of 1689, perhaps the revolutionaries and their subsequent followers sought to instill their own particular conceptions of social norms and common practices on the populace.[10] In order to pursue this possibility, I propose to study as a group the "revolutionaries" between 1689 and 1715. Were they Calvinists or Free Will Christians? How did they distribute their property in their wills and what can this tell us about their conceptions of womanhood in addition to women's roles in the family and society? Did their legislation differ substantially from that of their predecessors? Stated simply, did this new political order seek to generate social change predicated upon an oppressive reconstruction of gender relations based on their conception of womanhood? I believe that it did just that.

Lois G. Carr and David Jordan in *Maryland's Revolution of Government, 1689–1692* make a persuasive argument that the colonial government was stable both before and after the "revolution." Carr and Jordan draw this conclusion from the continuity of legal and political institutions at the local level.[11] They point out that county courts continued to serve justice during and after the revolution and, ultimately, the Associators reallocated only twenty-three percent of the local civil posts. Carr and Jordan claim that 1689 represented a shift in power from a largely Roman Catholic governing body to an Anglican one as the predominant religious affiliation of the population shifted to Anglicanism.[12] Carr and Jordan rightly point out that "although a majority of the Associators had served in some office of responsibility, very few of them had enjoyed proprietary patronage beyond the position of justice or had much confidence of receiving such favors in the future."[13] Thus, the pervasive discontent seemed to center on the unsatisfied cravings of the "outside" elites—since most of the Associators were wealthy landholders—faced with the entrenched landed "insiders" and their self-interests. This redistribution of power and wealth, associated with lucrative provincial posts, did not represent an overthrow of the social order or a subsequent reallocation of land from the old gentry to a new elite, according to Carr and Jordan.

Regardless of their emphasis on continuity, Carr and Jordan suggest that the revolution of 1689 really was a revolution that brought about some radical social changes. This upheaval in Maryland was a direct result of the Glorious Revolution in England that replaced the Catholic King James II with his Anglican daughter Mary and her Dutch Protestant husband William. As such, the Glorious Revolution ushered in major changes for Maryland Roman Catholics. When things settled down, the new monarchs appointed a royal governor to Maryland in 1692 and an anti–Roman Catholic flavor permeated the provincial government, beginning with the exclusion of Roman Catholics from official positions in 1689. This action was followed by Governor John Seymour's (1704–1709) "Act to Prevent the Growth of Popery," which prohibited Roman Catholic priests from saying Mass in public. Seymour also encouraged the children of Roman Catholics to rebel against their parents, and he discouraged Protestant widows from marrying Roman Catholics by threatening to remove their children from such a home.

As radical as these changes seem, it is important to point out that local authorities largely ignored anti-Catholic legislation. In fact, after the Catholics petitioned the Lower House, the Lower House suspended parts of the earlier act, thus allowing priests to say Mass in "private" homes.[14] Indeed, on several occasions, the Lower House (filled with the Arminian-Anglican relatives of the Roman Catholics) obstructed Governor Seymour and the council's anti-Catholic proposals.[15] The Catholics' carefully cultivated alliances with their Anglican kin in the Lower House proved advantageous time and again. Perhaps Arminian-Anglican affinities saw the threat to their Roman Catholic relatives as a foreshadowing of their own precarious position in society.[16]

Carr and Jordan's argument rests firmly upon the assumption that the Assoc-iators were wealthy Anglicans. There can be no doubt that they were landed elites: roughly ninety percent owned more than five hundred acres of land. Yet, can we assume they professed the Anglican faith? Many of them served as vestrymen or claimed allegiance to the Church of England, but is this enough evidence to con-firm their Anglicanism? The term itself is too imprecise for our purposes. Angli-cans fell along a spectrum that included those who leaned toward Roman Catholic doctrine (Arminians), those persuaded by Calvinism (Predestinarians), and those who cared little about theology and merely attended to their religious duties for social, economic, and political gains. Nineteenth-century historians often recognized this distinction as did George Davis when he argued that while the Catholics "were heartily opposed to the political party represented by the Puritans" in the province, "the administration of the proprietary's government was not shaped by any very great fear of [them]."[17] What we need to do is estab-lish the percentage of Predestinarians, the percentage of Free Will Christians, and where possible, the number of political trimmers within Maryland's Anglican church.

Some Associators were quite vocal about their Calvinist leanings. We know that Ninian Beale, David Browne, Samuel Hopkins, and Francis Jenckins all claimed to be Presbyterians with a Predestinarian soteriology. The known Presby-terian Associators constituted ten percent of the forty-one revolutionaries. Taking into account the religious language in the preambles of their last wills, we can increase this number of Calvinist members. Fortunately, an inordinate number of Associators' wills have survived; nearly eighty percent of Associators wrote wills compared to perhaps thirty percent of the total population. After examining the spirituality expressed in their last wills and testaments, we find that more than half of the Associators did, in fact, hold Calvinist values and belief systems that place them squarely in the Predestinarian cohort.

The wills these Calvinists left can tell us much about their understanding of womanhood. Nearly thirty percent of the married Associators followed the Predestinarian bequest patterns, leaving their wives personal goods rather than real estate. These wealthy Calvinists chose to distribute the family's most valuable asset—land—to males rather than females. Tellingly, only forty-five percent of the married Associators named their wives sole executrix compared to sixty-nine percent of the overall Predestinarian will-writing population. And unlike the larger will-writing population, the Associators were also much less likely to have females witness their wills. This strong propensity to favor males over females as influential authority figures suggests that these particular Calvinist Associators may have been more patriarchal than other Predestinarian men in the province.

In sum, the majority of Associators were Predestinarians who adhered to a patriarchal family structure that very well may have influenced the legislation that would follow.

Similar to the Calvinist men in New England, these Calvinist Associators most likely believed that a strong patriarchal family structure provided a firm foundation for a patriarchal social order at the provincial level. But what about the thirty-one Upper House members who followed the Associators after the appointment of a royal governor in 1692? Luckily, seventy-seven percent of the burgesses between 1692 and 1715 left wills in which seventeen members revealed their religious affiliations. Roughly half of these expressed Calvinist convictions. At a time when perhaps less than a quarter of the population was Predestinarian, Calvinist Associators and Upper House members who occupied posts during the subsequent royal period were present in vastly disproportionate numbers compared to the overall population. These Predestinarians brought to their new positions of power their distinctive worldviews, including their conception of womanhood that placed females in dependent positions rather than authoritative ones in the family; this outlook is manifest in the bequest patterns. If these Predestinarians embraced a vision of womanhood antithetical to the previous Free Will Christian paradigm established by the old gentry, did they use their newfound governmental power and authority to reconstruct social norms on a massive scale in accordance with their own patriarchal value system?

If Mary Beth Norton's work comparing the "Filmerian" families of New England with the "Lockean" families of Maryland had taken religion into account, her data would support the argument that New England Calvinists and Chesapeake Free Will Christians in positions of power aimed to construct societies that reflected their understandings of male/female power relations. Norton argued that the Filmerian system—adhered to by the Calvinists in New England—was predicated upon the idea that families were microcosms of the patriarchal state. Accordingly, judges ordered parents to whip servants and other dependents as part of their efforts to treat "the household power structure as an arm of the State and masters of families as semi-official constables." This was not the case for Maryland. Although she did not distinguish between the Maryland governments led by Free Will Christians and later by Calvinists, Norton's work tends to support the idea that Free Will Christian Marylanders held very different ideas about how much influence the government ought to impose upon the family. Norton suggested that "the Chesapeake governments, especially Maryland's, did not supervise their resident families with the same vigilance used in New England." Maryland's authorities did not get involved "in the day-to-day governance of families, as did New Haven authorities in particular." Primarily, Maryland judges "contented themselves with overseeing two crucial turning points, the formation of families in marriage and their cessation through death or divorce. The Chesapeake governments intervened in disorderly households only when asked to to [sic] come to the aid of beleaguered masters or when excessive abuse of subordinates was alleged." Overwhelmingly, Maryland "legislators were simply not as concerned as New Englanders with the internal functioning of families within their jurisdictions."[18] The legislators acted this way with good reason. Norton argues that Marylanders were influenced by a modern, enlightened "Lockean" sensibility. By and large, Norton's point that Marylanders were more modern than their New England counterparts is very persuasive and when we take religion into consideration, we can increase the value of Norton's study.

The Calvinists' city planning of Annapolis also points to continuity with New England and the Calvinists' conceptualization of their ideal relationship between church and state. Accordingly, a cursory glance at Annapolis' early State House and church locations underscores the extraordinary differences between the ideology concerning the separation of church and state adhered to by the Roman Catholics of St. Mary's City and the Calvinists' insistence on a government understood in theological terms. Five years after the 1689 Associators' revolution, state Governor Francis Nicholson relocated the capital of the province from St. Mary's City to Providence, first settled in 1649 by the Calvinist refugees from Virginia. While it is doubtful that Nicholson was a Calvinist himself, the inordinate number of Predestinarians who surrounded him as government officeholders surely influenced the development of Annapolis. Why else would the center of government move to an area that had been home to a large Calvinist community for decades? The Calvinist influence on the governor seems plausible since the plan for Annapolis was very different from the other capitals, like Williamsburg, that Nicholson developed. Moreover, the new city's name indicates a revelatory shift in focus. The Calvinists changed Providence's name—that had signified the new Israelites' commonwealth under God's care—to Anne's Polis after their new Protestant queen. The shift suggests some tie to ancient Greek civilizations in which religion and politics were conflated in a way similar to the New England Puritan theocracy. In this new capital that would support a more heterogeneous population than Providence had, perhaps the Calvinists saw a rare opportunity to impose their theocratic ideals upon non-Calvinists in the hopes of creating a well-ordered society.

Toward this end, Annapolis touted a "State House Circle" in the center of the city that dominated the landscape with its elevated prominence, massive scale, and central location (see Figure 8.1). The stately government buildings fit into a 528-foot diameter (approximately one acre) that comprised about 15 percent of

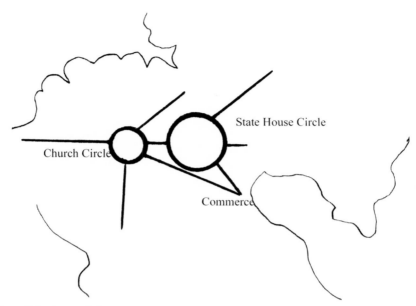

Figure 8.1   Annapolis Layout

the town.[19] The Church Circle—located just to the west of center and at a slightly lower elevation—was approximately two-thirds the diameter of the State House Circle.[20] Joined by a short thoroughfare where the schoolhouse once stood, the circles create an image not unlike two wheels held together by an axle. Metaphorically speaking, the Calvinists must have thought that these institutions would work in tandem. This configuration emphasized the close relationship between the church, the state, and the school much like the meetinghouse had in Calvinist New England. We should note, however, that in Maryland's case church and state were not conflated into a single source of authority as they were in Calvinist New England. While the Annapolis Calvinists hoped that the laws and mores initiated by the state would be predicated upon church doctrine, they simultaneously recognized a hierarchy of authority. Indicative of its supremacy, the state overlooked—both literally and figuratively—the affairs of the church. In fact, from the elevated State House one could have looked directly down into the front door of the original church. In keeping with this hierarchic ideal, both the church and the state had an equal influence upon public education since the schoolhouse was located between the two elemental institutions. Thus the schoolhouse figured prominently in the city's layout, mirroring the central role education was to play in the Calvinists' future plans.

Schools, for the Calvinists, played an instrumental role in the new government. Indeed, the number of schools in the province increased twofold after the Calvinists seized control. In 1696, the assembly petitioned the king for "Free-Schools" for teaching "the Gospel . . . Latine, Greek, Writing and the like," with more than one hundred scholars in attendance for each county.[21] The schools would not advocate instruction "contrary to your Majesty's Prerogative Royal, nor to the Laws and Statutes of your Majesty's Kingdom of England or Province of Maryland aforesaid, or to the Canons and Constitutions of the Church of England by Law Established." We cannot be sure of the extent of the Calvinist government's success in this plan for countywide "Free-Schools," but the new government did establish specific fines and duties designated to support these institutions.[22] The Calvinists' agenda becomes clearer when we examine their insistence that guardians were to provide an education for orphaned children. Lois Carr has noted, "By the beginning of the eighteenth century, guardianship agreements began to specify education. The change may have been partly the result of pressure from the royal governor Francis Nicholson, who was active in improving administration during the 1690s."[23] Just as likely, however, the Calvinists may have insisted on forced schooling because schools have often been used as an effective means to inculcate children with the values of the ruling elites with the hope of producing changes in cultural values and behavior. Surely, the English Roman Catholics had fully intended such instruction when they sent their own children to the Continent.

The Calvinists modeled their education legislation on Elizabethan wardship laws. During Elizabeth's reign, when approximately thirteen percent of the elites' children became orphans during their minority, the government passed laws requiring guardians to appoint Anglican, rather than Roman Catholic, tutors. We might assume their insistence on Protestant tutors indicated their desire to influence the future religious beliefs of orphans. Whether or not this proved to be an efficacious method of inculcating doctrine and values is unknown. However, the intent is clear. Similarly, by imposing Calvinist ideas on orphans through tutors in Maryland, the government ultimately hoped to change the mores of the larger culture over time. Perhaps this scheme proved rather successful in light of the cultural shifts of the eighteenth century.

Other aspects of the Calvinists' city planning in Annapolis also edify their notions of power relationships. Within Annapolis's city gates, a logical grid pattern of lots radiated from the church and state circles, reminiscent of its Greek antecedent. For both the Greeks and the Calvinists, the state-sponsored religious bureaucrats formed the nucleus of a government with the support of the citizens and slaves surrounding the elevated government buildings and church. A conspicuous—and, I would argue, conscious—deviation from this Greek renaissance was the location and relative importance of the marketplace, or agora. In ancient Greece the agora housed merchants and bankers alongside magistrates and council members as it served as the center of politics, trade, and oft times, worship. Conversely, the Calvinists of Annapolis believed government and the church—rather than the marketplace—defined their culture; this attitude is indicated by the elevated position and geographical location of the public and church circles. Commercial activity took place at a significantly lower elevation and at a distance from the two prominent circles. In fact, the Calvinists placed the business district at the very edge of the city. Of course, the harbor with its direct access to shipping was a logical place to locate the city's commercial activity. Yet the planners could have easily erected the State House or the church closer to the water at a lower elevation. Their conscious decision to place the agora outside of the preeminent circular centers of influence—indeed, on the very margins of the city—suggests that the economy did not define the new Calvinist society, and the agora's location served to underscore the prominent positions of church and state.

Calvinist city planning in Annapolis—while similar to the New England Puritans' reliance on the intertwining interests of church and state—stands in stark contrast with the layout of the Roman Catholic city of St. Mary's. When the province began in 1634, the Free Will Christian founders created St. Mary's City with a precise geometric pattern indicative of their political and religious ideology. The planners were influenced by the renaissance ideals adopted in Catholic Europe, where many of the founding fathers received their education. Henry Miller's account, "Baroque Cities in the Wilderness: Archaeology and Urban Development in the Colonial Chesapeake," employs archaeological evidence to illustrate the founders' conscious effort to secure the separation of church and state.[24] We can take Miller's insights a step further to show just how significant city planning might be. The Roman Catholic founders had thought of the correlations between business, politics, and religion as equally important contributions to the society with none unduly influencing the other two. Therefore, they placed these institutions in a triangular layout—upon a level plane—that presupposed a point of convergence, but not direct linkages of intertwining interests (figure 8.2). As typical English Roman Catholics, the colonists let their piety shape their personal relationships and their sense of right and wrong, but they did not rely on the Pope, the Maryland Jesuit priests, or indeed any other institution, person, or group to dictate state policy.[25] Thus, the State House was located as far from the first Roman Catholic chapel as logistically possible. Most of the society's supporting buildings, such as ordinaries (taverns with sleeping accommodations), shops, the printing office, storehouses, and the homes of aldermen, fit within the

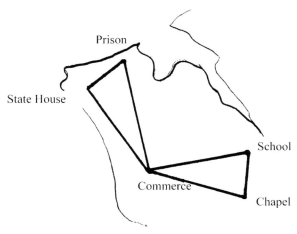

Figure 8.2   St. Mary's City Layout

triangular pattern anchored down by the imposing brick edifices of church and state.[26] Far from the marginalized agora of Annapolis, the commercial center of St. Mary's formed one corner of the large triangle that defined the city. And unlike the short thoroughfare connecting the public and church circles of Annapolis, the roads between the State House and chapel were not directly connected, nor was the chapel visible from the State House. Certainly, the men who attended Mass on Sunday at the Roman Catholic chapel on the other side of the city were the same men who served the province as council members, judges, and assemblymen during the rest of the week. Indeed, during the early years of settlement even the Jesuit priests were summoned to serve in some official provincial capacity.[27] Yet these men could not walk in a straight line between the two buildings nor could they see the State House while they attended church. If one of these men wanted to walk from the chapel to the State House, he would have passed through the commercial center at the halfway point. The physical distance between the State House and chapel in addition to the nonlinear layout of the roads must have been intentional, with the planners hoping that the layout would encourage these men to separate their religious obligations from their civic ones.

To emphasize their separate but equal influence on the society, the two-story State House and Roman Catholic chapel were comparable in size and style, both having been built upon massive cross-shaped brick foundations with low-pitched tiled roofs. These two visually similar structures, however, served very different and clearly defined social functions as institutions. On the one hand, the ruling elites considered education and religion closely tied to each other, so the Jesuits built the first official school adjacent to the chapel. There is evidence to suggest that the early Jesuits educated both English boys and girls (in addition to Black slaves and Native Americans) before they officially opened their school in 1677. When it did open, the school was quite successful; one priest noted how "The native youth, applying themselves assiduously to study, make good progress. Maryland and the recently established school sent two boys to St. Omer [to be educated for the priesthood], who yielded in abilities to few Europeans when competing for the honour of being first in their class."[28]

The Free Will Christians believed that civil justice should be grounded in their religious moral code, but they did not criminalize sin. Unlike the Puritans in New England who used words like "unclean carriages" and "filthiness" that indicated their theological concerns, the Maryland Free Will Christians (when they were sitting in the State House) did not equate breaking the law with sinful behavior.[29] Thus, the prison was erected in close proximity to the State House indicting that provincial criminal acts were civic matters. Although the cruciform layout of the State House's massive foundation served to remind civic leaders that state laws and civil justice must be grounded in God's moral code, civil leaders believed that only God punished sinners; Maryland judges punished civil criminals. To symbolically represent this point in the city's layout, the distance between the State House and economic center was exactly the same as the distance between the chapel and the center. This plan reminded community members to act honorably in their business dealings with one another. If they chose not to act this way, they faced punishment from both church and state. Unjust merchants would have to answer to God for their sinful behavior when they violated the Laws of Moses, and these sins in turn jeopardized their eternal salvation. Temporal punishment for sins might have included penitential prayers or even excommunication from the church. In addition, reprobates also faced fines, disfigurement, or public whippings for disrupting social order in their community when they broke the civil laws of the state. These two punishments were kept separate in the minds of the community members, the church, and the courts. Unlike New England judges, Marylanders sitting in the State House focused on their secular duties and were uninterested in the fate of a criminal's soul. Here in the temporal world judges were intent on securing reparations for the victims and sufficient punishment for the offender to deter him or her from repeating the offense that had disrupted social order. This separation of church and state served a very practical function in this heterogeneous community. Those colonists who were not Roman Catholics could serve the state and conform to its laws without having to accept (or even respect) the Roman Catholic Church's views on sin, punishment, and salvation. In stark contrast with the Calvinist New Englanders' conflation of church and state, Roman Catholic Marylanders answered to two very different and distinct authorities, those of the temporal world and those of the spiritual world. Each one required community members to understand their purpose and duties and each one enforced compliance using very different methods.

This fundamental disparity between the Free Will Christians and the Predestinarians can also be seen in Maryland legislation. Prior to 1689, when members of Lord Baltimore's kinship network controlled the province, little legislation was enacted to regulate either marriage or morality—both of which were traditionally placed under the church's control and governed largely by Canon Law. Since the settlers were not obligated to uphold church law in the civil courts, Maryland's governing elites focused their attention on land acquisition, government-enforced protection of personal property, and maintaining social order with minimal governmental interference.[30] Public ledgers record property disputes, the settlement of debts, and the government's tenacious attempts to maintain a stable economy. Accordingly, the Free Will Christian government rarely attempted to regulate marriage even though the society often faced the social chaos European historians believe stimulates that type of legislation. Cognizant of the upheavals at home with respect to power and religious struggles, the colonists responded with legislation calling for religious tolerance and provided settlers with more opportunities to trade with the Indians.[31] The provincial government met the threat of social chaos with an effort to reassert a calm, nonhostile commercial environment without overtly regulating gender relationships. Free Will Christians continued to see marriage as a private affair between two consenting adults that did not require governmental intrusion unless one or both of the adults were servants under contract. Thus the legislators passed laws to continue collecting fees for the privilege of marrying and the publication of the names of individuals who wanted to marry.[32] Both of these examples illustrate a desire to avoid the pervasive problem of indentured servants marrying before their contracts had expired; this action would, in turn, diminish a master's profits.

Regardless of the Free Will Christians' focus on economic issues, several laws passed during the Catholic administration might at first glance be considered morality legislation or legislation aimed at altering gender structures. The act of 1639, for instance, made it illegal to cohabitate with non-Christian Indians. While it is plausible to think that the legislators wanted to prevent marriages between the moral white Europeans and the darker-skinned savages, a more reasonable explanation rests on the founders' religious beliefs. If we consider the historical context that formed the backdrop for this law, we find that the Roman Catholics probably shared (or were influenced by) the Jesuits and Lord Baltimore's missionary zeal to enlarge the English Roman Catholic community.[33] By restricting the marriage pool to only baptized men and women, the legislators sought to increase the numbers of Roman Catholics in the province. These legislators, then, were not acting to alter gender structures, redefine racial relationships, or institute new morality codes. Quite simply, they were attempting to build a stable Anglo-Catholic province in the New World.

Similarly, the 1650 act regulating fornication seems to have been directed at controlling the sexual activity of servants with the hope of circumventing the rising number of bastards in the province, rather than serving as an example of legislating morality.[34] The act stipulated that "Every person or persons that shalbe found or proved by confession of either party to have comitted Adultery, or fornicacon, such Offender or Offenders shalbe censured or punished, as the Governor and Counsell or other cheife Judge and Comissioner pr[e]sent in court" shall think appropriate as long as the punishment did not include death or maiming.[35] Quite plausibly, then, one of the individuals involved in the sexual liaison would have to make a confession before legal action was taken. If this were so, the law would have functioned quite differently from morality legislation that sought to alter social codes of behavior affecting gender relations in order to conform to the moral values of the legislators. Mary Beth Norton's work on Maryland court cases suggests that very few individuals took these types of cases to court during the seventeenth century, as the surviving county records indicate that merely seventy-six women and thirty men were tried for such offenses.[36] Norton has also argued, "The community's primary concern in bastardy cases was not morality, but rather ensuring that the public would not have to bear the cost of raising bastard children." Here again we find economic concerns dominating the thoughts of government officials. Norton confirms this when she points out that most of the cases involved "unmarried maidservants whose babies survived infancy."[37] Masters, in these cases, were not only deprived of their maidservants' labor for a time, but they also had to shoulder the financial burden of sheltering, feeding, and clothing nonproductive babies. This law allowed masters to recover some of their financial losses by forcing the babies' fathers to support their children. In other words, Free Will Christian legislators attempted to control their economic assets, not morality and gender construction.

It seems clear that Maryland's Free Will Christian governing bodies endeavored to provide commercially minded planters and merchants—both male and female—with a hospitable environment in which to conduct their business. They strove to secure their personal property and wealth by passing acts relating to land boundaries, the killing of livestock, perjury, debts, and restricting the procreative behavior of indentured servants. They searched for the right balance in maintaining cordial relations with the neighboring Indians by allowing only certain colonists the right to trade with the Indians and outlawing their enslavement. And the governing bodies fought with other colonies to establish their borders with an eye on future land development, expansion, and rent payments. Maryland elites hoped to worship and conduct business in peace, with minimal interference from a governing body—be it provincial, proprietary, papal, or royal. They desired and secured a government dedicated to upholding this decidedly laissez-faire philosophy.[38] The question then becomes, did the Associators who took control of the province in 1689 share this vision?

Carr and Jordan suggest that the revolution of 1689 changed little outside of a few faces. However, an examination of the legislation after the Calvinist coup reveals a somewhat different picture. Carr herself notes the change in the laws governing orphans in her article, "The Development of the Maryland Orphan's Court, 1654–1715." It seems that the Free Will Christians in 1681 continued to focus on property and profits when they passed an act concerning orphans. Carr pointed out that "The courts not only appointed guardians; they set the terms of guardianship, supposedly within limits set by law. Solvent security had to be given to pay the orphan his portion and rules were laid down for preserving the property; orphans had to be educated according to their estates and, if bound out for a maintenance, were to be taught a trade; and children could not be placed with families of a religion different from that of their parents."[39] But Carr observes that after 1690—when the Calvinists controlled the government—"An orphan was considered to be a child whose father had died. His mother could be guardian, but not for the property, unless she could find the sureties required for her bond to pay the child's portion, and she was accountable to the court for the care of the child and his estate."[40] These Calvinists did not share the Free Will Christians' view of womanhood that placed mothers in positions of authority in the home and expected them to act on the family's behalf, when necessary, in the legal and economic arenas. On the contrary, the management and control of both dependents and valuable property was a distinctly male responsibility for these Calvinists. Thus when an adult male could no longer supervise his dependents, the state would take his place. Women were the bearers and nurturers of sons, not substitute patriarchs when fathers died. In sum, the change in a widow's status within her family had been legislated by the new Calvinist administration.

This paternal philosophy of the Calvinists manifested itself in other ways. Widows who remarried represented a threat to society in the minds of the Upper House members during the royal period.[41] They wrote: "And whereas many Orphans have greatly suffered by the second Marriages of such Widows, who having Estates in Possession by Will or Right of Administration, either by such Widows, while sole [unmarried], or their [new] Husbands, during the Coverture, the same have been Wasted and Embezeled; and if the woman [should] die, the said [second] Husband refuses to render an Account of such Estate, alledging that he is neither Executor nor Administrator to his Wife, nor of her former Husband."[42] According to the Calvinists, when women controlled real estate, they tended to pay little regard to the true heir's rights—those of the testator's eldest son. In an attempt to bring order from the chaos, the government wanted widows and their new husbands to post bond to insure the "Heir at Law's" legacy. They would also have to regularly report on the condition of both the estate and heir to the governmental body that would stand in as a substitute father. Their statement regarding a second husband's refusal "to render an Account of such Estate" underscores the Calvinists' patriarchal notions. These Calvinists seemed particularly vexed with a second husband's reluctance to assume his rightful place as master and protector of his new family.[43]

By 1696, the orphan's court explicitly perceived itself as a "father" to all orphans.[44] Carr and Walsh explain that at this time, "the assembly declared that orphans of intestates were often better cared for than orphans of testators. From that time forward, orphans' courts were charged with supervision of all orphans and were soon given powers to remove any guardians who were shown false to their trusts, regardless of the arrangements laid down in a will."[45] A governmental body—acting as the society's powerful "father"—had taken on the responsibilities and management of a decidedly private family matter in the eyes of the old Free Will Christian government. In so doing, it attempted to reconstruct women's roles consonant with the Calvinists' view of women as dependents and the nurturers of sons. Not surprisingly, the government followed this legislation with a law in 1715 allowing the government to remove children from their Roman Catholic mother if the father had been a Protestant, thus recognizing once again that a fatherless child was indeed an orphan in need of state protection.[46] While the government probably humiliated the Roman Catholics with the enactment of this legislation, perhaps it was the strong Arminian-Anglican kinship networks (constructed by the Catholics) that prevented the government from enforcing it.

In addition to their attempts at redefining womanhood, widowhood, and women's roles within the family in their legislation, the Calvinists initiated morality laws to impose upon the population the new government's patriarchal view of the ideal social order. We find that the Calvinists enacted morality legislation as a matter of course, addressing, in particular, "Adultery and Fornication," polygamy, blasphemy, cursing, drunkenness, "Prophaeness," gambling, usury (in excess of eight percent interest rates), and, of course, the all-inclusive "Sunday to be kept Holy." Essential to this process of criminalizing sin, the legislators instructed ministers to read the laws to their congregations four times per year.[47]

The law admonishing "Adultery and Fornication" defined a fornicator (or adulterer if married) as a man who enjoyed the company of, or who frequented, "Lewd women." These men would first be accessed and accused by "Church-Wardens," a minister or the upstanding male citizens who formed the church vestry. The accused then faced the provincial or county court and a jury of "Twelve Men." Fornicators got off pretty easily with a fine of "Thirty Shillings" while an adulterer paid sixty shillings. If the convicted man had no money, for his first transgression he would receive thirty-nine lashes "till the Blood do appear."[48] The "Lewd woman" faced the same fines or whipping as her coconspirator did, depending upon her marital status. We can assume that the pious churchmen who passed judgment on these sinners classified prostitutes as "Lewd" women, but they also could point fingers at promiscuous females, women who were "Cohabiting" with men, or those merely engaging in sexual intercourse outside of marriage.

Much like their brethren in New England, Maryland Calvinists understood women to be evil, wanton, lustful creatures who willingly led men astray. The Calvinists' conception of womanhood manifests itself in both morality legislation and the prosecution of sexual transgressions. Literally thousands of New Englanders were charged with lewd speech, fornication, and adultery during the colonial period when Calvinists were in power. In fact, just in New Haven alone, "sexual offenses outnumbered all other categories of criminality handled by the county court."[49] The patriarchal presuppositions behind Calvinist morality legislation were a dramatic departure from the Free Will Christians' conceptions of women as capable and trusted companions, confidantes, and partners. Contrary to the Free Will Christians' narrow focus on indentured servants in their regulation of sexual relations, Maryland Calvinist legislation attempted to redefine womanhood and normative behavior for *every* member of the society.

As advocates for a patriarchal society as a means for maintaining social order, Calvinists expected male heads of household to oversee the behavior of all their dependents. In particular, this expectation extended to the head of the household who ran an ordinary. As patriarchs who had to maintain order within their homes, keepers of ordinaries could not sell liquor "unless in Cases of absolute Necessity" (presumably for medical purposes) on the Lord's Day. The government made the patriarch responsible for ensuring that everyone in his household observed the Lord's Day properly by preventing people from consuming "strong Liquor," gambling, swearing, or engaging in a "Pastime." Moreover, "Tipling," that is to say, temperate drinking, and "Exercise" were also forbidden on Sundays.[50] If an ordinary keeper failed to maintain order by enforcing this law, he faced stiff fines and the possible loss of his tavern license, which was often his primary source of income. The government required men and women to respect the Lord's Day as a day of prayer in the home and at church; it was not a day for frivolous entertainment, drinking, or work. This sobering message from the government resembled Calvinist English Interregnum and New England legislation much more than it did the Free Will Christians' laws. Indeed, one of Maryland's most esteemed nineteenth-century historians remarked that legislation after 1689 "against immorality, profaneness, and breaking the Lord's day . . . only lack[ed] the word 'Sabbath' to have quite a Puritan flavor."[51]

The Calvinists' legislation also mandated that individuals refrain from cursing, swearing, and excessive drunkenness at all times—not just on Sundays—or they faced fines and whippings.[52] But men and women could expect the worst punishments for blasphemy. The charge could be levied against anyone who might: "Curse him [God], or deny our Saviour JESUS CHRIST to be the son of GOD, or shall deny the Holy Trinity, the Father, Son and Holy Ghost, or the God-Head of the three Persons, or the Unity of the God-Head, or shall utter any Prophane Words concerning the Holy Trinity, or any the Persons thereof."[53] For an individual's first offense, a hole "shall be bored through his, her or their Tongue" in addition to a fine of twenty pounds sterling. A second offense provided the accused with a "B" branded on his or her forehead along with a forty-pound sterling fine. If the criminal/sinner could not come up with the money, he or she served time in prison ranging from six months to a year. A third violation meant "DEATH without any Benefit of Clergy."

Calvinists were diligent in pursuing sinners/criminals who chose to ignore such legislation. Charles Arrabella, for instance, was imprisoned for quite some time for "Blasphemy."[54] These actions followed closely those prescribed by John Calvin himself. One of Calvin's biographers tells us, "The Church provides the environment in which mutual fraternal correction without resentment or alienation becomes possible; each helps his fellow as they move on together toward an unattained perfection of faith and works."[55] In sum, the Calvinist government in Maryland sought to conflate sin with civil criminal acts in keeping with the Calvinists' ideas about the intertwining relationship between church and state. In so doing, these Calvinists hoped to create a patriarchal society where women would experience far less freedom than they had under the Free Will Christian government.

Of course, the Catholic government also legislated against offensive acts of "Swearing, cursing, Adultery" and "Drunkenesse."[56] But the Free Will Christian laws sought to provide an environment suitable for conducting business; this goal contrasted with the Calvinists' criminalization of sin.[57] In part, the distinction to be made rests upon who was ultimately responsible for accusing the transgressor and enforcing the law. For the Calvinists, men in power implemented the patriarchal norms: keepers of ordinaries, clergy, and church officers—as "father" figures—kept order in the society and brought sinners/criminals to court. In particular, clergymen as community fathers stood out as the primary enforcers of moral behavior; they assessed the innocence or guilt of men and women involved in affairs of the heart and regularly stood in the pulpit (mandated by the Calvinist Assembly) to remind congregates of the law. We can only assume that Maryland's Calvinist magistrates, like their New England counterparts, were committed to the redemption of the sinner/criminal, urging "malefactors to ponder the spiritual implications of their crimes and to mend their ways."[58] Recognizing the need for laws restricting public drunkenness, swearing, and the like, assorted Catholics and their Quaker allies and kin, on the other hand, passed laws that encouraged social stability, but did not go so far as to dictate appropriate behavior for the private lives of individuals. What people did behind closed doors, for the most part, was a family's concern. If men and women wanted to "tip" a few, "Exercise," gamble, or engage in a "Pastime" on Sunday, it was not the concern of the community. The Free Will Christian government was not in the habit of intruding into private affairs. Only when a person's behavior threatened public peace, principally in a public space, did the government intervene. Men and women who placed others in imminent danger (like beating one's servant to a bloody pulp) or who threatened to complicate the distribution of family property because of an adulterous relationship might have provoked the Free Will Christian government into action.

Free Will Christian legislators, moreover, appear to have held a more modern sense of responsibility for the social order than did their Calvinist counterparts. Since these criminal acts were transgressions against society rather than sins, religious leaders such as ministers, "Church-Wardens," and church vestrymen were not primarily responsible for identifying the accused or judging his or her actions. For Free Will Christians, any two witnesses—male or female—could bring charges of "frequent Drunkenes" against a fellow colonist and information regarding adultery was expected to come from female midwives, not the community's "fathers." Essentially, the authority to identify a criminal lay in the hands of any man or woman in the community.[59] Thus while both Catholics and Calvinists shared a high moral code, they differed appreciably in the choice of accusers and prosecutors. The reconstruction of social norms and the transformation of sin into crime punishable by the patriarchal government of the Calvinists indicate a willingness and desire on the part of the new political order to reorganize the public and private spheres consonant with their own worldview.

In their quest to construct a new dominant paradigm, the Calvinists needed to reach the entire society from the elites down to the lowliest of servants. The Calvinist legislation aimed at "Negroes & Mullattoes & Mungrels" illustrates this point succinctly.[60] Prior to 1689, the Free Will Christian provincial government passed some legislation directed at black servants and slaves. Thus as early as 1664 the government mandated that a black person could serve for life and the condition was hereditary. The law also attempted to define the boundaries of slavery by describing exactly who could be classified as a slave. A white woman who willingly married a black slave had to serve her husband's master for life (as did their children). Her ignorance of the class hierarchy, rather than her race, could transform a free woman into a slave. However, if the white woman had been forced to marry the slave by her employer, the woman and her children would be free. Principally, provincial legislators were concerned with a woman's conscious decision to ignore cultural norms regarding class. If a white woman freely chose to take an enslaved black man for her husband, she threatened the "natural" order of English society; a white English woman was not supposed to select a socially "inferior" husband. Significantly, this new law did not apply to white women already married to "negros or other Slaves." Women who had previously chosen black mates (either free or slave) before this law was passed would continue to be legally recognized as free married women. Moreover, white women, under this law, could still choose to marry a free black man because as a free man, he enjoyed a higher status than both white servants and black slaves did and the children from these unions would be free.

Not surprisingly—given their proclivity to safeguard personal property rights—Free Will Christian legislators were particularly concerned with coerced marriages. If a rapacious man—seeing the financial advantage of prompting the creation of slave children bound to him for life—forced a white woman to marry a black slave, then certainly, the woman could not be held responsible. Nor should the incredulous master reap any profits from his behavior; the children from this forced marriage would not serve him as slaves. Arranging marriages between white women and black male slaves for profit must have been a problem for the society for we see another law passed in 1681 imposing an additional 10,000-pound tobacco penalty on any master who coerced such a union. On the one hand, this Free Will Christian legislation regulating marriage probably indicates an awareness of the disparate sex ratio between white males and females as well as a sense of class (if not racial) inferiority in the white male's mind. These legislators must have believed that white women, in short supply, ought to marry white men. If not, at least they should choose free men. On the other hand, it also attests to the white females' sense of solidarity with their husbands in the unions they voluntarily entered into. As indentured servants coming from a class-based hierarchic social background, these women must not have perceived any great disparity between their own status and that of the black males.

This type of mixed-marriage legislation continued after the Associators' revolution. By 1715, the language of the laws had changed significantly and it reflected the patriarchal nature of the new government. The act of 1715 states: "That all Ministers, Pastors and Magistrates, or other Person whatsoever, who, according to the Laws of this Province, do usually joyn People in Marriage, shall not upon any Pretence joyn in Marriage any Negroe whatsoever [free or slave], or Mulatto Slave with any White Person, on the Penalty of Five Thousand Pounds of Tobacco."[61] The anomaly of course is that this fine in 1715 is a fifty percent reduction from the 1681 statute. Still, the church ministers had become the paternal keepers of social order and as such took on the responsibility of controlling the behavior of others. The act also represents a change in attitude toward white women marrying free black men. Prior to this, the government restricted white women from marrying black slaves, not free black men. The Calvinist legislation, however, demanded that a free white woman become a servant for seven years if she "shall suffer herself to be got with Child by a Negroe or other Slave, or Free-Negro."[62] If the male accomplice to such an offense was "a Free-Negroe he shall become a Servant for and during the Term of Seven Years." In 1717, the legislation became more explicit. The previous laws had not addressed the marriages of "Negro" and "Mullatto" women to white men. The new act stated "That if any Free Negro or Mullatto Inter-marry with any white Woman, or if any white Man shall inter-marry with any Negro or Mullatto Woman, such Negro or Mullatto shall become a Slave during Life excepting Mullattos born of white Women, who for such inter-marriage shall only become Servants for Seven Years."[63] This represents a profound shift in the ruling elites' notions of womanhood, marriage, and the family. The Calvinist state's insistence upon placing limits and restrictions on mate selection between free people was unprecedented in the province (outside of the early law against marrying a non-Christian Indian). Indeed, the new government had gone so far as to redefine "family"; interracial unions were forbidden regardless of the partners' free or servile status. The "normal" family, then, would be white, free, and legally sanctioned.

Commensurate with their Roman Catholic predecessors, the Calvinist Associators brought their value systems with them to their new powerful and lucrative governmental posts in 1689. They appropriated the power of the Roman Catholic proprietor as well as that of his Maryland kinship network, and when they—and the Calvinists who would follow—held the authority to do so, they attempted to mold society according to their patriarchal beliefs and values to create a new dominant paradigm. They utilized the means available to them—including the provincial legislature—to revise the customs and laws and thus to legally redefine what it meant to be a family, a woman, an orphan, a guardian, a criminal, and a sinner. Ideally, the churchwardens and Calvinist Upper House members joined forces to insure a social order consonant with their worldview. Given that Maryland Calvinists believed in a government predicated upon church doctrine (manifest in their city planning), we are not surprised to see their stalwart efforts to legislate morality in a manner that reflected their firm belief in patriarchy. The revolution of 1689 did not signify a mere shift to an Anglican representational government as Carr and Jordan have argued. The Calvinist leaders, with their specific social agenda, aspired to bring about revolutionary social change. To be sure, Calvinists shared some of the fundamental views of their predecessors as they continued to initiate and enforce legislation for the expansion of the economy. Yet they parted company with the Free Will Christian government when it came to the roles they would willingly accord the female population.[64]

Since Free Will Christian families (who made up the majority in Maryland throughout the colonial period) were generally established with the understanding that marriage was a partnership between two authority figures in the household, legislators respected the right of the "yoke-fellows" to govern their new family. Governmental interference would have undermined the power and authority a married couple could wield over their dependents. Free Will Christians adhered to this model primarily because direct governmental intrusion into family governance stood in opposition to English custom and Canon Law. It was the church's responsibility to influence family life—mate selection, eligibility, marriage ritual, infant baptism, mediating discord, and divorce—not the state's.[65] Conversely, Calvinists believed in a theocracy in which the state's micromanagement of marriage eligibility, ceremony, and divorce was both welcomed and encouraged. Marriage, for the Calvinists, was a civil affair, not a religious one. English Calvinist families recognized the value of a strong patriarch at the provincial and local levels and, of course, within the family. And since well-ordered families would undoubtedly produce well-ordered societies, Calvinist judges and other governmental authorities had a moral and ethical responsibility to see that families were monitored closely.

We might ask whether or not the Calvinists' attempt at constructing a new paradigm proved effective in producing new roles for women or curbing the behavior of recalcitrants. There is no evidence to suggest that government officials ever took minor children from their Roman Catholic mothers when their fathers died. And certainly Roman Catholics (and Quakers for that matter) continued to practice their religion and assert creedal beliefs in their wills. Further, David Jordan suggests Quakers continued to exert power in politics after the 1680s when "Quaker minutes articulate a clear prohibition against oathtaking." Jordan asserts that because Quakers were essentially prevented from holding office, they invented "new tactics of political pressure and mobilization, including lobbying, special interest legislation, and shrewd employment of the vote."[66] Of course, the Catholics and Quakers would have found these achievements during the Calvinists' reign impossible had it not been for their carefully constructed prior connections to prominent Arminian-Anglican families. Yet, the exclusion of Quakers and Roman Catholics from governmental posts probably benefited some of these families in the long run. Contingent upon the continued support of Catholic and Quaker interests by these groups' Arminian-Anglican affinities, these developments proved instrumental in the rise of the very wealthy Quaker and Roman Catholic families, such as the Chews and Carrolls. Since the Associators had not confiscated Catholic and Quaker land and because they were no longer compelled (by family and society) to allocate precious time and resources toward public service, these elite Catholic and Quaker families channeled their energy and funds into profitable commercial enterprises. Their forced absence from the assembly made the countinghouse their prime business. Not coincidentally, John Bossy notes the increased wealth for Roman Catholics in England after their exclusion from politics. He wrote, "After 1750 many [English Catholic] landowners became extremely wealthy out of industrial expansion and property development, and the congregations and chapels of its towns grew rapidly, laity and clergy stretching their muscles in a general climate of optimism and improvement."[67]

Indeed, the Calvinists' agenda appears to have had a less-than-devastating impact at the provincial level. The majority of court cases continued to deal with property rights rather than moral delinquency. I know of no case where a court ordered an individual killed for blasphemy, nor did the church spend its time hunting down fornicators. The important consideration remains the intent of the Calvinists to indoctrinate the larger society with their own worldview. While it is hard to assess the extent of the Calvinists' success in their efforts to inculcate their values and displace the previous dominant cultural paradigm of the Free Will Christians, it was their intention to do so. The extent of the success or failure in reconstructing social conventions by the Calvinists is beyond the scope of this essay. It may be that local politics continued the old customs and laws with little regard to the new provincial powermongers.

Yet, some social restructuring did occur; there was a marked shift in cultural bias after the Calvinists gained control of the province. Historians have shown the adoption of a decidedly Calvinist behavioral pattern by the second half of the eighteenth century when the majority of men willed real estate to sons and only personal goods to their wives. But we must also point out that Calvinist behavioral patterns did not completely replace those of the Free Will Christians; aggressive authoritative women could always be found in the region. Indeed, if one statement can be made with certainty, it is that patriarchy never dominated

Maryland society as it did in New England, regardless of all the attempts made by Calvinists after the revolution of 1689.

Notes

The author would like to thank Lois Carr, Lorena Walsh, John Waters, and the members of the Kentucky Early American History Seminar for their helpful comments and suggestions.

1. There continues to be a great deal of ambiguity over what constitutes the "state" in early modern times. See for instance: Giorgio Chittolini, "The 'Private,' the 'Public,' the State," *The Origins of the Modern State in Italy*, supplement to *The Journal of Modern History* 67 (Dec. 1995): S34–S61; Stanley Chojnacki, "Measuring Adulthood: Adolescence and Gender in Renaissance Venice," *Journal of Family History* 17 (1992): 371–95; Georges Duby, "Introduction: Private Power, Public Power," *A History of Private Life*, vol. 2, Arthur Goldhammer, ed., Cambridge, Mass.: Harvard University Press (1988) 3–31; Jean-Philippe Genet, "Introduction: Which State Rises?" *Bulletin of Historical Research* 65, no. 157 (June 1992): 119–33; and Guido Ruggiero, "Marriage, Love, Sex, and Renaissance Civic Morality," *Sexuality and Gender in Early Modern Europe: Institutions, Texts, Images*, James G. Turner, ed., Cambridge: Cambridge University Press (1993) 10–30.

2. Of course, no consensus about this relationship has been established. Susan Amussen's model in "Gender, Family and the Social Order, 1560–1725" examines the relationship between social disorder and government's desire to manage and enforce patriarchy in the family in an effort to restore order. [Susan Amussen, "Gender, Family and the Social Order, 1560–1725," *Order and Disorder in Early Modern England*, Anthony Fletcher and John Stevenson, eds., Cambridge: Cambridge University Press (1985) 196–217]. A small sample of work addressing this issue includes: Philippe Aries, "Introduction," *A History of Private Life*, vol. 3, Roger Chartier ed., Cambridge, Mass.: Harvard University Press (1989) 1–11; Stanley Chojnacki, "Marriage Legislation and Patrician Society in Fifteenth-Century Venice," in *Law, Custom and the Social Fabric in Medieval Europe: Essays in Honor of Bryce Lyon*, Bernard Bachrach and David Nicholas, eds., Kalamazoo, Mich.: Medieval Institute Publications (1990) 163–84; Martha Howell, "Citizenship and Gender: Women's Political Status in Northern European Cities," in *Women and Power in the Middle Ages*, Mary Erler and Maryanne Kowaleski, eds., Athens, Ga.: University of Georgia Press (1988) 37–60; Diane O. Hughes, "Sumptuary Law and Social Relations in Renaissance Italy," in *Disputes and Settlements: Law and Human Relations in the West*, John Bossy, ed., Cambridge: Cambridge University Press (1983) 69–99; Julius Kirshner and Anthony Molho, "The Dowry Fund and the Marriage Market in Early Quattrocento Florence," *Journal of Modern History* 50 (1978): 403–38; and Anne Norton, "Liminality: Identity and Difference," in *Reflections on Political Identity*, Baltimore: Johns Hopkins University Press (1988) 53–94.

3. Stanley Chojnacki, "Subaltern Patriarchs: Patrician Bachelors in Renaissance Ven-

ice," in *Medieval Masculinities: Regarding Men in the Middle Ages*, Claire A. Lees, ed., Minneapolis: University of Minnesota Press (1994) 74.

4. Chojnacki, "Subaltern Patriarchs," 75.

5. The Catholic Irishman, Charles Carroll, was educated in France and continued his studies at the Inner Temple in London. He went on to serve as secretary to Lord Powis in the court of James II. Prompted by Powis, Charles Carroll immigrated to Maryland in 1688 at the age of twenty-eight. In Maryland, he served as "Lord Baltimore's Agent, Receiver-General, Keeper of the Great Seal, and Register of the Land Office," until 1717. He married a relative of Baltimore's—the young Mary Darnall—after his first wife died in 1690. Mary and Charles had ten children. Their eldest son, Henry (named after his maternal grandfather), had been sent to Europe for his education and died on his trip home. Henry's younger brothers Daniel and Charles studied at St. Omer's in Flanders—a Jesuit college. When the young Charles returned to the province, he married his cousin Elizabeth Brooke and settled into their home at Doughoregan Manor. Their only son, Charles (III), left for St. Omer's at the age of eleven with his cousin John Carroll, America's first Roman Catholic bishop. [Marion Harland, *More Colonial Homesteads and Their Stories*, New York: G. P. Putnam's Sons (1899) 224–84. See also Ronald Hoffman, Sally Mason, and Eleanor Darcy, eds., *Dear Papa, Dear Charley: the Papers of Charles Carroll of Carrollton*, Chapel Hill: Omohundro Institute of Early American History and Culture (2001) 3 vols.]

6. As a feudal socage, a vassal of Lord Baltimore's owed him homage in terms of legal tender rather than military service, though Baltimore's palatine status entitled him to ask colonists to take up arms against outside attackers. For more detailed information about the early feudalism of Maryland, see Constance Lippincott, *Maryland as a Palatinate*, Philadelphia: J. B. Lippincott (1902) and William Hand Browne, *Maryland: The History of a Palatinate*, Boston: Houghton Mifflin (1899). While the charter conferred royal powers on Lord Baltimore, he acquiesced in 1638 to the assembly's insistence on its right to initiate legislation. And by 1641, the assembly decided neither the governor nor the proprietor could adjourn its sessions.

7. Among these ladies and lords were Mary Brent, Margaret Brent, Robert Brooke, Charles Carroll, Nicholas Causine, Thomas Cornwallis, Thomas Gerrard, Augustine Herman, Thomas Matthews, Nicholas Sewall, and Abell Snow [Paul Wilstach, *Tidewater Maryland*, New York: Tudor Publishing (1931) 49].

8. Debra Meyers, "The Civil Lives of White Women in Seventeenth-Century Maryland," *Maryland Historical Magazine* 94 (1999): 309–28.

9. Debra Meyers, *Common Whores, Vertuous Women, and Loveing Wives: Free Will Christian Women in Colonial Maryland*, Indiana University Press (2003) chapter 5. All the surviving wills between 1634 and 1713 [N = 3,190]—including married, single, and widowed women and men—were systematically analyzed using the SAS Institute's JMP program designed for Macintosh.

10. Lord Baltimore continued to collect quitrents and other provincial revenues even though his political power to govern had been prorogued between 1689 and 1715. Similarly, William III abrogated William Penn's right to govern Pennsylvania.

11. Lois Carr and David Jordan, *Maryland's Revolution of Government, 1689–1692*, Ithaca, N.Y.: Cornell University Press (1974). For a general overview of Maryland politics, see David Jordan, *Foundations of Representative Government in Maryland, 1632–1715*, Cambridge: Cambridge University Press (1987) and Carl Everstine, *The General Assembly of Maryland, 1634–1776*, Charlottesville, Va.: Michie (1980).

12. Carr and Jordan, *Maryland's Revolution of Government*, 79–83.

13. Carr and Jordan, *Maryland's Revolution of Government*, 72.

14. Priests like Bennett Neale constructed large homes—referred to as Mass Houses—where they celebrated on Sundays with numerous parishioners. [Wilstach, *Tidewater Maryland*, 195].

15. When the Church of England was officially established in Maryland in 1702, the government imposed a universal tax for its support; Roman Catholics were expected to pay a double tax. Frequently Catholics avoided paying this, but it was strictly enforced between 1756 and 1763. To add insult to injury, Roman Catholics lost their right to vote in 1718.

16. In 1715, Lord Baltimore converted to the State Church of England and regained his province though he never reestablished the strong family-based government that had existed before 1689.

17. George Davis, *The Day-Star of American Freedom; or the Birth and Early Growth of Toleration, in the Province of Maryland*, New York: Scribner (1855) 256–57.

18. Mary Beth Norton, *Founding Mothers and Fathers: Gendered Power and the Forming of American Society*, New York: Alfred A. Knopf (1996) 48 and 146.

19. Anne Yentsch, "An Interpretive Study of the Use of Land and Space on Lot 83, Annapolis, Md.," *New Perspectives on Maryland Historical Archaeology* 26 (1990): 31.

20. The original church—probably a brick T-shaped structure—was begun after 1699, it measured sixty-five by thirty feet and the front entrance faced the State House.

21. John D. Cushing, *The Laws of the Province of Maryland*. Wilmington, De.: Michael Glazier (1978) 7–11.

22. Cushing, *The Laws of the Province of Maryland*, 16, 28, 201.

23. Carr, "The Development of the Maryland Orphan's Court," 52.

24. Henry Miller, "Baroque Cities in the Wilderness: Archaeology and Urban Development in the Colonial Chesapeake," *Historical Archaeology* 22 (1988): 57–73.

25. This was an English Catholic tradition. Hugh Trevor-Roper suggests, "Irish Catholicism . . . [during William's reign] had no influence on the Catholics of England, whose Catholicism was of a very different and far less dangerous kind . . . they no more allowed the right of the Pope to decide the matter for them than any of their fellow countrymen." [Trevor-Roper, "Toleration and Religion after 1688," in Peter Grell, Jonathan Israel, and Nicholas Tyacke, eds., *From Persecution to Toleration: the Glorious Revolution and Religion in England*, Oxford: Clarendon Press (1991) 400]. Thomas O'Brien Hanley has argued that Catholic Marylanders had come from a long tradition, commencing with Thomas More, of believing they "could be both God's servant and the king's without any conflict of loyalty . . . [if] the king did not tamper with [a Catholic's] conscience and

beliefs, which were committed by God to a spiritual authority distinct from the king and the State." [Thomas O'Brien Hanley, *Their Rights and Liberties: The Beginnings of Religious and Political Freedom in Maryland*, Chicago: Loyola University Press (1984) 42].

26. Most colonists built structures that modern-day archaeologists refer to as "Virginia Houses"—small wooden homes supported by posts set in the ground. Rarely more than one and a half stories high, these impermanent dwellings were constructed quickly and cheaply. [Dennis Pogue, *King's Reach and 17th-Century Plantation Life*, Annapolis: Jefferson Patterson Park and Museum Studies in Archaeology (1990)]. For more information on the largest structure in St. Mary's City, see Henry Miller, "The Country's House Site: An Archaeological Study of a Seventeenth-Century Domestic Landscape," in *Historical Archaeology of the Chesapeake*, Paul Shackel and Barbara Little, eds., Washington: Smithsonian Institution Press (1994) 65–83.

27. Jesuits John Altham, Thomas Copley, and Andrew White voted in the 1638 assembly meetings. [See Edward Neill, *The Founders of Maryland as Portrayed in Manuscripts, Provincial Records and Early Documents*, Albany: Joel Munsell (1876) 96, and William Treacy, *Old Catholic Maryland and its Early Jesuit Missionaries*, Baltimore (1889) 21]

28. Treacy, *Old Catholic Maryland*, 83–84. In 1671, the Assembly considered the act for the founding and erecting of a school or college with two schoolmasters, one for the Catholic and the other for the Protestant children [William Hand Browne, ed., *Archives of Maryland*, 73 vols., Baltimore: Maryland Historical Society (1883–1973) 2: 263].

29. Richard Godbeer, *Sexual Revolution in Early America*, Baltimore: Johns Hopkins University Press (2002) 101.

30. In a letter from Father Andrew White to his superior (Henry More) in England, he asked for the church's clarification in regard to what extent Roman Catholic legislators in Maryland ought to include Canon Law into their provincial laws since the province would not be establishing an ecclesiastic court. Some of his most important questions involved the control of testamentary cases and the interference in the matter of marriage [Rev. Theodore C. Gambrall, *Studies in the Civil, Social and Ecclesiastical History of Early Maryland*, New York: Thomas Whittaker (1893) 221].

31. The significance of this legislation is highly contested. See, for instance, Carl Everstine, "Maryland's Toleration Act: An Appraisal," *Maryland Historical Magazine* 79 (1984): 99–115; John Krugler, "With Promise of Liberty in Religion: The Catholic Lords Baltimore and Toleration in Seventeenth-Century Maryland, 1634–1692," *Maryland Historical Magazine* 79 (1984): 21–43; and Maxine Lurie, "Theory and Practice of Religious Toleration in the Seventeenth Century: The Proprietary Colonies as a Case Study," *Maryland Historical Magazine* 79 (1984): 117–25. The province also experienced within its borders that added to the social discord.

32. See, for instance, Browne, *Archives of Maryland*, 1: 428, 433, 434, 468, and 469.

33. Meyers, *Common Whores, Vertuous Women, and Loveing Wives*, chap. 1.

34. Browne, *Archives of Maryland*, 1: 286 and 10: 558. Other acts modified previous ones "concerning Servants that have Bastards." The law in 1662 punished both parties [Browne, *Archives of Maryland*, 1: 428].

35. Browne, *Archives of Maryland*, 1: 286.

36. Mary Beth Norton, "Gender, Crime, and Community in Seventeenth-Century Maryland," *The Transformation of Early American History*, eds. James Henretta, et al., New York: A. A. Knopf (1991) 135.

37. Norton, "Gender, Crime, and Community in Seventeenth-Century Maryland," 127. For Calvinist New England, Richard Godbeer found that "More than a hundred women were convicted for that offense in Essex County [alone] between 1640 and 1685" [Godbeer, *Sexual Revolution in Early America*, 20].

38. Of course, these elites adhered to a hierarchical society based on class; they were interested primarily in their own ability to increase wealth.

39. Lois Carr, "The Development of the Maryland Orphan's Court, 1654–1715," *Law, Society, and Politics in Early Maryland*, Land, Carr, and Papenfuse, eds., Baltimore: Johns Hopkins University Press (1977) 52.

40. Carr, "The Development of the Maryland Orphan's Court," 44.

41. The legislation noted thus far dealing with death and estate management seems all the more extraordinary when we consider that the provincial government passed it *after* the population began to reproduce itself. We could rationalize the existence of volumes of laws dealing with intestate, orphans, and will administration if they appeared when mortality rates were extremely high prior to 1689. We need to seek other explanations when faced with the fact that it was only after the Associators' revolution that they appear with any frequency.

42. Cushing, *The Laws of the Province of Maryland*, 163–64.

43. Perhaps conscious of their own efforts to reconstruct the dominant paradigm, the patriarchy assured citizens that "nothing shall be done by Virtue of this Act which shall seem repugnant or Contradictory to the last Will or Testament of any Person Deceased." One wonders how reassuring women found this caveat [Cushing, *The Laws of the Province of Maryland*, 164].

44. Carr and Walsh, "The Planter's Wife," reprinted in *In Search of Early America: The William and Mary Quarterly, 1943–1993*, Richmond: Institute of Early American History and Culture (1993) 198.

45. Carr and Walsh, "The Planter's Wife," (1993 reprint), 197.

46. Carr, "The Development of the Maryland Orphan's Court," 41–62.

47. Perhaps related to this was the importation of secularized Societies for the "reformation of manners" and the "propagation of the gospel," which began in earnest in England during the 1690s. These groups attempted to unite all Protestants (within the English empire) around moral activism targeting the lower classes and women in particular in regard to lewd behavior and amoral activities.

48. Cushing, *The Laws of the Province of Maryland*, 88–89.

49. Godbeer, *Sexual Revolution in Early America*, 20–21.

50. Cushing, *The Laws of the Province of Maryland*, 6–7.

51. John T. Scharf, *History of Maryland: From the Earliest Period to the Present Day*, Baltimore: John B. Piet (1879) 374.

52. Cushing, *The Laws of the Province of Maryland*, 96–100.

53. Cushing, *The Laws of the Province of Maryland*, 96–97.

54. Anne Pauley, Richard Love, and others diligently petitioned the governor's English superiors in 1710 hoping that "the Fine set upon [Arrabella] for the said Crime may be remitted & he discharged out of Prison" [Public Record Office: Board of Trade and War and Colonial Department: General Registers (CO 326/20) found on pages 16, 21, and 89 of the Index to Original Correspondence, Maryland].

55. John T. McNeill, *The History and Character of Calvinism*, London: Oxford University Press (1954) 221.

56. The act "concerning Religion" in 1649 also outlawed "blaspheme" and cursing [Browne, *Archives of Maryland*, 1: 244].

57. James Farr argues that in Burgundy "because justice was viewed as sacred, one important result of the sacralization of society was the criminalization of sin." This might apply to Calvinists in Maryland and New England as well [Farr, *Authority and Sexuality in Early Modern Burgundy (1550–1730)*, New York: Oxford University Press (1995) 33].

58. Godbeer, *Sexual Revolution in Early America*, 99.

59. A thorough examination comparing the prosecutions for these offenses before and after 1689 has yet to be completed.

60. This type of legislation needs to be used with care since Marylanders owned few Black servants or slaves prior to 1689; surely this fact had some influence on whether or not legislation was passed. Yet, I would argue that the language used in the laws governing the marriages of "Negroes & Mullattoes & Mungrels" allows us to understand the new government's intentions.

61. Cushing, *The Laws of the Province of Maryland*, 124. Note that if one were willing to pay the minister more than the fine, one could probably obtain a legal marriage. Penalties for deviant behavior were not always as onerous as actual legal prohibitions.

62. Cushing, *The Laws of the Province of Maryland*, 124.

63. Cushing, *The Laws of the Province of Maryland*, 200.

64. Surely, not every woman experienced a dramatic change in her status within the family and community during the second half of the eighteenth century. Sydney Fisher told us in his 1897 book on colonial manners that elite women in Maryland enjoyed the same pleasures their husbands did—eating, drinking, sailing, and dancing after a day at the horse races or hunting. He added, "They lived in the saddle; rode to balls in the evening, with a scarlet riding-habit over their white satin ball-dress, most extraordinary figures, with handkerchiefs tied over the enormous mass of their puffed and pomaded hair." Yet, we must seek to understand the distinctive change in bequest patterns by the mid-eighteenth century [Sydney Fisher, *Men, Women & Manners in Colonial Times*. Philadelphia: J. B. Lippincott Co. (1902 originally published in 1897) 191].

65. Meyers, *Common Whores, Vertuous Women, and Loveing Wives*, chapter 2.

66. David W. Jordan, "'Gods Candle' Within Government: Quakers and Politics in Early Maryland," *William and Mary Quarterly* 3d ser., 39 (October 1982): 634 and 639.

67. John Bossy, "English Catholics after 1688," in Peter Grell, Jonathan Israel, and Nicholas Tyacke, eds., *From Persecution to Toleration: the Glorious Revolution and Religion in England*, Oxford: Clarendon Press (1991) 370.

"The Fruit of Nine, Sue kindly brought": Colonial Enforcement of Sexual Norms in Eighteenth-Century Maryland[1]

9

CATHERINE CARDNO

URING THE EIGHTEENTH CENTURY, Maryland's adaptations to its moral regulations created a world that was less and less focused on publicly shaming those who transgressed the newly re-created sexual boundaries and produced illegitimate children, while at the same time holding them accountable for their actions—but only if those transgressors were part of a white pairing. The changing focus in thinking about white relationships paralleled an unchanging strictness in the colony's dealing with miscegenation, and while it became acceptable during Maryland's golden age of bellastristic literature to poke fun at sexually straying couples, illegitimacy, sex, lust, and virtue, this changing value structure did not extend to interracial relationships.[2]

In Maryland, men and women could be presented to court and convicted on two different types of illegitimacy charges: a standard charge of "bastardy" or a charge of "mulatto bastardy." The former did not involve interracial coupling, while the latter did. Neither type distinguished punishments between men and women. As the century progressed and the courts moved away from punishing white illegitimacy offenses with the public shame of corporal punishments, a court appearance became unnecessary. The concept that criminals could be rehabilitated gained strength after the century's midpoint and emblematized a marked shift from previous views of punishment as retributive.[3] In Maryland this shift occurred in white illegitimacy trials with a move away from court toward private appearances in front of individual magistrates, and in punishments for such behavior from the publicly shaming corporal punishment of lashes toward the equally punitive, but more private, punishment of fines and potential incarcera-

tion. Even the terminology adopted by the courts bowed to the niceties of perception, and after 1731 a bastard child increasingly became one who was simply
termed "base born."[4]

This essay examines changing attitudes toward standard illegitimacy charges
and illicit sex in eighteenth-century colonial Maryland, using Charles County
Court records to examine how the courts treated illegitimacy and premarital sex;
slander suits to see how men and women defended their sexual reputation; and
the available print material to reveal the social view of such transgressions. In
addition to providing an analysis of the numbers, this essay is designed to help
to better understand the intellectual environment of colonial eighteenth-century
Maryland and how colonists felt and joked about standard illegitimacy, compared
to how the courts treated it. The criminalization of immorality that had taken
place at the turn of the century brought a new facet to the experience of bearing
an illegitimate child within the province. Maintenance requirements for bastard
children became increasingly frequent after midcentury, illustrating a continuing
concern with the economic ramifications of bearing a child outside of wedlock.
Throughout the eighteenth century bearing an illegitimate child stood as a crime,
and as such, it carried a distinct immorality component that had not existed for
most of Maryland's seventeenth century.[5]

With the flowering of belletristic literature in Maryland and elsewhere in
colonial America by midcentury, straying husbands and wives, premarital sex, and
illegitimacy joined the ranks of permissible story and conversation material in the
Maryland *Almanack* and the *Maryland Gazette*, as they did elsewhere in the colonies.[6]
This development did not mean that society accepted such behavior, but merely
that joking about it was not taboo. Undoubtedly influenced by his participation
in the Tuesday Club of Annapolis,[7] Jonas Green, in "A Case to the Civilian,"
treated his readers to a question that in everyday life would have kept gossips and
neighbors talking:

> NOKES went, he thought, to *Style's* Wife to bed,
> Nor knew his own was laid there in her stead:
> Civilians, Is the Child he then begot
> To be allow'd Legitimate, or Not?[8]

The question here is focused on the straying husband, but implicit in the "case"
is the question of a straying wife. Both Nokes and his unnamed wife thought they
were enjoying someone else's company. Exactly what constituted a legitimate
child, Green asks—intent, or action? A debate for neighbors to argue over, for
sure. With this lighthearted question it is evident that straying husbands and
wives were certainly part of everyday life—uncommon enough to be gossip wor-

thy but certainly not unheard of. Cuckolding humor in comic literature had a basis in matrimonial comedy from England, and the ridicule that such pieces offered on correct male and female behavior allowed inappropriate conduct to be the basis of jokes even if it was not socially (or even legally) acceptable.[9]

Oblique jokes poking fun at the ill informed when it came to contraception also made it into print during this period.[10] In 1747 a poem, "The Undecided Case," appeared in the *Maryland Gazette*, and Jonas Green repeated it by inserting it into the Maryland *Almanack* in 1758. The poem offered a scenario in which a child was born to a couple four months after their wedding:

> DICK join'd in nuptial Conjugation
>   With *Susan*, whom he long had sought:
> But four Months after Cultivation,
>   The Fruit of Nine, *Sue* kindly brought.
> *Dick* scolded: She was in a Swoon:
>   About their Case the Neighbours varied:
> Some urged that *Susan* came too soon;
>   Others—that *Dick* too late was married[11]

The author purposely left the "case" up to the reader to decide. Was Susan's child a premature baby, or had the two been married too late? The poem illustrates that by the mid-eighteenth century, even though legal codes might permit a child to be born less than nine months after a wedding without criminal action being taken against the couple, social mores did not accept the birth so quietly. Community gossip about whether or not the child was born prematurely or whether the couple had had premarital sex was fully acceptable, and indeed expected. This was a fact Green himself would have been all too familiar with: he and his wife, Anne Catherine, were married only six months before the birth of their first child.[12] Community participation in regulating acceptable sexual behavior meant that neighbors, and the readers of the paper and *Almanack*, could, and should, have opinions about the actions and behavior of other community members in circumstances similar to those of Dick, Sue, Nokes, and his unnamed wife.

Five years after the second appearance of Dick and Susan's "case" in 1763, and sixteen years after its first appearance, Green treated the readers of the Maryland *Almanack* to an epigram about Florimel's two births—one legitimate and one illegitimate.

> Ten Months after *Florimel* happen'd to Wed,
> And was brought, in a laudable manner, to Bed;
> She warbled her Groans with so charming a Voice,

> That one half of the Parish was Stunn'd with the Noise:
> But when *Florimel* chose to lie *privately* in,
> Twelve Months before She and her Spouse were akin,
> She chose, with such prudence, her Pangs to conceal,
> That her Nurse, nay her Midwife, scarce heard her once Squeal.
> Learn Husbands, from hence, for the Peace of your Lives,
> That *Maids* make not half so much Tumult as *Wives*.[13]

This epigram, focusing on Florimel's efforts to conceal her labor pains through silence before marriage while publicly expressing them after marriage, shows the continuing stigma attached to illegitimacy. But is also suggests that while women like Florimel could go on to lead normal, acceptable lives, early slips in their behavior provided permissible material for wits to mock.

Women could turn to slander suits to protect their sexual reputation, as two women in Charles County did. Elizabeth Wilkinson and her husband took Mary Godshall and her husband to court in 1705 for spreading gossip that Wilkinson had borne a bastard and been whipped for the crime. Wilkinson and her husband sought damages, but they left the county before the resolution of the case and so lost by default.[14] Fifty-six years later another slander case involved much stronger language and a much vaguer accusation. In 1761 Margaret Key slandered Mary Magdelin Sotherland, "in the Presence and hearing" of various people, by uttering in a loud voice that "you (the said Mary Magdelin meaning) are a Rotten Whore and the said Margaret will Prove it."[15] In this case the court awarded damages to the wronged party, Sotherland, in the form of eight pounds current plus the costs and charges of her suit. In a community that relied heavily on a system of credit for an individual's economic health, the victims of slander couched their suits in terms of monetary damages. The loss of their good name and reputation could shut people out of social circles and out of economic ones, hampering their capacity for self-sufficiency.[16] Proving highly damaging rumors false could thus be critical to an individual's economic and social stability. With much riding on one's good name, victims challenged gossip or claims that besmirched their reputation in the public forum of the courtroom, where justices and a jury settled the matter once and for all.

The scandal of a conviction or the damage gossip may have caused did not mean that Marylanders did not joke about sex and illegitimacy. By the mid-eighteenth century a certain familiarity with issues of illegitimacy, sex, and male and female lust and virtue resulted in a few overt, and bawdy, references in printed matter designed for mass consumption. As discussed earlier, in 1747 a poem about Dick and Susan's unfortunate timing appeared in the *Maryland Gazette*, only to reappear eleven years later in a Maryland *Almanack*. In the same issue in 1758, "The Poetic Couple" of Richie and Pattie were caught midfrolic in the lines of a short ditty. While playing crambo, Patti offers to rhyme "Bliss" was "A-kiss." With this flirtatious overture, "The Prologue begun, no more to be said:/They stripped, and soon finishe'd the Poem in Bed."[17]

By 1764 Green felt secure enough in his purchasing, and reading, public to devote an entire almanac to a twelve-stanza poem about a wanton maiden, before ending with a strong statement about other vices. "The Mad-Dog: A Tale" traced a prudish maiden from church, where "Pale Penitence had mark'd her Face/With all the meager signs of Grace" to her weekly confession where she thrice confessed to illicit sex, forcing the minister to ask:

> Madam, I grant there's something in it
> That Virtue has the unguarded Minute;
> But Pray now tell me what are Whores,
> But Women of unguarded Hours?
> Then you must sure have lost all Shame,
> What ev'ry Day and still the same,
> And no Fault else! 'tis strange to find
> A Woman to one Sin confin'd!

Our one-time prudish maid traced the fault of her vice-ridden spree to a "sad Disaster." Bitten by a favorite lap dog, the only cure for the bite which had "set her youthful Blood fermenting" was to be dipped into icy seawater. "Naked in the Face of Day," our maid asks:

> What Virgin had not done as I did
> My modest Hand, by Nature guided,
> Debarr'd at once from human Eyes
> The Seat where Female Honour lies,
> And though thrice Dipt from Top to Toe,
> I still secur'd the Post below,
> And guarded it with Grasp so fast
> Not one Drop through my Fingers Past;
> Thus owe I to my bashful Care
> That all the Rage is settled there.

As a result of her commitment to securing "the Post below . . . with Grasp so fast/Not one Drop through my Fingers Past" our maiden inadvertently ruined the efficacy of the sea cure. Her confession to the minister as to the reasons for her actions and the failure of her immersion in seawater ends with the statement that "Thus owe I to my bashful Care/That all the Rage is settled there."

This poem portrayed the picture of maiden lust openly. Immediately after the maiden's first confession to the minister, the narrator tells us:

> Away she Trips; perhaps to Prayer.
> 'Twas no such Thing. Why then this haste?
> The Clock has struck, the Hour is past,
> And on the spur of Inclination,
> She scorn'd to Bilk her Assignation.

The narrator counters the maiden's desire to continue her wanton ways with a view of the minister that likens his motivation to the "wanton thought" of questioning justices in illegitimacy charges:

> The Father ask'd her where and when?
> How many? and what Sort of Men?
> By what Degrees her Blood was heated?
> How oft' the Frailty was repeated?
> Thus have I seen a pregnant Wench
> All flush'd with Guilt before the Bench,
> The Judges (wak'd by wanton Thought)
> Dive to the Bottom of her Fault,
> They leer, they simper at her Shame,
> And make her call all Things by Name.[18]

Bawdy references in the Maryland *Almanack* to the wantonness of men were not limited to this poem. In 1763, "On a Civilian" poked fun at lawyers through the story of "A Wealthy, old, grave, and grey-headed Sire,/Stole to a Wench, to quench his Lust's desire."[19] The infamous Nokes from "A Case to the Civilian" is yet another example of a man portrayed in an unflattering light because of his desire for illicit sex.

If female virtue was the product of guarded hours, as the poem claimed, female lust and wantonness were then linked to unguarded hours and actions. Though the poem clearly likens a woman's virtue to her genitalia and spells out the loss of that virtue as ultimately her own fault, medical problems or debauchery by a man promising marriage could underlie a maiden's wandering and be understandable reasons for "all the Rage" to be "settled there." Green's inclusion of such poems and ditties by no means celebrated wanton women or men. Though relatively graphic at points, "The Mad-Dog" illustrated the shame that followed a fallen women—regardless of the explanation for her fall from virtue.

Social views of illegitimacy and premarital sex thus allowed open discussion and joking about promiscuity, but such verbal permissibility did not equate with social acceptance of the actions themselves. As long as a marriage took place roughly around the time of conception, or even before birth, such premarital sex was not a legal issue, even though it may have been a social one. While the normative treatment of illegitimacy may have been moving away from public shaming and toward more private punitive measures, gossip and shame could still follow such women.

Legislation dealing with standard bastardy in Maryland underwent a triphasal shift during the eighteenth century as the colonial punishment of lashes went from being a requirement that the court could waive with an offender's request, to an alternate only if the offender could not pay the fine, to being outlawed altogether as a form of punishment in pre- and extramarital sex cases.

Punishment for standard bastardy charges in eighteenth-century Maryland followed seventeenth-century colonial traditions[20] in assuming until 1715 that lashes would be the punishment (though the offender could request a fine). Service time for servants continued to be assessed throughout in order to recoup her (or his) master's economic costs in the pregnancy, childbirth, and early years of the child's life. In the second eighteenth-century development, which took place with the 1715 legislation, the courts had the right to decide if a woman who bore an illegitimate child would be assessed the fine or lashes if she refused to name her partner. Otherwise the court could assess lashes only if the offender could not pay the fine.[21] As the eighteenth century progressed, the assembly began to shy away from public punishments and ended corporal punishment as an option for a conviction. After 1749, the standard bastardy punishment for having an illegitimate child stood at a fine, or upon failure to pay that fine, incarceration for the transgression. Lashes had totally been phased out of the punishment structure.

In the vast majority of bastardy cases women and men pleaded guilty. As a result, an impaneled jury acquitted a woman charged with bastardy only six times during our entire period.[22] The court entered "nolle prosequi"[23] and discharge decisions more commonly than flat acquittals, but a combined total of only nine instances of all of these occurred during our time period for women. The court failed to convict eighteen more women for a range of reasons—including four who died after being presented to court in the first place. The court failed to convict only seventeen men on bastard-begetting charges. Overall, then, the court did not convict six percent of the women and fifteen percent of the men.

Though rare, the aquittals, nolle prosequi, and ignoramus decisions indicate that a bastardy or bastard-begetting trial did not always dictate a conviction when an alleged offender appeared in court. The court almost always convicted offenders because of their own admissions of culpability—only a very small portion of women challenged their guilt by failing to plead guilty. Once the women were presented by the grand jury on a bastardy charge, the court usually tried and convicted in another court session within about a year, but convictions of men could take longer.

Table 9.1 shows the rate of women and men presented and convicted in Charles County between the years of 1696 and 1770. The conviction numbers for women begin with the normalized rate[24] of 46 convictions in the 1690s, and, after an initial peak in the 1700s, a steady increase through the 1750s when they topped 100 per year for both the 1740s and 1750s.[25] Looking more closely at the one year, 1755, where the at-risk population of free white women can be calculated tells us that these are not high numbers: In 1755 the normalized per-year average of convictions was 10, while the number of free white or mulatto women who could have gotten pregnant stood at 1,997.[26] This means that even though 100 women were convicted of bearing a bastard child over the course of the decade, only .5 percent of the at-risk women were convicted of bearing illegitimate children in Charles County that year. While bastardy may have been visible and joked about, it was clearly not a widespread problem. Convictions of men occurred on an even smaller scale.

Table 9.1.   Actual and Normalized Numbers of Convicted Women and Men in Standard Bastardy Cases

	Actual numbers[1]		Normalized[2] numbers	
	Women	Men	Women	Men
1690s	23		46	
1700s	77	1	77	1
1710s	54	7	70	9
1720s	68[3]	17	70	17
1730s	77	13	93	16
1740s	106	14	109	14
1750s	90	44[4]	100	49
1760s	52	15	53	15
Total:	547	111	618	121

Source: Charles County Court records, 1696–1770

1. Numbers include the 98 men convicted of begetting bastard or base-born children, as well as the 13 men convicted solely on adultery or fornication charges if an illegitimate child resulted from their transgression.

2. Since the county court met quarterly and 43 of the 320 court sessions are missing, the numbers have been normalized by finding the per-quarter average for the extant session records in each decade and multiplying that by the number of quarters (40) meant to be in a decade.

3. Includes two sets of twins.

4. One man, Thomas Miller, was convicted for begetting two children in the same court appearance (1758,0808,491-018).

The situation with men was quite different. No men were convicted of begetting illegitimate children in the 1690s and just one was convicted in the next decade. After the 1715 change in legislation threatened women with lashes if they did not name their partners, the number of male convictions rose to 16–17 in the 1720s and 1730s. The 1740s saw a modest drop, but the numbers more than tripled in the 1750s after the assembly passed legislation doubling the punishment for women who refused to name their partners. After this 1749 act, the Charles County Court convicted almost 50 men, roughly half of the 100 women it convicted during the same decade. These numbers stand in stark contrast to what was occurring in New England, where prosecutions of men ended at mid-century.[27] Despite the fact that one out of every two children causing an illegitimacy conviction had both their fathers and mothers convicted in that decade, on average the court only convicted 4.9 men a year out of an at-risk population of 2,425; this made convictions of men a microscopic .2 percent of the nonslave adult male population in 1755 Charles County.[28] The court may not have convicted men at the same rate as it convicted women, the result in no small part of many women's refusal to name their partners, but it still held eighteenth-century men responsible for their actions when possible, especially in the 1750s.

The line between legitimate and illegitimate sex between a free couple lay in their status with regard to marriage. Were they already married to each other, or to different spouses? Were they getting married? Or were they not married at all? The court dealt with each category differently, as it tried to keep colonists moral by punishing transgressors.

In 1706 the court convicted Abigaill Dyamond on a bastardy charge where she named Thomas Dyson Jr. as the father of her child.[29] Her brother, George Dyamond, came to her defense swearing "on the Holy Evangelist . . . that the said Thomas Dyson had fraudeulently Deceived and Deluded the said Abigaill under a Promise of Marriage." As a result, the court assessed the damages caused to Abigaill's reputation and required Dyson to pay Abigaill 1,200 pounds of tobacco for the "abuse of her body," to give her 900 pounds of tobacco annually for five years, to pay all the court fees, and to enter into a recognizance to indemnify the county from any charge relating to the child.[30] Despite the court's public defense of her reputation with its decision, within three years Abigaill had borne another bastard child to a different man, Matthew Tennison.[31]

Over fifty years later in October 1759, the court recorded that John Winter, a justice of the peace in Charles County, fined Elizabeth Dent on a bastardy charge. She had confessed her guilt in the relative privacy of her interview with the justice, swore the child to planter Peter Dent, and Winter fined her thirty shillings according to the law.[32] A month later, Peter Dent appeared before Justice

Winter and, after confessing his guilt, received a thirty-shilling fine according to law. Justice Winter also required Peter to enter into a recognizance to indemnify the county from any charge related to Elizabeth's bastard child.[33]

This case is representative of standard bastardy convictions after the 1740s for a number of reasons—both Elizabeth and Peter were free, both appeared in front of a single justice of the peace rather than in court, both were fined the same amount, and Elizabeth named the begetter of her child, Peter, whom the justice bound to a recognizance in addition to his fine. Elizabeth did not suffer the loss of her reputation lightly, and in November 1760 she brought Peter to court seeking damages for his breach of promise to marry her, charging that he acted "fraudulently[,] Intending to deceive and defraud" her and keep her from the benefits of marriage after she had "faithfully Promised the said Peter that she the said Elizabeth would take the said Peter to be her Husband in lawfull matrimoney" and he "faithfully Promised the said Elizabeth that he the said Peter would take her . . . wife." Elizabeth had trusted him, and "refused to Contract Matrimony with other Persons who had offered to Marry her," though her pregnancy and giving birth to a bastard child the year before must have weighed heavily on her mind. Despite frequent requests to Peter that he "be joyned to her in lawfull matriomony the said Peter hath further Altogether refused and still doth refuse whereby the said Elizabeth saith she is injured and hath damage to the value of ninety nine Pounds Sterling." Though Peter pleaded not guilty, the court found him at fault and awarded damages to Elizabeth in the sum of forty pounds sterling plus the costs and charges of her court case.[34]

If Dyamond's and Dent's suitors had not broken their marriage promises, the illegitimate children would have probably been born around the time of their parents' marriages—an acceptable situation in colonial eighteenth-century Maryland. The occurrence of childbirth shortly after marriage did not result in punishments for either the new husband or wife in Maryland, unlike the situation in Connecticut.[35] For those unfortunate women who had to appear in court on charges at all, the court itself protected women who were married for a reasonable amount of time before or after the birth of the child by either acquitting them of the crime or discharging them altogether.

The court also acquitted women who could prove that they were married at the time of the conception of their child, regardless of their status at the child's birth. Such was the case of Elizabeth Fardinando, presented in November 1712. The court acquitted her in June 1713 after she had "Proved In Court that at ye tyme of her supossing to bring forth said Bastardy Child shee was married to a Certayne John Wood junior since dead." Even women such as Hester Grumball who "Cometh and Saith shee is In No wise Guilty of the Trespass and Misde-meanour . . . and that her Child is a lawfull and True begotten Child" were acquit-ted because of a lack of positive evidence.[36] The court also acquitted women who married after the birth of the bastard child, such as servant Mary Simpson, who was acquitted from her June 1696 presentment in August 1696.[37]

As is seen in the cases of Abigaill Dyamond and Elizabeth Dent, the promise of marriage was not a promise easily broken. The courts accepted premarital sex and conception as long as the couple married around the time of the child's birth. Though the court convicted both Elizabeth and Abigaill of bastardy, by taking the men to court for damages both women publicly asserted themselves as acting in an acceptable manner and placed the blame for the illegitimate child directly on the father's broken marriage promise. By awarding both Elizabeth and Abigaill substantial amounts of money in damages, the jurors and court exhibited the legitimacy of the women's actions and the illegitimacy of the men's. The courts even accepted premarital sex and conception as long as a marriage took place roughly around the time of the birth, illustrated clearly when the court acquitted Mary Simpson in August 1696 because of her marriage after the birth of her child. Unlike their eighteenth-century New England counterparts,[38] Charles County men and women in 1760 were held equally responsible in a bastardy case, while men were also held ultimately responsible for the child if a promise to marry had been involved. The problem for the courts was getting women to name their partners at all.

Despite a gender-blind law when it came to adultery, marriage did not play the beneficial role for men that it did for women if a child resulted. The law passed by the General Assembly did not differentiate between men and women, stating that "every Person or Persons that shall commit Adultery, and shall be thereof convict . . . shall be Fined by the Justices."[39] Considered a graver crime than an illegitimate birth, adultery merited twice the monetary fine as did bearing or begetting a bastard child. Adultery was notoriously difficult to prove, and con-victions for adultery (or for that matter, fornication) that had not produced off-spring occurred only a few times a decade, unlike illegitimacy charges.[40]

A married woman who succeeded in keeping an illicit adulterous relationship secret was almost impossible to convict on a bastardy charge. Her husband would have had to have been away for more than nine months before the birth of the child, and especially during the early months of the pregnancy, to render improb-able the possibility that the eventual child was born prematurely and conceived without the participation of her husband. A married man named in a bastardy case was easier to convict, as happened in the 1732 case of Issabella Cubbison, a servant to Marcelius Littlejohn. Patrick Connelly, a blacksmith, came to pledge the security for Cubbison's court fees. Since Cubbison was unable or unwilling to pay the fine, or procure security for its future payment, the court sentenced her to ten lashes.[41] There is no way to know if she chose to receive lashes rather than to borrow money from Connelly, but in the same March 1732 court session at which the grand jury presented her and the court convicted her, she acted as witness to the grand jury in their presentment of Connelly as the begetter of her bastard child.[42] Connolly confessed, and after doing so it became "Manifest to the Justices here that the same Patrick at the time of begetting the bastard Child afsd was and still is a married person."[43] As a result, the court doubled his fine from the usual 30 shillings current or 600 pounds of tobacco for fornication, to the fine for adultery: 3 pounds current or 1,200 pounds of tobacco.[44]

Cubbison's employment as a servant brings up the question of status: the court convicted servant and free women in roughly even numbers for the first forty years of the century, until a sudden change in the 1740s when the proportion of free women made up almost two-thirds of the total numbers.[45] It is difficult to link the later acceptance of print jokes and references to illegitimacy to this shift in the offending woman's status because of the few issues that remain of an earlier run of the *Maryland Gazette*. However, based on the issues that do remain from the 1720s and 1730s, it is safe to say that bawdy jokes and references to marriage and premarital sex did not make a noticeable appearance before the late 1740s. Despite its subject matter, Ebenezer Cook's *Sot-weed Factor* was published in England in 1708, and its satirical curse on the province of Maryland "Where no Man's Faithful, nor a Woman Chast"[46] did not appear in the 1731 Maryland reprint.[47] Increasing references and the acceptability of jokes came about during the period of increasing literary output after midcentury, and paralleled the shift to free women, rather than indentured servant women, offenders.

The changing status of convicted offenders by the 1740s points to a clear difference between eighteenth-century and seventeenth-century Maryland.[48] Mary Beth Norton adeptly shows that Virginia's and Maryland's higher conviction rates for bastardy over fornication charges, as opposed to the opposite case in Massachusetts, resulted from the fact that servant women made up most of the single women in the seventeenth-century Chesapeake. Since servant women could not marry without their masters' permission, a stable relationship between a man and a woman had the potential to proceed long enough without marriage that a bastard child could result. This situation changed during the eighteenth century, with the convictions of free women ranging between forty-five percent and ninety-eight percent per decade during the eighteenth-century.

Table 9.2 shows the number of bastardy convictions and is broken down by the offenders' status as free or bonded. Except for the first decade of the eighteenth

Table 9.2. Actual and Normalized Numbers of Convicted Women in Standard Bastardy Cases, by Status

	Actual Numbers				Normalized Numbers			
	Free	Hired or living with	Servant	Total	Free	Hired or living with	Servant	Total
1690s	12		11	23	24		22	46
1700s	17	18	42	77	17	18	42	77
1710s	28	3	23	54	36	4	30	70
1720s	38[1]	4	26	68	39	4	27	70
1730s	41	2	34	77	50	2	41	93
1740s	60	11	35	106	62	11	36	109
1750s	77		13	90	86		14	100
1760s	51		1	52	52		1	53
Total:	324	38	185	547	366	39	213	618

Source: Charles County Court records, 1696–1770.
1. Includes two sets of twins.

century, the number of servant women convicted on bastardy charges never outweighed the number of free women convicted. Despite the direction of Norton's findings for the seventeenth century, then, servant women were not the majority of the offenders convicted in the eighteenth century under the revised legislation. The decreasing importance of servant women within the eighteenth-century Maryland labor pool accounted for the dropping numbers over the course of the entire century, especially so after the century's midpoint.

While slave labor began to replace servant labor in Maryland, another important demographic trend was underway.[49] Imports of servant women as either indentured servants or convict servants never reached the numbers of imported male laborers, but during the early years of the eighteenth century both male and female free laborers increasingly made up an important part of the Maryland labor pool.[50] These increasing numbers of free female laborers, when added to the fact that the average marriage age for women was rising in Maryland during the 1730s,[51] means that a growing body of free unmarried women were at risk for premarital pregnancy, and thus also for illegitimacy presentations and convictions by the courts. These were not widowed women—only three widows appeared in court convicted on bastardy charges—but rather single, never-married women.[52] As the court increasingly convicted free women, then, demographic trends explain the trend toward free women rather than a change of focus by the courts themselves, while at the same time the high remarriage rate of widows explains their absence on bastardy charges.[53]

The status of convicted men is harder to pinpoint. Out of the 111 convictions from the entire 1696–1770 period, the court labeled three men as both
planters and servants and two as both laborers (a term usually used to denote free
agents) and servants.[54] Blurring the meaning behind assigned statuses even more,
the court referred to Joseph Bladen as a planter but then listed his master as
Thomas Luckett. A similar situation involved James Knowland: the court listed
him as a laborer and his master as James Semmes, planter.[55] The confusion over
a worker's appellation centered in the 1720s and 1730s, and confirms Christine
Daniels's findings for Kent County that during this time men were increasingly
choosing to be called "laborer," rather than planter, because laborer was becoming
a recognized, and separate, status.[56]

As table 9.3 shows, the court convicted free men of bastard begetting much
more frequently than it convicted either indentured or hired servants. Although
the number of free men convicted by the court parallels the upward swing in
convictions of free women, the court still convicted men in much smaller numbers
than women, despite the overall increase in male conviction numbers over the
course of the decade. Women's refusal to name their partners explains, in part,
the smaller conviction rates of men.

Despite this evolution in an offender's status, the court still punished servants
differently than it did free people. The court generally assigned equal or fewer
lashes to women than their male counterparts regardless of the woman's status.
Under law, the court needed to assign the moiety for damages to convicted servant men, but hold free men responsible for all the costs of pregnancy, childbirth,
and the early years of the child's life. This practice, combined with the potential
embarrassment of the master's family (if the woman bearing the child was a ser-

Table 9.3.   Actual and Normalized Numbers of Convicted Men, by Status

	Actual Numbers			Normalized Numbers		
	Free	Servant	Total	Free	Servant	Total
1690s						
1700s	1		1	1		1
1710s	2	5	7	3	6	9
1720s	13	4	17	13	4	17
1730s	8	5	13	10	6	16
1740s	12	2	14	12	2	14
1750s	40	4	44	45	4	49
1760s	15		15	15		15
Total:	91	20	111	99	22	121

Source: Charles County Court records, 1696–1770.

vant), indicates that the court took more than gender into consideration: it also looked at a person's status. Free men often had to pay all the costs and expenses for women convicted on bastardy charges. As the status of female offenders shifted during the eighteenth century and the possibility of assigning extra servitude time to recoup the economic considerations of supporting an illegitimate child no longer existed, the court after 1742 increasingly required free men to enter into recognizances to indemnify the county from charges associated with a free-born illegitimate child as it grew up.[57] Although maintenance requirements were always rare for women, they began to occur in a few cases after 1745.[58] The courts' equality in assigning parental responsibility to two servants indicates an equality of status on the part of a servant couple, a perception that did not hold true for free men and women. In the case of a free couple the punishment became strikingly gendered, with the court requiring the man to pay both his and the woman's costs, plus the monetary burden of raising the child.

As stated previously, punishment for bastardy in Maryland underwent a triphasal shift during our time period: from 1694 until 1715, from 1715 until 1749, and from 1749 until past the end of our period, in 1781. The punishment for illegitimacy moved from the court's making the decision to assess a fine or lashes, to a 1715 law that first required a fine. Upon a person's inability to pay that fine, the court would then substitute lashes. Even though the assembly intended this 1715 change to apply only to fornicators and adulterers, with the courts still choosing bastardy punishments, in practice the number of corporal punishments decreased over the years as the Charles County court gave all women the choice of a fine. The assembly took away the corporal punishment option in 1749, and imprisonment became the penalty if a person could not pay the fine.

In 1749, when the assembly repealed the corporal punishment section of the 1715 act, it also updated the fine itself on three major points. The revised law brought the monetary fine in line with current exchange rates, giving the court even more leverage in attempting to force a woman to name the father of her child. The newly gendered act now squarely addressed that group easiest to convict of illegitimacy, women, and stipulated that "Every Free woman convict[ed] of fornication, in any county court, shall be fined 30 s. current Money." In 1749 Maryland, thirty shillings current was worth 240 pounds of tobacco rather than the 600 pounds of tobacco that had remained unaltered in the act's wording since 1715. Despite the tremendous fluctuation in the tobacco market over the intervening years, reworking the punishment for bastardy had not been a high priority for the General Assembly.

The 1749 revision also stated that a woman who refused to name the man who begat her "base-born" child should be assessed his thirty-shilling fine as well, bringing her fine up to the total of three pounds current. Furthermore, if the woman refused "to discover" the child's father, she was responsible for entering into a security to "keep the Child from becoming a Charge to the County." If she did name the man and the court convicted him, he would be responsible for his thirty shillings, "together with all Charges of Prosecution."[59] In cases where the woman "discovered" the father of the child, he was also to be legally responsible to enter into a recognizance to indemnify the county from charges relating to the child, and she would be discharged from the responsibility. If either party was unable to pay the fine immediately upon conviction he or she was allowed to offer a security for payment within the space of twelve months, or stand committed to the sheriff's custody as a debtor would have been.[60]

Table 9.4 shows the influence of the 1749 law: with the legal doubling of the fine if the woman concealed the father, the normalized number of women who named their partners jumped from twenty in the 1740s to 48 in the 1750s. The sudden jump in naming as a result of the doubled fine makes a persuasive argument that from the 1690s through the 1740s women were choosing to conceal the names of the involved men. We can see that table 9.1 also supports this theory, showing that the number of men convicted in the decade immediately following the law change quadrupled, jumping from fourteen to forty-nine.[61]

Table 9.5 shows the complexity of the issue. While the eighteenth century began with fifty-two percent of the women naming their partners, no men were convicted. The numbers of women who named men sank to eighteen percent in the decade immediately preceding the 1749 law change, and the number of men

Table 9.4.   Actual and Normalized Numbers of Convicted Women Who Named Their Partners in Standard Bastardy Cases

	Actual named numbers				Normalized named numbers			
	Free	*Hired*	*Servant*	*Total*	*Free*	*Hired*	*Servant*	*Total*
1690s	4		8	12	8		16	24
1700s	11	2	16	29	11	2	16	29
1710s	7	2	8	17	9	3	10	22
1720s	17[1]		9	26	17		9	26
1730s	8		13	21	10		16	26
1740s	17		3	20	17		3	20
1750s	40		4	44	44		4	48
1760s	16		1	17	16		1	17
Total:	120	4	62	186	132	5	75	212

Source: Charles County Court records, 1696–1770.
1. Includes two sets of twins.

Table 9.5. Normalized Number of Convicted Women, and Named and Convicted Men in Standard Bastardy Cases

Decade	Women[1]	Men			
		Named	Percentage[2]	Convicted	Percentage[3]
1690s	46	24	52%	0	0%
1700s	77	29	38%	1	1.3%
1710s	70	22	31%	9	13%
1720s	68	26	38%	17	25%
1730s	93	26	28%	16	17%
1740s	109	20	18%	14	13%
1750s	100	48	48%	49	49%
1760s	53	17	32%	15	28%
Total:	616	212	28.5%[4]	121	14.6%[5]

Source: Charles County Court records, 1696–1770

1. Total number of women convicted (normalized).

2. The percentage is made up by comparing the number of women who named men, to the total number of women who were convicted. For example, in the 1700s 29 women named men and 77 women were convicted. So 37.7% of the women named men.

3. This percentage is made up by comparing the number of men convicted to the total number of women convicted in that decade. For example, in the 1700s 1 man was convicted despite 29 being named. So while 37.7% of the women named men, compared to the total number of convicted women the number of convicted men made up only 1.3% (rather than the 37.7% of them who were named).

4. The average per decade of named men (using normalized numbers).

5. The average per decade of convicted men (using normalized numbers).

convicted relative to the number of women dropped to thirteen percent. While this number of male convictions was not the lowest number that occurred during the first half of the eighteenth century, the ratio of men to women convicted had been steadily declining from a small peak in the 1720s. With the new 1749 legislation, however, the percentage of women naming their partners jumped to forty-eight percent, with the percentage of bastardy cases where the court also convicted a man increasing to forty-nine percent, meaning that if a woman named her partner, the court was almost certain to convict him.

The General Assembly's further punishment for women who concealed begetters post-1749 would not have been implemented if the court had not felt it necessary. However, the journals of the upper and lower houses are surprisingly quiet regarding the assembly's motivation in suddenly repealing the corporal punishments relating to illegitimacy charges. The appearance of Benjamin Franklin's "The Speech of Polly Baker" in the *Maryland Gazette* two years before the law change, when combined with the law change itself, suggests that more and more people within Maryland were questioning the legitimacy of the bastardy law itself during and after the 1740s.

In 1747, Jonas Green reprinted "a correct Copy" of Miss Polly Baker's famous "speech" in Connecticut.[62] Green prefaced the front-page reprint with the remark that "I cannot think it amiss, to [give] it [to] my Readers, not doubting it's [sic] favourable Reception." Benjamin Franklin's now-famous hoax was a parody of the fallen woman, and Polly "enhances her image by showing that vice is but another facet of virtue."[63] The speech itself, however, reinforced the notion that current colonial bastardy laws were unreasonable. Baker was "recorded" as saying that "since Laws are sometimes unreasonable in themselves, and therefore repealed," she will take the liberty of saying that:

> I think this Law, by which I am punished is both unreasonable in itself, and particularly severe with regard to me, who have always lived an inoffensive Life in the neighborhood where I was born and defy my Enemies (if I have any) to say I ever wrong'd Man, Woman, or Child. Abstracted from the Law, I cannot conceive (may it please your Honour) what the Nature of my offense is.

Franklin, as Baker, justifies her indiscretions by pointing out that she has fulfilled her womanly and biblically commanded "Duty" to procreate by bringing five more healthy children into a land in need of more people. Her downfall began with a breach of promise and was not her fault: she was doing her duty to the land as a womanly woman by bringing more healthy children into the world to populate it.

Despite being understood as purposefully provocative, underlying the satire was Franklin's discontent with current legislation.[64] Baker blamed illegitimacy laws for driving women to abortions and infanticide and so entreated the justices (and the reading public) to reflect on the unnaturalness of the laws themselves:

> But if you, great men, must be making Laws, do not turn natural and useful Actions into Crimes, by your Prohibitions. Reflect a little on the horrid Consequences of this Law in particular: What Numbers of procur'd Abortions? and how many distress'd Mothers have been driven, by the Terror of Punishment and public Shame, to imbrue, contrary to nature, their own trembling Hands in the Blood of their helpless Offspring!

Baker blamed the Law for "all these Barbarities and Murders" in the form of abortions and infanticide, and finally questioned the justices whether or not bachelors who refused to marry were not actually committing a "greater Offense against the Public Good, than mine."

Though the piece was designed as a hoax, it serves nonetheless as an indicator of the intellectual environment. Its appearance in the *Maryland Gazette* acted as a reflection of prevailing thoughts in Maryland, which followed the lines—developing elsewhere in the colonies—that questioned the immorality of bastardy. Franklin's Polly had strong views, and presented them in a way meant to titillate the audience, but the existence of the speech, its reprint in Maryland (and elsewhere), and the content of it, satire and parody aside, represented the changing values of the mid-eighteenth century. The piece gave satirical voice to the eighteenth-century trends that questioned the reasoning behind illegitimacy legislation. Questioning of the legislation, while not immediately apparent in the written records, must have occurred because of the overhaul of bastardy legislation in Maryland, and the General Assembly's removal of corporal punishment for illegitimacy charges as of 1749.

No further laws passed concerning illegitimacy in colonial Maryland. The next time the Maryland General Assembly addressed the issue, in 1781, it only set out a procedure requiring securities from either the mother or father to ensure that the illegitimate child would not become an economic burden on the community.[65] The law made no mention of a fine or of illegitimacy's being a misdemeanor offense.

Pairings that involved a free couple and a standard bastardy conviction were criminal in Maryland for eighty-seven years. Rather than being based on the economic burden posed for communities by an unsupported illegitimate child, the Maryland General Assembly's 1694 criminalization of illegitimacy was based firmly on morality. While courtroom references to sin and offenses against God faded as the century passed, bearing or begetting a bastard child continued as a criminal offense. That the assembly tried to make both men and women equally culpable can be seen in the gender-blind laws that it passed, and the increased punishments levied upon women who refused to name their partners. That the Charles County Court held men and women equally culpable for the moral offense can be seen in the equality of lashes given to men and women punished corporally. At the same time, the economic opportunities available to men meant that they could afford to pay the fine much more frequently, and so the court assessed lashes on women much more often than on their male counterparts.

Despite the laws' lack of a gender bias, the court could not convict men and women at the same rate. The assembly and Charles County Court's efforts to reverse that trend are visible, and caused one of every two illegitimate children born in the 1750s to have both its parents punished for their offense. People recognized that premarital sexual activity took place and forgave it, as long as a marriage took place during the pregnancy or around the birth of the child. The economic considerations that had motivated the General Assembly to pass law after law in the seventeenth century continued in importance for servants who were convicted on standard bastardy charges, but a distinct moral component had entered into the equation in the 1690s as Maryland worked to criminalize a variety of immoral activities. Women who bore illegitimate children, and the men who begat those children, had transgressed acceptable moral boundaries. But as demonstrated through print material, such offenses could be socially forgivable, acceptable targets for wits to mock, and food for gossip.

Notes

1. Jonas Green, "The Undecided Case," *The Maryland Almanack* (1758): August.

2. For a discussion of interracial illegitimacy, please see Catherine Cardno, "Community, Morality, and Violence: Crime and the Construction of a British-American Society in Eighteenth-Century Charles County, Maryland." (Ph.D. diss., Johns Hopkins University, 2004).

3. For example, see Michel Meranze, *Laboratories of Virtue: Punishment, Revolution, and Authority in Philadelphia, 1760–1835*, (Chapel Hill: University of North Carolina Press, 1996) for an examination of Benjamin Rush and developments in Pennsylvania.

4. In the course of this study the author constructed a database of the criminal court records from the Charles County Court (1696–1770) in Maryland. Each reference was assigned a unique identification number based on the year it appeared in the records, the month and day of the court session, the beginning page number it can be found on, and its number within the court session. For example, the first appearance of "base born" appears in servant Jane Curry's presentment (1731,0309,469–004), which is immediately followed by Eleanor Hand's presentment (1731,0309,469–005). Both appeared in 1731, at the March 9 court session of the Charles County Court. They appear on page 469 of the court records, and Curry's presentment is the fourth record of the session, while Hand's is the fifth. Hand's presentment is notable because "bastard child" was written in first, then crossed out, and "base born" entered above it.

5. Mary Beth Norton, *Founding Mothers and Fathers: Gendered Power and the Forming of American Society* (New York: A. A. Knopf, 1996), 336–37.

6. J. A. Leo Lemay, *Men of Letters in Colonial Maryland* (Knoxville: University of Tennessee Press, 1972); David Shields, *Oracles of Empire: Poetry, Politics, and Commerce in British America, 1690–1750* (Chicago: University of Chicago Press, 1990). Clare Anna Lyons, "Humor and Anxiety: Sexuality in Popular Print," chap. 2 in *Sex Among the "Rabble": Gender Transitions in the Age of Revolution, Philadelphia, 1750–1830* (Ph.D. diss., Yale University, 1996).

7. Elaine G. Breslaw, "Wit, Whimsy, and Politics: The Uses of Satire by the Tuesday Club of Annapolis, 1744–1756," *William and Mary Quarterly* 32, no. 2 (1975): 298; Elaine Breslaw, ed., *Records of the Tuesday Club of Annapolis 1745–56* (Chicago: University of Illinois Press, 1988), 110.

8. *The Maryland Almanack* (Annapolis, 1763): October.

9. David M. Turner, *Fashioning Adultery: Gender, Sex and Civility in England, 1660–1740* (Cambridge: Cambridge University Press, 2002), chap. 3.

10. See also "The Female Caution, Or, Pair of Stockings" in *The Maryland Almanack* (1762): January. In it, Mother Breedwell's attempts to find a method of birth control cause a joke at her expense when the doctor tells her to wear one hose over both legs in bed every night. The humor lies in Breedwell's misunderstanding of the doctor's direction to keep her legs together in bed, and she requests the second hose thinking that if one can be so successful, two must be doubly so.

11. *The Maryland Gazette*, 14 October 1747. Also found in *The Maryland Almanack* (1758): August.

12. Lemay, *Men of Letters*, 195 and 201.

13. *The Maryland Almanack* (1763): January.

14. Taylor Wilkinson and Elizabeth his wife against John Godshall and Mary his wife (1705,0313,081–055). For a discussion of slander suits in colonial North Carolina see Kirsten Fischer, "False, Feigned, and Scandalous Words: Sexual Slander and Racial Ideology Among Whites in Colonial North Carolina," in *The Devil's Lane: Sex and Race in the Early South*, eds. Catherine Clinton and Michele Gillespie (London: Oxford University Press, 1997), 139–53. Fischer notes that male defense of their sexual reputation when it involved sex with white women ended at about the turn of the century (140); after that date men sued over business dealings while slander suits to defend sexual reputation became the province of women.

15. Mary Magdelin Sotherland against William Key and Margaret his wife (1761,0809,338–015).

16. Trevor Burnard, *Creole Gentlemen: the Maryland Elite, 1691–1776* (London: Routledge, 2002), chap. 3 "'A species of Capital attached to Certain Mercantile houses:' Elite Debts and the Significance of Credit," 61–102.

17. "The Poetic Couple," *The Maryland Almanack* (1758): July.

18. "The Mad-Dog: A Tale," *The Maryland Almanack* (1764): January–December.

19. "On a Civilian," *The Maryland Almanack* (1763): October.

20. Robert V. Wells, "Illegitimacy and Bridal Pregnancy in Colonial America," in Laslett et al, eds., *Bastardy and its Comparative History: Studies in the History of Illegitimacy and Marital Nonconformism in Britain, France, Germany, Sweden, North America, Jamaica and Japan* (London: Edward Arnold Publishers, 1980), especially 358–59. Norton, *Founding Mothers and Fathers*, 338–40.

21. "An Act for the punishing of the Offences of Adultery and ffornication" (1715) reads "And in Case the said Offenders or any of them shall not have wherewith to pay the Sevll fines by this Act Imposed then the said Offenders shall be Adjudged to suffer Corporall punishmt by whipping upon his or their bare bodys 'till the blood Doe appear soe many Stripes not Exceeding thirty nine as the Justices before whome such Conviction shall be shall Adjudge. Provided that this Act shall not be Construed to Extend as to the fine for Women who have bastards And Doe refuse to Discover the father or begetter of

such Children but that in such Cases it shall be in the Discretion of the Justices before whome such Woman or Women shall be Convicted Either to take the fine by this Act Appointed or to Award Corporall punishmt," *Archives*, 30:234. For a further discussion of lashes, see Cardno, "Community, Morality, and Violence," 148–55.

22. Once the grand jury presented a man or woman, the court then commanded the sheriff to bring the defendant to court for a trial. If the defendant failed to confess his or her crime, a jury was impaneled to make the decision for a conviction or acquittal. Juries very rarely acquitted either women or men, but in 1700 Magdalene Thomas pleaded not guilty to the charge of having a bastard child and was cleared by a jury of twelve men. Abigail Gaby presented (1737,1108,382–004), acquitted (1738,0808,499–032); Mary Simpson (1696,0811,025–003); Mary Salt (1698,0111,298–008); Hester Grumball (1708,0608,470–039); and Mary Frawner (1727,0808,005–026).

23. Abandonment of the case by the prosecution.

24. Because the Charles County Court records are not extant for 1690–1695, I have begun with the 1696 records (the year the boundary lines were redrawn) and normalized the numbers for that decade to reflect a full ten years. The adjusted rates for the other decades normalize the data to account for the few missing court sessions.

25. The numbers for the 1760s are skewed in part because of a faulty clerk who did not record all of the court's decisions into the existing record book.

26. "The Population of Maryland, 1755," *Gentleman's Magazine* 34 (1764), in Edward C. Papenfuse and Joseph M. Coale, III, eds., *The Hammond-Harwood House Atlas of Historical Maps of Maryland, 1608–1908* (Baltimore: Johns Hopkins University Press, 1982), 37. There were 1,777 free women, 106 indentured or hired women, 78 convict women, and 36 free mulatto women identified in the census of 1755 for Charles County.

27. Cornelia Hughes Dayton, *Women before the Bar: Gender, Law, and Society in Connecticut, 1639–1789* (Chapel Hill: University of North Carolina Press, 1995), 159. Laurel Thatcher Ulrich, *A Midwife's Tale: The Life of Martha Ballard, Based on Her Diary, 1785–1812* (New York: Knopf, 1990), 148. William E. Nelson, *Americanization of the Common Law: The Impact of Legal Change on Massachusetts Society, 1760–1830* (Cambridge, Mass.: Harvard University Press, 1975), 110–11; Lincoln County Court of General Sessions of the Peace, Books 1–2. Found in Ulrich, p. 148, note 18.

28. "The Population of Maryland, 1755," *Gentleman's Magazine* 34 (1764), in Papenfuse and Coale, eds., *The Hammond-Harwood House Atlas*, 37. There were 1,929 free men, 173 hired or indented men, 205 convicts, 60 free mulattos, 3 free blacks, 4 clergymen, and 51 poor men reported in Charles County for 1755.

29. Abigaill Dyamond's conviction (1706,0813,245–020), Thomas Dyson Jr. named as the father of her child. Nothing points to her being a servant, though she was living at Henry Norris's house.

30. Thomas Dyson Jr. conviction for damages (1706,0910,254,017). Thomas Dyson Jr.'s recognizance for £40 jointly with Thomas Dyson Sr. (1706,0910,254–018).

31. Abigaill Dyamond conviction (1709,0809,609–020), Matthew Tennison named as the father of the child.

32. Elizabeth Dent conviction (1759,1113,405–027).

33. Peter Dent conviction (1759,1113,405–028).

34. Elizabeth Dent presenting Peter Dent for damages, (1760,1112,105–023).

35. See Dayton, *Women before the Bar*, p. 182–83, tables 7 and 8, for comparison of fornication rates for married couples and singles. Prosecutions of couples in the New Haven County Court peaked in the 1730s with a total of 107 prosecutions of couples.

36. Elizabeth Fardinando's presentment (1712,1111,189–001), acquittal (1713,0609,257–018); Hester Grumball's presentment (1708,0309,448–051) and conviction (1708,0608,470–039).

37. Mary Simpson's presentment (1696,0609,001–001) and acquittal (1696,0811,025–003).

38. See Cornelia Hughes Dayton's findings for Connecticut, where "In the 1750s and 1760s the calculus of accountability for sexual transgressions had shifted to suggest that women bore almost the entire responsibility for guarding female chastity." Dayton, *Women Before the Bar*, 161.

39. The law also stipulates that the fine in cases of adultery is three pounds current or 1,200 pounds tobacco. "An Act for the Punishing the Offences of Adultery and Fornication" (1715), *The Laws of the Province of Maryland Collected into one Volume By Oath of the Governor and Assembly of the Province At a General Assembly begun at St. Mary's* (May 1692–1718), 88.

40. See Cardno, "Community, Morality, and Violence," chap. 2.

41. Isabella Cubbison's conviction (1732,0314,093–049).

42. Patrick Connelly's presentment by Isabella Cubbyson (1732,0314,080–005).

43. Patrick Connelly's conviction (1732,0314,094–051).

44. Patrick Connelly's conviction (1732,0314,094–051). Chances are good that he paid the fine in currency rather than tobacco. The fluctuating price of tobacco and currency meant that almost as soon as the 1715 law equated 30 shillings current with 600 pounds of tobacco, 600 pounds of tobacco became worth much, much more. The law was not revised until 1749 when 30 shillings currency became equated with 240 pounds of tobacco according to current equivalents. During the 1730s tobacco crisis most people began paying their fines with currency directly to the sheriff in court.

45. In order to be categorized as a free woman, three criteria had to be met. The first two are a given: a woman could not be listed as either a servant or having a master in the presentment, conviction, or any other applicable record during or around the trial proceedings. The third criterion is less so: statutes passed in 1715 laid out the method of punishment to be followed by the county courts. It was stated that in cases of a servant woman's being brought to court on a bastardy charge, if the father was not named (or if he was not proven to be the father) "the Mother of such Child shall be lyable to satisfy the Damage so sustained [by masters or mistresses], by Servitude or otherwise, as the Court before whom such Matter is brought shall see convenient," *Laws of the Province of Maryland*, 125. Thus, my third criterion for deciding whether or not a woman was free or a servant was if she had been assessed extra time to serve "for trouble on the house," as

it was called, in her trial or at any other point in the extant court records. Motions or petitions brought to the court for satisfaction for bastardy fees or trouble on the house to be assessed on a woman thus categorized the woman as a servant even if she had not been listed as one at any other point during her presentment or trial.

46. Ebenezer Cook, *The Sot-weed Factor* (London, 1708), line 708.

47. James Talbot Pole, "Ebenezer Cook and The Maryland Muse," *American Literature*, vol. 3, no. 3 (Nov, 1931), 296–302, quote from p. 301.

48. Norton, *Founding Mothers and Fathers*, 336.

49. See Russell Menard, "From Servants to Slaves: The Transformation of the Chesapeake Labor System," *Southern Studies* 16 (1977): 355–90 for a discussion of the transition of the labor population in Maryland from one based on indentured servitude to one based on slave labor. Menard places the transition in the labor supply to the declining numbers in the traditional labor supply as increasing numbers of slaves appeared on the colonial labor market. See also David Galenson, *White Servitude in Colonial America: An Economic Analysis*, (New York: Cambridge University Press, 1981), especially part 4 "White Servitude in the Colonial Labor Market," pp. 117–70, for the turn-of-the-century transition from servant to slave labor in the colonies.

50. See Galenson, "Patterns of Servant Migration from England to America," *White Servitude*, chap. 6, 81–96, for proportions of indentured servant women imported to Maryland. See A. Roger Ekirch, *Bound for America: The Transportation of British Convicts to the Colonies, 1718–1775* (Oxford: Clarendon Press, 1987), 50, for numbers of convict women imported. See Abbot Emerson Smith, *Colonists in Bondage: White Servitude and Convict Labor in America, 1607–1776* (Chapel Hill: University of North Carolina Press, 1947), 325 and 329 for numbers of servants and convicts imported into Maryland. See Christine Daniels, "'Getting his [or her] Livelyhood': Free Workers in Slave Anglo-America, 1675–1810," *Agricultural History* 71, no. 2 (Spring 1997), esp. 129–30, and Daniels, "Gresham's Laws: Labor Management on an Early-Eighteenth-Century Chesapeake Plantation," *Journal of Southern History* 62, no. 2 (May 1996): 208, for discussions of the increasing numbers of free women laborers and their duties on plantations.

51. Allan Kulikoff, *Tobacco and Slaves: The Development of Southern Cultures in the Chesapeake, 1680–1800* (Chapel Hill: University of North Carolina Press, 1986), 54–60. Figure 4, p. 56, shows an increase in the age at which women married: in Southern Maryland the numbers rose from around 18 to 22 in the 1730s.

52. The only three widows convicted on standard bastardy charges were: Elizabeth Bryant presented (1729,0812,307–006) and convicted (1729,0812,314–041); Elinor Sanders presented (1742,1109,450–001) and convicted (1743,0308,514–054); and Elizabeth Gray/Grey, listed as NEJ five times (1744,0814,087–012; 1744,1113,192–021; 1745,0312,256–014; 1745,0611,355–030; and 1745,0813,368–002) before her conviction (1745,1112,479–019). An Elizabeth Grey, widow, is presented for bearing an illegitimate child in 1742 (1742,0608,371–009), but this may or may not have been the same woman eventually convicted in 1745. There is also a 1737 presentment (1737,1108,382–008) of an Elizabeth Grey, as well as a 1754 report of a fine paid to a

justice of the peace upon confession of bearing a base-born child (1754,0813,368–002), but without any specifics linking the cases together, it is difficult to say if the 1737 and 1742 presentments and the 1754 conviction are at all linked to the 1745 conviction.

53. Burnard, *Creole Gentlemen*, 103–38.

54. John Atchison (1720,0614,339–018) planter with Francis Adams planter his master; John Huson (1732,0613,160–038) planter also called a servant with Richard Speake as his master; Patrick Matthews (1720,0614,340–019) planter with Thomas Mitchell planter as his master. Benjamin Thompson (1735,1111,103–083) laborer and servant with Richard Chapman as his master, William Dungen (1727,0314,424–056) laborer and servant with Thomas Matthews as his master.

55. Joseph Bladen (1723,1112,163–045) and James Knowland (1720,0809,012–050).

56. Christine Daniels, "'Getting his [or her] Livelyhood,'" 134.

57. Benjamin Partee (1742,1109,454–019). It is possible that the vestry took care of securities informally before the court took an official role in the 1740s. Norton, *Founding Mothers and Fathers*, 336, and Mary Beth Norton, "Gender, Crime and Community in Seventeenth-Century Maryland," James A. Henretta, Michael Kammen, and Stanley N. Katz, eds., *The Transformation of Early American History: Society, Authority, and Ideology*, 136–38. Despite earlier concerns with economic cost in the seventeenth century, which Norton addresses and which are also made very clear in 1658, 1662, and 1674 legislation, by the eighteenth century an important moral component came into play that lasted throughout the colonial period. While the child's existence still raised the issue of the cost of raising that child, by the mid-eighteenth century, recognizances for the support of illegitimate children became common, indicating that while the numbers of servants bearing illegitimate children may have been declining, there were now increasing numbers of free women bearing children whom they could not afford to support.

58. See Mary Chrismond (1745,0312,256–018) regarding the beginning of frequent recognizances. Pricilla King (1744,0612,001–001) illustrates that they do occur, but it is the sole entry of a recognizance for a women in 1744.

59. *Archives*, 46:319 "An Act for taking off corporal Punishment inflicted on Females having base-born Children, and other Purposes therein mentioned" (1749), ch. 12 paras. 1 and 4.

60. *Archives*, 46:319 "An Act for taking off corporal Punishment inflicted on Females having base-born Children, and other Purposes therein mentioned" (1749), ch. 12 paras. 2 and 3.

61. See normalized numbers in table 9.1.

62. "The Speech of Miss Polly Baker, before a Court of Judicature, at Connecticut in New England, where she was prosecuted the fifth Time for having a Bastard Child: which influenced the Court to dispense with her Punishment, and induced one of her Judges to marry her the next Day," *The Maryland Gazette*, 11 August 1747, front page.

63. Daniel Royot, "Long Live *La Différence*: Humor and Sex in Franklin's Writings," in *Finding Colonial Americas: Essays honoring J. A. Leo Lemay*, eds. Carla Mulford and David S. Shields (Newark: University of Delaware, 2001), 307–15. Quote found on page 308.

64. Described as "erectile," in Royot, "Long Live," 308. On provocative puns, see J. A. Leo Lemay, "The Text, Rhetorical Strategies and Themes of 'The Speech of Polly Baker,'" in *The Oldest Revolutionary: Essays on Benjamin Franklin*, ed. J. A. Leo Lemay (Philadelphia: University of Pennsylvania, 1976).

65. *Archives* 203:294 (1781) "An ACT directing the proceedings against persons guilty of fornication."

CONTRIBUTORS

James D. Alsop is professor of history at McMaster University, Hamilton, Ontario. He is coauthor of *Seamen and Traders in Guinea, 1553–1565* (1992). The focus of his current research is disease and health in modern Atlantic maritime history.

Angelo T. Angelis is an assistant professor of history at Hunter College, New York. His scholarly interests include the American Revolution, Constitution, and popular political movements.

Thomas F. Brown is assistant professor of sociology at Lamar University. His research interests are in symbolic ethnicity, ethnic nationalism, and African-American class formation.

Catherine Cardno is currently a visiting assistant professor of history at Goucher College. She received her Ph.D. in history from Johns Hopkins University in 2004.

Kathleen Fawver is assistant professor of history at California State University, Dominguez Hills. She received her Ph.D. in history from the University of California, Riverside in 2002.

Seth Mallios is associate professor of anthropology and director of the South Coastal Information Center at San Diego State University. He is the founding editor of the *Journal of the Jamestown Rediscovery Center* and the *San Diego State University Occasional Archaeological Papers*. Mallios has two manuscripts currently under review: *Gifts and Bloodshed* and *Beware the Gift, Revere the Gift*.

Sarah Hand Meacham is an assistant dean at the University of Virginia. She recently received her Ph.D. in U.S. and women's history from the University of Virginia.

Debra Meyers is associate professor of history at Northern Kentucky University. She recently published *Common Whores, Vertuous Women, and Loveing Wives* (2003) and coedited *Women and Religion in Old and New Worlds* (2001), which includes her essay, "Gender and Religion in England's Catholic Province."

Melanie Perreault is associate professor of history at Salisbury University in Maryland. She recently published *Early English Encounters in Russia, West Africa, and the Americas, 1530–1614* (2004).

Leah C. Sims is a history student at Lamar University. Her research interests are in deviance, and in the social history of slaves and free people of color, focusing on nineteenth-century North Carolina.